MW01628390

Published in association with the Buddhist Society Trust.

The publisher gratefully acknowledges the generous contribution
to this book provided by the Japan Foundation.

The publisher gratefully acknowledges the generous contribution to this book provided by the Great Britain Sasakawa Foundation.

The publisher gratefully acknowledges the generous support of the Humanities Endowment Fund of the University of California Press Foundation.

Selected Works of D. T. Suzuki, Volume II

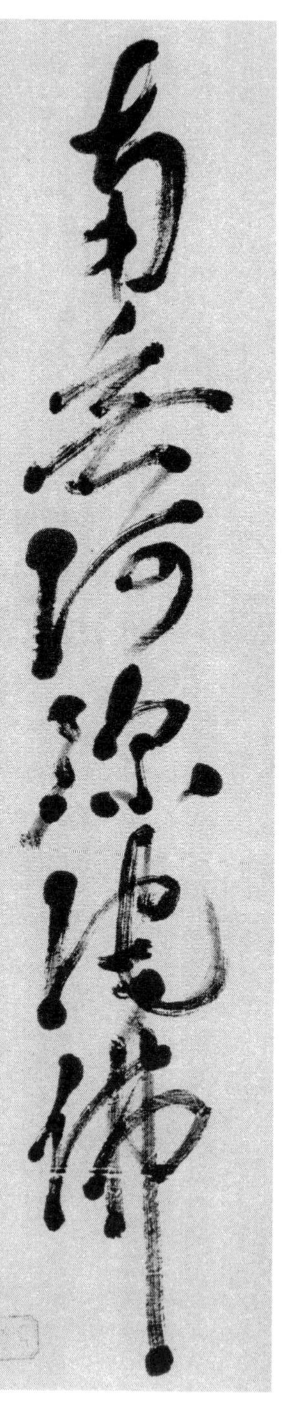
南無阿弥陀佛

Selected Works of D. T. Suzuki, Volume II

Pure Land

Volume Editor

James C. Dobbins

General Editor

Richard M. Jaffe

Published in association with the Buddhist Society Trust

UNIVERSITY OF CALIFORNIA PRESS

University of California Press, one of the most distinguished university presses in the United States, enriches lives around the world by advancing scholarship in the humanities, social sciences, and natural sciences. Its activities are supported by the UC Press Foundation and by philanthropic contributions from individuals and institutions. For more information, visit www.ucpress.edu.

University of California Press
Oakland, California

Frontispiece: *Namu Amida Butsu* 南無阿彌陀佛 ("I take refuge in Amitābha Buddha"). Calligraphy by Suzuki Daisetsu. Courtesy of the Matsugaoka Bunko.

Library of Congress Cataloging-in-Publication Data

Suzuki, Daisetz Teitaro, 1870–1966, author.
[Works. Selections. English. 2014]
Selected works of D. T. Suzuki / edited by Richard M. Jaffe.
volumes cm.
Includes bibliographical references and index.
Contents: Volume 1. Zen.—Volume 2. Pure Land.
ISBN 978-0-520-26919-4 (cloth : v. 1)—ISBN 978-0-520-26893-7 (cloth : v. 2)—ISBN 978-0-520-95961-3 (ebook : v. 1)—ISBN 978-0-520-95962-0 (ebook : v. 2)
1. Suzuki, Daisetz Teitaro, 1870–1966—Translations into English. 2. Zen Buddhism. I. Jaffe, Richard M., 1954– editor of compilation. II. Title.
BQ9266.S93 2014
294.3′927—dc23 2014012088

Manufactured in the United States of America

24 23 22 21 20 19 18 17 16 15
10 9 8 7 6 5 4 3 2 1

In keeping with a commitment to support environmentally responsible and sustainable printing practices, UC Press has printed this book on Natures Natural, a fiber that contains 30% post-consumer waste and meets the minimum requirements of ANSI/NISO Z39.48–1992 (R 1997) (*Permanence of Paper*).

CONTENTS

ACKNOWLEDGMENTS

When I embarked on this project, my knowledge of D.T. Suzuki was limited largely to several of his writings that I had read casually and uncritically early in my career. Hence, I faced a challenge equipping myself with a sufficient understanding of his life, thought, historical circumstances, and intellectual climate to undertake this work. I am indebted to my home institution, Oberlin College, for providing a sabbatical leave in 2010–2011 during which this project was begun. I am equally grateful to Otani University in Kyoto, where Suzuki was a professor, for hosting me during that year, and to its Shinshū Sōgō Kenkyūjo and *The Eastern Buddhist* office, which provided additional support. Special thanks also go to Norman Waddell, who updated his translation of excerpts from Suzuki's *Japanese Spirituality (Nihon teki reisei)* that appear in this volume, and to the American Buddhist Studies Center in New York and its president, Hoshina Seki, for permission to publish Suzuki's public talk of September 11, 1955. I would also like to thank Caroline Chen who, supported by Oberlin College, assisted me in the early production of the manuscript—creating electronic versions of Suzuki's essays, making the first wave of editorial changes to them, and producing preliminary versions of Japanese, Chinese, and Sanskrit glossaries. In addition, I want to express appreciation to the Matsugaoka Bunko for permission to publish Suzuki's essays. There are also several organizations who provided financial support for the production of this volume and of the series in general: the Buddhist Society of London; Duke University's Asian-Pacific Studies Institute and Trinity College of Arts and Sciences; the Japan Foundation of New York (through a grant to the Triangle Center for Japanese Studies) and the Japan Foundation of Los Angeles; Mr. Luke Ding;

and the Great Britain Sasakawa Foundation. Finally, I must acknowledge the expertise and help of Wayne Yokoyama and Richard Jaffe who became frequent conversation partners concerning Suzuki and who offered valuable suggestions and information at all stages of the project. And of course I wish to thank my wife Suzanne Gay for her patience and support throughout the process.

INTRODUCTION

Suzuki Daisetsu Teitarō (1870–1966), known popularly in the West as D. T. Suzuki, is famous for his writings on Zen, but he also had a long and abiding interest in Pure Land Buddhism, particularly Jōdo Shinshū, or Shin Buddhism. This interest arose from a combination of circumstances—his upbringing in Kanazawa, his encounter with various Pure Land adherents and thinkers, and his appointment at Otani, a Shin Buddhist university—but it also stemmed from his own curiosity, both intellectual and religious. From the time he began writing and throughout his publishing life, Suzuki wrote about Pure Land repeatedly, and during certain phases of his career he concentrated on it heavily. Some people think that in the last decade or two of his life Suzuki was more attracted to Pure Land Buddhism than to Zen. This may be wishful thinking though, for Zen always held a special place in Suzuki's heart, epitomizing for him the essence of Buddhism. But Pure Land Buddhism was never far behind, for he considered it the complement of Zen—the other side of the Buddhist coin, so to speak. Just as he gave Zen a unique and powerful interpretation in the modern world, likewise he gave Pure Land a distinctive reading. It is Suzuki's interpretation of Pure Land Buddhism that I would like to explore here. In doing so, my goal is to historicize Suzuki—that is, to situate him amid the intellectual and historical trends of his times, for he was both a product of them and a contributor to them.

Suzuki emerged as a well-known public intellectual in the last two decades of his long life. In the 1950s, while he was living in America, he was catapulted to fame as a world-renowned authority on Buddhism. With fame in the West came fame in Japan, where he thence received greater adulation than he ever had earlier in his career. In some ways Suzuki was an unlikely candidate to become such a prominent figure in Buddhism because he was not reared in a Buddhist temple, nor did he receive formal training in traditional Buddhist texts and doctrine. But from a young age he showed great resourcefulness in his studies—he was bright and energetic and autodidactic. Suzuki also had the good fortune to receive scholarly advice and financial support at various junctures in his life that allowed him to become a unique scholar, different from his contemporaries in the way he combined Buddhist subject matter with Western approaches. The distinctive character of Suzuki's scholarship also applied to his work on Pure Land Buddhism. Because he stood outside of the sectarian structures and doctrinal factions of Shin Buddhism, Suzuki did not feel beholden to any particular line of thought. He read the texts that interested him and reacted to them with candor. Shin Buddhist scholars have sometimes looked upon Suzuki as a Zen partisan in his views of Pure Land, and Suzuki himself acknowledged that his ideas represented no more than his own humble perspective.[1] But as an outsider, Suzuki could march to his own drum, unafraid to be daring in his thinking. As a result, his work on Pure Land Buddhism was often eye opening, sometimes idiosyncratic, and ultimately influential in both Japan and the West.

SUZUKI'S LIFE

Biographically, we can divide Suzuki's life into distinct phases according to where he was and what he was doing.[2] The first phase was his childhood and youth in Kanazawa. He was born in 1870 into a well-educated and previously elite family, but became impoverished as a young child after his father died. He nonetheless grew up in the glow of his mother's love and amid her devout, though unorthodox, Pure Land beliefs. In middle and upper school Suzuki excelled in his studies, particularly in English at a time when few other Japanese were proficient in the language. But because of limited finances he was forced to drop out of school and to seek his livelihood as an English instructor. Soon afterward, at the age of twenty, Suzuki lost his mother, a devastating blow that nonetheless allowed him to leave Kanazawa and seek higher education.

The next phase of Suzuki's life commenced when he traveled to Tokyo in 1891 to take classes first at Waseda and then at Tokyo Imperial University, studying Western philosophy and other subjects. More importantly, Suzuki began Zen practice at the Engakuji monastery in Kamakura and came under the influence of Shaku Sōen (1859–1919), the brilliant but unconventional Zen master who was committed to a modern, international understanding of Buddhism. Suzuki became his disciple and intellectual protégé, on the one hand training in meditation and koan under his direction and on the other assisting Sōen in his promotion of a worldwide Buddhism, since Suzuki's English ability was superior. Under Sōen, Suzuki is said to have experienced Zen enlightenment, satori, in December 1896, and he departed for America in February 1897 to work for Sōen's intellectual acquaintance Paul Carus (1852–1919) at Open Court Publishing in LaSalle, Illinois.

Suzuki's twelve-year stay overseas, primarily in LaSalle, marked the next stage of his life. He worked as a translator and editorial assistant for Open Court, but at the same time he studied assiduously, receiving advice from Carus, who was a recognized scholar of religion. During this period Suzuki was exposed to all manner of Western learning—philosophy, religion, literature, psychology, and Western scholarship on Buddhism. He encountered the writings of William James (1842–1910) and was heavily influenced by his psychology of religion. Suzuki also began to publish translations and other works in English on Buddhism. In 1905–1906, while interpreting for Shaku Sōen, who was on a lecture tour of America, Suzuki met Beatrice Erskine Lane (1878–1939), a brilliant and highly educated American who was fascinated with the "Orient" and Asian religions. She would become an important contributor to Suzuki's success as a scholar. He returned to Japan in 1909 after traveling for a year mostly in Europe, spending a long period in London translating a text for the Swedenborg Society.

After Suzuki's return to Japan he managed to get a position at first temporarily and then permanently as an English professor in the preparatory division of Gakushūin, the Peers School, in Tokyo. Within a year Suzuki came into contact with Sasaki Gesshō (1875–1926), the future president of Otani University, who hired him to assist with an English work on Shin Buddhism, the first of their collaborations. In February 1911, Beatrice Lane arrived in Japan and in December she and Suzuki were married. Throughout this decade Suzuki seemed to be engaged more by his work on religion than by his English teaching at Gakushūin. He made frequent and extended visits to Kamakura not only to practice Zen but also to assist Sōen with Zen publications and projects on Buddhism. Sōen's death in 1919 in a sense marked the end of a long period of intellectual incubation—beginning with Suzuki's student days in Tokyo and Kamakura, extending through his lengthy sojourn overseas, and culminating in his Gakushūin years—which prepared Suzuki for his life's work, interpreting Buddhism for modern Japan and the West.

Suzuki's career as a professor at Otani University, negotiated by Sasaki Gesshō in 1921, represents the next phase of his life. His official letter of appointment listed his academic field as English first and "Indian philosophy" (that is, Buddhist studies) second.[3] This was actually the first position that Suzuki had ever occupied in Buddhist studies, even though he was already fifty years old. Otani proved to be an excellent setting for Suzuki to pursue his work on Buddhism. At his behest it established the English journal *The Eastern Buddhist,* edited by Suzuki and his wife Beatrice, in which he published some of his earliest and most influential essays. Also, with the patronage of his longtime friend Ataka Yakichi (1873–1949), a wealthy Osaka businessman, Suzuki published numerous English books overseas, thereby fostering his reputation abroad as an important scholar of Buddhism.

Suzuki's Otani years, extending through the Pacific War, during which he resided principally in Kamakura, were a period of prolific scholarship (though he concentrated on Japanese publications, rather than English ones, after his wife's death in 1939). During that time Suzuki attained wide recognition in Japan as a scholar of Buddhism.

The next phase in Suzuki's life extended from the end of the war in 1945, when he was seventy-five years old, until 1958. This was the period when he became an academic celebrity. During the postwar American occupation of Japan, Suzuki emerged as a public figure after he was invited to give lectures to the Emperor of Japan in 1946.[4] But in 1949 he traveled to the United States, where he stayed until 1958, visiting Japan only intermittently. There he taught first at the University of Hawaii and Claremont, but principally at Columbia in New York thereafter. His fame in the West arose in part from the republication of his earlier English books at a time when there was a surging interest in Buddhism in America and Europe. It was in this period that Suzuki participated in the Eranos Conference of world-class intellectuals in Switzerland in 1953 and 1954. During Suzuki's brief visits back to Japan, he was always welcomed with great fanfare.

The last phase of Suzuki's life began with his return to residency in Japan in 1958. At that point he was treated as one of Japan's greatest scholars of Buddhism. In his twilight years Suzuki was in great demand for lectures, interviews, publications, and translations. He also continued an ambitious scholarly agenda, including Zen projects, at the Matsugaoka Bunko in Kamakura, a research library for Buddhism that he founded in 1945, where he resided. It was during this period that Suzuki translated a large portion of the Pure Land doctrinal classic *Kyōgyōshinshō* at the behest of the Shin Buddhist headquarters in Kyoto. After Suzuki's death in 1966 he was honored as one of Japan's best-known and most respected Buddhist thinkers.

INTELLECTUAL INFLUENCES ON SUZUKI

Suzuki's interpretations of Pure Land Buddhism arose as a result of a wide variety of influences on him. Some were from things directly connected to Pure Land—practices, ideas, texts, and people. But others were more indirect influences—for instance, Zen themes and Western concepts of religion. Identifying these influences helps us see how Suzuki arrived at his Pure Land ideas and why he presented them in a nontraditional way.

The first influence on Suzuki was his mother and his upbringing in Kanazawa. Though his family did not have historical ties to Pure Land Buddhism,[5] his mother was attracted to it after her husband died in 1876. Specifically, she gravitated to Shin Buddhism, which was widespread in the Kanazawa area. Her connection, however, was to an insular and covert religious group that espoused "secret teachings" *(hiji bōmon),* a strain of Shin Buddhism that was disavowed by ecclesiastical authorities in Kyoto. According to one account given by Suzuki in old age, he underwent a special initiation, what he called a baptism *(senrei),* into this group when he was young:

> When I was a child, it seems that secret teachings were widely practiced in Kaga [the traditional province of Kanazawa]. This was when I was perhaps seven or eight, but not yet ten—after my father died. My mother seems to have joined such a group at some point. Because of that I apparently received a baptism into those secret teachings. That occurrence, which I remember even now, was at my house. My mother's friends came and offered a candle at our Buddhist altar. I don't remember whether they recited scriptures or not. There was a man who was apparently the leader, and he had us chant *Namu-amida-butsu, Namu-amida-butsu,* repeatedly and incessantly. I forgot whether I was chanting it or the man was saying it, but at any rate we chanted *Namu-amida-butsu* incessantly. All the while, the man took hold of my upper body as I sat [on the floor formally] with my legs folded under me, and he swayed me backward and forward. I felt no need to think about the time or how long we were doing this—whether it was thirty minutes or an hour. But just in the midst of doing so, about the time he brought everything to an end, he happened to stop his movement [of my body]. At that moment a psychological change *(shinri teki na henka)* occurred. The instant that this steady rhythmic motion was interrupted, somehow from it there emerged a change in my psychology, and a certain sensation *(kankaku)* arose. It seemed to say, "There! You are saved!"[6]

Throughout Suzuki's long life he seldom spoke of this event, but it is hard to believe that it did not make a strong impression on him as a child. This was his personal introduction to the nembutsu, the Pure Land practice of chanting the name of Amida Buddha. It is also possible that this episode functioned as a subconscious template for Suzuki's later experience of Zen enlightenment, satori, which became central to his Zen writings, for both experiences are structurally similar: a period of intense repetitive practice culminating in a sudden awakening or a changed state of mind. Suzuki's exposure to Pure Land beliefs and practices, including several Shin Buddhist temples and priests, continued throughout his youth until his departure for Tokyo in 1891.

Another major influence on Suzuki's thought was his Zen master, Shaku Sōen. He was probably the most important mentor to Suzuki in the formative years of his intellectual development, specifically at the Engakuji monastery in Kamakura before his departure for America and again after his return from America when he was an English professor at Gakushūin in Tokyo. Suzuki's original attraction to the Engakuji was for Zen training, since the monastery, unlike some traditional ones, was quite welcoming to lay Zen practitioners, including and especially intellectuals with modern Western interests. Sōen was a fully certified Zen master, having risen quickly and brilliantly through the Zen hierarchy, but he was also an unconventional master.

He received a Western-oriented education at Keiō University, he trained as a Theravada monk in Sri Lanka, and he developed a strong commitment to modernizing and internationalizing Buddhism. From this background Sōen was invited to participate in the World's Parliament of Religions in Chicago in 1893, and he recruited Suzuki to translate the text for his lecture into English for the meeting.[7] Suzuki, of course, underwent traditional Zen training with Sōen, including koan examination, but he also received Sōen's guidance on a variety of Western subjects, particularly the writings of Paul Carus, whom Sōen met at the Parliament in Chicago. Under Sōen's direction Suzuki translated Carus's *The Gospel of Buddha* into Japanese, and Suzuki's own first book, *Shin shūkyō ron* (A New Interpretation of Religion), published in 1896, was influenced by Carus's theories.[8] Over the course of their long association, Suzuki inherited Sōen's goals: to make Buddhism relevant in modern Japan; to develop a trans-sectarian, pan-Asian understanding of Buddhism; and to articulate Buddhism in a way that would be comprehensible and attractive to interested Westerners. Sōen and Suzuki ultimately sought to situate Zen within this framework. And likewise Suzuki applied these same principles to his interpretation of Pure Land Buddhism.

Another important influence on Suzuki was Paul Carus and, by extension, Western concepts of religion. When Suzuki arrived in America in 1897 to work for Carus at Open Court Publishing, he began a long period of exposure to Western learning, building on his university studies in Tokyo. Suzuki's letters from this period contain references to a variety of philosophers, religious thinkers, psychologists, and literary figures whom Suzuki read: Immanuel Kant (1724–1804), Friedrich Schleiermacher (1768–1834), Arthur Schopenhauer (1788–1860), Victor Hugo (1802–1885), Ralph Waldo Emerson (1803–1882), Henrik Ibsen (1828–1906), William James (1842–1910),[9] and others. Carus had a large personal library, and Suzuki apparently borrowed books from him frequently.[10] To the extent that the academic study of religion was just emerging as a scholarly field in the West, this was a vibrant time for Suzuki to immerse himself in religious scholarship. Carus was an accomplished, though somewhat unusual, scholar and his primary intellectual objective was to reconcile religion to rational thought and science. He argued that genuine religion, like science, is simply the recognition of truth, and hence the two are compatible. To advance this viewpoint, Carus coined the expression "religion of science."[11] Suzuki was originally attracted to these ideas, but in America he found other ways of interpreting Buddhism to which he felt a greater affinity. Thus, he gradually and discretely moved away from Carus's rationalist approach toward a nonrationalist interpretation of religion inspired in part by the Romantic and Transcendentalist traditions in the West. Of all the Western scholars Suzuki studied, the one that attracted him the most was William James, the psychologist of religion. He found his concept of "religious experience" to be especially persuasive and felt it explained cogently his own Zen satori. Suzuki recommended James's book *The Varieties of Religious Experience* to his lifelong friend, the Japanese philosopher Nishida Kitarō (1870–1945),[12] and he also taught it in his classes at Otani throughout his career.[13] The concept of religious experience also became crucial to his interpretation of Pure Land Buddhism. Notwithstanding his nonrationalist approach, Suzuki retained a rationalist outlook to the extent that he sought to differentiate true religion from so-called superstition just as Carus and other rationalists did.

Another influence on Suzuki's thinking was his wife, Beatrice Lane Suzuki, though in a more indirect and subtle way. Beatrice was a remarkably well-educated woman for her generation. She received an undergraduate degree from Radcliffe, the women's college affiliated with Harvard. There she took classes with William James himself, and also with the philosophers Josiah Royce (1855–1916) and George Santayana (1863–1952). Later she completed a master's degree at Columbia University in social work. Beatrice was a voracious reader and widely knowledgeable. From the time she married Suzuki in 1911, she became his partner for life in the publication of English works on Buddhism. She apparently edited and polished all his books in English up to the time of her death in 1939, and as the coeditor of *The Eastern Buddhist* she was largely responsible for making it into a high-quality English journal. Both Beatrice and her mother were unusual for their generation in their discontent with conventional Christianity and their yearning for religious alternatives. A certain segment of educated Westerners in the eighteenth, nineteenth, and twentieth centuries had such sentiments, and they gravitated toward Unitarianism, Swedenborgianism, and Theosophy. All these modern intellectual movements were eclectic and syncretic in their outlook, drawing bits and pieces from different traditions and amalgamating them into a new religious synthesis. Asian religions—especially Hinduism, Buddhism, Baha'i, and Islamic Sufism—became points of interest for such Westerners. Hence, it is not surprising that Beatrice first met Suzuki while attending a presentation by Shaku Sōen at the Vedanta Society in New York in April 1906, when Sōen was on his lecture tour of America.[14] After they married, Beatrice showed a deep commitment to Theosophy even while living in Japan, joining a Theosophy lodge in Tokyo and later establishing a lodge in Kyoto. Though she generally described herself as Buddhist, she tended to view Buddhism through a Theosophical lens. To that extent, Beatrice was never a conventional Buddhist, but rather she picked and chose elements of Buddhism that appealed to her, and treated them as identical to the best elements of other religions. Suzuki himself was sympathetic to Swedenborgianism and Theosophy, and actually served as the president of their Theosophy lodge in Tokyo briefly.[15] He seemed comfortable with its eclectic and syncretic outlook, and was thus more open-minded to Christianity than many of his contemporary Buddhist reformers were. This eclecticism appeared in varying degrees in Suzuki's scholarship on Buddhism. It allowed him to combine ideas in interesting ways, though it sometimes resulted in peculiar or unconventional depictions of Buddhism. Suzuki's interpretations of Pure Land Buddhism were affected by this outlook also.

Finally, another influence on Suzuki's Pure Land thought was the various Shin Buddhists that he met during his lifetime, especially those at Otani University. He of course encountered Shin adherents while growing up in Kanazawa, not only those in his mother's secret nembutsu circle, but also knowledgeable priests and devout believers of mainstream Shin temples.[16] While living in America, Suzuki also spent time with immigrant Shin Buddhists from the Nishi Honganji branch of the school and assisted them with their English-language journal *The Light of Dharma* in San Francisco.[17] But the most important influence on Suzuki came from Sasaki Gesshō and other Buddhist scholars at Otani University. Suzuki's association with Sasaki began in earnest very soon after he returned from America in 1909. Otani, then known as Shinshū University, was located in Tokyo and Sasaki, who was on the faculty, recruited Suzuki to assist in two English publications on Shin Buddhism: *Principal Teachings of the True Sect of Pure Land* (1910) and *The Life of the Shonin Shinran* (1911).[18] Through his association with Sasaki, Suzuki apparently became more interested in Shin Buddhism, for around that time he read a short collection of five popular Shin texts, including the *Tannishō* (Tract on Deploring the Heterodoxies) and the *Anjin ketsujō shō* (On the Final Peaceful Settlement of Mind), which made a lasting impression on him.[19] And in 1911 he published his first essay on a Shin topic, self-power and other-power, "Jiriki to tariki."[20]

Suzuki's work on Pure Land Buddhism unfolded steadily and consistently after he moved to Otani University in Kyoto in 1921. There Suzuki found a welcoming circle of like-minded scholars at *The Eastern Buddhist* that included not only Sasaki but also Akanuma Chizen (1884–1937) and Yamabe Shūgaku (1882–1944), both of whom had experience living in South Asia and England. Their interest was, like Suzuki's, to understand Buddhism broadly and deeply in its development across Asia and to promote its recognition in the West. But unlike Suzuki, they came out of the Shin tradition and sought to secure a place for it in the modern world of Buddhism. Suzuki, as he put down roots at Otani, gradually adopted these Shin sympathies as his own and advanced Shin Buddhism in his own distinctive way, even though he was an outsider.

Beyond this close circle of colleagues, Suzuki found a lively and diverse community of scholars and students of Pure Land Buddhism at Otani. Needless to say, many had been disciples of the first president, Kiyozawa Manshi (1863–1903)—not just Sasaki, Akanuma, and Yamabe, but also Soga Ryōjin (1875–1971) and Kaneko Daiei (1881–1976), radical modern thinkers of Shin doctrine who were forced out of Otani for a number of years because of their provocative claims.[21] Though some of Suzuki's ideas about Pure Land were just as provocative, he seemed to arrive at them by his own logical path, rather than in formal collaboration or exchange with these scholars. Because Suzuki stood outside the Shin sectarian organization, he was beyond the reach of ecclesiastical authorities. The general approach of Kiyozawa's disciples, focusing on the inner spirit *(seishin)* of each person, coalesced well with Suzuki's emphasis on the individual and religious experience. In time, younger faculty members and students became Suzuki's protégés, such as Sugihira Shizutoshi (1899–1984) and Yokogawa Kenshō (1904–1940), and likewise adopted religious experience as a theme for interpreting Pure Land Buddhism.[22] Otani thereby stimulated Suzuki's interest in Pure Land and provided a congenial environment for him to pursue his own unique interpretations. Suzuki, however, did not belong to any particular scholarly clique or school of thought, but formulated his ideas about Pure Land independently, if not idiosyncratically.

SUZUKI'S CONCEPT OF RELIGION

The starting point for Suzuki's interpretation of Pure Land, and of Zen as well, was the crisis that Buddhism faced in Japan during the Meiji period (1868–1912). It was treated as an antiquated and benighted worldview that was incompatible with a new and modern Japan, and it actually underwent persecution, the so-called *Haibutsu kishaku,* as a result. Buddhism's loss of credibility in many ways paralleled the destabilization of religion worldwide during the eighteenth, nineteenth, and twentieth centuries. Religion was typically depicted as irrational and unscientific, and hence as antithetical to a modern secular society. As Japan rushed headlong toward modernization, adopting science and rational argumentation as authoritative modes of discourse, Buddhism appeared as an obstacle to modern thought. In response to this crisis a generation of young Buddhist reformers, who actually embraced modernization instead of resisting it, rose to the fore. They sought to highlight elements in Buddhism that were compatible with this new worldview and to discount or repudiate those that were not. Though different reformers interpreted Buddhism in different ways, compositely they succeeded in reconstructing Buddhism as a credible and compelling discourse in modern times. Suzuki was one of these reformers, and his interpretations of Pure Land and Zen, as well as Buddhism and religion generally, were part of this grand and heroic effort to preserve and advance Buddhism.

Suzuki sought to articulate a new hermeneutical framework in which to interpret Buddhism. His search ultimately led him from a rationalist approach to a nonrationalist one, specifically to the concept of religious experience. The idea of religious experience has become so pervasive and unquestioned in our present culture that it is hard to imagine interpreting religion in any other way. Though experience, *keiken* or *taiken,* was not strongly embedded in the premodern Japanese vocabulary (nor in the pre-Enlightenment European vocabulary), it gained tremendous acceptance and recognition in modern times for explaining certain types of events in human culture.[23] Especially with the rise of scientific thought, which tended to atomize events into objective causes and effects, the concept of experience became one way to insulate humans from such mechanistic analysis, ascribing to them inward freedom, autonomy, and agency. Suzuki and countless other religious thinkers, in both Japan and the West, adopted the language of experience to claim that religion is a real and legitimate dimension of humans, which lies outside the reach of scientific scrutiny and reductionism. Suzuki essentialized religion as the inner core of humans, and he considered religious experience to be the place or event where that core erupts into the world.[24] Suzuki adopted this concept very early in the development of his religious thought, and he subsequently elaborated and refined it with other concepts such as mysticism and spirituality. These ideas, which Suzuki developed in interaction with Western scholarship, became central to his interpretation of Buddhism, Zen, and Pure Land.

Suzuki's emphasis on religious experience emerged out of a combination of his own Zen background and the ideas of William James's *The Varieties of Religious Experience.* Suzuki presented experience as the core component of Buddhism, without which scriptures, rituals, and other aspects of religion have no meaning. Religious experience arises not out of reason or intellection, but out of "feelings"—to use William James's explanation.[25] In short, it is a nonrational activity or event. Suzuki equated Zen satori to religious experience and, following James's analysis, characterized it as a psychological transformation or internal reorientation of one's outlook on the world.[26] For Suzuki, to undergo this experience is the most crucial event in the life of a Buddhist. He mapped it onto his own satori experience of identification with the trees one night while he was training at Engakuji in late 1896.[27] The net effect of emphasizing religious experience as the essence of Buddhism—the idea of *shūkyō teki keiken,* a term that hardly existed in the Japanese vocabulary before Suzuki's generation—is that it shifted the focus away from the idea of Buddhism as a multifaceted way of life, one that encompasses ritual actions, etiquette and comportment, mastery of ideas, new insights, participation in a community, and a code of behavior. Such an understanding of Buddhism dominated Japan for centuries and, to the extent that religious experience was recognized, it was embedded in this broad and diverse religious lifestyle. Suzuki's emphasis on religious experience thus represented a paradigm shift aimed at defining Buddhism first and foremost as a valid, nonrational, interior mental state and deemphasizing the external dimensions of Buddhism.[28] It proved to be a winning strategy for Suzuki and others defending Buddhism against its secular critics in the Meiji period and against scientific and rationalist attacks.

Another concept that Suzuki adopted to explain Buddhism, which was again influenced by James and other Western scholars of religion, was mysticism. It was treated as a natural extension or subcategory of religious experience, though in this case the experience was recognized as especially profound or overwhelming or transformative. In his writings Suzuki typically linked mysticism, like religious experience, to satori or *kenshō* in Zen or to enlightenment (S. *saṃbodhi*) in Buddhism.[29] The aspects of mysticism that fit best with Suzuki's image of Buddhist enlightenment were the sudden and unexpected character of the experience and the profound sense of knowing arising from it—namely, the irrational, noetic, and instantaneous quality of the occurrence. These characteristics are analogous to ones that James attributed to mysticism.[30] In Suzuki's analysis of this event, he developed the standard explanation that in a mystical state one loses all sense of separation from the thing encountered, though without obliterating one's individual identity.[31] Such a sense of merging with the other or of nondualism can be found in accounts of mysticism around the world, though Suzuki identified it as an essential aspect of Buddhist enlightenment. His adoption of mysticism as a conceptual model for explaining Zen served his needs well. But its application to Pure Land Buddhism was more complex. Suzuki nonetheless used this concept in his own comparative study, *Mysticism: Christian and Buddhist* of 1957, which contained numerous examples from the Pure Land tradition.[32] Late in life Suzuki expressed some misgivings about mysticism as a way to explain Buddhism and some regrets about his own use of the concept, but not enough to undo his decades of scholarship propounding Buddhism as mysticism.[33]

Religious experience and mysticism tended to be identified with sudden and profound moments of religious awakening, but over time Suzuki sought to expand his definition of Buddhist experience to include religious consciousness in everyday life, thereby reconciling it more to the earlier understanding of Buddhism as a multidimensional way of life. The primary form that this expanded interpretation took was as "Japanese spirituality," elucidated in Suzuki's book *Nihon teki reisei* in 1944. The term *reisei* was extremely rare in earlier Japanese writings. Suzuki appropriated it and singlehandedly infused it with a Buddhist and religious meaning of his own choosing. In a nutshell he explicated the term in the following way:

> As long as two things oppose each other, contradiction, rivalry, mutual suppression, and annihilation cannot be averted. In such situations, it will become impossible for human beings to carry on. What is needed is something that can encompass both of them and understand that the two are really not two, but one, and that the one is, as it is, two. *Reisei* accomplishes this. If we want the rivalries of the existing dualistic worldview to cease and become conciliatory and fraternal, and mutual interpenetration and self-identity to prevail, we have no choice but to await the awakening of man's religious consciousness, *reisei*.[34]

This idea of nondualistic identity was consistent with Suzuki's earlier interpretations of religious experience and mysticism, but in this case he did not limit it to a sudden or momentary realization. The concept of *reisei* received as its defining characteristic the idea of *sokuhi no ronri*, "the logic of simultaneous identification and differentiation," a theme that began to appear in Suzuki's writings shortly before this work was published.[35] As in the case of religious experience and mysticism, he treated *reisei* not as a rational or intellectual occurrence, but as a state arising from a more elemental experience, interaction with the earth. Of all the forms of Buddhism in Japan, Suzuki considered Zen and Pure Land to exemplify *reisei* the most. He considered aristocratic forms of Buddhism too effete and removed from the earth to manifest this spirituality. But Zen and Pure Land, through their association with samurai and peasant culture respectively, had strong ties to the earth.[36] Thus, they were the ones that embodied *Nihon teki reisei,* Japanese spirituality, the best, including and especially its core experience of *sokuhi,* simultaneous identification and differentiation. One outcome of Suzuki's idealization of this spirituality was his expanded interest in *myōkōnin*—lowly and sometimes illiterate exemplars of Shin Buddhist piety—as models of *Nihon teki reisei.*[37] They would become an increasingly prominent subject in Suzuki's scholarship.

These three concepts—religious experience, mysticism, and Japanese spirituality—shaped and informed most of Suzuki's interpretations of Buddhism. The first two emerged principally from his attempt to explain Zen, and the third from his desire to include Pure Land as well. But Pure Land Buddhism presented special challenges. First, it was at odds with the modern mindset more than most other forms of Buddhism—tethered to the myth of an other-worldly Buddha and his paradise where one would be born after death, and grounded in the seemingly mindless and ineffectual ritual of chanting the Buddha's name. Second, Pure Land Buddhism did not lend itself as readily and felicitously to the idea of sudden religious experience and mysticism as Zen satori did. Hence, it would require some experimental probing and interpretive license on Suzuki's part to attach his definition of Buddhist experience to the Pure Land case. Other modern interpreters of Pure Land, including Suzuki's Shin Buddhist colleagues at Otani, also experimented with new concepts and approaches. But Suzuki's own combination of ideas and explication of the Pure Land tradition generally put him in a category of his own.

PURE LAND BUDDHISM

The historical development and content of Pure Land Buddhism are too complex to describe in depth here, but suffice it to say that as a branch of Buddhism it focused on the transcendent Buddha Amida and the miraculous realm he has created in a distant western sphere of the universe, known variously as paradise or "the land of bliss" (J. *gokuraku,* S. *sukhāvatī*) or as the Pure Land (J. *jōdo*). These core elements and themes are traceable to the so-called three Pure Land sutras, which largely became the authoritative scriptures for various strands of Pure Land Buddhism in Japan. The message of these texts in their most literal and rudimentary form is that, among the countless "Buddha-lands" in the universe, the one established by Amida in the remote western direction is the most appealing and spiritually compelling, and that sentient beings should aspire to be born there in their next life, where liberation and enlightenment are assured to all. The miraculous characteristics of Amida, his Pure Land, and the path that sentient beings follow to attain birth there are elucidated in a series of forty-eight vows that Amida made vouchsafing this path to enlightenment. They indicate, among other things, that Amida is the Buddha of infinite light and eternal life, that the features of the Pure Land are paradisiacal and perfect, that all the Buddhas of the universe sing and praise Amida's name, that sentient beings who are sincere and have faith and desire birth in the Pure Land and perform the nembutsu are all born there, and that Amida and his celestial host will appear at the deathbed of the faithful to usher them into the Pure Land. The sutras thus convey the idea of a life of piety in this world and of birth in Amida's Pure Land in the next life where enlightenment occurs.[38]

The core themes and motifs of the Pure Land sutras underwent explication in China and Japan, where a variety of Pure Land beliefs and practices unfolded. One strand of the tradition tended to emphasize meditative visualization of Amida and the Pure Land, based on the literal meaning of the word "nembutsu," "thinking *(nen)* on the Buddha *(butsu)*." Another interpreted the nembutsu to mean invoking or chanting the name of Amida with the syllables *Namu-amida-butsu,* "I take refuge in the Buddha Amida." Some encouraged a life of structured religious practice. Others stressed faith and sincerity more. Most held the view that enlightenment does not occur in this life, but in the next in the Pure Land, though some occasionally conflated this world and Amida's paradise conceptually or rhetorically. Hōnen (1133–1212), the great founder of an independent Pure Land (or Jōdo) movement in Japan, is well known for advocating the "exclusive nembutsu" *(senju nenbutsu)*—specifically, the verbal invocation of Amida's name—as the central practice. His disciple Shinran (1173–1262), the founder of Shin Buddhism, was a major proponent of faith in addition. Ippen (1239–1289) and Shōkū (1177–1247), who represent other branches of Pure Land Buddhism, taught the inseparability of the Buddha and the believer in the practice of the nembutsu. And virtually all Pure Land Buddhists in Japan's medieval period subscribed to the idea of *mappō,* the decline of the Dharma, or *masse,* the age of decline. This was the notion that our world has entered a dark period when the teachings of the historical Buddha will disappear and people will be bereft of enlightenment. Pure Land beliefs and practices were presented as the only viable alternative in such a desperate age.[39]

These were the Pure Land teachings that Suzuki and his peers inherited as Japan emerged from a premodern mindset at the beginning of the Meiji period. Suzuki, as part of a new breed of modern Buddhists, approached these ideas with wariness and suspicion. This can be seen in a theoretical study of religion that he published in 1896 at the tender age of twenty-six, before he had even departed for America. In it he outlined the modern critique of traditional Buddhism from the standpoint of materialism and the pursuit of happiness, which were on the rise in Japan's new secular society:

> If people construct an icon of the Buddha, enshrine it in a chapel, offer flowers and burn incense, prostrate themselves and perform the nine reverences, and thereby pray for immediate happiness in this world and ethereal happiness after death, can we necessarily say there will be a divine response to this? Thus, if human life always attains just what it wishes by rituals such as these, then one might dare to believe that it is not difficult to make fire flow and water burn. Wouldn't such delusions be abundant? Likewise, can we say that there is a paradise in the western Pure Land and that, if people rely on the original vow of Amida and do not harbor thoughts of self-power, they will be enveloped in his light and will be able to go to that land of bliss without fail after death? But what exactly does this land that is ten trillion [lands] away in the west refer to? And what kind of personage does this Amida refer to? And how is it possible that his original vow has the magical power to save sentient beings? With delusional decision-making such as this and superstitions such as these, based on what type of logic could we arrive at any deduction? In no way is it possible for science to believe that there is such a thing as this.[40]

In this passage Suzuki identifies the challenge to Pure Land Buddhism in the modern world. Its rituals and cosmology were at odds with science and reason, and its aspirations for paradise after death seemed delusional or superstitious. For premodern believers, it was probably inconsequential whether they understood the Pure Land sutras literally or figuratively, since both offered a valid avenue to a fulfilling religious life. But for Suzuki, these ideas represented a stumbling block not only to scientific rationalists and materialists, but also to modern Buddhists. As a result, he attempted to articulate Buddhism in a way that would not be an affront to the modern mind, adapting some of its traditional themes and abandoning others.

SUZUKI'S IDEAS ON PURE LAND BUDDHISM

Suzuki's contribution to the emergence of Pure Land Buddhism in the modern period is reflected symbolically in the fact that he coined, or at least popularized, the term "Shin Buddhism" to convey the teachings of Pure Land to the West. This pithy title, which has rhetorical symmetry to "Zen Buddhism," allowed Shin to take root in the Western mind as a coherent and distinct category of Buddhism, albeit in contrast to Zen. In his English writings Suzuki talked about Shin Buddhism as often as, if not more than, Pure Land or Jōdo Buddhism, thus reflecting his partiality toward Shin among the various forms of Pure Land Buddhism. Even when Suzuki cited Hōnen and other non-Shin figures, he tended to explicate their ideas from a Shin perspective or in a Shin interpretive framework. Though some of Suzuki's ideas about Pure Land actually resembled the historical teachings of Ippen of the Jishū tradition and Shōkū of the Seizan branch of Pure Land Buddhism, more than those of Shinran and Shin Buddhism, Suzuki ascribed them to Shin as if they were completely compatible. Hence, Suzuki's claims about Pure Land Buddhism were associated first and foremost with Shin Buddhism, either by presupposing a Shin point of view or by projecting ideas onto the Shin tradition.

Suzuki's treatment of Shin Buddhism tended to be selective and idiosyncratic rather than comprehensive and systematic. Generally speaking, he was an eclectic and syncretic thinker. But he always had the best interests of Shin Buddhism at heart: to articulate it in such a way that it would be a persuasive and compelling viewpoint in the modern world. To do so, Suzuki felt compelled to interpret some ideas in a radical new way and to deviate from certain time-honored themes in the Shin tradition. A good example is the concept of *mappō* or *masse,* the idea of the inexorable decline of Buddhism and the disappearance of a path to liberation in this world. Historically, this belief was widespread in medieval times and was closely linked to the efflorescence of Pure Land Buddhism as an alternative path. Despite its prominence in the writings of Hōnen and Shinran, Suzuki dismissed *mappō* as irrelevant to true Pure Land spirituality.[41] Certainly in the eyes of Suzuki and other modern reformers, materialism and secularism posed a greater threat to Buddhism than did the archaic notion of *mappō.*

Another example of Suzuki's departure from tradition was his idealization of the *Tannishō* and even the *Anjin ketsujō shō,* both texts with obscure origins in Shin Buddhism, above Shinran's magnum opus, *Kyōgyōshinshō.*[42] In the case of the *Tannishō,* Suzuki was influenced no doubt by other Shin Buddhist reformers, especially disciples of Kiyozawa Manshi, who treasured the *Tannishō* as an inspiring digest of Shin beliefs. Suzuki himself seems to have had a preference for succinct expressions of religious truth over complex expositions of doctrine. That may have predisposed him more to the aphoristic style of the *Tannishō* and the *Anjin ketsujō shō*—which may have sounded faintly like the terse, pithy sayings of Zen masters to Suzuki—than to the long doctrinal discourses of the *Kyōgyōshinshō.* Though he was persuaded late in life to undertake an English translation of the *Kyōgyōshinshō,* it is not clear that Suzuki ever considered it the most important statement of Shinran's teachings.[43]

Suzuki's presentation of Pure Land Buddhism was not so much a tightly argued and logical exposition, but rather a collection of explications of Pure Land themes that attracted his attention. In expounding on them, he did not feel constrained by established doctrine. There are several trends that we can detect in his approach to Pure Land ideas. One was to shift the focus from the afterlife and the other world to the present life and this world. This helped to deflect the modern rationalist criticism of Pure Land's premodern cosmology. Shin Buddhism contained traditional ideas affirming the present as much as the afterlife, so there was a solid basis for Suzuki to pursue this line of thinking. But he placed such a heavy emphasis on the present that he excluded virtually any consideration of the afterlife.

A second trend in Suzuki's interpretations was to highlight religious experience as the crucial component in Pure Land Buddhism. As in the case of Zen, Suzuki sought to locate the essence of Pure Land in the subjective interior of humans, thereby insulating it from the reductionistic analysis of the objective world. As a result, he attempted to identify elements in the Pure Land tradition that reflected this inner experience. One side effect of Suzuki's idealization of religious experience is that it shifted the emphasis away from the community, which had long been a focal point of Shin Buddhism, and located it in the individual instead.

A third trend in Suzuki's explication of Pure Land Buddhism was to highlight nondualistic aspects of the tradition. His theoretical basis for this was the so-called logic of simultaneous identification and differentiation, *sokuhi no ronri,* propounded in his work on Japanese spirituality. This concept worked well when applied to Zen satori. But the Pure Land tradition contained strong dualistic motifs—for instance, the juxtaposition of this world to the Pure Land and of humans to Amida Buddha. Suzuki sought interpretive ways to counter or neutralize these dualisms and to give primacy to nondualistic experiences in Pure Land Buddhism.

Among Pure Land themes that captured Suzuki's imagination, the first was the twin concepts of self-power and other-power, *jiriki* and *tariki.* These tropes were well established in Pure Land discourse. Shinran of course emphasized the primacy of *tariki,* the power of Amida Buddha, over *jiriki,* the efforts of sentient beings. It is the Buddha's power, he declared, that unilaterally brings living beings to enlightenment, not their own effort and exertion.[44] Suzuki understood the logic of this argument, but he also acknowledged the importance of the *jiriki* standpoint, especially as exemplified in Zen Buddhism. While recognizing the validity of each side, Suzuki ultimately treated *tariki* and *jiriki* as coterminous with each other. His analysis faintly resembles William James's explication of two types of conversion, volitional and self-surrender, in *The Varieties of Religious Experience.*[45] The place where *tariki* and *jiriki* converge, according to Suzuki, is experience, specifically a mystical experience in which differentiations fade and opposites meld. This Suzuki regarded as the ground of all religion, authenticating *jiriki* and *tariki* experiences alike and unifying them even amid their differences.[46]

A second Pure Land element that fascinated Suzuki was the nembutsu, the chanting of Amida Buddha's name. As a child he had encountered it in his secret nembutsu initiation, and underwent a psychological change as a result. That event no doubt remained with him, at least subconsciously, throughout his life. Suzuki was interested, on the one hand, in the nembutsu's mechanical workings—its rhythmic and repetitious structure and its spellbinding and mesmerizing effect on the body and mind. He focused specifically on the psychological dynamics by which one's empirical consciousness of ordinary objects is somehow subverted and a different type of consciousness arises. Suzuki observed that a similar outcome arises in Islamic Sufism when the name of Allah is chanted, and also in Zen koan practice, though the actual workings of koan are considerably different.[47] On the other hand, Suzuki was also interested in the nembutsu as religious experience, whether manifested as a momentary mystical event or as an ongoing spiritual state. In this experience there is a coalescence of Amida Buddha with the person who intones his name so that, in a sense, only the nembutsu exists. This dimension of nonduality is, in Suzuki's estimation, what makes the nembutsu a religious experience. In interpreting it this way, Suzuki shifted the focus away from the more pedestrian understanding of the nembutsu as a practice assuring birth in the Pure Land after death. Instead, it is to be experienced here and now.[48] Suzuki's interpretation had a basis in certain doctrines of Shin Buddhism, but it was actually more akin to Ippen's view of the nembutsu in the Jishū tradition.[49] Suzuki searched assiduously for good examples of this in the Shin tradition proper, and he finally discovered it in the *myōkōnin* Asahara Saichi (1850–1932).[50] There are few other *myōkōnin* that fit Suzuki's model as closely as Saichi did. Suzuki singlehandedly raised him up in scholarship as a paradigm of Shin Buddhist spirituality.

The third theme that Suzuki was drawn to was the concept of the Pure Land paradise. His interpretation had the effect of countering the traditional and entrenched cosmology of the Pure Land as a place in the universe where one is born after death. Such a view was no longer tenable in a world of modern astronomy and scientific observation. Suzuki thus sought to give the Pure Land a symbolic or experiential meaning, instead of a locational one. Specifically, he identified the Pure Land as a state or domain of spirituality. To be born in the Pure Land is to reside in a realm of spirituality in which one feels harmonized with all things rather than at odds with them. And since this state can and does occur in this life, it does not belong to the future but to the present. As a result, Suzuki equated the Pure Land to this flawed and tragic world in which humans live, the so-called *sahā* (S.) or *shaba* (J.) world. Thus, Amida's paradise can be experienced here and now if one abides in this spiritual state.[51] Suzuki's interpretation of the Pure Land was to a certain extent a variation of ideas found in the *Platform Sutra (Rokuso dangyō)* of Zen and in the *Vimalakīrti Sūtra (Yuimagyō),* both of which lay outside Pure Land Buddhism's textual and exegetical tradition.[52] But more importantly, as an explanation it brought together all three of Suzuki's interpretive goals: emphasis on the present, on religious experience, and on nonduality.

The next theme that Suzuki singled out in his interpretation of Shin Buddhism was the doctrine of *kihō ittai,* the idea that humans with all their shortcomings and the Buddha with his Dharmic perfection are actually one inseparable substance. This concept had a complex history in Shin Buddhism. It was articulated most cogently in the *Anjin ketsujō shō,* a text that did not have Shin roots, but was nonetheless embraced and promoted by Rennyo (1415–1499), the greatest promulgator of

Shin Buddhism. It now seems clear that the text reflected ideas of the Seizan branch of Pure Land Buddhism, founded by Shōkū, more than the teachings of Shinran. Nonetheless, Suzuki treated the *Anjin ketsujō shō* as one of the most important works of Shin Buddhism, citing it more frequently than many mainstream sources. The reason no doubt was that the *kihō ittai* doctrine coalesced well with Suzuki's own interpretive agenda. The nondualistic message of the doctrine—the unity of Buddha and sentient beings—conformed felicitously to his trademark "logic of simultaneous identification and differentiation," *sokuhi no ronri.* In his explication of this doctrine, Suzuki elaborated on the various expressions of these unified pairs: Amida and devotee, all-saving Buddha and sin-laden individual, subject and object, supreme enlightenment and human yearnings.[53] All are united as one substance. Most prominently, Suzuki emphasized—in a statement consistent with both the *Anjin ketsujō shō* and Shinran's teachings—that the paramount example of this nonduality is found in the nembutsu. The invocation *Namu-amida-butsu* brings together sentient beings on one side, with their dependence expressed in the word *Namu,* and the Buddha on the other side, with his identity embodied in the name *Amida-butsu.* This invocation functions as a seamless whole in religious practice, in a sense actualizing the unification of the two. In this way Suzuki again sought to highlight the nondualistic quality of the Shin Buddhist experience.[54]

One more theme that attracted Suzuki's attention was the Shin Buddhist concept of faith, expressed variously in religious texts as *shin* (faith), *shinjin* (mind or heart of faith), *isshin* (oneness of mind or heart), *ichinen* (one thought), and other terms. Suzuki focused on this theme after finally reading Shinran's *Kyōgyōshinshō* in depth in the early 1940s.[55] This concept seemed to provide an excellent example of Suzuki's idea of an inner religious dimension of humans that is immune to the intrusions and analyses of the external and objective world. To the extent that Shin Buddhism traditionally emphasized faith as the crucial aspect of religious life, it also fit well with Suzuki's model of experience as the defining characteristic of religion. As in the case of Zen satori, Suzuki interpreted Shin Buddhist faith in terms of religious experience, mysticism, and spirituality, *reisei.*[56] The fact that the Shin tradition considered faith to be the point of intersection between the heart or mind of humans and that of the Buddha also lent itself to the nondualistic motif Suzuki sought to advance.[57] One point of ambiguity that arose from Suzuki's interpretation is whether Shin faith is actually the experience of Buddhist enlightenment. That assumption seems implicit in Suzuki's treatment of faith as the Shin analogue of Zen satori, which is unequivocally identified as Buddhist enlightenment.[58] In the Shin tradition, however, there was a tendency to use more indirect and elusive language, for instance, describing the person of faith as a bodhisattva at the highest stage, "equivalent to enlightenment" *(tōshōgaku),* but not to take the final step of proclaiming faith to be enlightenment.[59] Suzuki's interpretation seemed to push beyond these limits and to conflate faith with satori itself.

One final theme from Shin Buddhism that intrigued Suzuki was the idea of *jinen hōni,* which roughly means the natural way for things to be. Shinran used this expression to refer to the state of complete reliance on the power of Amida by the person of faith, devoid of any individual contrivance or calculation *(hakarai).*[60] Suzuki was drawn to the idea of *jinen hōni* as an example of mysticism or spirituality, replete with its nondualistic dimensions and overtones. He identified *jinen hōni* as the spirituality of *myōkōnin* saints in their day-to-day and moment-to-moment life. Suzuki's treatment of this theme suggests that he perceived religious experience as encompassing not just momentary mystical occurrences but also ongoing spiritual states. As in the case of mysticism, he considered *jinen hōni* to be a positive, immediate experience in this world.[61] In terms of sectarian Shin Buddhist doctrine, Suzuki's heavy emphasis on spirituality and *jinen hōni* would probably classify him as a partisan of the *hō no jinshin* doctrine, the idealization of faith as a state of identification with and inseparability from the Buddha. By comparison, the *ki no jinshin* doctrine, the characterization of faith as a realization of one's own profound and insurmountable shortcomings, is less prominent in Suzuki's treatment, even though it is given equal weight in Shin Buddhism.[62]

The composite effect of Suzuki's interpretation of these various Pure Land themes was to create a version of Pure Land—and of Shin Buddhism in particular—that focused overwhelmingly on the present, on religious experience, and on nonduality as defining characteristics. He was not the only modern Buddhist thinker to emphasize these motifs. But he presented them in a cogent, distinctive, and thought-provoking way, such that his portrayal of Pure Land Buddhism, while not emerging as the dominant interpretation in traditional sectarian circles, helped to stimulate new understandings quite different from before.

SUZUKI'S CONTRIBUTIONS

Suzuki and his generation of Buddhist reformers succeeded beyond their wildest expectations in articulating a Buddhism that could weather the storm of rationalism, science, and materialism, and that could actually flourish in the modern world. Not only was Buddhism reestablished in Japan as a viable and influential tradition, but it also gained credibility among Westerners searching for new religious alternatives. Suzuki was a bridge figure in this process. Because he published so much in English, he emerged as one of the primary authorities on Buddhism in the West. And because he couched it in terms that Westerners already recognized and appreciated—principally, "religious experience," "mysticism," and "spirituality"—he facilitated the integration of Buddhism into Western circles as a new religious discourse. To this day, some of the expressions that he (and his wife Beatrice) selected for Buddhist ideas remain as standard terminology in English. As in the case of other formulations of religion in the early twentieth century, there are aspects of Suzuki's interpretations that may now seem dated, especially in the light of postmodernism's trenchant critique of the essentialisms of religion. But whatever criticism his ideas have sustained in the present, it is clear that the West could not have arrived at its current understanding of Buddhism without the views he propounded.

In terms of Pure Land Buddhism specifically, Suzuki left a distinct mark there also. His legacy in Japan is complex and diffused. Though we could not describe Suzuki's understanding of Pure Land as the mainstream interpretation, it helped create an alternative discourse and acted as a catalyst for rethinking the tradition. Certainly the motifs that he advanced—his focus on the present, on religious experience, and on nonduality—have gained traction in many arenas of modern Pure Land thought. In addition, he opened up a new avenue of Shin Buddhist scholarship in the form of *myōkōnin* studies. Documentation and explication of their sayings lay at the fringes of scholarship before Suzuki's time. By force of his own innovative examination of *myōkōnin* sayings, this genre of literature has emerged as a focal point in Shin Buddhist studies.

Suzuki's contribution to Pure Land Buddhism in the West is, in a sense, simple and straightforward. He caused Westerners to take Pure Land Buddhism seriously even though they were not inclined to do so. The allure of Buddhism in the West during the nineteenth and twentieth centuries was born out of a discontent that many Westerners felt toward their own religious traditions, particularly Christianity. Hence, when they encountered Pure Land Buddhism, they tended to stereotype it as a Buddhist aberration that resembled the religion they had rejected: the myth of an all-merciful deity taking pity on sinful humans, who surrender to him in faith and perform acts of devotion, resulting ultimately in their salvation in heaven after death. Suzuki, by contrast, always treated Pure Land as an authentic and compelling expression of Mahayana Buddhism. He presented parallels between it and Zen, and highlighted ways in which Pure Land seemed to outstrip Zen in Mahayana values. And his modernist interpretation of Pure Land—emphasizing the present, religious experience, and nonduality—sparked the interest of Westerners in ways they never imagined. In short, it is unlikely that Pure Land Buddhism would have ever received a fair and open hearing in the West without the writings and interpretations of D. T. Suzuki.

James C. Dobbins

EDITORIAL NOTE

The essays by D. T. Suzuki contained in this volume are based mostly on previously published texts that are cited in the introduction to each essay. As much as possible, we have adhered to Suzuki's original text, although we have made some changes according to the following editorial principles:

- British spellings and punctuation have been changed to American.
- Chinese and Japanese characters are deleted from the text and assembled in a glossary at the end of the volume.
- Romanization of Japanese and Chinese terms conforms to the modified Hepburn and the pinyin system respectively.
- Romanization of Sanskrit and Pali terms follows the conventions of Nakamura Hajime's *Bukkyōgo daijiten.*
- The spelling, hyphenation, capitalization, and italicization of a few specialized terms (for example, *Namu-amida-butsu*) are standardized throughout the volume even though they vary in Suzuki's original texts.
- In places where Suzuki gives dates for people, events, historical periods, and so on that have been revised by contemporary scholars, we have noted the correct date in a footnote with the initials of the volume editor making the emendation to the original text.
- Foreign words are changed to their anglicized form if they appear in *Webster's Third International Dictionary,* except for ones specifically presented as foreign terms.
- Corrections are made to misspellings and missing words where they are obvious or where they are confirmed in later republications of the same essay or translations of it into Japanese.

- Slight changes are made to the punctuation to correct obvious errors or nonstandard and misleading punctuation.
- Square brackets indicating text inserted by the editor or translator into the essays are identified by the editor's or translator's initials. Suzuki's own square bracketed interpolations into the text have been left as in the original source text. Other editorial changes noted in the text are as they are in the published version of the text used as the basis for the essay in the current volume.
- In most cases capitalization of words (for example, Vow vs. vow, or Gatha vs. gatha) follows Suzuki's original texts despite their inconsistencies.
- Lengthy quotations have been reformatted as block quotations.
- In a few rare cases, corrections are made to content, especially where those corrections are confirmed in later republications of the essays or in Japanese translations of them.

1

The Development of the Pure Land Doctrine in Buddhism

This essay is one of Suzuki's earliest detailed treatments of Pure Land Buddhism. It gives a brief overview of its core concepts and themes: Amida Buddha, Pure Land paradise, vows of Amida to deliver all beings to enlightenment, karmic wrongdoing or sin that hinders humans from attaining enlightenment, nembutsu practice of invoking the Buddha's name, and the religious life of relying on the power of the Buddha, tariki, instead of one's own power, jiriki. Suzuki presents these ideas as fundamental to the Jōdo school of Hōnen (1133–1212), the Shin school of Shinran (1173–1262), and the Ji school of Ippen (1239–1289), but among them Shin Buddhism seems to have exerted the greatest influence on his thinking.

Suzuki seeks to situate the Pure Land sutras and its doctrines in the broader context of Mahayana thought, including the bodhisattva path and the twin ideals of wisdom and love (or compassion). As in the case of Mahayana, he attempts to defend Pure Land from disparagement as an inferior or inauthentic form of Buddhism compared to Theravada, which dominated the scholarly understanding of Buddhism in the early twentieth century. He does so in several ways. First, he identifies similarities between early Buddhism and Pure Land, suggesting that Pure Land in fact embodies the spirit and essence of the historical Buddha Śākyamuni. Second, he argues that historical truth does not necessarily trump mythic truth, propounded in the Mahayana sutras. Third, he differentiates the inner spiritual dimension of humans from the world of intellection and mechanistic causation—a strategy similar to the West's modern attempt to define religion as a nonrational experience operating outside of reason and science. Finally, he offers his own interpretation of the Pure Land paradise as a mystical world that can be experienced in this life rather than after death. The extent to which Suzuki's argument departs from established Pure Land doctrine is reflected in his citation of the *Vimalakīrti Sūtra* near the end of his essay to support his claim, a text that plays virtually no role in traditional Pure Land hermeneutics. Suzuki's essay, in short, represents a new style of argumentation to defend Pure Land in the modern period as an authentic form of Buddhism.

The base text for this essay is "The Development of the Pure Land Doctrine in Buddhism," *The Eastern Buddhist* 3, no. 4 (1925): 285–326. It was republished with slight editorial changes in Daisetz Teitarō Suzuki, *Collected Writings on Shin Buddhism* (CWSB), ed. The Eastern Buddhist Society (Kyoto: Shinshū Ōtaniha, 1973), 3–31. A Japanese translation by Kusunoki Kyō was published as "Bukkyō ni okeru Jōdo kyōri no hattatsu," in Suzuki Daisetsu, *Nihon Bukkyō no soko o nagareru mono* (Kyoto: Ōtani Shuppansha, 1950), 61–138. See SDZ 11:352–400.

. . .

If we believe, as we must from the modern critical point of view, that the history of any religious system consists, partly, in the exfoliation of the unessential elements, but, chiefly, in the revelation and the constant growth of the most vital spiritual elements which lie hidden either in the words of the founder or in his personality, the following question naturally comes up for solution in our investigation of the history of Buddhist dogmatics: "How much of the Pure Land *(jōdo)* idea is deducible from the teaching of primitive Buddhism so-called, or from the personality of Śākyamuni Buddha himself?"

This is one of the most important and fundamental questions in the history of Buddhism, seeing that the majority of Japanese Buddhists are adherents of the Pure Land teaching. Indeed, the origin of the Pure Land idea is simultaneous with the general growth of Mahayana Buddhism itself, which evidently took place within a few centuries after the passing of the Master. At the present stage, however, of our knowledge of Indian thought and culture generally, the solution of the question above cited will be necessarily philosophical and psychological rather than strictly historical. There ought to be more materials at our disposal before we can objectively trace every step of development in reference to historical facts. Therefore, what I have attempted in the following pages may be said to be a philosophy of religious experience which has been gone through with by the followers of the Enlightened One; that is to say, it will be the interpretation of the Pure Land teaching as a formulation of the experience which has so far unfolded itself in the Buddhist life.

For the benefit of readers who are not well acquainted with the characteristic features of Japanese or Eastern Buddhism, a few introductory remarks concerning the teaching of the Pure Land school may not be out of place here. Without some knowledge of this, the purport of the present article will be more or less unintelligible.

I

By the Pure Land school of Japanese Buddhism[1] I mean the Buddhist doctrine that teaches the invocation of the name of Amida Buddha in order to be saved from an imperfect and sinful life which we all lead, and be taken up after death into the abode of the Buddha, which is known as the Land of Purity or Land of Bliss.[2] This school is also called the Nembutsu school, *nembutsu* being Japanese (*nianfo* in Chinese) for the invocation of the Buddha's name. *Nen* or *nian* (*smṛti* in Sanskrit) literally means "to recollect," "to remember," "to reflect upon," or "to think of," and consequently *nembutsu* is to think of the Buddha, and as far as its literal sense is concerned it is not the invoking of his name as is understood at present. This was no doubt all true, primarily; but as the doctrine of Nembutsu began to unfold all its implications, it came to be synonymous with the reciting of the name of the Buddha, for the intense thinking of the Buddha with all his moral and spiritual qualities would inevitably burst out in a loud call on his name. Later, the vocal accompaniment was isolated[3] and given an independent program in the progressive development of the doctrine of Nembutsu. Nembutsu was then no more "meditative recollection" but "vocal recollection." And at present as all the aspirants for the Pure Land of Bliss are taught to resort to this "vocal recollection" as the means of rebirth there, they are followers of Nembutsu.

There are three or four sects now in Japan that are to be classed under the Pure Land school: they are the Jōdo, Shin, and Ji. The Yūzū-nembutsu may also be brought under this category, as it teaches the nembutsu and the possibility of rebirth in the land of Amida. But as it will grow clearer later, this sect is based on the philosophy of identity and interpenetration as is expounded in the *Avataṃsaka Sūtra* and not on the Original Vows of Amida which are detailed in the *Sukhāvatī-vyūha Sūtra,* and this latter constitutes the foundation of the Pure Land sects. While the Yūzū no doubt precipitated the development of the Pure Land school proper as we understand it, the Yūzū stands by itself when we consider its peculiar features; and it may be best not to group it with such purely Pure Land sects such as the Jōdo, Shin, and Ji. We shall later treat of its tenets in connection with the history of the Pure Land teaching in Japan.

The following are the main ideas which support the structure of the great Pure Land edifice. While each Pure Land sect may differ in its way of upholding certain aspects of the doctrine more emphatically than others, all the sects agree in recognizing the following elements as essential to their faith and incorporating them in the system of their teaching. When we are therefore acquainted with these factors as enumerated below, we know in what respects the Pure Land teaching varies from other Mahayana systems, in other words, how in spite of its assumption of such an apparently un-Buddhist complexion it is essentially Mahayanistic.

1. *Amida.*[4] Amida occupies the center of the Pure Land doctrine and we must know who he is. According to the *Larger Sukhāvatī-vyūha,* he was a king in one of his former incarnations, and moved by the sermons of the Buddha Lokeśvara who was the reigning Buddha of that age; he conceived the idea of becoming a homeless sramana and later realizing Buddhahood.

His monkish name was Dharmākara. He meditated for five kalpas before he made a certain number of vows *(praṇidhāna)* as conditions of his attainment of enlightenment. When these vows were declared in the presence of Buddha Lokeśvara, the earth shook in six different ways. After this, the Bhikshu Dharmākara devoted himself to the practice of all kinds of virtues and meritorious deeds for a period of incalculable kalpas. He went through many an incarnation as kings, lay-disciples of the Buddha, celestial gods, etc. He finally attained enlightenment, and became the Buddha of infinite light *(amitābha)* and eternal life *(amitāyus)*. It has now passed ten kalpas since then.

2. *The Pure Land.* This is the country where the Buddha of Eternal Life and Infinite Light is abiding and is described minutely in the *Larger Sukhāvatī-vyūha* and the *Smaller Sukhāvatī-vyūha*. In the main it is the world in which "there is neither bodily nor mental pain for living beings, and where the sources of happiness are innumerable." While Buddha Akṣobhya has his Buddha-land in the east, Amida has his in the west, distant from this world by a hundred thousand *niyuta*s of *koṭi*s of Buddha-countries. And the Pure Land school teaches that Amida Buddha is awaiting us there and that we must cherish the desire to be born in his country. The object, however, is not necessarily to enjoy happiness pure and simple in that world, but to attain enlightenment which is impossible for ordinary mortals to realize while on earth. For they are fettered on all sides by things finite and imperfect, indeed they are themselves all this, and have no way to attain their ideals of freedom and perfection except by going out of this *sahāloka* (world of endurance) and being taken up by Amida into his world. He made his Vows and reached his enlightenment proving that all the Vows were fulfilled, and therefore if we only invoke his name and ask him to be helped in our trials here, he will undoubtedly listen to us and carry us up into his own abode. In fact, he is constantly calling out to us to come to him, and what we have to do is just to pay attention to the fact and hear his voice.

3. *The Original Vows.* The fact that he is calling out to us is established by the fulfillment of all his Original Vows *(pūrva-praṇidhāna)*, which he made after meditation for five long kalpas. There are, according to Saṃghavarman's Chinese translation of the *Sukhāvatī-vyūha*, forty-eight[5] Vows made by Amida. While some of them have apparently no practical bearings on our modern conception of life and salvation, there is one most important and most significant Vow, without which the whole system of the forty-eight *praṇidhāna*s would collapse. This is known as the Eighteenth Vow, which reads:

> If all beings in the ten quarters, when I have attained Buddhahood, should believe in me with all sincerity of heart, desiring to be born in my country, and should, say ten times, think of me, and if they should not be reborn there, may I not obtain enlightenment, barring only those who have committed the five deadly sins and who have abused the Good Law *(Dharma)*.

That the Bodhisattva will practice the virtues of perfection *(pāramitā)* not merely for his own benefit but for others as well is one of the original ideas in Buddhism, which grew up in the course of development in India. And with Amida this thought of benefiting others was made the condition of enlightenment, for he vowed that he would not be enlightened unless the conditions were not fulfilled. In Hinayana Buddhism Arhatship was the ideal of the Buddhist life and the Arhat was satisfied with his own enlightenment. Naturally as a social being, he wished to see others enlightened as himself, but this was in no wise thought of in connection with his own attainment. His individuality did not extend so far as to embrace others in it. But Amida's love for all beings was so intense and all-embracing that even when he could have for himself all he aspired to in the way of Buddhahood, he postponed it until his fellow creatures were also assured of a share in his attainment.

4. *The conception of sin.* Now that Amida has fulfilled his part, what shall common mortals have to do in order to respond to his call? That is, how are we to be reborn in his Land of Purity? First, we have to realize that we are sinful beings due to the karma of innumerable evil deeds committed by us in our former lives, and that if we are left to ourselves we shall have no chance whatever to be delivered from this life of misery and suffering. In this, the Pure Land followers are sometimes apt to run to an extreme by drawing a too sharply defined line between Amida and ourselves. Amida is love, they would say, and light and goodness and has nothing evil in himself, while common mortals are so depraved that, by themselves, they are destined nowhere else than to purgatory. Practically, however, when this remorseful attitude is the more intensely realized, the more earnest and sincere a man will be in his desire to be born in the Pure Land of Amida. Thus three things are considered most necessary for rebirth in the other world: 1. Sincerity of heart, 2. a deep (believing) heart, and 3. desire to be reborn in Amida's Pure Land.

5. *Nembutsu.* The nembutsu is the expression of a man's complete dependence on Amida as far as his salvation and rebirth are concerned. When he is sincerely awakened to the fact that his moral depravity finally condemns him to purgatory *(naraka),* this, according to Pure Land scholars, is the time he hears the call of Amida, and the nembutsu is the natural outcome of this awakening and hearing. Whatever the historical meaning of nembutsu might have been, it is now no more mere thinking of the Buddha and his virtues, but, as was explained above, it is the invocation of the name of Amida as one whose forty-eight Original Vows were fulfilled ten kalpas ago. The name Amida itself has now come to have a mysterious meaning charged with a power to save all who uttered it with sincerity of heart and singleness of thought. This is the most remarkable part in the development of the *tariki* (other-power) system in Buddhism.

6. *The moral life.* That moral perfection is not essential, i.e., not absolutely needed, for salvation, is one of the principal keynotes in all the Pure Land schools

of Buddhism. Even in primitive Buddhism mere morality was not regarded as sufficient for the attainment of Arhatship; for meditation *(dhyāna)* and spiritual intuition *(prajñā)* were also strongly inculcated upon the minds of the Bhikshus and Sramanas. The contention most emphatically set forward by Pure Land devotees is that we are fundamentally imperfect, and therefore that no amount of our human and unaided efforts to perfect ourselves morally, if that is the only condition for enlightenment and deliverance, will ever lead to the attainment of the end. The will as expressed in the Original Vows of Amida is thus absolutely essential to lift us from this hopeless situation. Our own efforts called *jiriki* (self-power) always contain in them something, however minute or faint, of the residual idea of ego, and the basic teaching of Buddhism in whatever form is that we must be free from the thought of ego if we really desire for Nirvana or *Saṃbodhi* (enlightenment). We often have, principally I think in Mahayana literature, that the Bodhisattvas ask questions of the Buddha through his grace or power *(tathāgata-dhiṣṭhāna* or *-anubhāva)* and not of their own accord. If this can happen, that is, if the Buddha has the power to move others as he wills, and if common mortals are not their own saviors, it seems to be natural for certain Buddhists to arrive at the conclusion that *tariki* and not *jiriki* is the condition of salvation, and that faith and not morality is what is absolutely required of Pure Land aspirants. At all events, teachers of the Pure Land school look askance at the doctrine of self-reliance or self-power *(jiriki)* as the assertion of egoism, and strongly insist on *tariki,* other-power, or on the unparalleled superiority of faith and passivity. The following passage from Tauler is in full agreement with the view held by the Pure Land advocates: "Alles das Gott von uns haben will, das ist, dass wir müssig seyen und ihn Werkmeister seyen lassen; wären wir ganz und gar müssig, so wären wir vollkommen Menschen." ["All that God would have from us is that we be idle and allow him to be the master craftsman; were we to be completely and utterly idle, then we would be perfectly human" (JCD).][6]

These six factors or ideas are closely interwoven into the fabric of the Pure Land teaching, determining in various ways the relationship of Amida and all sentient beings *(sarvasattva)* and thereby the conditions of rebirth in the Pure Land.

The questions may be raised: How do we come to know about Amida, his all-embracing love, his Original Vows, his Pure Land, and his realization of enlightenment? How are we justified in placing our spiritual destiny entirely into the hands of Amida? How do we come to be assured of the fulfillment of his Vows? How is it that Amida whose existence seems to be altogether mythical and not at all historical can exercise such an exalted spiritual influence over human souls which seem to be so really sinful and under the sway of karmic law? These are all profound questions relating to the bases of our religious consciousness, and when they [are (CWSB)] fully answered a book on the philosophy of religion would be written. In the following pages some phases of these questions are touched upon, though necessarily cursorily; and further investigation is reserved for future articles.

There are three principal sutras constituting the Pure Land group of Mahayana literature: The *Larger* and the *Smaller Sukhāvatī-vyūha*[7] *Sūtra* and the *Sutra of the Meditations on Amitāyus;* and they conjointly make up the foundations of the doctrine of Amida. The Jataka story of Amida and his forty-eight Original Vows are detailed in the *Larger Sukhāvatī.* The scenes in the Pure Land are minutely described in the *Larger* and the *Smaller Sukhāvatī.* The *Meditation Sutra* gives an account of Śākyamuni Buddha's vision as it appeared to Queen Vaidehī in her imprisonment and his sermon to her on the various forms of meditation, of which the most important is the one on the Buddha of Infinite Light and Eternal Life. The sutra also tells in detail as to the plans or grades in the Pure Land, which are assigned to different classes of the aspirants according to their ways of living and understanding while in this world.

As long as those Original Vows are the living source of *tariki* faith, one may say, the *Larger Sukhāvatī* ought to occupy, as with the Shin sect, the most central position in its teaching, but this is not always the case; for the Jōdo tends to emphasize the importance of the *Meditation Sutra* more than the *Larger Sukhāvatī,* while the Ji apparently upholds the *Smaller Sukhāvatī* as the chief scriptural authority for its doctrine.

The fact is that while Amida and his attributes including his Pure Land are topics common to these three sutras, each has its own peculiar way of dealing with the subject matter. For instance, while the Original Vows are not at all the subject of the *Meditation Sutra* or of the *Smaller Sukhāvatī,* they are fully described in the *Larger Sukhāvatī,* in fact they are the chief topic of the first part of the sutra. Meditations on Amida are highly recommended in the *Meditation Sutra,* reminding one strongly of the five or ten subjects of meditation[8] suggested already in the Agamas. There is no doubt that the idea of the compiler of this sutra was to teach the doctrine that the perfections of the Pure Land presided over by Amida are realizable by the strength of mental concentration and not by the mysterious *tariki* power of Amida as the author of the forty-eight Vows. The *Smaller Sukhāvatī* shares in this respect the tendency of the *Meditation Sutra,* but with this difference that while the latter relies on the power of self-concentration to realize Amida and his Pure Land, the *Smaller Sukhāvatī* makes most of the holding in thought of the *name* of Amida.

It is likely that these three Pure Land sutras were complied at different times, and with different objects in view. For this reason, when the three Pure Land sects came each to emphasize its own special teaching in the system of Amida doctrine, each took up the one most suited to its purpose, thus distinguishing itself from the others; but when they wished to elucidate generally the Amida doctrine, they systematically and uniformly upheld the three sutras as unfolding in a most specific sense the mystery of Amida. We can thus readily understand how easy it was for the Pure Land school to be differentiated into the Jōdo, Shin, and Ji.

This was still more so when such strong and independent souls as Shinran or Hōnen with their own deep religious experiences read and interpreted the scriptures in their own original way and were not always scrupulous to follow literally the traditional reading. Naturally, they would not ignore the authority of Śākyamuni Buddha, through whom they were first made acquainted with Amida and his Vows; indeed they never neglected to bring Śākyamuni forward as the source of their inspirations. But they interpreted this source with their own experiences. We can say that the latter were really of the first importance to them—how could it be otherwise?—and that the scriptural authority was used to support them. This is the way we would now judge the matter before us, but as far as their own consciousness went they must have sincerely believed that everything they had in the way of *tariki* faith came from the teaching of Śākyamuni himself. This being the case, at least with modern critics of the Pure Land faith, some of the questions raised above are to be answered in terms of the inner experience of a highly spiritual character, and not in the conventional manner of professional scholars bent on defending their faith on scriptural authority.

Incidentally, let us note here that the idea of scriptural authority in whatever form is no more tenable and therefore that whatever ideas that have proved vital, inspiring, and uplifting in the history of religion must find another way of establishing themselves as the ultimate facts of the religious consciousness. Scriptures, Christian or Buddhist, are divine revelations inasmuch as they tally with the deeper experiences of the soul and really help humanity to break through the fetters of finitude and open up a vista full of light and life. In other words, authority must come from within and not from without. The conception of an external God who revealed himself only at a certain time and place cannot be maintained in the face of science and philosophy. The real God is revealed not only in history as it unfolds itself in time, but especially in the human heart when it dives down into itself. This being our standpoint, the Pure Land teaching is to be interpreted, as I said before, in terms of religious consciousness, and not, as is done usually by its orthodox followers, in terms of scriptural authority or special revelation.

Before we proceed farther, let us define the use of the two commonest words which will arrest our attention in every work dealing with the Pure Land teaching. They are *tariki* (literally, other-power) and *jiriki* (self-power), to which reference has already been made in the present article. Broadly stated, *jiriki* means individual human efforts and *tariki* divine grace. These terms have come in vogue since the day of Donran (C. Tanluan) when he illustrated the *tariki* method of salvation by the analogy of a weak man going about everywhere in the world when he attaches himself to the Lord of the Universe, Cakravartin. In contrast to this, *jiriki* is relying on one's own moral and spiritual discipline by which he would practice meditations for the acquisition of miraculous powers. This latter is however too hard a task to be accomplished by ordinary mortals; for they are imperfect in every way and full of sinful thoughts and desires, which the harder they try to eradicate the stronger the evils seem to grow. In Self there is nothing that will lead one up to Buddhahood. The latter is to be attained only by the grace of a higher or "other" being whose wise and compassionate spirit-power works even in sinful human hearts. Truly, without this mysterious power working in them, they are unable to achieve final salvation when they are left to themselves, that is, when they endeavor to attain Buddhahood by *jiriki.* In order to make the mysterious power of a higher being work within ourselves, we must abandon *jiriki* and resort entirely to *tariki* which will effect its own end by itself.

To express the idea in Christian terminology, "This inward work of God, though never ceasing or altering, is yet always and only hindered by the activity of our own nature and faculties, by bad men through their obedience to earthly passions, and by good men through their striving to be good in their own way, by their natural strength, and a multiplicity of seemingly holy labors and contrivances." "Their own way" here corresponds to *jiriki. Tariki* is the spirit of faith, or the ultimate perfection of piety, "which not here, [or there, (CWSB)] or now and then, but everywhere, and in all things, looks up to God alone, trusts solely in Him, depends absolutely upon Him, expects all from Him, and does all it does for Him."

The difference between Christian and Buddhist mysticism is perhaps that Buddhists do not regard the whole nature of man as "consisting in its being fallen from God into itself, into a self-government and activity, under its own powers broken off from God."[9] They realize that karma works either way, good or bad, according to the direction we give to it, and however tremendous the work may be to counterbalance the evils of the past accumulated karma-force, we can still accomplish it if we would apply ourselves to it most assiduously through countless ages. But the Christians seem to think that the first karma [is (CWSB)] committed by our first father by deviating from a fall, absolute dependence upon God can never be made good until we are brought out of ourselves by a power from Christ living in us; for otherwise our lost goodness could never come back to us. That is to say, while the Christians uphold *tariki* and leave no room for *jiriki,* the Buddhists recognize the possibility of a purely *jiriki* school under the name of the Holy Path or Difficult Practice. Therefore, when Buddhism is taken as a whole, we note that there are two systems apparently contradicting each other but really working in unison.

Below is the most noted parable of the "Two Streams and a White Path"[10] given first by Zendō (C. Shandao) in his commentary to the *Sutra of the Meditation on Amida.* Zendō of the seventh century in the Tang is one of the seven patriarchs of the Pure Land school, and his commentary constitutes one of the main springs of its teaching. As the parable graphically represents the position of the *tariki* follower as he stands related to Amida, to Śākyamuni Buddha, to this world of defilement, and to himself, it is reproduced here from Zendō's text.

> Here is a man wishing to travel in the western direction on a road extending over a hundred or even a thousand *li*.[11] Suddenly he descries in the way two streams, the one of fire and the other of water: the fire is on the south and the water on the north. Both are one hundred steps wide but the depths are unknown. How far they extend northward and southward nobody can measure. Just between the fire and the water there lies a white path about four or five *sun* broad and running from the east bank to the west; its length is also one hundred steps. Not only the waves rising in succession from this water sweep over the path, but the flames of the fire also reach up and scorch it. The path is thus found washed by waves and flames, alternately and without cessation.
>
> A traveler, already in the midst of the wilderness far away from human habitations, is now detected by highway robbers and ferocious beasts. Taking advantage of his helpless situation they vie with one another to lay their murderous hands on the poor victim. He is mortally afraid and runs at full speed in the western direction until suddenly he finds himself confronted by the great river. He thinks within himself: "This river extends without bounds to the south and to the north, with just one white path cutting through the middle. The passage is extremely narrow. Though the further bank does not seem to be very far from here, how can I cross it? No doubt I am going to die this very moment. If I should turn back, the highwaymen and the wild beasts are steadily approaching. If I should run south or north, the wild beasts and the poisonous reptiles are ready to devour me. But if I should attempt to find my escape to the west, in all probability I should be drowned in these streams of fire and water."
>
> At this moment his terror is beyond description. However, he reflects again: "To go back means death, to stay here means death, to go ahead means death: if death thus inevitably threatens me on all sides, why not rather try the path before me, and run on straight ahead? The path lies anyhow right in front, and surely it is possible for me to cross it."
>
> When the traveler comes to this resolution, he suddenly hears a voice coming from the east bank, which urges him to go ahead, saying, "You be only resolute and go ahead along this path and you will be delivered from death. But if you tarry here death will be your fate." There is another voice at the time reaching him from the west bank, which calls out to him, saying, "With singleness of thought and with a rightly directed heart, come straight to me. I will protect you, you need not at all fear falling into the abyss of water and fire."
>
> Hearing an order to go on this side and a summoning call on the other, the traveler is fully determined with his body as well as in his mind to proceed along the path. He now goes on straightforward without entertaining either a doubt or a backsliding thought. As he thus goes along a little way, the robbers on the east bank call out loudly, saying, "The path is stormy and full of dangers, you cannot possibly cross it, and there is no doubt about your meeting a certain death. We are all far from having

an evil design on you." The traveler hears the calling voice but never turns his head back. He keeps on his way with singleness of heart and with his thoughts fixed on the path. Before long he reaches the west bank where, eternally released from all ills, he is greeted by all good friends and blessed forever more.

Now to explain the meaning of the parable. The east bank is likened to the fiery residence of this world of endurance, while the west bank is likened to the treasure-land of happiness. A number of the highway robbers, wild beasts, and their treacherous intimacy are likened to the six sense-organs, six consciousnesses, six sense-objects, five *skandhas*, and four elements, with which all sentient beings are constituted. The wilderness with no inhabitants is likened to our being constantly attended by evil advisers and being kept away from good sincere friends. The two streams of water and fire are likened to the desires and cravings of all sentient beings, which resemble water, and to their anger and hatred which resemble fire. The white path in the middle which is four or five *sun* in width is likened to one's heart pure in itself and desiring to be born [in the Pure Land], which is awakened even in the midst of our cravings, hatreds, and evil passions. As our cravings and hatreds are powerful, they are likened to water and fire, while the faintness of the devotional heart resembles the white path. The waves constantly sweeping over the path are likened to our cravings, which, being constantly stirred within us, defile the devotional heart. The flames always ablaze on the path are likened to our dislikes and hatreds which burn up the spiritual treasure of merit. The traveler's going west straight along the path is likened to a man's turning all his deeds right toward the west [to be born in the Pure Land]. That the traveler hears a voice on the east bank urging him to go ahead along the path means that after the death of Śākyamuni those who follow him are unable to see him except through the teaching left by him, which resembling the master's voice they can hear. That after going a little way the man is called back by the band of robbers means that there are some people whose understanding and behaviors are at variance [with those of the Pure Land followers] and whose views are not at all true and that they get themselves and others into confusion by their false views and arguments, ending finally in the commission of sinful deeds which make them go backward [in their spiritual progress]. That there is a voice calling from the west bank refers to Amida's Vows. That before long the man reaches the west bank and there greeted by all his good friends is made happy means that all beings who have long been sinking in [the sea of] birth-and-death, transmigrating from time immemorial, binding themselves in errors and falsehoods, and knowing no way to emancipation are now mercifully directed by Śākyamuni to proceed westward and then summoned by Amida whose loving heart is ever beckoning them, and that they, now in faithful obedience to the intentions of these two Honored Ones, pay no heed to the two streams of water and fire, and, ever in remembrance of Amida's Vows, walk on the path led by the strength of the Vows, and that when they abandon this life they are born in his land and coming into his presence are exceedingly made happy.

Having explained what is meant by the Pure Land doctrine generally, and hoping that the above is enough to acquaint the reader with its principal elements, let us proceed to the main subject which is to trace the growth of this doctrine in the body of Buddhism.

II

There is no doubt that Buddhism has been throughout its history a religion of enlightenment *(saṃbodhi)* and emancipation *(vimutti* or *vimokṣa),* and in the beginning there were no indications in the teaching of the master, which betrayed the "other-power" *(tariki)* elements of later Buddhism. Everything the Buddha taught tended toward self-reliance, self-realization, and self-emancipation. To be dependent upon another in any sense of the word was eschewed. Even relying on the Buddha was interdicted. "Be ye lamps to yourselves; be ye a refuge to yourselves; betake yourselves to no external refuge!" *(Attadīpā viharatha attasaraṇā anaññasaraṇā!)*[12] This was the keynote of his spiritual discipline; and after his death the Dharma was to be represented as the master himself by the disciples. So he told them, *Yo kho dhammam passati so mam passati* ("He who sees the Dharma sees me.") And this Dharma, as was proclaimed by the Buddha, was *sandiṭṭhika, akālika, ehipassika, opanayika, paccattaṃ veditabbo viññūhi.*[13] The Arhat who subdued all his *āśravas* (depravities), who destroyed the bonds of birth-and-death, and was completely detached from the intellectual and affectional hindrances, was the one who grasped the Dharma by his own mental efforts *(sayam abhiññāya),* devoting himself to meditation *(jhānānuyutta),* in some secluded spot remote from the haunts of men *(gaṇamhā vūpakaṭṭho).* He was alone *(eko),* earnest *(appammato),* zealous *(ātāpī),* and master of himself *(pahitatto),* walked in the middle path *(majjhena dhammaṃ),* and enjoyed the twofold emancipation *(ubhato-bhāga-vimutto)* which was the product of the intellectual and the spiritual discipline. There was no room in his heart for the faith-element to enter as developed soon after the passing of the master. Mysticism was there and asceticism too, but the entire outlook of Arhatship consisted in the most vigorous self-discipline, intellectual as well as moral.

How could this *jiriki* religion of enlightenment and emancipation be turned into that of *tariki* faith and salvation? How could this teaching of the Buddha which when mastered enabled one to realize the truth in this world of ours *(diṭṭhadhamma)* transform itself into a faith in another world, that is, the Land of Bliss *(sukhāvatī),* in which its followers concentrate all their mental efforts to be reborn after death? They are after enlightenment, it is true, as other Buddhists are, but they have decided to postpone its attainment until they reach Amida's Land of Purity and Perfect Bliss. How did they come to create such a being as Amida when to the Buddha even the highest god of the heavens bowed low and offered their homage most reverently? As there was no ego *(ātman)* from the very beginning, it was perhaps natural enough in one sense to abandon the thought of "self-power" *(jiriki),* but to establish "other-power" *(tariki)* in its stead was in a way creating another self, not as narrow indeed, not so limited, and perhaps not so irrational, but was it not against the Buddha's teaching to put faith in anything not realizable *yathābhūtaṃ* [in accordance with reality (JCD)] by *sammappaññā* [true insight (JCD)]?[14] When the nembutsu idea is contrasted in more details to Buddhist thought generally as it developed in India early in the history of Buddhism, we find an almost impassable chasm dividing one from the other: there seems no way to reconcile them harmoniously and naturally. It is not strange that some Buddhist critics regard the Nembutsu schools as degeneration and refuse to recognize them as pursuing the orthodox course of development.

When we carefully turn over the pages of the history of Buddhism, however, the following lines of development suggest themselves to our minds. They are no more than suggestions at present, but as we grow in historical knowledge as regards things Indian, they may be more definitely verified. When the doctrine of Nembutsu is analyzed we may find many elements going into its makeup, but, generally stated, we can distinguish at least the following five factors constituting its essentials: ethico-mythical, metaphysical, religious, psychological, and historical. These five factors are so inseparably and organically interwoven into the system of *tariki* salvation that when we try to single out one element after another for analytical inspection, the others are invariably found attached to it. Therefore, this enumeration of the various factors must be regarded as merely set up for the practical purpose of this study.

1. By the ethico-mythical factor I mean the Jataka element which has so largely entered into the notion of Buddhahood. Every Buddha was a Bodhisattva in his former life and while in this stage of spiritual discipline he practiced most vigorously all the virtues of perfection *(pāramitā).* And it was due to the cumulative effect of these virtues or merits that the Bodhisattva could finally realize the ultimate end of his life, which was the attainment of supreme enlightenment. If not for his spiritual perfection realized only after a strenuous moral life through a series of rebirths, he could not hope for such a culmination as the realization of Buddhahood.

Amida had thus also to go through with the same process of discipline as the Bodhisattva Dharmākara in his previous life, and performed innumerable deeds of charity, morality, energy, patience, meditation, and supreme wisdom. And so far the upward course of his life was normal and in full accordance with the ideas of early Buddhism. But in the beginning of his career he made what is known as "Original Vows," *pūrva-praṇidhāna,* and this was something not to be literally traceable in the Agamas or Nikāyas. As far as the Jataka idea is concerned, it is old enough, for this is the direct practical application of the theory of karma to our moral life. Without the accumulation of moral merit in our previous lives, we could not hope for the attainment of anything highly spiritual in the present existence. This is intelligible enough. But when we come to the conception of Amida's *Pūrva-praṇidhāna* in which he makes his realization of Buddhahood conditional on the fulfillment of the Vows, we have here something quite new and original germinating in the mere Jataka idea—something more than mere karma could comprehend in itself. This infusion of a new element transcending the law of causality marks the beginning of Mahayana Buddhism.

While Amida's forty-eight Vows are mixed up with many unessential, and to us moderners nonsensical, *praṇidhāna*s or vows, the most significant one, that is, the eighteenth *praṇidhāna,* is really of great religious importance, and by virtue of this in fact all the Pure Land sects are justified for their existence. While the Jataka requires a severe moral and ascetic discipline, the condition implied in the *praṇidhāna* is an absolute faith in the mysterious virtue of Amida. And this simple faith is enough to lead all sentient beings to his Land of Purity and to make them attain the Supreme Perfect Enlightenment of the Buddha.

This making of the *praṇidhāna*s or vows is what distinguishes Amida from Śākyamuni and other Buddhas prior to him; for none of the latter ever expressed any strong desires other than the attainment of their own enlightenment before they entered into the life of a Bodhisattva. It is evident that the idea of *praṇidhāna* did not develop until sometime after the passing of the Buddha as we have no mention of it in Pali literature. One of the Tathagatas who appeared, according to some scholars, before Amida in the literature of Mahayana Buddhism, is known as Akṣobhya Buddha, and in the sutra detailing his Jataka and his country a number of "Original Vows" is made by him before his enlightenment. Probably this is one of the precedents of the *praṇidhāna* idea. The Bodhisattva Maitreya has his Pure Land in Tuṣita Heaven and the sutras relating his life assure our rebirth in that heaven if we sincerely believe in him; but as far as literature goes we are not acquainted with any definite *praṇidhāna*s made by him. In fact Maitreya has not yet attained his Buddhahood, and his work as savior of mankind, we can say, has not yet really started among us. Bhaiṣajyaguru Buddha has his *praṇidhāna*s, twelve in number; while he seems to have been taken notice of by the Mahayanists later than Amida, his vows make no reference to the idea of universal salvation by faith. In this respect, the vows of Bhaiṣajyaguru are like those of Akṣobhya; both wish to pave the way smoothly for the followers of their Buddha-lands so that they would not encounter too many and too formidable obstructions in their upward course of spiritual discipline. But the faith-element, that is, what is technically known by Buddhist scholars as the *tariki* element, has not found its way into the *praṇidhāna*s of these two Buddha-Tathagatas. All the other Buddhas that are mentioned in Mahayana literature as having their Pure Lands somewhere in the spiritual universe do not stand in any intimate relationship to our human world of patience and misery. They are all too mythical. Akṣobhya and Bhaiṣajyaguru have the nearest approach to us next to Amida, but neither of them can replace the latter to any degree of human satisfaction.

The question now is, How did this notion of *praṇidhānas*, especially those made by Amida, come to the minds of earlier Buddhists who did not know much about achieving universal salvation by this means? Their motto was: "Be ye lamps to yourselves" *(attadīpā viharatha),* and enlightenment, if they at all realized it, was the product of a long spiritual discipline by themselves. But here is an element precluded from the original sphere of their thought, but evidently forcing itself into it. How was this?

When the Buddha attained the Enlightenment, he realized that it was too exalted a state of consciousness for common souls to aspire after, and he was for a moment full of the idea of himself disappearing from the world. But this was the intellectual side of his realization in which however there was something very much deeper than the mere intellect, and it was this deeper side that kept him on earth and made him work hard for the edification of his fellow beings. He could not help this. According to his penetrating metaphysical insight, he knew too well that it was far beyond the reach of the average understanding, and consequently that it was of no use for him to attempt to induce others to come up to the giddy height of enlightenment, but something in him impelled him to go ahead and mix himself up in the world and to lead it toward the higher ideals of life, if necessary, even by means of contrivance or expediency *(upāya).* What was this impelling force, let me ask, which the Buddha failed to keep in check?

In the Agamas we read about two kinds of emancipation, *cetovimutti* and *paññāvimutti,* and he who has achieved the first kind of emancipation—emancipation of the heart acquires four qualities of the heart, which are: love *(mettā),* sympathy *(karuṇā),* impartiality *(upekhā),* and soft-heartedness *(muditā).* If the Buddha was the king of all the emancipations, was he not also the great possessor of love, amity, kindness, and other cognate feelings in the most boundless measure? While he reasoned somewhat coldly on the surface, his heart always betrayed itself, and if not for this, his moral influence could never be what it actually was as evidenced in the history of Buddhism. This awakening and assertion of *mahākaruṇā* which proved such a powerful factor in the molding of later Buddhism was a new element infused into the system of the so-called primitive Buddhism. This was the most impelling force the Buddha released in himself. When his mind was still under the spell of enlightenment, he probably failed to be cognizant of this altogether too powerful life-energy which later grew in him ever stronger and ever more inevitable. And it was this indeed that was most operative in the formulation of Amida's *praṇidhānas*. If this were the case as I think it was, we must say that there was something in the enlightenment-consciousness of the Buddha far more than the earlier Buddhists could have imagined or analyzed.

In the history of Buddhism, the Jataka represents the ideal of Hinayana Buddhists who have amassed an immense treasure of tales and parables, all richly illustrating the laborious course of ascent in the life of a Bodhisattva. The scene however changes when we come to Mahayana literature. There are Jataka tales here no doubt, but they are no more so interesting, they are not at all told in the way as to be so persuasive and enticing as in the Hinayana Jatakas. According to the Mahayanists, this is due to the lack of love-factor in the Jatakas. Every deed of sacrifice for instance performed by the Bodhisattva has for its ultimate object his own attainment of Bodhi and not necessarily the salvation of all sentient as well as non-sentient beings. The Jatakas must develop into the *Pūrva-praṇidhāna,* if Buddhism has to unfold all that is implied in the Buddha's Enlightenment; for the Enlightenment which is the dispelling of ignorance releases not only a man's intellectual faculty but his noblest emotional energy. When Prajna goes hand in hand with Karuna, the Buddha ceases to be a mere Pratyekabuddha but grows to be a great perfect being, Mahāsattva and Bodhisattva in the meaning as we understand it and not in that of the Jatakas.

2. The Supreme Perfect Enlightenment which was the greatest event in the life of the Buddha and in the history of Buddhism was not after all so intellectual as is ordinarily interpreted by scholars. It goes without saying that it was far more than the discovery of the law of causality which prevails only in the phenomenal world and not in a realm where the deepest religious consciousness obtains. The latter transcends the principle of causation; the idea that "as this is, that is, and as this is not, that is not," is to be abandoned when one wants to meet the deepest longings of our hearts. Did enlightenment satisfy these requirements as well as intellectual speculations? As I take it, enlightenment is negatively the dispelling of ignorance and positively the restoring of freedom to the Will, that is to say, the awakening of the "original vows" *(pūrva-praṇidhāna)* hitherto dormant in the deepest recesses of our being. The removal of ignorance did not mean a state of emptiness, the emancipation of the void, *suññatācetovimutti;* for enlightenment had an altogether positive content and released all the energy that had hitherto been utilized for the pursuit of egotistical interests and aspirations arising from ignorance. The Enlightenment of the Buddha is not to be interpreted merely as an intellectual insight into the thusness of things *(tathatā),* this would make him a passive onlooker at the mad dancing of primordial forces. It is on the contrary the revealing of a creative and self-regulating principle and makes the Will master of itself, giving it back all the native and spontaneous activity stored up primarily in it. This idea later developed into that of *Anutpattikadharmakṣānti* by the Mahayanists.

What does the Will accomplish by itself when it is released from all the crippling and cramping notions and desires? According to Buddhist interpretation, the first thing the Will as embodied in an individual being wishes to achieve after the release is to do to others what it has done for itself. As enlightenment has made it known to the Will that there is no real and impassable gap between oneself and others, the Will feels now no need of asserting itself blindly, that is, of following the dictates of the principle of individuation. While the Will does not ignore the latter as the condition of intellection which is its servant, it knows now how to make him obedient to itself, instead of reversing the position as is ordinarily done by the ignorant. In other words, the efforts of an enlightened consciousness are to lead others to the realization of a similar state of release. As long as one remains ignorant and under the bondage of the principle of multitudinosity, one is never able to rise above the interests of the ego, but when the chain is cut asunder and one is uplifted to a realm where one can survey the world *yathābhūtaṃ* [in accordance with reality (JCD)] in the absolute sense of the word, every act of such a spirit most felicitously hits off the harmonious relation between *meum et tuum* [mine and thine (JCD)]. When Amida Nyorai (Tathāgata Amitābha) made his forty-eight Original Vows, he must have been right in the midst of enlightenment, though the attainment of the latter was made conditional on the fulfillment of the Vows. Unless there were some inevitable interrelation between the Enlightenment and Original Vows, it were altogether useless for Amida to make such vows as detailed in the sutra. Indeed when he attained enlightenment, the entire universe was released from ignorance and bondage; and as he is still quietly abiding in his own Land of Purity, the entire universe including all its beings sentient and non-sentient must be said also to be abiding right in the state of enlightenment, no matter what miserable things we are to the eyes of the ignorant and confused. Thus we find the idea of the Original Vows justified in the metaphysical significance of enlightenment.

3. But to make this metaphysical significance workable in our everyday practical life, another concept is needed, by which I mean the doctrine of *Pariṇāmana*. So far as we can trace in Pali literature there is no approach to this doctrine which really caused an epoch-making revolution in the history of Buddhist thought; but the conception of *Pariṇāmana* was the logical outcome of enlightenment-consciousness which transcends the category of causality. What made Buddhism great as a universal religion responding to the still small voice of the soul was due to the discovery of this principle. *Pariṇāmana* means to turn one's own merit over to others, just the reverse of karmic law. According to the latter, every Bodhisattva is to accumulate his own virtues in order to acquire a capacity for the Supreme Perfect Enlightenment of the Buddha. He went thus through many a rebirth putting himself under the severest moral discipline he was capable of. If every sentient being has to be a Buddha or an Arhat or somebody finally leading up to such, before he can attain to full enlightenment and emancipation, he will have to be thoroughly trained in the Eightfold Path of Righteousness or the Six Virtues of Perfection and

completely purgated of all the traces of *kāma* (desire), *bhāva* (becoming), and *diṭṭha* (intellection), and *avijjā* (ignorance). This discipline, if absolutely and universally required of all candidates for Buddhas or Arhats—which was the case with the earlier Buddhists—may prove too formidable and impossible for most common mortals, and the world may be full of unsaved souls with no hopes for ultimate deliverance. This is an unbearable state of things for anyone whose heart generously opens to all the sufferings and depravities that are going on in the world. There ought to be some way to mend it. The Buddha-nature or enlightenment-consciousness ought to be present in all sentient and even non-sentient beings, and when this is directly awakened or shown the way to be awakened, the world may have some prospect of being saved in spite of its evils. There ought to be some way to do this, and the way is to make others share in the benefits accruing in any manner from the accumulation of merit and the realization of enlightenment. If they fail to come up to the mark even when they try hard to accomplish impossibilities, owing to their innate weaknesses, they must be helped out by such as are capable of spiritual discipline. The gifted are not to be left with themselves, love is to make them come out of their selfishness, and let others also come into the treasury-house of merit. The law of karma may be true and should be made to work in our practical and intellectual plane of life, but it is too rigid, too exclusive, too individualistic, and above all goes against our religious yearnings. While our individualism wishes for self-interest and self-preservation, we have another order of impulses to sacrifice ourselves for others. We want to suffer for others, and when this is not practicable we want to send out our thoughts and sympathies to them. If we are at all spiritual beings capable of enlightenment, this thought-communication or mystical interpretation must be possible though this of course cannot take place in the way of material things. The possibility of the Original Vows is based upon this theory of *Pariṇāmana,* which in turn derives its metaphysical reasonableness from the signification of enlightenment.

4. When the doctrine of *Pariṇāmana* is thus established, enlightenment grows in its *tariki* significance and the Buddhism of *attadīpā* ["Be ye lamps to yourselves." (JCD)] gradually and inevitably transforms itself into that of the Original Vows *(pūrva-praṇidhāna).* Aristocratic Arhats are now democratic *Sarvasattvas.* An infinite perfectibility of moral character which means a life of unending strenuosity and asceticism ceases to intimidate weak-hearted ones *(bāla* or *pṛthagjana).* Instead of trying to attain what is almost utterly beyond their powers, they now look up to one whose wisdom and love are strong enough to embrace them. They do not now attempt to attain enlightenment in this life, but would postpone it until they are reborn in the Land of Purity presided over by Amida, they would rest assured, while here, in his promise to take them to his own abode. They will do all they can to lead a morally pure life, but they will never rely upon their moral supe-

riority for final salvation. They have found someone who will look after their spiritual welfare if only they accept him and place their whole-souled faith in him by invoking his name. If we were all perfect, there would be no need for us to look around and discover an external aid. But we are in most varied ways weak, imperfect, and always ready to fall away from the high ideals and if we were to be dwelling constantly upon these shortcomings and moral deficiencies, there would never be a chance for us to enjoy spiritual rest and happiness. While the *jiriki* side of our life means eternal perfectibility of our character, the *tariki* side whispers to us in a most assured manner that with all our failures and unattained aspirations we are finally to be saved as we are abiding right in the midst of enlightenment.

Why? For enlightenment itself has a double aspect, *jiriki* and *tariki,* when it is intellectually analyzed. The *jiriki* aspect of enlightenment is the consummation of our spiritual efforts throughout innumerable lives of the past, while its *tariki* aspect is the fulfillment of all the *praṇidhāna*s vowed not only by Amida but by all the Buddhas and Arhats and all common mortals. We usually imagine that the Eighteenth *Praṇidhāna* is the monopoly of Amida, but in fact what he did was merely to give expression to what lies deeply and inarticulately hidden in the heart of every sentient being. While it is a great achievement on the part of Amida to be able to give vent to this inmost feeling of ours, we must not be blind to the fact that the feeling of *praṇidhāna* is not the exclusive possession of any one highly endowed mind. For this reason we are able to respond to the call of Amida. If there were nothing in our consciousness which answers to his *praṇidhāna*s, the latter would surely fall flat on us like gold coins thrown before a cat. The ultimate truth is that we common mortals are all capable of attaining the Buddha's Supreme Perfect Enlightenment with its double aspect, *jiriki* and *tariki.* This being so, when we think we are saved by the grace of Amida, we are really saving ourselves, and when we think we are hearing his call, we are in fact listening to our own *praṇidhāna*s which have been planted in our consciousness ever since its awakening. But as it was Amida who pointed them out and gave them a name, he is our savior. In a book called *Anjin ketsujō shō*[15] we read that in the *Namu-amida-butsu,* Amida and ourselves are united as one and that the one from the other cannot even for a moment be separated, so that every thought we have is of Amida and every breath we breathe is of his virtue. To be separate in oneness and to be one in separation, or, more personally, that Amida is his own savior by saving others—this is indeed the mystery of mysteries.

Jiriki (self-power) is the *adhipaññā* aspect of enlightenment and *tariki* (other-power) is the *mahākaruṇā* aspect of the same. By *adhipaññā* we transcend the principle of individuation, and by *mahākaruṇā* we descend into a world of particulars. The one goes upward while the other comes downward, but this is our intellectual way of understanding or interpreting enlightenment, in whose movement however there is no such twofold direction discernible. Amida himself sitteth forever immovably in his lotus-seat, but from the human point of view we speak of his *praṇidhāna*s directed toward us and our longings going up to him.

5. But, historically speaking, how did a religion of the threefold discipline *(sikkhā* or *śikṣā)* consisting of *adhisīla, adhicitta,* and *adhipaññā* develop into the teaching of salvation by faith? The latter may have its metaphysical ground in the Buddha's enlightenment, but in point of history how did it come to happen? Let me see into the course of events after the Buddha's Nirvana or even into the psychology of his followers while he was yet alive among them.

There is no doubt that the Buddha was a wonderfully inspiring personality. When we know that no religious system has ever been built upon logical reasoning however subtle and thoroughgoing it might be, and again that all religion is a kind of edifice constructed around a person who is its animating center, the fact grows evident that the center-force supporting the huge structure known as Buddhism must have been a grand figure. Even while still walking among his fellow beings, the Buddha was an object of adoration and attracted many followers to him who were content just to be with him and to look at him. Something of the magnetic rays of divinity must have emanated from his person, and to those who were struck with them it did not probably matter very much whether his teaching was logically true or not. They were eager to accept it just because it came from the golden lips of such a personality as the Buddha. Even when things are systematically presented and logically tenable, we are often reluctant to accept them abstractly. We may be convinced intellectually of their validity, and nothing may be left for us to say against it. But singularly enough there are so many cases in life in which we feel undecided as to their being final truths. Why? Because life is more than reasoning and personality deeper than mere syllogistic consistency. Therefore, let there be a living spirit behind verbalism and every word dropping from its mouth vibrates through the entire being of the hearer. That such was the case with the Buddha, the early literature of Buddhism eloquently testifies. The Agamas relate of his having been invited into a village infested with an epidemic, for the villagers thought that the Buddha so full of wonderful personal power would be able to keep all the evil spirits away from the village, to whom they ascribed the cause of the disaster.

When the Buddha passed into Nirvana, his followers were thrown into excessive grief and did not know how to control their feelings. This fact is taken notice of, for herein lies at least one most important happening in the life of the Buddha in connection with the development of later Buddhist thought. His Nirvana means so much to all Buddhists. The two most fruit-bearing and thought-provoking events in the Buddha's life were Enlightenment and Nirvana. His teaching naturally supplied material for Buddhist philosophy, but the latter could be delineated only on the canvas woven of Nirvana and Enlightenment, so much so indeed that when these two grand facts are taken away from Buddhism, nothing is left behind which is strong and vital enough for the cogitation of Buddhist thinkers. This is also the origin and meaning of the Nirvana figure and the Nirvana picture we see so much in Buddhist temples and monasteries. When Christians kneel before the crucified figure of Christ, I believe, it is not from the sense of lamentation, but from that of reverential gratitude and adoration. To Buddhists the Nirvana picture, as it is painted by Japanese or Chinese painters, represents the peaceful termination of a great historical character whose departure from us could not be stopped even with the earnest entreaties and heart-rending wails of his disciples and followers, including all creatures human as well as nonhuman. How was it that such a great soul as the Buddha had to pass out? Why did he not prolong his life to the utmost limit, which he said he could if he wished? Is it then that he did not really die as all mortals do but just appeared to be dead to our mortal sense? What is then his true body? His immediate disciples must have reasoned in some such wise while their hearts were filled with grief and adoration and while the living memory of the late master left such a deep stamp in their minds.

The doctrine of the universal transitoriness of things could not check the outbursts of their lamentation; the master's personality appeared to his disciples too great, too superhuman, to be regarded as one of their kind; the feelings they entertained toward him were altogether out of the ordinary, and must have had much deeper meaning, probably as deep as the personality of the master. There was no violence connected with his death as was the case with that of Christ, but this peaceful ending impressed the minds of his disciples intellectually rather than affectively. They did not give themselves away altogether to the feeling of loss and grief, however great this was, but there was room left for them to reason quietly about the whole proceeding and about the significance of the Buddha's life on earth and his departure. The reasoning backed by the emotion gradually developed into faith. They now came to consider Gautama, the Muni of the Śākyas, as the eternal Buddha who was manifested temporarily among them in order to enlighten us, to deliver us from the bondage of all sorts, and if needed by some of us, to lead them to his own abode of purity and happiness. This idea is strongly developed in the *Saddharma-puṇḍarīka.*

In the Nikāyas, the Buddha is made to have advised his disciples to think of him and his virtues as if they saw his body before their eyes, whereby they would be enabled to accumulate merit and attain Nirvana or be saved from transmigrating in the evil paths of existence and be born in the heavens. Though there is much distance between this and the doctrine of the Pure Land school, it is quite a start toward the latter, and if any thought or belief popularly accepted or beginning to move the masses, which closely approaches to that of the Amida faith, happens to lie athwart in the course of Buddhist history, it will very readily have the chance to get planted into the soil thus prepared by the immediate and early disciples of the Buddha. As some scholars suggest, something like the Vishnu cult as is accepted by the author of the *Bhagavadgītā* might find ready sympathizers among such Buddhists. And as the outcome of such contact, the creation of Amida Buddha as eternal being with his Sukhāvatī might have been effected. When rival thoughts are to be disposed of, the favorite Indian way, I am told, is to swallow them up as the larger and stronger snake does its enemy, and turn them into an organic part of the victor's system. In this respect, Buddhism has never been behind other systems; wherever and whenever it thought it opportune and helping its own growth it was ready to swallow and assimilate any healthy thought with which it came in contact. While we are still unable to trace every step Buddhism took in its course of development, something like the foregoing may fairly be considered true in its general outlines.

. . .

To put the whole story as above analyzed in a constructive form: Here is Śākyamuni ready to be apotheosized with all his human qualities, his Enlightenment, and his practical assertions of love *(mahākaruṇā);* and, at the other end, a group of devout disciples trying to get all their doubts, sufferings, and yearnings solved in the teaching and personality of their master; and, further, the fact that no religion can hold itself up without a consolidating, unifying, and vivifying personal power as its center or as its foundation—with all this ready, is there not the way perfectly open and without any obstructions directly leading to the *tariki* conception of salvation? In fact, the logical conclusion of the interplay of the various forces above delineated is the growth of the Pure Land teaching with Amida as its source of aspirations.

The myth of Amida might have been an exotic growth or a foreign transplantation into the native soil of primitive Buddhism. If this were the case though we have no historic facts for this hypothesis, Buddhists could not find anything more suitable than this myth, for a nucleus around which they could develop all that was needed for the theory of *tariki* salvation. As I said before, especially for the Indian mind, no historicity was needed to construct a vital religious belief; for to it as well as to other Oriental minds spiritual facts were more real and fruit-bearing than what is known as objectively historical. As long as history remained external, that is, as long as it stood outside of our inner life, it had no reality with the power to affect us. To be real and historical meant to be innerly experienced by a pious and earnest soul, and therefore an objective world with all its so-called facts and laws was something that had no living connection with the soul, it was as if it never existed. The Jataka of Amida and his *Praṇidhāna*s (vows) were true and real to his devotees no matter how they originated.

From the Supreme Perfect Enlightenment there flowed an emotional spring of *Mettā, Karuṇā, Upekhā,* and *Muditā;* for it laid low all the barriers constructed by the ego-soul to check the free movement of the original willpower. The Will was not to be overruled by the law of karma or that of moral causation; on the contrary it wished to revoke the law or rather to make it serve its own purpose, that is, for the accomplishment of its Original Vows. Thus it created the principle of *Pariṇāmana* [transference of merit (JCD)] to replace the law of karma. Karma was indeed primarily the agent to bring about the Enlightenment, as it was the outcome of a long and arduous spiritual discipline: but once the end was gained, the spirit burned the bridge behind it, and all its merits, virtues, powers, and concentrations were now turned over to all sentient beings, who were thus enabled now to share in them and to achieve with ease and trust what Amida achieved after great sacrifices. The principle of *Pariṇāmana* was not however an absolutely new creation, but it lay from the beginning in the Enlightenment itself as its content, and what Buddhists had to do, that is, to make it work in a world of particulars, was simply to grow conscious of the fact and draw it out as it were from its primordial bed. This drawing-out took the form of the forty-eight *Praṇidhāna*s on the part of Amida.

There is no reason to suppose that because primitive Buddhists failed to draw out all the contents of the Enlightenment and remained satisfied with the Fourfold Noble Truth, or the Twelvefold Chain of Origination, or some other formulas, the *tariki* teaching was something externally grafted into the system of Buddhism. The thing required for the adequate reading of the history of the spirit is to get the scales off one's mental eye which is really made to look inward as well as outward, for the outward is inward and the inward outward. When this is done we are initiated right into the mysteries of the Supreme Perfect Enlightenment of Śākyamuni, which he realized while sitting under the shade of the Bodhi tree, and which we today can also attain by delving into the depths of our being.

Thus we can say that while there was something historical or mythical which contributed to the formulation of the Pure Land doctrine, the idea itself principally developed out of the inwardness of the Buddha's Enlightenment and of the eternal yearnings of the soul. The distance from the doctrine of self-discipline and Arhatship to that of salvation by faith seems to be a very long one, but the *tariki* followers have not abandoned enlightenment and in fact what is considered salvation is enlightenment under the disguise of faith. Professedly, they do not seek enlightenment while in this world, but only wish to attain it in the Pure Land where resides Amida; they are thus contented with the assurance that Amida will take them up after death to his Land of Purity and Bliss. But as this Land is no more than the projection of Amida's Enlightenment, the assurance of one's rebirth there amounts to this, that one can share in the Enlightenment itself. The objection that the assurance is a kind of promise and must not be identified with the fact of enlightenment is not a serious one. For we can for all practical purposes regard this assurance as the fact itself as long as the assurance implies the spiritual recognition of Amida's grace on our part while this grace grows operative only as the outcome of Amida's Enlightenment. There is a process indeed, logically stated, between the two notions, assurance and enlightenment, but psychologically the assurance on the part of sentient beings as the objects of the Original Vows is identical with Enlightenment on the part of Amida. This is the basic idea of the *tariki* teaching in which the self-attained enlightenment of primitive Buddhists has taken the form of faith in Amida's Enlightenment. The difference lies in the approach and not in the substance.

Thus we can see that to trace the development of the Pure Land idea or *tariki* teaching is really writing the history of Mahayana Buddhism. If the essence of Mahayana Buddhism consists in the upholding of infinite Karuna lying deep in the enlightened Buddha-heart and making it overflow the narrow and self-murdering limits of intellectual individuation, the Original Vow of Amida is no more than the surest grasp of this essence. To be reborn in the Pure Land by embracing Amida in absolute faith means nothing more, nor less, than our being all one in the Supreme Enlightenment of the perfect Buddha. What generally distinguishes the Mahayana from the Hinayana is chiefly discernible in the teaching of the Pure Land school of Buddhism. In contrast to the metaphysical and moral outlook characterizing other schools such as the Tendai, Kegon, or Zen, the Jōdo is emotional, appealing strongly to the affective side of human life. Emotion is always symbolical and artistic and wants to express itself in pictures. Hence the creation of the Pure Land presided over by Amida. And as art has a realm of its own apart from that of reality, so stands the religion of the Pure Land outside the ken of intellectual criticism.

Before concluding this article, I must not forget to say a word concerning the Buddhist conception of the Pure Land. So far I referred to it as if it made up the entirety of Buddhist eschatology, that is to say, some of our readers may be led to think that the sole object of the Pure Land devotees is to be born in Amida's Land of Bliss and Purity, which is described in detail in some of the Pure Land sutras. But the fact is that the birth itself (which is technically called *ōjō* in Japanese and *wangsheng* in Chinese, literally meaning "to go and be born") is not the object, but to attain enlightenment in the country of Amida where conditions are such as to insure a ready realization of the true Buddhist life. The Pure Land school in this respect shows no deviation from the main current of Buddhist thought; indeed if it did it could not at all go under the name of Buddhism. Enlightenment is the one fundamental note that reverberates through all the branches of the teaching of the Buddha; whether Mahayana or Hinayana, enlightenment is the consummation of Buddhist discipline. It is true that the difficulties of the Holy Path are very much talked of by the followers of the Pure Land school as if the object of the Holy Path were something unrealizable for us poor sinful mortals. But what they really advise us is to take another way than the one chosen by the holies; as to the object itself the Easy Doctrine is in perfect agreement with the Difficult One. If we can say so, to be born in the Pure Land is the means to the end; for Buddhism in whatever form is the religion of enlightenment and emancipation.

Properly speaking, the Pure Land school is a misnomer, it may better be called the Nembutsu school, for the nembutsu is of more significance and characterizes the school more appropriately. What would the followers do after they are actually born in the Pure Land if just to be born there were their only object in view? It makes one feel happy to think that there is an ideal world somewhere within our reach where all the ills of this earthly life are kept away; but to be personally there in all reality and to be doing nothing after the birth, as this is evidently the case if we believe literally all that is described in the sutras, must be, to say the least, a dull and tedious business, and I am sure that we shall all be longing again to be born into this world of patience, *sahāloka*. Unless we are altogether deprived of humanity, the Pure Land is no place for us. The most desirable thing for us to attain will be to descend on earth as soon as we have attained enlightenment through the grace of Amida and to work again among our still benighted brothers and sisters. And it is indeed for this reason that Shinran has a doctrine known as *gensō-ekō,* which means "to return and transfer," that is, to come back to this life and to dedicate all one's merits toward the enlightenment of one's fellow beings, sentient and non-sentient. He knew well that the Pure Land was meant either for beings far above ourselves or for those far below. For beings such as we ourselves are, life must contain something stimulating, something that will make us struggle and conquer; if things come to materialize as soon as desired, the Will is an empty term, and without the Will what are we? The Pure Land is the annihilator of the Will and consequently of the human soul. The Buddha wants to save it and not to annul it. The reason why the Bodhisattva wishes to descend to Hell instead of going up heavenward is mainly due to the fact that in Heaven he has no occupation for his faculties to exercise. Love dormant is the same as love dead. Therefore, what even the adherents of the Pure Land school long for and endeavor to realize through the easy practice of the nembutsu is no other than enlightenment.

Here the question is: What is the Pure Land? Is it an objective reality? or does it belong to the same category as the Platonic world of ideas? Those who rely on scriptural authority of course cherish no doubt as to the objectivity of the Pure Land; for according to them Śākyamuni the Buddha is no storyteller and all the sutras beginning with *evaṃ mayā śrutam* ["thus have I heard" (JCD)] are truthful records of his sermons. To raise any doubt about their genuineness will be an unpardonable sin. The Buddha tells us all about Amida, his country, his Vows, his Jataka, etc., and if we did not accept these stories as they are narrated in the Pure Land sutras, where does our faith in the nembutsu come? And the forty-eight Original Vows will be mere empty talk. Any criticism, higher or lower, will mean the destruction of the foundation of the school. When the nembutsu is accepted, everything else must come along with it. But this position of the defenders of scriptural authority is not countenanced by modernists.

The latter being naturally critically inclined refuse to swallow the scriptures bodily, they would appeal first either to their intellectual judgments or their individual religious experiences, before they accept the scriptures; for after all no outside authority or historical conventionalism can stand in the way of personal conviction. An idealistic interpretation of the scriptural legends concerning the Pure Land is thus the inevitable consequence in these modern days. What is true and vital in religion is not its tradition, literary or otherwise, but its essential inwardness whose expressions are subject to constant modification, but which remain ever the same in its spirit and meaning. The Pure Land in the form as it is given in the sutras may vanish, but the Original Vows of Amida will retain their validity and the nembutsu school will not lose any signification in its essential features. Whatever this may be, the main point is whether the nembutsu is the "Easy Practice" leading to enlightenment, and not whether the Pure Land really or objectively exists to receive us after death. When we are actually enlightened and our *prajñā-cakṣu* [wisdom eye (JCD)] is opened we shall know where we are and what is expected of us. Even the idealists who attempt to interpret the Pure Land platonically may have missed the point really at issue; for they are more concerned with the Pure Land than with enlightenment, which should be regarded as the most fundamental in the teaching of "Easy Practice" as it truly is.

One reason at least why the conception of the Pure Land is apparently made so much of and often, though erroneously, as we have seen, brought out to the center of interest as if the sole object of the nembutsu were to be born just in the Land of Purity and Happiness presided over by Amida, and nothing else, is partly because some of the Chinese and Japanese leaders of the Pure Land school laid too much stress on the idea of the land of defilement in contrast to that of the Pure Land, and partly because Hōnen, the founder of the Jōdo sect, preferred to designate his teaching as such. To take our thoughts away from sensuosity and worldliness with which we are ordinarily found deeply engaged, the leaders dwelt too strongly upon the defiled and disgusting conditions of existence here. Their main idea was to impress us common mortals with the futility of our attempts to satisfy our innermost yearnings with things mundane and "defiled." Our souls which are ever seeking for rest and peace cannot be appeased with the limitations and defilements of a dualistic world. When the latter are transcended, we have what our hearts have been hungering after. Therefore, we may say that the Pure Land symbolized a mystical world of transcendental idealism where all traces of dualistic defilements are wiped off and where souls move with their native freedom hindered or stained in no way by limitations of the senses. Or we may say that the Pure Land is the shadow of enlightenment cast over a world of name-and-form *(nāmarūpa)*. Those who are told by Hōnen and Shinran and other spiritual leaders to seek rebirth in

Amida's kingdom are not really seeking after a Western world lying so many thousands of *koṭis* of miles away from this earth of ours, but an inner illumination which has a miraculous power to transform or rather transfigure every object it touches into that of the Pure Land. In this sense, Amida and his worshipers are one just as Christ and his Father are one, and this conception of oneness is one of the most fundamental tenets of the Shin. The greatest happiness one can have in the Pure Land and which constitutes the object of rebirth there is to see Amida face to face and to listen to his personal sermons.

Wherever its historical development may be traced, the Pure Land is not a world existing in space-time but an idealistic world of enlightenment, or, to use the phraseology of the Pure Land sutras, a world illumined by the eternal light of Amida and subsisting in it. In one sense, it has nothing to do with this world of dualistic limitations and defilements, but in another sense it is right here with us and has reality as we read in the *Vimalakīrti Sūtra* that "Wherever your hearts are pure there is a Pure Land."[16] The Land of Purity is not to be sought outside this land of defilement and patience; when it is thought of as independent of the latter, it is sheer emptiness; all the inhabitants of the Land of Purity are recruited from those of this earth and the Land has a signification as long as its earthly archetype, however defiled, is suffered to exist. Amida himself once belonged to this world of particulars and that is the reason why he knows all our passions, failings, defilements, bondages, and sufferings and could make his forty-eight Vows. Moreover, for this reason these vows are proving wonderfully efficacious and soul-saving.

2

Zen and Jōdo, Two Types of Buddhist Experience

The two forms of Buddhism that Suzuki most frequently expounded upon were Zen and Pure Land (Jōdo). Though his commitment was first and foremost to Zen, arising from his monastic training as a young adult, he nonetheless felt a lifelong sympathy to Pure Land, fostered first in childhood and deepened during his career at Otani University. This essay is an attempt to compare and contrast these two types of Buddhism.

Underlying Suzuki's elucidation of them is his conviction that the highest form of Pure Land is mystical, rather than devotional, and that in this mysticism Pure Land and Zen merge. In the essay Suzuki dwells more on Pure Land concepts and issues than on Zen. He adopts the classical Pure Land distinction between *jiriki*, self-power, and *tariki*, other-power, as a rubric for characterizing Zen and Pure Land respectively. But unlike traditional Pure Land apologetics, which recognizes *tariki* as superior, Suzuki treats both as valid expressions of Buddhist experience. He portrays Zen as speculative, intellectual, and self-reliant and Pure Land as devotional, emotional, and dependent on the Buddha. He acknowledges that devotionalism has been the prevailing outlook of Pure Land practice: relying on the other-power of Amida (S. Amitābha) Buddha for salvation, invoking his name in the form of the nembutsu, and aspiring for birth in his Pure Land paradise after death where enlightenment is assured. Suzuki argues, however, that the real meaning of Pure Land Buddhism is different, and he singles out examples from the Pure Land tradition to make his case. He cites, for instance, Shinran's (1173–1262) commitment to practice the nembutsu whether it leads to birth in the Pure Land or to hell in the next life. He also points to Ippen's (1239–1289) declaration that a person should merge into the nembutsu when chanting it instead of thinking of rebirth. And he quotes the obscure Pure Land text *Anjin ketsujō shō* (On the Final Peaceful Settlement of Mind) that emphasizes the unity between sentient beings and the Buddha *(kihō ittai)* and between the nembutsu here and now and the Pure Land paradise after death. These examples reflect a nondualist outlook that is different from the dualism typically associated with devotionalism.

By advancing this interpretation of Pure Land Buddhism, Suzuki portrays it as a type of mysticism analogous to Zen. In reference to Christianity, Suzuki notes that it is dominated by devotionalism (though mysticism has occasionally appeared in it), and hence it stands in contrast to Buddhism, which he claims is grounded in the monistic and mystical outlook of ancient India.

The base text for this essay is "Zen and Jōdo, Two Types of Buddhist Experience," *The Eastern Buddhist* 4, no. 2 (1927): 89–121.

• • •

Those who have studied Eastern or Mahayana Buddhism, even superficially, will at once notice that there are at least two distinct types of it, the devotional and the speculative; and that they are so sharply and almost so radically distinguished the one from the other that they may be regarded as not belonging to one and the same system known as Buddhism. Compare, for instance, the quotations from Hōnen (1133–1212) and Shinran[1] (1173–1262) with the one from Rinzai (C. Linji, died 867):

> "The reason I founded the Pure Land sect," says Hōnen, "was that I might show the ordinary man how to be born into the Buddha's Real Land of Compensation. According to the Tendai (C. Tiantai) sect, the ordinary man may be born into the so-called Pure Land, but that land is conceived of as a very inferior place. Although the Hossō (S. Dharmalakṣaṇa)[2] sect conceives of it as indeed a very superior place, they do not admit that the common man can be born there at all. And all the sects, though differing in many other points, agree in not admitting that the common man can be born into the Buddha's Land of Real Compensation. . . . And so I inquired of a great many learned men and priests whether there is any other way of salvation than the Threefold Discipline *(śikṣā)*, that is better suited to our poor abilities, but I found none who could either teach me the way or even suggest it to me. At last I went all by myself and with a heavy heart into the Library at Kurodani on Mount Hiei, where all the Scriptures were kept, and read them all through. While doing so, I hit upon a passage in Zendō's[3] *Commentary on the Meditation Sutra* (C. *Guanjingshu*, J. *Kangyōsho*) which runs as follows: 'Whether walking or standing, sitting or lying, only repeat the name of Amida with all your heart. Never cease the practice of it even for a moment. This is the very work which unfailingly issues in Salvation, for it is in accordance with the Original Vow of that Buddha.' On reading this I was impressed with the fact that even ignorant people like myself, by reverent meditation on this passage and an entire dependence on the truth in it, never forgetting the repetition of Amida's sacred name, may lay the foundation for that good karma, which will with absolute certainty eventuate in birth into the Blissful Land. And I was led not only to believe in this teaching bequeathed by Zendō, but also earnestly to follow the great Vow of Amida. And especially was that passage deeply inwrought into my very soul which says, 'For it is in accordance with the Original Vow of that Buddha.'"[4]

According to Shinran, we have this:

> When the thought is awakened in us to recite the nembutsu,[5] believing that our rebirth in the Pure Land of Amida will surely take place by virtue of the miraculous power of his Vow, we then come to share in his all-embracing grace. The Original Vow makes no distinctions whatever as to age or moral merit; all that is needed is a believing heart. For the Vow is to save us—those sentient beings who are deeply immersed in sins and incessantly burning with passions. This being the case, when we believe in the Original Vow, no other merits are needed, for there are no merits that excel the nembutsu; nor are we to be afraid of evil deeds, for no evils are strong enough to stand in the way of Amida's Original Vow.[6]

These quotations are representative of the devotional type of Buddhist life, which is led by Donran (C. Tanluan, 476–542), Dōshaku (C. Daochuo, 562–645), Zendō, Jimin (C. Cimin, 679–748), and others in China, and by Genshin (942–1017), Hōnen, Shinran, and Ippen (1239–1289) in Japan. The authority for this they find in the so-called Three Sutras of the Pure Land school: the *Daikyō* (that is, *Sukhāvatī-vyūha*), *Kangyō (Meditation Sutra),* and *Shōkyō (Smaller Sukhāvatī-vyūha).* When we peruse their works such as Zendō's *Commentaries,* Hōnen's *Compilation (Senchakushū),* or another by Shinran *(Kyōgyōshinshō),* we observe how firmly their thoughts are fixed on being born in a better world, because they describe themselves as hopelessly sinful mortals whose peace and happiness is entirely depending on being embraced in the love of Amida and born in his Land of Bliss and Purity. Now compare this deeply religious sentiment and devotional attitude with the following passage from Rinzai, one of the foremost Zen masters in the Tang dynasty:

> Those who wish to study Buddhism these days must seek a true understanding of it. When they have it, they are not defiled by birth-and-death; to stay or to go, they are at liberty; while not seeking after anything superior and unusual, it comes to them by itself. O friends of the truth, the masters of old all had their specific ways of instructing their disciples, and as regards my way of illustrating [the truth of Zen], it simply consists in not letting you be confounded by others. If you wish to use it, use it,[7] and have no hesitation whatever.
>
> Where is the trouble with students of Buddhism these days that they do not attain to it? The trouble lies in their not having faith enough in themselves. For when you have not faith enough in yourselves, you are always kept busy and annoyed, as you are controlled by your external conditions; and when you are thus turned round by all kinds of external circumstances, you will never be free, independent masters of yourselves. Only let your thoughts cease from pursuing things external, and you will not be any different from the Buddhas and fathers.
>
> Do you wish to know the Buddhas and Fathers? They are right here with you listening to my discourse. As long as students not having faith enough run after things external, they will never attain to the living spirit of the Fathers, and all that they grasp will be the literary beauty of expression and nothing else.
>
> Don't be deceived, O venerable followers of Zen! If you fail to avail yourselves of this chance, you will have to be going around through the triple world forever

> so many kalpas and so many lives; and when you are thus swept off your feet by agreeable circumstances in this life, your next birth will be inside a cow or an ass.
>
> O friends of the truth, as far as I can see, in my understanding of the truth there is nothing different from that of Śākyamuni himself. Whatever activity shown by me today, is there anything not sufficient unto itself? All the mysterious light illumining the six forms of existence has not for a moment ceased to shine. When you gain this understanding, you will be leading a quiet, undisturbed life all the time.
>
> O venerable ones, there is no place for rest in this triple world which is like unto a house on fire. This is not a place for you to stay long; when a devil known as Impermanence comes around, all will be carried away in an instant, no respect will be paid to age, young or old, and to social rank, high or low. If you want to be like unto the Buddhas and Fathers, only pursue not things external.[8]

The devotional type as represented by Zendō and other saints of the Nembutsu is technically known among Buddhist scholars as the *tariki* ("other-power") branch of Buddhism, while the speculative or intellectual type as illustrated by Zen is called *jiriki* which literally means "self-power." For Zen relies on one's own efforts to reach the goal set up by its teachers, while Shin and Jōdo ask Amida to help his devotees in their rebirth in the Pure Land where they expect to realize the Supreme Enlightenment. When practical difficulties involved in self-discipline are considered, the Jōdo is said to be the path of Easy Practice in contradistinction to the path of Difficult Practice, which is trodden by the followers of Self-power. The Self-power school is also called the Holy Path as it is meant only for those holy Bodhisattvas who are richly endowed due to their previous karma and are thus able to climb the rungs of perfection by their own moral effort *(vīrya)*.

Overwhelmed with the wickedness of this world, the helplessness of sinful mortals, and the immensity of moral efforts one has to exercise for Enlightenment and freedom, the Jōdo followers were placed in a situation of utmost despondency and untold agony. The drowning souls did not have even a fragment of straw to take hold of, when they caught sight of a shining one enveloped in infinite light. The Original Vow of Amida was the last refuge to which they could go. In spite of the Buddha's injunction, "Be ye your own lamp," they rushed toward the Infinite Light, immersed in which they felt strong, efficient, blessed, and enlightened. They felt and reasoned that whatever teaching left by the Buddha for his disciples was not meant for the weak-minded and heavily burdened with sins, who came to this world long after the master and could not come in personal touch with him. Their spiritual experience called for something else than the Nikāyas or Agamas, they tried to find what they wanted among all the scriptures which claimed to come from the Buddha; if such documents were not in actual existence in the form of literature or oral transmission, they did not hesitate to compile one as based upon the inner spirit of the master whose love made him go through an infinite round of transmigration for the sake of sentient beings as told in the Jatakas and demonstrated in his last earthly life itself.

In this respect the speculative or intellectual type of Buddhism as exemplified by Zen is in better accord with the teaching of the Buddha, which is, as far as is observable in the earlier literature, highly characterized by its meditative and self-reflective mood of mind. In many respects the Bodhisattva is not an Arhat, perhaps the gap between the two conceptions is just as wide as that between the Holy Path and the Easy Practice; but as long as the Bodhisattva is a self-reliant and self-disciplined follower of the Buddha, he is essentially an Arhat; both are striving after the realization of the Supreme Enlightenment. They do not mind how long they have to transmigrate in their earthly lives, if they attain to self-realization by constant striving and indefatigable energy. They are such believers in individualism and moral perfectibility that they never think of availing themselves of a stock of merit accumulated by others; their view of the moral law of causation is exclusive and self-containing and not at all so diffusive and all-embracing as that entertained by followers of the Nembutsu. The Holy Path is thorny and paved with the sense of moral responsibility, in which one side of human nature finds satisfaction. We are a strange combination of contraries; solitary aloofness appeals to us as much as social gregariousness.

It may not be out of place here to see how teachers of the Jōdo doctrine survey the whole system of Buddhism from their particular angle of observation; for the reader will thus be enabled to understand by himself the history of relationship as existing between the Zen and the Jōdo type of Buddhist experience, and such highly technical terms as "Self-power" and "Other-power," "Difficult Practice" and "Easy Practice," "Holy Path" and "Pure Land" will also become more intelligible.

According to Shinran,[9] the founder of the Shin branch of the Jōdo doctrine, Buddhism is divided into two grand groups, Mahayana and Hinayana; and Mahayana into two further sections, the one to be known as Abrupt and the other as Gradual. In the Abrupt section of Mahayana Buddhism there are two Teachings and two kinds of Leaping: the two Teachings are the Difficult Practice which is the doctrine of the Holy Path, and the Easy Practice which is the doctrine of the Pure Land (Jōdo); two kinds of Leaping are Leaping Straight-ahead by which is meant enlightenment attained by the doctrine of identity, and Leaping Athwart by which is meant rebirth in the Pure Land through faith in the Original Vow of Amida. In the Gradual section of Mahayana Buddhism there are also two Teachings and two kinds of Outgoing. The two Teachings are the Difficult Practice which is the doctrine of the Holy Path as advocated by followers of the Hossō (Dharmalakṣaṇa sect), and the Easy Practice which is the doctrine of the Pure Land as explained in the *Sutra of Meditations,* for instance. The two kinds of Outgoing are Straight Outgoing by which is meant enlightenment attained after a laborious moral discipline for ages, and Athwart Outgoing by which is meant rebirth in the outskirts of the Pure Land.

This somewhat complicated classification may be rendered clearer when presented in a tabular schema as follows:

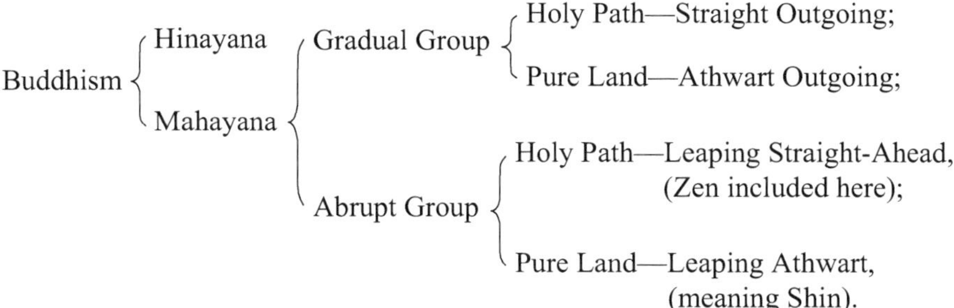

It is evident as is seen here that Shinran considered Zen occupying the same position in the Holy Path system as Shin does in the Pure Land system, as both belong to the Abrupt Leaping group though the one is the "straight-ahead" kind while the other is the "athwart."

Shōkū who was the leader of the Seizan branch of the Jōdo sect has also worked out his schema of the Buddhist schools, which is quite instructive and illuminating in regard to the relative position of Zen and Jōdo. The following list of contrasts is compiled after Shōkū, which he considers existing between the Holy Path and the Pure Land doctrine:

	Holy Path	Pure Land
What is the objective?	To get rid of Ignorance while here and attain Buddhahood;	To be born in the Pure Land after death.
By what means?	Self-power—wisdom—meditation—ascetic discipline;	Other-power—love—faith in the Original Vow.
How related to morality?	Relies on the accumulation of merit;	No such accumulation needed.
Route described:	Winding, tortuous road, on land;	Straightforward course, by water.
Teacher:	Śākyamuni;	Amitābha.
Meant for whom?	Wise men;	Plain ordinary mortals.
General characterizations:	Easy to believe, Difficult to practice, Gradual progress, Not meant for the present age, Limited application;	Difficult to believe, Easy to practice, Abrupt leap, Just meant for the present age, Universally valid.

However widely these two types of Buddhist experience, the Jōdo and the Zen, may thus differ in their method of achieving final deliverance, there is no doubt that they both start from the Buddhist view of life as suffering. They both want to get away from this suffering life in which they fail to find anything enjoyable. The Jōdo finds a better and purer life in the Pure Land of Amida who welcomes all to his land. The followers of Zen, on the other hand, take their refuge in a transcendental realm beyond the reach of birth-and-death, which is found within one's self when looked into it deeply enough.

By suffering, however, the Buddhists do not mean that life is psychologically explained as pain, and that therefore it is to be shunned. Most of unreflective critics regard Buddhism as pessimistic and world-flying because of its view of life as suffering. But in fact this Buddhist idea of suffering is the Buddhist way of judging life as it is lived by most of us who are finite, limited, relative, and conditioned; and therefore, this life is for Buddhists something to be transcended, or mastered, or expanded, or purified. The religious life with all its varieties starts from the consciousness of limitation and its consequent idea of bondage. This bondage is felt as pain. To escape from pain, therefore, is to be released from bondage, and when this assumes a positive sense, it is to get unified with the infinite, or to be embraced by an unconditioned being. Every religion ought to start pessimistic inasmuch as it feels the necessity of breaking through the limitations of this present life.

Though the Jōdo and the Zen start from the same view of life as suffering, the Jōdo has developed the emotional side of Buddhist experience more emphatically than its intellectual side. Suffering is thus conceived by Jōdo followers as due to their moral imperfection, that is, due to their sinfulness, which is the outcome of their previous karma. They want to be perfect, to be freed from sin, but as they realize that in consequence of their heavy karma-burden, too heavy to be carried on by themselves, they seek someone who is thoroughly free from it and able to help them out of their difficulties. This they find in Amida.

Amida is not a historical personality in the sense that he once lived in human history as limited in time and space, but a living being in a transcendental realm of spiritual aspirations and longings. He may not be real in the same sense as the objective world is, but just because of this he is more real than anything existing in time-space relations. If it is an incontestable fact that we are more than merely physical or biological realities, it is an equally incontestable fact that Amida is more real than a merely historical personality. This Amida has his Pure Land, also not limited by space-time relations though the descriptions of it sometimes suggest its being a spatial existence. He willed this Land of his for the sake of all sentient beings as a place or community where they could have all their deepest spiritual longings fulfilled, and it came to be realized as he attained his Supreme Enlightenment. This being the case, every suffering, pining, helpless mortal who wishes to be a member of this community can now be one and share in Amida's love and wisdom.

The Jōdo is thus dualistic with Amida on the other shore of the ocean of transmigration and sinful mortals on this side. The distance between the two increases the more in one sense as the latter—sinful mortals—grow the more conscious of their sinfulness and defiled conditions; but in another sense this distance grows the shorter and there takes place the most intimate relationship between Amida and his devotees. Therefore, the greatest stress the Jōdo places in its teaching is on the sinful life we all are leading here on earth. We are sinful, according to its teaching, because of our previous karma and not necessarily because we commit so many different kinds of evil deeds one after another. When this is realized, we are inevitably thrown back on the infinite love of Amida and will most fervently long for his merciful embrace.

The gap between Amida and his devotees is never to be closed up as long as the consciousness of sin is made the basis of the religious life. The devotees may feel the closest possible relationship to their object of appeal, but the dualistic sense will remain with them to the end of their earthly lives. They may recognize the fact of consubstantiality existing between Amida and themselves; for if there were not something in Amida that is of the same nature with the human, he could never understand the sufferings of his worshipers, he could never listen to their appeal and send to them whatever help they are in need of; and this ability on the part of Amida to read the thoughts of his followers shows that there is something common to them and Amida. Indeed, Amida was once one of us, and it was through the perfect maturing of his Buddha-nature that he thoroughly got rid of his earthly passions and became the savior of his former fellow beings who are now his devotees. The fact that Amida suffered once as we suffer now brings him most intimately to our hearts, and perhaps the very possibility of salvation is due to the awakening of our consciousness to the presence of Amida himself in us. If this really be the case, the theory of consubstantiality will now turn into that of self-identity, and dualism will cease to exist in the minds of Jōdo and Shin followers. But as long as "faith alone" is the key to salvation Amida will forever stand in contrast to the defiled condition of karma-ridden creatures.

Compared with this dualistic and devotional type of Buddhism, the Zen type is unquestionably intellectual and monistic. The view of life as suffering is taken up intellectually by Zen. The cause of suffering is referred to the fact that we are finite and living under various conditions of limitation. To reach a state of rest, freedom, and perfect bliss, therefore, Zen followers try to grasp the infinite. They know that deeply buried underneath their consciousness of finitude there lies something infinite; for otherwise they would not even be conscious of their being finite and under bondage. They also know, therefore, that when this infinite is brought out clearly in consciousness and the feeling of identity is firmly established, they are no more sufferers of the passions and desires classified under various headings by Buddhist philosophers.

Zen Buddhism is thus naturally speculative and mystical. Its gaze is fixed more on "the other shore" than "on this shore." It perceives infinity in a particle of dust and knows that this very moment is confluent with eternity. If its followers have Amida, he is at once identified with themselves. He is not quietly sitting cross-legged on the lotus-flower in the Land of Purity, but he is right with them and in them and moves his hands as they move theirs and walks as they walk. His Pure Land is not so far away as 100,000 × 100,000,000 lands in the West, but right here on this earth. Thus instead of duality, unity is the keynote of Zen Buddhism.

Contentment is a sentiment common to Zen and Jōdo; but the Zen remains cool as if there were nothing in life to disturb its serenity, while the Jōdo is full of grateful feelings, even for the smallest things in life. If Zen is a towering solitary winter mountain covered with snow, Jōdo is the spring ocean with its broad swelling waves. Zen contemplates, Jōdo appreciates; Zen is intoxicated with the sense of identification, Jōdo is constantly aware of its overflowing joys; the Zen master comes out into the world and is looked up to as almost a superior being who has already gone over to the other shore *(pāraṃ),* the Jōdo devotee is mixed up from the beginning with the world and takes everybody for a fellow being suffering like himself; Zen rejects the worldly life as not conducive to the realization of enlightenment, Jōdo accepts the worldly life as a thing inevitable to a being living in bondage from which it expects to be freed only after death. The Zen follower disciplines himself to the utmost of his capacity in order to reach the highest stage of self-identification; the Jōdo gives himself up to his life as he finds it making Amida shoulder all the burden inherent to it.

A Christian counterpart to the Zen form of Buddhist mysticism may be found in the sermons of Eckhart, while the Jōdo, especially the Shin form of it, finds its Christian correspondent in the *sola fide* ["faith alone" (JCD)] teaching of evangelicalism. Zen has a practical method of training the mind in order to bring it to a state of concentration, from which there ensues an intuition of the truth. This is lacking in Eckhart for all his sermons are concerned with the realization itself and not with the way to it. Being in the direct line of Indian thought and culture, Zen differs from Christian mysticism especially in its practical training. So with the Jōdo, it has its own formula which has no parallel in Christianity.

The Jōdo formula of faith is *Namu-amida-butsu (namo amitābha-buddhāya),* technically known as "nembutsu" (thinking of the Buddha). It literally means "Adoration (or homage) to Amitābha Buddha," but the formula as it is repeated these days has no special reference to its original meaning, for the name of the Buddha is invoked in the main as expression of one's devotion.

As to the way this formula, *Namu-amida-butsu,* is interpreted, we may distinguish different tendencies of thought existing side by side in the Pure Land school, that is, in the devotional type of Buddhist experience. The formula may be repeated by the devotee without his really being conscious of all its implications, but when his psychological attitude is analyzed, we grow aware of the following three motives or ways of approaching the nembutsu, and these motives determine the different tendencies of thought in the understanding of its signification. The first is to think of the Buddha as a being fully enlightened and emancipated from fetters of various kinds; the second is to recite or invoke the name as itself containing innumerable merits in accordance with the scriptural authority; and the third is to call upon his name, as when a distressed child calls upon its mother, as the last refuge from all the worldly sufferings and spiritual tribulations.

Historically, the nembutsu *(buddhānusmṛti)* meant to think of the Buddha as possessor of all the virtues Buddhists could think of. When he was thus thought of, the corresponding virtues would gradually grow in the hearts of his followers. The nembutsu was thus the means of moral training. We may understand the nembutsu in this way whenever reference is made to it in the early or Hinayana literature of Buddhism.

The second form of invocation developed perhaps when the mystery of name came to be recognized. In fact, the Indians had been from their early history great advocates of incantation; they had been cognizant of the mysterious powers concealed in names, and this is the reason why we find so many magical formulas quoted throughout the classical literature of India. Probably this also explains why we read in the Jōdo sutras that Amida wished to have his name resounding all over the chiliocosm and that there are innumerable merits contained in the name of Amida or Amitābha. Thus there was a time when the question was most heatedly discussed by scholars of Shin philosophy whether its devotees were to believe in the mysterious power of Amida's Original Vow or of his name.

Most Jōdo followers believe in the mysterious power of the name and consequently that the more frequently is the name repeated the more meritorious one's life will be and the more assured of one's birth in the Land of Purity. Hōnen is said to have repeated the nembutsu more than fifty thousand times a day;[10] but according to Shukō (C. Zhuhong), a Zen master of the Ming dynasty, who was experimentally inclined, the nembutsu cannot be repeated more than one hundred thousand times for every twenty-four hours. When, however, the formula is pronounced in full and when some time is given up to eating and other physical requirements, the number will considerably be reduced. It is readily seen that in this kind of invocation there is no thinking about the virtues of the Buddha, the repetition being altogether mechanical; and therefore this practice tends to produce a hypnosis in the consciousness of the devotee-invoker. Could we say that the final result of the nembutsu in this case is to clear up the field of consciousness ready for the awakening of a hidden truth?

The genuine devotional type of Buddhism is represented by the third form of the nembutsu, in which Amida is appealed to as the real rescuer of sinful mortals who look up to him as children do to their father or mother. The nembutsu for this class of devotees is the last cry they utter in their desperate efforts to be delivered from the miserable situation in which they are. It is a cry in which the last citadel of egoism is given up, that is, the old Adam dies and the new man is born, and the very moment the cry is uttered, the devotee is embraced in the light of Amida. In his consciousness, this cry is felt as if he were compelled to utter it by another, and at the moment a light comes to his passive mind. The nembutsu in this case is not thinking of the Buddha, nor is it for the inducement of an ecstatic condition of mind, but it is simply calling upon Amida as the last appeal from a spirit in indescribable anguish. It is just one call, and there is no room in such a soul for repetition or for deliberation. When a rope is at the last-stage of tension, it snaps with a sound, which is, translated into Shin terminology, *Namu-amida-butsu!*

Besides these three ways of saying the nembutsu, we have another form in which the devotional type of Buddhist experience sometimes comes closely related to the speculative type, showing their common origin at least psychologically, in spite of their apparent polarization. This form may be termed the Zen nembutsu, for it is the nembutsu practiced by some of the later Zen masters in China. It is distinct, however, from the foregoing three forms in this respect that the Zen adept treats it intellectually and not devotionally or psychologically. He tells his followers to find out who is the one that invokes the name of the Buddha. Historically, this way of treating the nembutsu must have developed when the nembutsu as a repetitive formula was very much in vogue, and when on the part of Zen history what is technically known as "Koan" (C. *gong'an*) was resorted to as the means of opening the mind to the truth of Zen.

Instead of mechanically repeating the nembutsu, the Zen master wants to have an interview as it were with the inner man who does this repetition. Zen always insists to have an intellectual insight into the innermost recesses of consciousness. Its method is like peeling the onion; taking off every skin of logical complication, it wants to see face-to-face the last man if there is any. It is never satisfied with mere reasoning or mere metaphysical inference, it wants to lay its hand on the thing itself. This is where Zen is a personal experience and not a philosophy. It is thus ever pressing inward until it goes through the bottomless abyss of human consciousness. Therefore, when the Zen student repeats the nembutsu we know that he is knocking at the gate of the invoker himself. Which is to say, he is doing his utmost to look into the secrets of his own being. The Zen master sometimes regards this form as the true meaning of the nembutsu; but in this he is mistaken, for there are three other ways of invoking the Buddha's name, each representing a type of religious experience in Buddhism.

As to the relations between being born in the Pure Land and the reciting of the Buddha's name, the general idea entertained by scholars is that the nembutsu is the condition for such a rebirth, that the nembutsu is said with the sole purpose of assuring oneself of the rebirth. This is what is expressly taught in the Sutras and what the Jōdo devotees confessedly aim at. As this is a hopeless world as far as the attainment of purity and perfection is concerned, they desire to have their ideal world realized in the dominion of Amida where everything is granted to them as it is desired. Life there unfolds itself on the basis of eternity and infinitude, of light and love, quite unlike this world of limitations and hence of imperfections and defilements. When, however, this idea of being born in the Land of Purity through the mysterious virtue in the name of Amida is closely studied, I doubt whether this is really the case with the actual psychology of the nembutsu devotee who claims to have been saved by the grace of Amida. The point awaits further investigation and I will not enter here into a discussion. This much I wish to say that in the Zen type of nembutsu there is no thought of being born in the country of Amida. The motive of the Zen follower is to penetrate into the secret of the nembutsu itself and has no ulterior aim to attain beyond that. When the realization dawns upon him that he himself is the bearer of the Buddha-name and that infinite light shines out of his own inner man, he knows that there is no Pure Land to seek after. This is usually expressed in the following phrases: *Koshin no Mida, yuishin Jōdo,*[11] "The self-body is Amida, mind only is the Pure Land."

These four approaches to the nembutsu are distinct enough as they have been defined here, but in our practical lives they are more or less mixed up and difficult to separate one from another, except the Zen type which is quite apart from the rest, especially in this that it entertains no desire for the Pure Land. While this is true of most Zen masters, there are a great deal of individual variations. Some of the masters express a desire for the Pure Land where they pray to be born after this life. But the peculiar feature we have to recognize about them is that they do not say the nembutsu conditionally for the attainment of their wish. The nembutsu is quite a separate thing with them, perhaps it is a recollective type making them think of the attainment of perfect Buddhahood. Read the following prayer by Daie (C. Dahui, 1089–1163):

> This is my prayer: May I be firm in my desire for the truth, showing no retrogression in the long pursuit of it, while my physical body remains in health, free from all disease, with my mind strong and striving, neither scattered nor listless! May I be free from disaster and undisturbed by evil ones, and, not turning toward a wrong path, directly enter upon the right path! May my selfish desires be destroyed and my wisdom increase so that coming soon to the realization of the great truth I may inherit the Buddha's spiritual life, and, by delivering all sentient beings from misery, requite the grace I have received from the Buddhas and Fathers!

Next, may I not suffer much at the time of death! Knowing its arrival seven days previously, may I quietly rest in the right thought and enjoy spiritual freedom, at the last moment! When this physical body is quitted, may I instantly be born in a [or the] Buddha-land where I come in the presence of all the Buddhas and, by them certified as to my realization of enlightenment, I may reveal myself all over the world in various forms and save all sentient beings. [I pray to you,] O all the Buddhas and Bodhisattva-Mahāsattvas, of the past, present, and future in the ten quarters of the universe; O *Mahāprajñāpāramitā!*

In a way it is strange that a Zen master should ever think of offering a prayer to the Buddha or Buddhas and also to *Prajñāpāramitā*. Does he not find himself well with the whole world with its multifarious contents? Has he not gained a transcendental view of life, from which he surveys undisturbed all the vicissitudes of human experience? Does he think that his prayer-offering has a power to move the course of things in the universe, which are evidently regulated by the law of causation, moral as well as physical? At all events Zen masters frequently offer prayers for various reasons in spite of their claim to have grasped the ultimate truth which makes the sun rise in the morning and the stars shine at night and which when grasped makes one free from all bonds of human ailments and trivialities. Daie however does not say whether he wishes to be born in the Land of Amida, for he simply wishes to be born in a Buddha-land; but in this respect the Chinese language leaves the reader in the lurch. *Fotu* is too indefinite, which may mean a Buddha-land or the Buddha-land. But the prayer of Irin (C. Weilin), another Zen master of Ming dynasty, is quite explicit in this respect:[12]

Homage to the Buddhas of the past, present, and future in the ten quarters; to the Honored One, Śākyamuni, who is my teacher and leader; to the Mysterious Gates of Truth which are of one vehicle but innumerable in number; to the Mahāsattvas such as Mañjuśrī and Samantabhadra; to such Great Sravakas as Mahākāśyapa and Ānanda and other Bhikshus of wisdom and holiness. I pray to hosts of the Triple Treasure and to the Nāgadevas that they would not forsake me from their mercy but embrace with pity this poor Bhikshu as well as all sentient beings in the universe. From beginningless time till this day they have all been drifting along in the triple world and transmigrating from one state to another in the five forms of existence. Not yet being able to realize the essential unity of things, they erroneously cling to the body made of the four elements. In the Dharma of identity, they make the mistake of cherishing the view of *meum et tuum* [mine and thine (JCD)], and to the world of unreality they are so insanely attached. They have no restraint over their passions: avarice, anger, and infatuation, which they assert with the body, mouth, and mind. All kinds of karma are produced, and evils in every form are committed. Through kalpas as numberless as atoms and dusts they have wandered in a cycle of births and deaths.

Fortunately, due to a seed of wisdom sown in my previous existence, I was now born as a human being in this Middle Kingdom. I am endowed with six complete sense-organs, and my body, mouth, and mind are in sound harmony. Borne by the right faith I am now a Buddhist monk; and under the guidance of a wise teacher have I entered the path. My effort is to master the Threefold Discipline, to comprehend most thoroughly the doctrine of One Vehicle, to penetrate into the real reality of all things, and to abide in the eternity of One Mind. What I fear, however, is that my steps are not steady enough to overcome my past evil karma and that my thoughts are not penetrating enough to reach the most subtle truth. If the dark storms are always disturbing the bottom of my mind and the four snakes are ready at any moment to devour this visionary husk of existence, when can I bring the fruit of truth to maturity and make the tree of enlightenment blossom out? I humbly wish by means of repentance to climb up the path of discipline and enlightenment.

I only pray that the Triple Treasure would embrace me under their truly merciful protection and let not only myself but all sentient beings be released forever from the bondage or karma-hindrance, and deeply penetrate into the great Dharma, and, furnished with great blissful wisdom and exhibiting great activities, perform great spiritual wonders. For thereby the Triple Treasure should flourish, the Mahayana be propagated, the Right Dharma prevail all over the world, the True Way be always conserved even to the last day, the Eightfold Path of Righteousness be brought out to view, the Fourfold Gate of Reception be kept open, and all sentient beings be brought under the Dharma so that they might universally be back at the home of Enlightenment.

When the day comes to quit this body of karmic effect, may my understanding of the doctrine of Emptiness *(śūnyatā)* be not obscured, but the spirituality of the Buddha-mind be revealed, and, being born in the Western World of Bliss, come in the personal presence of Amitābha Buddha, Avalokiteśvara, Mahāsthāmaprāpta, and other holy beings. And by them may I personally be respected and be allowed to listen to their own sermons on the mystery of the Dharma, and then being admitted into the congregation of the firmly established in the faith, attain to the meaning of the Dharanis, be furnished with the Ten Supernatural Powers, and open up the Three Secret Treasures. May I then sit on a lotus of the first order and realize the fruit of enlightenment in one birth. When this is attained, may my being be in accord with the nature of the universe and work with the activity of the universe. While not going away from the Land of Bliss, may my body be revealed all over the ten quarters; while waiting upon Amitābha Buddha may I also come in personal contact with all the Buddhas. Every land has a place for a Buddha to abide, and may I come in his presence wherever he may be, and being regarded as his eldest son, ask him to revolve the fundamental wheel of the Law.

There is not indeed a place in the universe which is not inhabited by sentient beings, and they are looking for a merciful one to come and help them, and may I in response to their call become a rescuing boat for them in order to take them safely to the other shore which is Nirvana. May I also reveal myself in all forms and be a helpful friend to the four classes of being.

May the Six Virtues of Perfection be fulfilled in every thought of mine and all kinds of Dharanis be attained by every function of my mind. When there is no Buddha, may I even become a Buddha and reveal myself like the moon which is uniformly reflected

> on one thousand lakes; where there is no Dharma may I preach it in such a way as an echo reverberates throughout ten thousand hollows. Wherever there is a call may I respond without fail, and whenever there is a wish may I fulfill it. May my pitying heart be equal to that of Avalokiteśvara, and my miraculous deeds be like unto those of Samantabhadra. Beginning today till the end of time, may my prayer be effective when there would be no more suffering beings anywhere in the universe. This alone is my earnest desire that the Triple Treasure have mercy on me and taking note of my sincerity fulfill all my wishes.

With the devotional type of the Jōdo the being born in the Pure Land is manifestly the object of the nembutsu, though in my view there is some confusion in the minds of its adherents as to the real signification of what they call salvation, that is, rebirth in the Pure Land. For instance, when they say they are assured of the rebirth, what guarantee do they have of a fact which has not yet taken place? How can they be absolutely or at least to a very high degree of anticipation sure of the promise or vow made by Amida to materialize successfully after their death? According to the Jōdo devotee, he is assured of his rebirth when his faith is firmly established, that is to say, when he is innerly convinced of the sincerity and genuineness as well as the efficaciousness of the Original Vow. He will then have not a shadow of doubt as to the wonderful power of the Vow which comes out of the mysterious depths of the will of Amitābha Buddha. It is this faith and not necessarily the fact of rebirth in the Pure Land that seems to be of every importance in the life of the Jōdo devotee. The rebirth is not yet a matured fact, for it is something to be realized after death; and who can be sure of a thing that is to happen after the dissolution of this relative existence when we have no absolute reason to expect even the sun to rise tomorrow as it did this morning? The faith thus naturally comes to be of more consequence than the rebirth itself, which is, however, confessedly the objective of the nembutsu. "When the faith is acquired, the rebirth is assured. When the rebirth is assured, one abides in the condition of no-retrogression. When one abides in the condition of no-retrogression, one is settled in the order of steadfastness *(samyaktvaniyatarāśi)*." And this "when" means simultaneity or instantaneousness and not succession in time.[13]

It is then evident that what the followers of the nembutsu are seeking after as a thing of foremost significance in their religious life is the faith in the Original Vow of Amitābha Buddha. If this is once firmly established, they would leave everything to the wisdom and love of Amida, for he knows what is the best for them to have. They would not mind even if they were sent to hell instead of their coveted Land of Bliss. The wisdom of Amida, who is the Buddha of Infinite Light, is altogether beyond the comprehensibility of finite mortals such as we are; it is the height of absurdity and presumptuousness on our part to try to guess at his wondrous ways of achieving our salvation. We must abandon all our finite thinking, all our individual reasoning, and give ourselves up absolutely to the mercy of the Buddha; for the faith is gained only thus. As to the rebirth, it takes care of itself. It does not matter indeed what will become of it so long as the Vow remains effective through faith. Read the following from Kakunyo,[14] one of the most illustrious and learned followers of Shinran, who quotes his master thus:

> To be reborn in the Land of Purity, all that is needed is faith, and nothing else matters. Such a great event as the rebirth is altogether beyond the limits of finite knowledge. The only thing we can do is to leave everything in the hands of the Buddha. Not only we who are finite but even Bodhisattva Maitreya who is to be a Buddha after another birth *(ekajātipratibaddha)* are unable to fathom the incomprehensibility of Buddha-wisdom. The limited intelligence of an ignorant being is of no avail. My repeated advice, therefore, is to trust ourselves entirely to the Original Vow of the Buddha. Such a trusting one is called one who has awakened faith in "other-power."
>
> Therefore, as far as we ourselves are concerned, let us not be troubled with the thought whether we should be reborn in the Pure Land or in *Naraka.* As I [meaning Shinran] was told by my late master just to follow him wherever he was destined, I am ready to go even to *Naraka* (hell) if he is to be there. In case I had no opportunity to meet my good master in this life, I as one of ignorant beings was sure to go to *Naraka.* But, instructed by the holy teacher, I have now learned of Amida's Original Vow, and his all-embracing love is cherished deeply in my heart; I have cut asunder the bonds of birth-and-death and know that my destiny is in the Pure Land where it is so difficult to obtain a rebirth. This surely cannot be the work of a limited being. It is possible that the taking refuge in the Buddha-wisdom of Amida and saying the nembutsu were really a deed destined for *Naraka;* misinterpreting which, however, my late master might have deceived me, saying that it would be the cause of rebirth in the Pure Land. Even in this case I have no regret whatever, for I should most willingly go to *Naraka.* Why? Because if I did not meet him my destination after death would have been nowhere else but *Naraka* itself; but if I go there now deceived by my wise teacher, I should be there with him, I should not be alone; and so long as I were with him it did not matter where I went, either to the Pure Land or to one of the evil paths; I am decided to follow him. The faith I now cherish is not most assuredly the designing of any finite being.

This idea of not caring for one's destination after death, if once faith is awakened in the Original Vow, is in most unmistakable manner expressed in the following passage taken from the *Tannishō,* in which are presented some of the most remarkable views held by Shinran, the founder of the Shin sect: "Whether the nembutsu is the seed from which a rebirth is obtained in the Land of Purity, or whether it is a deed meant for *Naraka,* I have no knowledge whatever. I only follow the teaching of my good master who told me to say the nembutsu and be saved by Amida. This is the whole content of my faith."

When the nembutsu goes beyond the idea of rebirth in the Pure Land, and gains a new signification in itself and for itself, the Jōdo school has to turn toward mysticism. The nembutsu is now no more the means of taking one into the promised land of bliss and purity, it is in itself an end, in the realization of which the dualism between the reciter of the nembutsu (i.e., the Jōdo devotee) and its listener (i.e., Amida) is finally obliterated. And in this obliteration we notice the strong mystic coloring of the Jōdo. In the beginning it was through the nembutsu that the Jōdo devotee brought upon himself all the favors that could issue from the Original Vow; but the moment he got assured of his rebirth, that is, the moment his faith was somehow established, the objective was forgotten, his consciousness dwelt only on the mysterious power of the Vow itself, and then the feeling of mystery developed and dwelt on an inexplicable state of identification now taking place between himself and the Buddha.

The Jōdo writers as a rule do not dwell so much upon the description of the Happy Land where they long to go, as the mystery of the Original Vow whereby they are so singularly, so wonderfully, so inexplicably saved in spite of all their past and present sinful life. According to the ordinary law of moral causation, sin multiplies itself, but the Original Vow breaks completely this eternal chain of cause and effect, of curse and damnation; for if one only believes in its efficacy, one is at once released from it and received into the Infinite Light and Eternal Life known as Amida. This is absolutely beyond the grasp of finite knowledge bound up in the principle of relativity. Shinran is never weary of talking about the unfathomable depths of Amida's wisdom deprecating all the petty contrivances of a finite and sinful being. The following is an abstract made out of one of his sayings[15] with the heading "On Being True to Self-Nature":

> By "being true to self-nature" is meant that the mysterious power of the nembutsu is wholly due to the virtue of the Original Vow itself and that the devotee's will or contrivance has no share in it. As the Buddha willed it so, so it is; there are no other wills entering into it. It is, therefore, said that the nembutsu transcends all determination as to its meaning, which is the very meaning of it. In other words, the nembutsu is not a matter of thought, it demands faith and not the understanding. Therefore, what the devotee has to do is simply to take in what Amida freely gives and not to put forward anything of himself, he need not think of what is good for himself or what is not, but just to abandon himself to the free natural working of the Original Vow. And as the Vow is to take every mortal being to Amida's own Land of Bliss and Purity where he can have a full realization of Buddhahood, it is said that the nembutsu works out itself, that is, true to its self-nature, and that its meaninglessness is the very meaning of it. Indeed, even where this much is asserted, something of meaning gets attached to the nembutsu. How beyond the ordinary comprehension of mortal beings is the Buddha-wisdom!

From this attitude the next step will be to grow more and more conscious of the mystery of the nembutsu itself. According to Ippen:[16]

> When one casts away the thought of this body and gets absolutely unified with *Namu-amida-butsu,* we have the so-called state of "undisturbed single-mindedness."

> Every nembutsu one would say at this moment of self-concentration is a repetition of itself by itself, for in it subject and object are identified. When the subject-ego is separated from the nembutsu and made a somewhat devising for the rebirth, this is asserting "self-power" and is a form of ego-attachment. Such nembutsu reciter will not probably be born in the Pure Land. To be merged single-mindedly in the nembutsu itself, paying no attention whatever to the dualistic determinations of thought, is what is meant by "saying the nembutsu with singleness of thought."

From the author of the *Anjin ketsujō shō*,[17] a short treatise on the attainment of spiritual peace, we have this:

> When your faith is established in a state known as "Nembutsu *Sanmai*"[18] your body as well as your mind turns into *Namu-amida-butsu,* leaving nothing behind but *Namu-amida-butsu.* The physical body is constituted of the four elements, earth, water, fire, and air; the Hinayanists consider it as made up of *aṇu* (infinitesimal particles). Let the body be crushed into infinitesimal dust and you will find every one of them colored with the virtues of Amitābha Buddha (i.e., Buddha of Enjoyment or *Saṃbhogakāya*). This being so, the physical body in which *ki* and *hō* are united is no other than *Namu-amida-butsu* itself. The mind is filled with the passions, major and minor, and with other things as well; it is born every minute and dies every minute, it is in a state of constant becoming. Analyze the mind into its component thoughts as they succeed in time one after another, and you will find that every one of them is filled with the Vow and the Deeds of Amitābha Buddha; the mind in which *ki* and *hō* are thus found united is no other than *Namu-amida-butsu* itself.
>
> As the great pitying heart of Amida is filled with thoughts about sentient beings who are ever sinking in the ocean of birth-and-death, in him you too will find the identity of *ki* and *hō;* and he is no other than *Namu-amida-butsu.* At the bottom of our hearts, however confused and distorted, we find them filled with the virtues of the Buddha whose body is the universe itself, and for this reason there is also in our hearts an identity of *ki* and *hō,* and they are no other than *Namu-amida-butsu.*
>
> The same can be said of the Land of Purity and of its Lord: For every leaf of the jewel-trees in the Land sways for the sake of mortal sinful beings such as ourselves, and for that reason in it too we find an identity of *ki* and *hō;* it is thus no other than *Namu-amida-butsu* itself. As to the Lord in the Land of Purity, every part of his body, from the white hair-tuft *(ūrṇākeśa)* between his eyebrows to the wheel with one thousand spokes on his hands and feet, is the form of perfection attained by the fulfillment of his Vow and Deeds, which he had for the sake of all sentient beings forever in transmigration; and for that reason in his form too there is an identity of *ki* and *hō;* and it is thus no other than *Namu-amida-butsu.*
>
> This being of ours composed of matter and mind and capable of acting in three ways[19] is pervaded throughout, whichever one you may assume of the four attitudes,[20] with the virtues of the Buddha in his state of enjoyment; and for that reason between us who turn toward the Buddha for salvation saying *Namu-* and the Buddha, i.e., *Amida-butsu* himself, there has never been a gap from the first; every thought of ours is thus *Namu-amida-butsu* itself. Since every breath indeed, inhaling

> or exhaling, has never had even for a moment been separated from the virtues of the Buddha, it is the embodiment of *Namu-amida-butsu.*

In these confessions of the great adherents of the nembutsu we notice that the devotional type is changing into the mystical type and closely approaching the Zen. While beginning intellectually, the Zen ends in transcending logic and philosophy, which is also the case with the Jōdo. For the Jōdo too ultimately casts off its dualistic attitude toward the object of its devotion as we have seen, and enters upon the phase of identification, growing thoroughly mystical. The difference between the two types is finally resolvable to this, that the one avowedly proclaims the identity of *Ki* and *Hō,* directing all its religious discipline toward the realization of the theory, whereas the other starts off with facts of experience in which realism is frankly acknowledged. The latter therefore tends to be dualistic, and insofar as this is the case the Jōdo stands in contradistinction to the Zen. But the essentially mystic tendency of Buddhism reappears in the Jōdo as well as in the Zen when they both claim to have realized their goal, the one in Satori and the other in *Anjin.* Compare thus the following stanza by a Zen master with the last quotation from the author of the *Anjin ketsujō shō,* in which indeed this is also quoted:

> Every night, embraced by Buddha I sleep;
> Every morning when I wake I am with him;
> Whether standing or sitting, I am forever accompanied by him,
> I am never away from him even for a second:
> It is like unto an object followed by its shadow.
> Wishest thou to know where the Buddha is this moment?
> Only this—hear thou this voice of mine!

We are now enabled to understand how the two types of Buddhist experience which are so manifestly diverse and apart from each other are merged in one, breathing the same original spirit of Mahayanism. The *jiriki* here becomes *tariki* and the *tariki jiriki,* that is to say, selfhood is revealed in otherness and otherness in selfhood, which means a complete interpenetration of subject and object, Amida and his devotees. And we can say that Buddhism is after all one and remains so in spite of its apparent diversity.

This is where Buddhism differs from Christianity. Christianity is essentially a devotional religion, and dualistic, holding fast to the irreconcilable gap as existing between the sinful mortal and the all-pardoning savior. The devout orthodox Christians would never think of crossing this gap in order to get unified with their object of worship. Mysticism was something foreign to Christianity in the beginning of its history; it was grafted into it later on when it came in contact with other forms of religious thought and experience. Buddhism on the other hand is truly Indian in its tenacious hold on the monistic view of life which is to be intuitively attained. While the bhakti [religious devotion (JCD)] type may not be said to be a foreign importation, it generally stands contrasted to the *vidyā* [clear knowledge (JCD)] type; and where it reaches its consummation it thoroughly merges into the latter, erasing almost all the individual traces of each type. So we observe that even the extremely devotional form of Buddhist life as revealed in the Jōdo begins in its last stage of "spiritual rest" *(anjin)* to approach the Zen type. Indeed here lies the unity of Buddhist experience throughout its varied expressions.[21]

3

Selection from The Koan Exercise

This essay is a long excerpt from Suzuki's monograph-length study of the Zen koan published in his renowned three-volume series Essays in Zen Buddhism. Though the primary focus of this work is the koan, Suzuki dedicates almost a third of it to the nembutsu, thus reflecting his fascination with Pure Land Buddhism as well. He uses Buddhological methodology to examine the nembutsu: identifying its origins in Buddhist texts going back to India, tracing its evolution across China and Japan, analyzing its terminology, parsing its meaning and uses in various traditions, elucidating the views of important Japanese Buddhists, and suggesting what the significance of the nembutsu is for religious practice in the Pure Land tradition. Interwoven into this meticulous study are Suzuki's own proposals about the psychological dynamics of the nembutsu and the mystical experience it triggers, which he considers the essence of religion.

Suzuki's study begins with the observation that the word "nembutsu" in Buddhist texts originally meant to think or meditate *(nen)* on the Buddha *(butsu)*, but over time came to signify *shōmyō*, uttering the Buddha's name. Thus, it shifted from a mental event to a verbal one. But that verbal act, Suzuki argues, has the capacity to provoke a mental state too. He points out that the syllables of the chanted nembutsu are simply a transliteration from Sanskrit rather than a translation of words that can be logically grasped by the chanter. That is, it is a repetitive verbal act with no cognitive content. As such, it has the capacity to arrest certain types of mental activity and to generate other states of mind—specifically, a mystical state. Hence, Suzuki sees the genealogy of the nembutsu as originating with a mental state (meditation on the Buddha) then evolving into a verbal practice (uttering the Buddha's name) and finally merging back into a mental state (mystical experience). Seeking to identify the varied ways that Pure Land Buddhism has expressed this mysticism, he singles out, among others, the emphasis on Buddha-name only by Ippen (1239–1289), the theme of no separation between devotee and Amida Buddha in the *Anjin ketsujō shō* (On the Final Peaceful Settlement of Mind), and the concept of faith *(shin)* in the teachings of Shinran

(1173–1262). Suzuki considers them all to be a mystical experience of nondualism in the present, and he suggests that this is the true significance of the nembutsu for Pure Land Buddhism.

There are several elements in this essay that are found in Suzuki's other scholarship. The first is Suzuki's nontraditional representation of Pure Land Buddhism. He goes to great lengths to shift the focus from the Pure Land paradise in the afterlife to a mystical experience in this life, even though the aspiration for paradise was always a prominent dimension of it. The second is Suzuki's attempt to find common ground between Zen and Pure Land Buddhism. Here his point of comparison is the nembutsu and the koan. He identifies both as verbal devices to confound reasoning and provoke mystical awareness. The third is Suzuki's use of approaches and terminology from religious studies in the West to elucidate Buddhism—in this case, the psychology of religion and the concept of mysticism. These were categories and interpretive strategies that circulated widely in the West during the first half of the twentieth century, used largely in an attempt to define the essence of religion. Suzuki was quite familiar with these Western approaches and deployed them in a similar way in his analysis of Buddhism. In the second half of the twentieth century, however, both the category of mysticism and the psychology of religion have undergone criticism and lost clout in some scholarly circles.

The base text for this essay is "The Koan Exercise," in Daisetz Teitaro Suzuki, *Essays in Zen Buddhism (Second Series)* (London: Luzac, 1933), 123–160. It was republished with editorial changes by Christmas Humphreys in Daisetz Teitaro Suzuki, *Essays in Zen Buddhism (Second Series)* (London: Rider, 1949), 154–194. A Japanese translation by Yokogawa Kenshō was published as *Zen to nenbutsu no shinrigaku teki kiso* (Tokyo: Daitō Shuppansha, 1937). See SDZ 4:305–343.

. . .

NEMBUTSU (C. *NIANFO*) AND *SHŌMYŌ* (C. *CHENGMING*)

Nembutsu or *buddhānusmṛti* literally means "to think of the Buddha," or "to meditate on the Buddha," and is counted as one of the six subjects of meditation in the *Mahāvyutpatti*. The six are as follows: 1. *Buddhānusmṛti*, 2. *Dharma*, 3. *Saṃgha* (Brotherhood), 4. *Śīla* (morality), 5. *Tyāga* (giving up), and 6. *Devatā* (gods). It is also one of the five subjects of mental discipline known as *wutingxin;* that is, objects by thinking of which the mind is kept away from erroneous views. The five are: 1. Impurity of the body, the thought of which reacts against greed and lust; 2. Compassion, as against anger; 3. Causation, as against infatuation or folly; 4. The six elements, as against the notion of an ego-substance; and 5. Breathing exercise, as against mental perturbation. Though I am unable to find out exactly how it came to pass, the fourth subject (that is, the six elements: earth, water, fire, air, the void, and consciousness) is replaced by "meditation on the Buddha" *(nenbutsu)* in Zhizhe's[1] commentary on the *Saddharma-puṇḍarīka*. According to a work[2] belonging to the Tiantai school of Zhizhe, this meditation is considered to counteract mental heaviness, evil thoughts, and physical calamities.

It is a very natural thing for the Buddhists to meditate on their teacher whose great personality impressed them in some way more than did his teaching. When they were not feeling energetic in their search after the truth, or when their minds were disturbed by all kinds of worldly temptation, the best way to strengthen their moral courage was, no doubt, to think of their teacher. In the beginning the Nembutsu was a purely moral practice, but as the mysterious power of a name came to claim a stronger hold on the religious imagination of the Indian Buddhists, the thinking of the Buddha as a person endowed with great virtues ceased and gave way to the uttering of his name. As a philosopher says, "Nec nomen Deo quaeras; Deus nomen est" ["Nor should we seek a name for God; God is his name" (JCD)].[3] Name is as good as substance; in some cases it works far more efficaciously than that for which it stands, for when we know the name, we can put a god into service. This has been so from the earliest days of every religious history all the world over. When Amitābha Buddha obtained his enlightenment he wished to have his name *(nāmadheya)* resound throughout the great chiliocosms, so that he might save any being that heard his name.[4]

But the sutra[5] makes no reference yet to the uttering of his name only. The phrases used are: *daśabhiś cittotpādaparivartaiḥ,*[6] which forms the nineteenth vow of the Sanskrit text, meaning "Ten times repeating the thought [of the Pure Land]"; *prasannacittā mām anusmareyuḥ,*[7] which is the eighteenth vow of the Sanskrit text, meaning "Remembered me with pure thoughts"; or *antaśa ekacittotpādam api adhyāśayena prasādasahagatena cittam utpādayanti,*[8] "[All beings] raise their thought, even for once only, raise their thought, with devotion and serenity." *Cittotpāda* or *anusmṛti,* "thinking of [the Buddha]," is not the same as "uttering the name." The *Pratyutpanna-samādhi Sūtra*[9] which was translated into Chinese as early as the second century by Lokarakṣa,[10] in which mention is also made of Amitābha Buddha in the West, and which is consequently regarded as one of the authoritative sources of the Pure Land school, refers to the name of the Buddha, saying, "The Bodhisattva, who hearing the name of the Buddha Amitābha wishes to see him, may see him by constantly thinking of the region where he is." The term used here is "thinking" (*nian* in Chinese) and not "uttering." Whenever the Buddha becomes an object of meditation, no matter to what school the devotee may belong, Hinayana or Mahayana, Zen or Shin, he has always been thought of as a personality, not only physically, but as spiritually inspiring.

In the *Sūtra of the Meditation on the Buddha of Eternal Life,* however, the devotees are taught to say, "Adoration to Buddha Amitābha"; for when they utter this Buddha-name they will be liberated from sins committed in their lives for fifty billions of kalpas. Again if a dying man cannot think of the Buddha owing to intense pain, he is told just to utter the name of the Buddha of Eternal Life *(Amitāyus).* In the *Smaller Sukhāvatī-vyūha,* or *Sūtra of Amitāyus,* the author advises people to hold in mind *(manasikāra)* the name of the blessed Amitāyus the Tathagata, which will make them depart with a tranquil mind from this life, when the time comes.

In accordance with these instructions in the sutras, Nāgārjuna writes in his *Commentary on the Daśabhūmika* (chapter 5, "On Easy Practice") that if one wishes quickly to reach the stage of no-turning-back, he should hold the Buddha's name in mind full of reverent thought. There may be some difference, as far as words go, between "holding in mind" and "uttering" or "invoking," but, practically, holding the Buddha's name in mind is to utter it with the lips, silently or audibly. The shifting of the center of devotional attention from thinking to utterance, from remembrance to invocation, is a natural process.

Daochuo[11] quotes a sutra[12] in his work called *Anleji*[13] which is one of the principal sources of the Pure Land doctrine: All the Buddhas save beings in four ways: 1. By oral teachings such as are recorded in the twelve divisions of Buddhist literature; 2. By their physical features of supernatural beauty; 3. By their wonderful powers and virtues and transformations; and 4. By their names, which, when uttered by beings, will remove obstacles and assure their rebirth in the presence of the Buddha.

To this Daochuo adds:

> To my mind the present age belongs to the fourth five-hundred-years after the Buddha, and what we have to do now is to repent our sins, to cultivate virtues, and to utter the Buddha's name. Is it not said that even once thinking of Amitābha Buddha and uttering his name cleanses us from all our sins committed while transmigrating for eighty billion kalpas? If even one thought achieves this, how much more if one constantly thinks of the Buddha and repents one's [sinful deeds]!

All the Nembutsu followers who came after him have eagerly accepted his teaching, and *nembutsu (nianfo),* "thinking of the Buddha," has become identified with *shōmyō (chengming),* "uttering the name." In fact, uttering the name contains more and functions more effectively than thinking of the various excellent spiritual virtues and physical qualities with which the Buddha is endowed. The name represents all that can be predicated of the Buddha. The thinking of him means holding up his image in mind, and all kinds of hallucinations are apt to appear before the eye. In the case of the name, the mental operations tend more toward intellection and a different psychology obtains here.

Here we can distinguish two ways in which the Buddha-name can be invoked; that is, when the name is announced, there are two attitudes on the part of the devotee toward the object of his adoration. In one case, the invocation takes place with the idea that "nomen est numen" ["name is spirit" (JCD)], or as a sort of magical formula. The name itself is regarded as having some mysterious power to work wonders. For instance, we read in the *Saddharma-puṇḍarīka,* Chapter XXIV, where the worship of Avalokiteśvara is upheld: "[Goblins and giants] would, by virtue of the name of Bodhisattva-Mahāsattva Avalokiteśvara being pronounced, lose the faculty of sight in their designs." Or, "Be not afraid, invoke all of you with one voice the Bodhisattva-Mahāsattva Avalokiteśvara, the giver of safety; then you shall be delivered from this danger by which you are threatened at the hands of robbers and enemies." In these cases the name of Avalokiteśvara has undoubtedly a magical power not only over one's enemies, but also over impure passions, hatred, infatuation, etc. It further enables the devotee to get whatever happiness he desires. The gathas in this chapter describe all the virtues issuing from him, and what the devotee has to do is just to think of him, that is, to utter his name. It was quite natural in the light here shed by the name of Avalokiteśvara that scholars of Shin Buddhism had once a heated discussion regarding the wonderful saving power of Amitābha, asking whether it comes from his name or from his vows.

The other attitude which may be assumed by the devotee toward the invocation, or Nembutsu, is especially represented by Tianru Weize,[14] a Zen master of the Yuan dynasty of the fourteenth century. He states in his *Some Questions Regarding the Pure Land Answered:*

> The Nembutsu consists in intensely thinking of the thirty-two marks of excellence possessed by the Buddha, by holding them in mind in a state of concentration, when one will see the Buddha all the time whether his eyes are closed or open. This seeing the Buddha while still in this life may also take place when the Buddha is invoked by name, which is held fast in the mind. This way of coming into the presence of the Buddha by invoking him by name is better than the Nembutsu. When you practice this invocation, the mind must be kept under full control so that it will not wander about; let your thought dwell without interruption on the name of the Buddha, audibly repeat *Emituo Fo*[15] (or nembutsu). Each sound must be distinctly presented to the mind. Do not mind how many times the name is repeated, for the main thing is to have thought and will, mind and lips, all in perfect union.

In the first case the name itself is regarded as having a wonderful power, especially over human affairs; it is a magic formula. When Amitābha wished to have his name resound all over the universe, did he want it to be a sort of talisman, or did he want it to be a moral force, that is, symbolic of something that is desirable in human life, so that whenever his name was heard his virtues and merits would be remembered, and would serve to incite the hearers to follow his example? Most likely the latter was in his mind. When the name is uttered, all that it stands for is awakened in the mind of the utterer; not only that, but finally his own mind will thereby open up its deepest resources and reveal its inmost truth which is no other than the reality of the name, that is, Amitābha himself.

In the second case, the name is pronounced not necessarily as indicative of things that are therein suggested, but in order to work out a certain psychological process thus set up. The name of the Buddha may now even be mechanically repeated without reference to the bearer of the name himself as an objective reality. This is what has actually taken place later in the history of the koan exercise. The following incident which took place in the mind of an old miser under the instruction of Hakuin, founder of the modern Japanese Rinzai School of Zen Buddhism, will supply us with a good illustration of what I mean by the psychological process induced by the recitation of the Buddha-name.

One of the numerous lay-disciples of Hakuin was worried over his old miserly father whose mind so bent on making money was not at all disposed toward Buddhism. He wanted Hakuin to suggest some method to turn his father's thought away from avarice. Hakuin suggested this proposal: Let the miserly old gentleman say the Nembutsu whenever he thinks of it, and have a penny paid for each recital. If he said the Nembutsu for one hundred times a day, he would have one hundred pennies for it. The old man thought that it was the easiest way in the world to earn his pocket money. He came each day to Hakuin to be paid for his Nembutsu as he was perfectly regular in his account, so much for so many repetitions. He was enchanted with his earnings. But after a while he ceased to come to Hakuin for his daily payment. Hakuin sent for the son to learn what was the matter with the father. It was found that the father was now so engrossed in saying the Nembutsu that he forgot to make a record of it. This was what Hakuin was all the time expecting of him. He told the devoted son to leave his father alone for some time and see what would become of him now. The advice was followed, and in a week the father himself with the beaming eyes came up to Hakuin, which told at once what a blissful spiritual experience he had gone through. There was no doubt that he had a kind of satori.

The mechanical repetition of the Nembutsu, that is, the rhythmic though monotonous utterance of the Buddha-name, *na-mu-a-mi-da-bu, na-mu-a-mi-da-bu* . . . over again and again, tens of thousands of times, creates a state of consciousness which tends to keep down all the ordinary functions of the mind. This state is very much akin perhaps to that of hypnotic trance, but fundamentally different from the latter in that what grows out of the Nembutsu consciousness is a most significant insight into the nature of Reality and has a most enduring and beneficial effect on the spiritual life of the devotee. In a hypnotic trance there is nothing of the sort, for it is a diseased state of mind bearing no fruit of a permanent value.

As regards the difference between the koan exercise and the Nembutsu, as was already repeatedly pointed out, in the one it consists in the absence of the intellectual element, and in the other in the presence of an inquiring spirit.

THE VALUE OF *SHŌMYŌ* ("UTTERING THE NAME") IN THE JŌDO SCHOOL

After the decease of the Buddha the earnest desire of his followers was to see him again. They could not persuade themselves to think that such a great personality as the Buddha had completely passed away from among them. The impression he had left in their minds was too deep to be wiped off so soon and so easily. This is generally the case with any great soul. We are loath to consider his physical death the ending of all that constituted him, all that belonged to him; we want to believe that he is still alive among us, not in his former worldly fashion but in some way, perhaps in the way we like to designate spiritual. Thinking so, we are sure to see him somewhere and sometime. This was true with the Christ as with the Buddha. But the Buddha had been living among a people who were trained in all kinds of concentration called Samadhi, and who were also perfect masters of practical psychology. The result was the production of such sutras as the *Meditation Sūtra (Kangyō)* or the *Pratyutpanna-samādhi Sūtra (Hanju zanmai)* in which directions are given in detail for having a personal interview with the Buddha or the Buddhas. First, there must be an intense thinking of the past master, an earnest longing to see him once more, and then the spiritual exercise in which the thinking and longing is to be visualized—this is the natural order of things.

This visualization seems to have taken two courses as time went on: the one was nominalistic[16] and the other idealistic. It is of significance that these two tendencies are traceable in one and the same sutra which is entitled *Saptaśatikā-prajñāpāramitā Sūtra,*[17] which was translated into Chinese by Mantuoluo Xian of Funanguo in A.D. 503, of the Liang dynasty. The sutra belongs to the Prajñāpāramitā class of Mahayana literature and is considered to be one of the earliest Mahayana texts. It contains the essence of Prajñāpāramitā philosophy, but what strikes us strange is that the two tendencies of thought, nominalistic and idealistic, apparently contradicting each other, are presented here side by side. I suspect the later incorporation of the passages referring to the nominalistic current of thought which is made so much of by the expositors of the Pure Land teaching. However this may be, the visualizing process of meditation is generally superseded in this sutra by the idealization of Buddhahood, which is typical of all the Prajna texts.

In the opening passage of this sutra, Mañjuśrī expresses his desire to interview the Buddha in his true aspect, thus:

> I desire to see the Buddha as he is in order to benefit all beings. I see the Buddha in the aspect of suchness *(tathatā),* of no-other-ness, of immovability, of doing-nothingness; I see the Buddha as free from birth and death, from form and no-form, from spatial and temporal relations, from duality and nonduality, from defilement and purity. Thus seen, he is in his true aspect and all beings are thereby benefited.
>
> By seeing the Buddha in this manner, [the Bodhisattva]is freed from both attachment and non-attachment, both accumulation and dissipation. . . .
>
> While thus seeing the Buddha for the sake of all beings, his [Bodhisattva's] mind is not attached to the form of all beings. While teaching all beings so as to make them turn toward Nirvana, he is not attached to the form of Nirvana. While arranging

varieties of things in order for the sake of all beings, the mind does not recognize them [as having individual realities].

In another version by Saṃghapāla which appeared a few years later than Mantuoluo's, we have this:

Buddha asked: "Do you really wish to see the Buddha?"

Mañjuśrī said: "The Dharmakaya of the Buddha is not really to be seen. That I come to see the Buddha here is for the sake of all things. As to the Dharmakaya of the Buddha, it is beyond thinkability, it has no form, no shape, it is neither coming nor departing, neither existent nor non-existent, neither visible nor invisible, it is such as it is, it is reality-limit. This light [that emanates from the Buddha giving a supernatural power to those who can perceive it] is Prajñāpāramitā, and Prajñāpāramitā is the Tathagata, and the Tathagata is all beings; and it is in this way that I practice Prajñāpāramitā."

In Mantuoluo's translation, this Prajñāpāramitā is defined to be "limitless, boundless, nameless, formless, beyond speculation, with nothing to depend on, with no anchorage, neither offensive nor blessed, neither darkening nor illuminating, neither divisible nor countable. . . . And when this is experienced, one is said to have attained enlightenment."

The thought expressed here is in perfect agreement with what generally characterizes the philosophy of the *Prajñāpāramitā Sūtras*. The Buddha is here described in highly abstract terms by a series of negations. While the idea Buddha thus does not appear to go beyond verbalism *(adhivacana)*, he is after all more than a mere name *(nāmadheya)*. Any amount of negations, it is true, fails to make one grasp the suchness of Buddhahood, but this does not of course mean that the Buddha, or what is the same thing, Prajñāpāramitā or supreme enlightenment, can be realized by merely repeating his name. If this is possible, the uttering of the Buddha-name must be considered in some other light, that is, not in the sense of abstract negation, but in the psychological process started by the repetition itself. It is interesting to see this shifting of thought from conceptualism to psychological realism. Let us see what Mañjuśrī has further to say about supreme enlightenment to be attained by means of the Buddha-name *(nāmadheya)*.

In the second half of the *Saptaśatikā-prajñāpāramitā* (Mantuoluo version) a Samadhi known as *yixing*[18] is mentioned, whereby the Yogin realizes supreme enlightenment and also comes into the presence of the Buddhas of the past, present, and future. The passage in the Mantuoluo runs as follows:

"Again, there is the Samadhi *yixing;* when this Samadhi is practiced by sons and daughters of good family, supreme enlightenment will speedily be realized by them."

Mañjuśrī asked: "Blessed One, what is this *yixing* Samadhi?"

The Blessed One said: "The Dharmadhātu is characterized with oneness, and as the Samadhi is conditioned by [this oneness of] the Dharmadhātu it is called the

> Samadhi of Oneness *(yixing)*. If sons and daughters of good family wish to enter upon this Samadhi of Oneness they must listen to the discourse on Prajñāpāramitā and practice it accordingly; for then they can enter upon the Samadhi of Oneness whereby they will realize the Dharmadhātu in its aspect of not-going-back, of not-being-destroyed, of unthinkability, of non-obstruction, of no-form.
>
> "If sons and daughters of good family wish to enter upon the Samadhi of Oneness, let them sit in a solitary place, abandon all thoughts that are disturbing, not become attached to forms and features, have the mind fixed on one Buddha, and devote themselves exclusively to reciting *(cheng)* his name *(ming*, or *nāmadheya)*, sitting in the proper style in the direction where the Buddha is, and facing him squarely. When their thoughts are continuously fixed on one Buddha, they will be able to see in these thoughts all the Buddhas of the past, present, and future."[19]

In Mantuoluo's text there is a strange mixture of Prajñāpāramitā philosophy proper with the visualization of the Buddha by means of his name which is recited with singleness of thought. Xuanzang's text refers to reflecting on the personality or personal features of the Buddha in connection with holding his name, which to a certain extent contradicts the idea of the first text. For the first one emphasizes the uttering of the name with no allusion whatever to visualizing the personal marks of Buddhahood, and yet it promises the Yogins their seeing not only one Buddha whose name they recite but all the Buddhas of the past, present, and future. And this is indeed the point upon which the Pure Land followers lay great emphasis in their teaching, that is, the sutra's preference given to verbal or nominalistic recitation rather than reflection or visualization.

In the *Pratyutpanna-samādhi Sūtra*[20] also, the visualizing meditation singularly blends with the nominalistic trends of thought. The subject of discourse here as given to the Bodhisattva Bhadrapāla is how to realize a Samadhi known as Pratyutpanna in which all the Buddhas of the ten quarters come and stand before the Yogin ready to answer all the questions he may ask them. The Yogin's qualifications are: 1. He must have great faith in the Buddha; 2. He must exert himself to the farthest extent of his spiritual energy; 3. He must be provided with a thorough understanding of the Dharma; and 4. He must always be associated with good friends and teachers. When these conditions are fulfilled, the Samadhi is matured, and then, first, because of the sustaining power of the Buddha which is added to the Yogin, secondly, because of the virtue of the Samadhi itself, and, thirdly, because of the virtue inherent in the accumulated stock of merit, all the Buddhas appear before the Yogin in such a manner as images are reflected in a mirror.

In the beginning the Yogin hears of the name of the Buddha Amitābha and his Land of Purity. By means of this name, he visualizes all the excellent and extraordinary features belonging to the Buddha such as his thirty-two major marks of manhood and eighty minor ones. The Yogin will also visualize all the resplendent glories of the Buddha while reflecting *(nian)* on his name with singleness of thought. When this exercise attains its fullness, the Yogin's mind is purgated of all its impurities. As it grows pure, the Buddha is reflected in it, and the mind and the Buddha are finally identified, as if the mind is looking at itself or the Buddha at himself, and yet the Yogin is not conscious of this fact of self-identification. To be thus unconscious is Nirvana. When there is the slightest stirring of a thought, the identification scale is tipped, and there starts a world of infatuations.

Strictly speaking, it is doubtful whether the sutra makes so much of the name and its recitation as is maintained by the followers of the Pure Land. As far as we can see, the visualization plays as much importance as thinking of the name. It is true that without a name our minds are unable to take hold of anything; even when there is really something objectively in existence, so long as it remains unnamed, it has no reality for us. When a thing gets its name, its relations with other things are defined and its value fully appreciated. Amitābha is non-existent when we cannot invoke him by a name; naming is creating, so to speak. But, on the other hand, mere naming does not prove to be so efficient, is not so effect-producing, as when there is back of it a corresponding reality. Mere uttering the name "water" does not quench the thirst; when it is visualized and there is a mental picture of a spring it produces a more physiologically realistic effect; but it is only when there is real fresh water before us which is quaffed that the thirst actually ceases. By means of sheer will and imagination, the mental picture can attain the highest degree of intensification, but there is naturally a limit to human powers. When this limit is reached, a leap into the abyss is possible only by the sustaining power which is now added to the Yogin by the Buddhas of the ten quarters. Thus, the name, reflection or visualization, and actualization are the natural order of things playing the most important role in the system of the Pure Land teaching.

It was owing to Shandao's[21] pietistic synthesis that the visualizing meditation, the nominalistic attitude, and the rebirth in the Pure Land were made to form a system, which was to be put into active service by means of the Nembutsu, that is, by constantly and single-mindedly pronouncing the name of Amitābha Buddha. After him, visualization gradually ceased to be upheld and nominalism came to reign over the entire school of the Pure Land. In China the koan exercise had about this time probably been gaining influence along with the prevalence of nominalism, but in Japan the establishment of the Pure Land school as an independent sect greatly helped the growth of the Nembutsu, that is, the vocal Nembutsu.

The transition of emphasis from idealism to nominalism, from the single-minded thinking to the vocal recitation, may be traced in the following passage from the *Anleji* of Daochuo, who answers the question how the Nembutsu is to be practiced:

> It is like a man traveling through the wilderness who happens to be attacked by a highwayman. The latter savagely threatens the traveler at the point of the sword and if his order is not obeyed, is ready to murder him. The traveler fleeing away from the

> impending peril observes a stream before him. Before reaching it, he reflects: "When I come to the river, should I cross it with my dress on or not? As to undressing myself there may not be time enough for it. But even when I jump into it with all my things on, my head and neck may not be safe enough from the attack." At this critical moment he has indeed no other thought than devising the way to get to the other side of the river. His mind is exclusively devoted to it. It is the same with the devotee of the Nembutsu. When he thinks of the Buddha Amitābha, his mind should be exclusively occupied with the thought, so that it has no room left for anything else. Whether he thinks *(nian)* of the Dharmakaya of the Buddha, or of his supernatural powers, or of his Prajna, or of the light issuing from his hair-tuft, or of his physical features, or of his Original Vow, let the devotee uninterruptedly pronounce *(cheng)* the name of the Buddha with singleness of thought so that no room is left in his mind for anything else, and he is sure to be reborn in the presence of the Buddha.

At such a critical moment as described here it is doubted whether the devotee has enough room left in his mind to do any sort of reflection. All that he can do will be pronouncing the name of the Buddha, for he cannot have any psychological time which is to be devoted to thinking of the Buddha's virtues or powers or features. In this case his Nembutsu (*nianfo,* literally, "thinking of the Buddha") cannot be more than a *shōmyō* (*chengming,* literally, "pronouncing or uttering the name"). For in the pronouncing of the name of the Buddha, that is, in reciting the Nembutsu, his whole being is absorbed; this is all he can do consciously, there can be no other thoughts in his field of consciousness.

Shandao[22] distinguishes, in his commentary on the *Sutra of Meditations,* two kinds of devotional practice for the Nembutsu devotee, "proper" and "mixed." The "proper practice" consists in thinking *(nian)* of the name of the Buddha Amitābha with singleness of thought. But here too "thinking of the name" has no meaning except when the name is deliberately pronounced. This kind of thinking is effective only when the vocal nerves and muscles are set in motion in accompaniment with the mental representation. In fact, it is doubtful whether any thinking high or low can be carried on without its muscular accompaniment, however slight and imperceptible it may be.

Adding to this psychological fact, the Pure Land philosophers propose the theory that the name *(nāmadheya)* is the repository of all the virtues belonging to the Buddha, that is to say, of all the inner attainments and virtues belonging to one Amitābha Buddha such as the fourfold knowledge, the triple body, the tenfold power, the fourfold fearlessness, etc. Together with all his external functions and virtues including his excellent features, his illuminating rays of light, his discourses on the Dharma, his deeds of salvation, etc.—they are all included in the name of the Buddha Amitābha.[23] Thus, as we see further on, psychology and philosophy have combined to lay entire stress of the Nembutsu teaching on the pronouncement of the name.

In the *Ōjōyōshū*[24] (Fas. II, Part 1), compiled by Genshin (942–1017), who was one of the forerunners of the Jōdo (Pure Land) school of Buddhism in Japan, the author raises the question: "Is Nembutsu-samadhi to be gained by mere meditation or by vocal recitation?" The answer is given by a quotation from Chisha Daishi's *Makashikan* (C. Zhizhe Dashi's *Mohezhiguan*)[25] Fas. II, Part 1: "Sometimes recitation and meditation go on hand in hand, sometimes meditation precedes and recitation follows, sometimes recitation comes first and then meditation. When recitation and meditation go on thus in constant succession and without interruption each thought as well as each sound is fixed on Amitābha."[26] In this, the vocal Nembutsu is not yet brought out sufficiently prominently.

It was Hōnen (1133–1212) who, following the teaching of Shandao, emphasized the Nembutsu, that is, the recitation of the Buddha's name. This was regarded as the most important practice in the Pure Land school when the devotees wished to be reborn in the Land of Amida. Praising his virtues, making offerings, bowing before him, reading the sutras, and meditating on him—these were by no means to be slighted, but the chief act of piety consisted in the recitation *(chengming)*. By constantly uttering his name with devotion, in whatever posture one may be in, whether sitting or standing, lying down or walking, he will surely, after some time has elapsed, be taken by Amida into his abode of happiness. For this, according to the masters of the Jōdo school, is in full accordance with the teachings of the sutras, that is to say, with the original vows of the Buddha.[27]

To confirm this view, Hōnen again quotes Shandao, according to whom the Nembutsu is easier to practice than any other deeds of devotion. The question as to why meditation is set aside in preference to single-minded recitation is answered thus:

> It is because sentient beings are all very heavily handicapped with hindrances, and the world in which they are living is full of subtle temptations; it is because their mind is too disconcerted, and their intelligence too clumsy, and their spirit too wandering. Meditation, therefore, is not theirs. Taking pity on them, the Buddha advises them to concentrate on reciting his name, for when this is practiced without interruption the devotee is sure of his rebirth in the Land of Amida.

Hōnen then proceeds to state that thinking or meditating is reciting—the two being the same—that to think of Amida is to recite his name and vice versa. *Nembutsu,* "thinking of the Buddha," has thus come to be completely identified with *shōmyō,* "reciting or pronouncing the name"; meditation has turned into recitation. What may be termed the Buddhist philosophy of nominalism has come to occupy the minds of the Pure Land devotees, for they now realize the presence in the name of something that goes altogether beyond conception. My object is now to study the psychological signification of this vocal Nembutsu and to see in what relationship it stands to the koan exercise as practiced by followers of Zen.

THE PSYCHOLOGY OF THE *SHŌMYŌ* EXERCISE AND WHERE IT BECOMES RELATED TO THE KOAN EXERCISE

With the vocalization of the Nembutsu on the one hand, Hōnen and his predecessors have not forgotten on the other hand to emphasize the importance and necessity of a believing heart. Meditating on the Buddha as one in possession of all the virtuous qualities and also of the thirty-two marks of a great being requires no doubt a great deal of concentration and may be beyond the psychic powers of an ordinary man. Compared to that, the recitation of the name is indeed much easier. A name is something like an algebraic symbol; as *a* or *b* or *c* may stand for any kind of number, the name Amida may be regarded as representing everything that is contained in the conception of the Buddha, not only of one Amida, but of all the Buddhas whose number is beyond calculation. When a man pronounces this name he digs down deeply into the content of his religious consciousness. Mere utterance, however, will be of no consequence being devoid of sense; the uttering must be the outcome of deep thinking, earnest seeking, and great faith; if it is not the outcome of such intense yearnings, it must be strengthened continuously by them. Lips and heart must be in full accord in its practice.

In this kind of Nembutsu the mind focuses itself on the name and not on the outward form of the Buddha. His thirty-two physical marks of greatness are not pictured out in the mind of the devotee. The name possesses the entire field of consciousness. So we read in the *Smaller Sukhāvatī-vyūha:*[28] *amitāyuṣas tathāgatasya nāmadheyam śroṣyati śrutvā ca manasikariṣyati. . . .* ("Let him hear the name of the Tathagata Amitāyus, and, having heard it, keep it in mind. . . .") The Chinese translator has *zhichi* for *manasikṛ,* meaning "to hold an object of thought fixedly in mind." The name itself is held at the center of attention, not mere lip repetition but an utterance of the heart. There is no doubt that this kind of Nembutsu is a great help to concentration. The calling-up of the form of the Buddha is pregnant with many psychological dangers or evils, and the devotee may become an incurable victim of hallucinations. The vocalization is a great step forward to the attainment of a true religious Samadhi.

The object of the Nembutsu, we see clearly, has gone through modifications. In the beginning it was remembering the Buddha, longing to see him again as he had lived among his followers—a desire entirely human and natural. Later, it came to mean the coming into the presence of an idealized Buddha, eternally living in the Land of Purity and Happiness. And, finally, by holding the name firmly in mind the explicit object became a desire to turn the gracious attention of the Buddha toward the sinful devotee. This modification is thus interpreted by masters of the Pure Land school to be in full accord with the teaching of the Buddha as expounded in the various sutras belonging to that school.

But the question that arises here is: Is there no psychological background which elicits this gradual modification? Has the vocal Nembutsu no implicit object? Has it no other object than to direct the devotee to the Pure Land of Amida? The masters might not have been conscious of the fact, but was there not a psychological experience on their part which made them teach the simple vocal Nembutsu instead of other religious deeds, such as sutra-reading, meditating on the Buddha, making bows to him, or singing hymns of praise?

If moral or spiritual enhancement is to be achieved, the mere uttering of the name, even though it be the name of the Holiest One, does not seem to elevate the mind so much as meditating on him and reading his sermons. The Pure Land teachers honestly believed in the sutras when the vocal Nembutsu was recommended. But as far as the sutras are concerned they teach many other things also, and if the teachers so desired, they could therein develop some other teachings than the Nembutsu. For a sutra or in fact any religious literature generally lends itself, according to the reader's personal experience, to varieties of interpretation. The development of the vocal Nembutsu, therefore, must be said to have its psychological ground as well as its philosophical and religious ones. It was, of course, the philosophical side that chiefly and therefore consciously governed the religious consciousness of the teachers.

It would be against reason to assert that the psychology of the vocal Nembutsu is all that constitutes the foundation of the Pure Land teachings. For such conceptions as sin, the reality of suffering, and the all-embracing love of Amida are also essential factors, but my present study is solely to analyze the psychological aspect of it.

To give a name is to discriminate; to discriminate is to recognize the reality of an individual object, and to make it accessible to the human understanding as well as to the human heart. Therefore, when the name is pronounced, we feel that the object itself is with us, and it was a most natural process of development that thinking of the Buddha gradually turned into pronouncing his name. But what we wish to examine now is that the name of the Buddha continued to retain its original Sanskrit form, or rather its transliteration, throughout its long history in China and Japan. Why was not the Buddha addressed by the Chinese or Japanese equivalent instead of by the original or modified Sanskrit? *Namu-amida-butsu* and *Namo-emituo-fo* are the Japanese and the Chinese way of reading *namo 'mitābhāya buddhāya. Namo* or *namas* means "adoration" or "salutation," and *amitābhāya buddhāya* means "to the Buddha of Infinite Light," which in Chinese is *guiyi wuliang guang fo.*[29] Why did they not say "Adoration to the Buddha of Infinite Light," instead of *Namu-amida-butsu* or *Namo-emituo-fo?* These transliterations give no sense ordinarily to the Japanese or Chinese mind, as they are modified Sanskrit sounds and apparently carry no meaning. It is to them a sort of Dharani or Mantram which is to be pronounced as it stands with no translation; for when translated a Dharani conveys no intelligent thought, being no more than a stream of jargon. What was the reason of this—intelligence giving way to non-intelligence, sense to nonsense, clearness to obscurity, discrimination to non-discrimination? Why all the time, *Namu-amida-butsu, Namu-amida-butsu?*

In my view, the reason is to be sought not in the magical effect of the name itself, but in the psychological effect of its repetition. Wherever there is an intelligent meaning, it suggests an endless train of ideas and feelings attached thereto; the mind then either becomes engaged in working a logical loom, or becomes inextricably involved in the meshes of imagination and association. When meaningless sounds are repeated, the mind stops there, not having chances to wander about. Images and hallucinations are less apt to invade it. To use Buddhist terminology, the external dust of discrimination covers the original bright surface of the inner mirror of enlightenment. To avoid this tragedy, it is necessary that sounds intended for the vocal Nembutsu should be devoid of intelligible meaning. When the reflective and the meditative Nembutsu developed into the vocal Nembutsu, there must have been some such psychological experience on the part of the masters who wanted to concentrate their minds on Buddhahood itself and not on the personality of the Buddha. The thought of the personality of the Buddha, as they saw it, demands a higher process of mentality and yet does not always yield genuine results.

The Jōdo masters are always quite emphatic on the triple attitude of mind which should always accompany the vocal Nembutsu: 1. sincerity of heart, 2. inwardness of faith, and 3. the desire for the Land of Amida. Without these subjective factors, indeed, no amount of Nembutsu will be of use to the devotee in gaining the object of his desire. But the masters in their apparently too earnest desire to propagate the so-called easy method of salvation and to bring out in the strongest possible light the necessity of the vocal Nembutsu, seem sometimes to set aside the importance of these subjective conditions. As a result the students of the Pure Land schools are often attracted too irresistibly to the vocal Nembutsu at the expense of the right subjective conditions. This is not right, but one may wonder whether there is not something in the attitude of the masters which will justify this erroneous assumption. Are they not emphasizing the importance of the subjective factors in order to make the vocal Nembutsu effective to its utmost extent? If a man had all these inner requirements fulfilled, it does not seem, as far as ordinary logic goes, to matter very much whether he was a devotee of sutra-reading, or of bowings, or of the vocal Nembutsu. But the masters, especially of the Jōdo school of Genkū[30] and Hōnen, are unmistakably insistent on uttering the name of the Buddha in the form of *Namu-amida-butsu* as the most essential practice, relegating all other devotional exercises to a secondary category. According to them, therefore, the *Namu-amida-butsu* is what finally guarantees one's rebirth in the Land of Bliss. How can this be so unless the vocal Nembutsu works in some mysterious manner in the consciousness of the devotee? When a certain state of consciousness is induced by repeatedly pronouncing the Buddha-name, it is likely that the Buddha himself comes to take possession of the mind, whereby the devotee is assured of his future destiny. Was this psychology what was aimed at by Shandao, Hōnen, and other teachers of the Jōdo school?

When such great Jōdo teachers as Shandao, Daochuo, and Huaigan give two ways of rebirth in the Pure Land, (1) Saying the Nembutsu and (2) Practicing other meritorious deeds, and prefer the first to the second as being more in accord with the teachings of the sutras, and further when they identify "thinking of" or "meditating on" (*nian* in Chinese, *anusmṛti* in Sanskrit) with "voicing" or "uttering" *(sheng)*, saying that to think of Buddha is to utter his name, do they find this reason for identification in logic or in psychology? Logically, to think intensely of an object does not necessarily mean uttering its name; the thinking is independent of the uttering of its name; the thinking is independent of the uttering especially when the mind meditatively dwells on an object of devotion and reverence. But as a matter of psychological fact, the thinking of abstract ideas is greatly helped by looking at some graphical representations, letters, or diagrams, and also by pronouncing names mentally or audibly. Grounded on this psychological fact, they must have come to the conclusion that thinking of the Buddha is uttering his name, that the thinking and the uttering are identical. And again, according to Huaigan's commentary[31] on the noted passage in the *Daji yuezang jing*:[32] "By great thinking *(nian)* one sees great Buddha, and by small thinking, small Buddha. Great thinking means calling out the Buddha[-name] at a high pitch; small thinking at a low pitch."[33] While I am not quite sure as to what is exactly meant by "seeing great Buddha and small Buddha," it is readily seen that the teachers are here making much of saying the Nembutsu loudly. The more muscular effort we make in uttering the name of the Buddha, the higher degree of concentration will be attained, and thus the holding in mind of *Namu-amida-butsu* will be the more effective.

Whatever doctrinal interpretations were given to the fact, the teachers must have had some psychological experience before they confirmed the identification of thinking *(nian)* and uttering *(cheng)*. Do we not see here something of Zen psychology in which "'*Wu*,' '*Wu*,' all day today, and '*Wu*,' '*Wu*,' over again all day tomorrow,"[34] is practiced? Hence their exhortation to say the Nembutsu all day, or every day regularly, or so many times a day—ten thousand times, fifty thousand, and even up to a hundred thousand times a day. There is a Jōdo temple in Kyoto, the name of which is "One Million Times," referring to the number of the vocal Nembutsu to be repeated. The mental fact that vocalization helps concentration is the basis of the doctrine of the vocal Nembutsu *(shōmyō*, or *shengming)*.

When the Buddha-name is so frequently repeated as ten or twenty thousand times at a stretch, the practice grows mechanical with no conscious effort, therefore with no conscious realization of the three factors of devotion. Is this mechanization to be considered the effective means of the rebirth? Is there no need of the devotee's making a determined effort to grow up in his belief and devotion? Does this constant muttering or uttering of meaningless sounds produce in the consciousness of the devotee a definite sense of assurance whereby he cherishes no doubt as to his rebirth in the Pure Land, or as to his salvation through the grace of Amida? When the Nembutsu is turned into pronouncing a Dharani without any conscious reference to its meaning literary and devotional, its psychological effect will be to create a state of unconsciousness in which ideas and feelings superficially floating are wiped off. Morally speaking, this is a condition of innocence as there is no discrimination of good and bad, and in this way the Jōdo teachers state that the Nembutsu wipes off all the sins accumulated during one's lives in countless past ages.

The perpetual reiteration of *Namu-amida-butsu*[35] has its parallel in Sufism whose followers repeat the name "Allah," as has been observed by R. A. Nicholson in his *Studies in Islam Mysticism,* "as a method practiced by Moslem mystics for bringing about *fana,* i.e., the passing away from self, or in Pascal's phrase, 'Oubli du monde et de tout hormis Dieu' ['Forget the world and everything except God' (JCD)]."[36]

We cannot think that the mere repetition of *Namu-amida-butsu* assures the devotee of his rebirth in the Pure Land in spite of all the guarantee that is given in the sutras and by the teachers of that school, unless the reiteration produces a certain mental effect wherein he attains the realization by himself. And is not this realization what is known as the Samadhi of Nembutsu or the Samadhi of Oneness *(ekavyūha)?*

In the *Anrakushū* (*Anleji,* Part II) by Daochuo, the passages bearing on this Samadhi are quoted from various sutras. The author's intention here is to prove the Samadhi to be the efficient means of bringing the devotee into the presence of all the Buddhas of the past, present, and future. But, from the point of view of salvation (or enlightenment), what is the use of seeing the Buddhas unless their assurance of salvation evokes the sense of its truth in the consciousness of the devotee? The seeing of the Buddha objectively must be in correspondence with the inner realization, and as far as psychology is concerned, inner realization is the more important topic of consideration.

There is a sutra entitled *Bosatsu nenbutsu zanmai (samādhi) kyō,*[37] first translated by Dharmagupta of Sui, in which all the necessary instructions concerning the practice of the Nembutsu Samadhi are given in detail. According to this work, the chief merit accruing from the Samadhi seems to be the realization of supreme enlightenment. Evidently the coming into the presence of all the Buddhas is not to see them in their company as spiritually enlightened beings, to be in communion with them in a world transcending all forms of corporeality. The devotee is persuaded to practice the Nembutsu in order to see the Buddhas, but when he actually enters into a Samadhi, he sees them in a way quite different from what he might have expected in the beginning.[38]

Hōnen quotes in his *Senchakushū,* Part II, a passage from *Lives of the Pious Followers of the Pure Land School,*[39] in which reference is made to Shandao's attainment of the Samadhi. According to this account, the Samadhi among other things seems to give one a prophetic insight into the spiritual condition of others; for the account reveals that Shandao could tell about the past lives of his own teacher, Daochuo, and also about the rebirth of the latter in the Land of Amida. But the fact that the Samadhi could not go any farther than the attainment of these miraculous powers, we may say that it has not much to do with one's spiritual enhancement and assurance of emancipation. There must be something more in the Samadhi acquired by means of the Nembutsu. The teachers of the Pure Land school have been too eager to advance their religious views regarding rebirth after death, ignoring the psychological effect which is sure to follow the constant reiteration of *Namu-amida-butsu.* They have been too busy reminding us of this degenerate age in which the pure form of Buddhism is too difficult to maintain itself, and, therefore, that the uttering of the Buddha-name is the best, easiest, and surest for beings of this degenerate age to come into the presence of the Buddhas and to be embraced in the arms of their infinite love. In this respect, Shinran pushed this idea to its utmost logical end; for he states in connection with one's rebirth in the Pure Land by uttering the name of the Buddha only ten times that "this does not mean to specifically and quietly meditate on the Buddha, or to think of him intensely, but merely to pronounce the name." With all their expostulations about the Nembutsu, about saying it once or up to ten times, which will surely be heard by the Buddha, I cannot imagine that the teachers were utterly unconscious of the psychology of the Nembutsu as has already been referred to.

WHAT IS THE OBJECT OF THE NEMBUTSU EXERCISE?

One may ask in this connection: whatever the content of the Samadhi, which is the real object of the Nembutsu, rebirth in the Pure Land or the Samadhi itself? Or is the Samadhi a kind of foretaste of the rebirth? No teachers of the Jōdo as far as I can learn make this point thoroughly clear for us. But if we can so view the matter, the Samadhi may be regarded as the subjective and psychological aspect of the Nembutsu exercise, and the rebirth as the objective and ontological aspect. In this case, the Samadhi and the rebirth are the same thing only described in two ways, but as the Samadhi is attainable in this life while rebirth is an affair taking place after death, the Samadhi must be said to be identical with the rebirth in a most specific sense, that is, the rebirth is not to be judged as an objective and temporal event, but as a form of subjective assurance of a thing that is surely to take place. If so, the rebirth means a spiritual regeneration and as such it can be regarded as identical with the Samadhi.

This view of the Samadhi is supported in the *Anjin ketsujō shō* by an unknown author, which is, however, one of the most significant books on the teaching of the

Jōdo school. In this the author states that the faith is to be firmly established by the realization of the Samadhi—the faith in the original vow of Amida whereby the devotee is assured of his future destiny. For the Samadhi obtains when the mind of the devotee is so perfectly identified with the mind of Amida that the consciousness of the dualism is altogether effaced from it. This conclusion, not only in logic but from the factual point of view, is inevitable, seeing that the entire structure of Buddhist philosophy is based on an idealistic monism, and no exception is to be made about the realistic Jōdo. Read this from the *Meditation Sutra:*

> The Buddha said to Ānanda and Vaidehī: "After you have seen these, you should think of the Buddha. You may ask, How? Every Buddha-Tathagata has his body in the spiritual world *(dharmadhātu)* and enters into the mind of every sentient being. Therefore, when you think of the Buddha, your mind itself becomes endowed with the thirty-two marks of greatness and also with the eighty secondary marks of excellence. This mind is transformed into Buddhahood, this mind is no other than the Buddha himself. The ocean of true all-knowledge possessed by the Buddhas grows out of your own mind and thought. For this reason, you should apply yourselves with singleness of thought to meditation on the Buddha-Tathagata, who is an Arhat and a Fully-enlightened One."

In the *Pratyutpanna-samādhi Sūtra,*[40] which is thought by the Jōdo teachers to be one of the sources of their teachings, we have this:

> "And again, Bhadrapāla, when a young man of fine mien wishes to see his own features, ugly or handsome, he takes up a vessel of refined oil or of clean water, or he brings out a crystal or a mirror. When either one of these four objects reflects his image in it, he definitely knows how he looks, ugly or handsome. Bhadrapāla, do you think that what the young man sees in these four objects has been already in existence there?"
>
> Answered Bhadrapāla, "O no, Blessed One."
>
> "Is it to be regarded altogether as a non-entity?"
>
> "O no, Blessed One."
>
> "Is it to be regarded as being within them?"
>
> "O no, Blessed One."
>
> "Is it to be regarded as outside them?"
>
> "O no, Blessed One. As the oil and water and crystal and mirror are clear, transparent, and free from muddiness and dust, the image is reflected in them when a person stands before them. The image does not come out of the object, nor does it get into them from the outside, nor is it there by itself, nor is it artificially constructed. The image comes from nowhere, vanishes away to nowhere; it is not subject to birth and death; it has no fixed abode."
>
> When Bhadrapāla finished thus answering, the Buddha said:
>
> "Bhadrapāla, so it is, indeed, as you say. When the objects are pure and clean, the image is reflected in them without much trouble. So is it with the Bodhisattva. When he meditates on the Buddhas with singleness of thought, he sees them; having

appeared to him, they stay with him; staying with him, they explain things to him that he wishes to understand. Being thus enlightened by them he is delighted; he now reflects: Whence do these Buddhas come? and whither does this body of mine vanish? When he thus reflects he sees that all the Tathagatas come from nowhere and go out nowhere. So it is with my own body; it has no definite path by which it comes, and how can there be any returning to anywhere?"

He reflects again: "This triple world exists only because of the mind. According to one's own thought, one sees oneself in one's own mind. My now seeing the Buddha is after my own mind; my mind becomes the Buddha; my mind itself is the Buddha; my mind itself is the Tathagata. My mind is my body, my mind sees the Buddha; the mind does not know itself, the mind does not see itself. When thoughts are stirred, there is Nirvana. All things have no reality in themselves, they take their rise owing to thought and laws of origination. When that which is thought vanishes, the thinking one himself vanishes. Bhadrapāla, you should know that all the Bodhisattvas by means of this Samadhi attained great enlightenment."

Viewing the Samadhi of Nembutsu from this absolute idealistic point of view—the Samadhi that is realized by constant reiteration of *Namu-amida-butsu*—we state that the Samadhi, and the establishment of faith in the Buddha, and the assurance of rebirth in his Land of Purity describe one and the same psychological fact which constitutes the foundation of the Jōdo (Pure Land) doctrine. Hōnen says in his commentary on the *Meditation Sutra* that the devotee should be like a man who has lost his senses, or like a deaf and dumb person, or like an idiot, when he devotes himself exclusively to the practice of the Nembutsu, pronouncing the name of the Buddha day and night, whether sitting or standing, lying down or walking, and for any length of time, one day, two days, a week, a month, a year, or even two or three years. When the practice is carried on in such wise, the devotee will surely some day attain the Samadhi and have his Dharma-eye opened, and he will view a world that is altogether beyond thought and imagination. This is "a mysterious realm where all thoughts cease and all imaginings are swept away, being in full correspondence with a state of Samadhi."

In this Samadhi where the devotee is fully confirmed in the faith, according to the author of the *Anjin ketsujō shō,* "The body becomes *Namu-amida-butsu,* and the mind becomes *Namu-amida-butsu.*" If so, is this not a mystic state of consciousness corresponding to that which is realized by the koan exercise?

The explicit claim made by the Jōdo teachers, that the repetition of the Nembutsu is the easiest method of salvation for all beings, is of course based on the original vow of Amida, in which the Buddha assures his followers of their rebirth in his Land of Bliss, if they only pronounce his name as showing their good faith and willingness to be thus saved. To reinforce or strengthen their teaching, they describe, on the one hand, in glowing terms the beauties of the Pure Land, while, on the other hand, they are never tired of picturing the miseries and horrors of this world and the sinfulness and the helpless ignorance of the beings therein. Therefore, those who wish to be helped by this doctrine will have to be earnest devotees of *Namu-amida-butsu* and be pronouncing and reciting the phrase all the time. But when they are doing this, their ultimate object of being members of the Pure Land community may gradually give way to the immediate daily practice itself of the Nembutsu. And even when their deliberate attention is focused upon it, their psychology of the unconscious may begin to function by itself independently of the ultimate aim, which is supposed to take place at the end of this life; for the nearer happenings always claim the more intimate and intense concentration of mind. Let this concentration be brought up to the highest pitch and there will be the intuition of such mystical truths as these: Rebirth is no-birth; to think of Buddha is not to have any thought; every moment is the last; this mind is no other than the Tathagata himself; while the body belongs to this world, the mind is enjoying itself in the Pure Land; this body, as it is, is of the same order as Maitreya Bodhisattva; etc. Such statements seem to be not so typically Jōdo, in fact they go much against its generally realistic tendency, but we cannot altogether ignore this mysticism entering into the structural foundations of practical Jōdo, and there is no doubt that this comes from the psychology of the Nembutsu.

The Shin Branch of the Pure Land sect emphasizes faith as the only condition of rebirth in the land of Amida. Absolute trust is placed in the wisdom of the Buddha which goes altogether beyond human conception. Put, therefore, your faith in this wonder-working wisdom of Amida and you will straightway be taken up by him; there is no need for your waiting for the last moment when a band of welcoming Buddhas comes down from above; nor need you entertain any anxious tears about your destiny after death, thinking whether or not you are after all bound for *Naraka* (hell). All that is required of you is to abandon all thoughts regarding yourself and to put your unconditioned trust in the Buddha who knows best how to look after your welfare.[41] You need not worry at all about the last hour when you have to bid farewell to this life on earth. If, while living, you had been instructed by a wise adviser and had awakened one thought of trust in the Buddha, that moment of awakening was for you the last moment on earth. When trusting the original vow of Amida *Namu-amida-butsu* is once pronounced, you are assured of rebirth in his Land; for this believing heart is the rebirth.[42]

But how can one really have this believing heart which raises the owner at once to the order of the fully-enlightened one, bringing him up to the company even of Maitreya?[43] Mere listening to the teachers will not do it. Nor will the mere saying the Nembutsu. How does one come to have this absolute faith—the faith which is evidently the same in substance as enlightenment? How can we be sure of our rebirth? How do we come to entertain no doubts as to our future destiny? A certain state of consciousness must be awakened within us whereby we can be confirmed in our faith. Reasoning, or reading the sutras, or listening to the discourses of the wise and enlightened will not induce this consciousness. As the history of religions tells us, there must be an intuitive insight into the truth, which is the abandoning of the self into the original vow of Amida. And is not this the moment when *Namu-amida-butsu* gushes out of one's inmost heart *(adhyāśaya)?* Is this not what the Shin teachers mean when they say, "Utter the Name once, and you are saved"?

MYSTICISM OF THE NEMBUTSU AND THE UTTERING OF THE NAME

When we thus interpret the Nembutsu, we are able to understand the discourse of Ippen:[44]

> The rebirth means the first awakening of thought, and this assumes an existence, i.e., one in whom a thought is awakened. The *Namu-amida-butsu* itself is the rebirth, and the rebirth is no-birth. When this realization takes place, I call it provisionally the first awakening of thought. When one is absorbed in the Buddha-name that is above time, there is the rebirth that knows no beginning, no end. Sometimes the distinction is made between the last moment of life and everyday life, but this is a teaching that is based on confused thought. In the *Namu-amida-butsu* itself there is no last moment, no everyday life; it is a reality abiding through all periods of time. As regards human life, it is a series of moments lasting only between an in-breath and an out-breath, and therefore the very moment of thought is the last moment of life. If so, every thought-moment is the last moment and every moment is a rebirth.

The meaning of this mystical utterance by Ippen will become more transparent when the following quotations are gone through.

> When one's mind (or consciousness) is all annulled by saying *Namu-amida-butsu,* this is the right thought for the last moment.
>
> There is the Buddha-name only, and beyond it there is neither the one who says it, nor the one to whom it is addressed. There is the Buddha-name only, and beyond it there is no rebirth. All things existent are virtues included within the body of the Buddha-name itself. If so, when you attain the perception of all things as unborn, where all traces of a conscious mind vanish, saying *Namu-amida-butsu,* a first thought then awakened is called the right thought of one's last moment; for this is no other than the thought of enlightenment, which is *Namu-amida-butsu.*
>
> Rather be possessed by the name than be possessing the name. All things are of one mind, but this mind is not manifested by itself. The eye cannot see itself, the wood cannot burn itself though it is by nature combustible. But hold a mirror before yourself and the eye can see itself—this is the virtue of the mirror. And the mirror is the one owned by every one of us and is known as the Great Mirror of Enlightenment; it is the name already realized by all the Buddhas. This being so, see your own original features in the Mirror of Enlightenment. Do we not read in the *Meditation Sūtra* that it is like seeing one's own face in the mirror? Again, wood will be burned when ignited by fire—the fire that burns is identical with the fire that is latent in the

> wood. It is thus through the concordance of causes inner and outer that all things are brought into actual existence. Though we are all endowed with the Buddha-nature, this of itself does not burn up the passions unless it be enkindled by the fire of transcendental wisdom which is the name *(nāmadheya)*. The Jōdo school teaches that to take hold of an object one has to get away from it. The injunction is to be called to mind in this connection.

Literally, *Namu-amida-butsu* is not the name *(nāmadheya)* itself; it contains more than that, because *Namu* (*namas* in Sanskrit) means "adoration" or "salutation"; but generally the whole phrase, *Namu-amida-butsu*, is regarded as the name, and its mysterious working is extolled. The masters of the Pure Land school exhausted their philosophical ingenuity on the subject, but strangely they keep quiet about the psychological aspect of the experience. Perhaps this silence comes from their conception of Amida, which is fundamentally ontological. But when it is asserted that the name alone exists and thus in it vanishes the dualistic contrast of the one who reiterates it and the one to whom it is addressed, this is the statement of a mystical experience and not of metaphysical reflection. The experience arising from the utterance of the name is of the same nature as that which ensues from the koan exercise. When the objective aspect of the experience is metaphysically interpreted, the name is objectified and Amida is absolute "other-power"; but, on the other hand, let the devotee be a follower of Zen, and his understanding of it will be thoroughly idealistic.

The author of the *Anjin ketsujō shō* may also, like Ippen, be considered an emphatic upholder of the name, for he says:

> As there is not a moment's separation between the devotee who says *Namu* and *Amida Butsu* himself, every thought cherished by him is *Namu-amida-butsu*. This being so, every breath of his has never even for a moment been separated from the virtues of the Buddha; his whole being, indeed, is the substance of *Namu-amida-butsu*. . . . When there is an understanding as to the meaning of the Nembutsu-Samadhi, both his body and his mind are *Namu-amida-butsu*. For that reason, when all beings of the past, present, and future raise one thought of faith [in the original vow of Amida], the very thought goes back to the one thought of Enlightenment [which was originally awakened in the Buddha]; and the minds of all sentient beings in the ten quarters, when they utter the name, also go back to the one thought of Enlightenment. No thought, no utterance ever issuing from the devotees remains with them [they all go back to the source whence comes Enlightenment]. As the original vow is an act in which the name and essence are synthesized, the name contains in itself the whole essence of Enlightenment, and as it is thus the essence of Enlightenment, it is rebirth on the part of all beings in the ten quarters.

Whether the masters of the Jōdo school, including the Shin, are conscious of the fact or not, there is something distinctly psychological in their metaphysical conclusions, or in their theology if that term could be used in Buddhism. Psychology cannot be said to be everything in religion, though it constitutes the groundwork of it. Thus even in Shin, where faith is made the chief principle of its teachings, there are many statements of Shinran, its founder, which are unintelligible unless his mystical experience is taken into consideration. For instance, when he teaches the identity of the name and the original vow in their going beyond human understanding, he bases it on the Buddha's teaching itself. The explanation is simple enough, but how do we get confirmed in our belief? Especially when the masters of Shin all exhort us to abandon learning and reasoning, how can we accept everything that is poured into our heads rather mechanically, that is, on what authority? Some psychological state must come to us, even to the most unlogical minds, that leads us to say "yes" to all that is told us to believe. Why is the name to be pronounced in addition to believing in the vow? It may be that the pronouncing is the believing and vice versa, but this identification, too, must be an outcome of experience and not a logical inference.

> The vow and the name are not two separate things, for there is no name apart from the vow, nor is there any vow apart from the name. Even making this statement involves human understanding. When, believing in the vow as beyond the understanding and also in the name as beyond the understanding, you utter the name in oneness of thought, why should you exercise your own understanding?[45]

The believing alone seems to be sufficient to guarantee a man's rebirth in the Pure Land, or in Enlightenment, and why should this uttering the name be considered essential too? There is no uttering the name, it is declared, separate from the faith, and also there is no believing thought disjoined from the name; but why such importance given to the name? Why is *Namu-amida-butsu* so essential to the confirmation of faith? The name, whose meaning consists in having no meaning as it transcends the relativity of human knowledge, must be once demonstrated in experience before one realizes that it is really so. *Namu-amida-butsu,* from the Zen point of view, is a koan given to followers of the Pure Land school. One day the mystery of the name is realized as it is uttered, and this is the moment when the key is delivered into the hand of the devotee, to whom the entire treasure of religious consciousness is now safely entrusted.

> The original vow of Amida is to welcome anybody to his Land of Bliss who should utter his name in absolute confidence; being so, blessed are those who utter the name. A man may have the faith, but if he utters not the name, his faith will be of no avail. Another may utter the name single-mindedly, but if his faith is not deep enough his rebirth will not take place. He, however, who firmly believes in the rebirth as the outcome of the Nembutsu and utters the name will doubtless be reborn in the Land of Recompense.[46]

It can readily be understood that without faith rebirth is impossible, but why the uttering of the name? To comprehend this mystery, which constitutes the transcendental wisdom of all the Buddhas, the depths of our own being must be penetrated, and there is no doubt, according to the Jōdo, that it is the *Namu-amida-butsu* which fathoms these depths.

EXPERIENCE AND THEORIZATION

All religion is built upon the foundation of mystical experience, without which all its metaphysical or theological superstructure collapses. This is where religion differs from philosophy. All the philosophical systems may some day be found in ruins, but the religious life will forever go on experiencing its deep mysteries. The Jōdo and the Zen cannot separate themselves from these mysteries. The Jōdo bases its theory on the Nembutsu, and the Zen bases theirs on the koan exercise. As far as their theoretical edifices are concerned they seem very dissimilar to each other. The Jōdo wants to see its followers reborn in the Land of Bliss and there attain their enlightenment. To do this they are taught about their sinfulness, about their intellectual inabilities to grasp the higher truths of Buddhism, and also about their being too heavily laden by their past karma to shake themselves free of their shackles by their own limited efforts. Amida is now held up before them, whose original vow is to give them a helping hand for crossing the stream of birth and death. But this helping hand cannot be reached unless they utter the name of their savior with singleness of thought *(ekacitta)*. To awaken this state of single-mindedness, that is, "one thought of faith," as it is technically termed, is the great problem of the Jōdo teaching. The vow, the name, the "one thought of faith," the uttering of the name, the rebirth—these are the links making up the chain of the Pure Land doctrine. When any one of these links is held fast, the entire chain will be in your hand, and the masters of the Jōdo have set up the uttering of the name in the most prominent position. In this the Jōdo experience is the counterpart of the Zen experience. The vocal Nembutsu and the koan exercise are here standing on a common ground.

Psychologically considered, the aim of the vocal Nembutsu is to do away with the fundamental dualism which is a condition of our empirical consciousness. By achieving this the devotee rides over the theoretical difficulties and contradictions that have troubled him before. With all intensity of thought and will *(adhyāśaya)* he has thrown himself into the deeps of his own being. He is not, however, a mere wanderer without anything to guide him, for he has the name with him. He walks along with it, he goes down to the abyss with it; though he finds himself frequently divorced from it, he always remembers it and keeps in its company. One day without knowing how, he is no more himself, nor is he with the name. The name alone there is, and he is the name, the name is he. Suddenly even this disappears, which is not a state of mental blankness or of total unconsciousness. All these psychological designations fail to describe the state of mind in which he now is. But he stays not even here, for he awakes from it as suddenly as before. As he awakes, he awakes with a thought, which is the name and the faith in the original vow of Amida and the rebirth. This emerging from a state of absolute identity is marked with the utterance of *Namu-amida-butsu,* because he comes to this awakening through the teaching of his school.

Religion is fundamentally a personal experience but the intellect enters into every fiber of the faith thus realized. For when the experience receives its name, that is, when it comes to be designated as faith, it has already gone through the baptism of intellection. Though the latter in itself is powerless, it gains authority as soon as it is combined with the experience. Thus we find almost all religious controversies centering about the philosophy of the experience, in other words, about theological subtleties and not about the experience itself. How to interpret the experience thus becomes frequently the cause of a most irreligious persecution or the bloodiest warfare. However this may be, the religious experience always remains the sustaining and driving energy of its metaphysical system. This explains the diversity of intellectual interpretations even within one body of Buddhism, the one as Zen and the other as Jōdo, while their experience remains as far as psychology is concerned fundamentally the same.

This also explains the historical connection that came to exist between Zen and Jōdo. Superficially or intellectually observed, take for instance one of the numerous Zen koans and compare it with the *Namu-amida-butsu,* how utterly unrelated they appear! "What is it that stands forever companionless?" "I'll tell you when you have swallowed up in one draught all the waves of the Xi!" "What was Bodhidharma's idea in coming from the West?" "The eastern mountains move over the waves." Between these koans and *Namu-amida-butsu* there is no possible relationship as far as their appeal to the intellect is concerned. *Namu-amida-butsu,* as literally meaning "Adoration to Amitābha Buddha," is intelligible enough; but as to the mountains moving over the waves, or one swallowing a whole river in one draught, there is no intelligible sense; all we can say about them is "nonsense!" How can these nonsensical utterances be related to the Nembutsu?

As was explained above, however, the Nembutsu ceased to mean "meditating on the Buddha" and came to be identified with the name *(minghao)*[47] or rather with "uttering the name" *(chengming).*[48] Meditation, or "coming into the presence of the Buddha," thus gave way to the constant reiteration of the phrase as not always or necessarily referring to any definite objective reality, but merely as a name somehow beyond comprehension, or rather as a symbol standing for something indescribable, unpredictable, altogether transcending the intellect, and therefore suggesting a meaning beyond meaning. When the Nembutsu comes to this, the name closely approaches the koan. Hitherto the Nembutsu and the koan exercise have been walking down their different routes of historical development, but now they find themselves near each other, and, as they look at each other, each most unexpectedly recognizes himself in the other.

Zen wants to clear one's consciousness of all its intellectual sediments so that it can receive the first awakening of thought in its purity, in its unaffected simplicity; for this purpose the koan, which is devoid of sense as ordinarily understood, is given to its followers. The idea is to go back to the original blankness in which there was as yet no functioning consciousness. This is a state of no-birth. Zen starts from it and so does the Jōdo.

4

The Shin Sect of Buddhism

This is the longest single essay that Suzuki wrote in English on Shin Buddhism, the Pure Land tradition attributed to Shinran (1173–1262). Certainly, Shin was the form of Pure Land Buddhism with which Suzuki had the greatest contact. This essay is extensive, but it is not necessarily systematic or conventional. It comprises several mini- and even micro-essays on different facets of Shin Buddhism. Some are largely descriptive, explaining the content and themes of Pure Land scriptures and doctrines. Others are highly interpretive, framing Shin ideas in the context of psychological dynamics and Suzuki's own theories about religion. Some sections are puzzling—for instance, his translation of all forty-eight vows of Amida Buddha from the Larger Pure Land Sutra, even though only a handful of them ever had exegetical prominence in Shin and Pure Land Buddhism. Certainly Suzuki knew what a conventional sectarian exposition of the Shin tradition looked like, for he had translated such a work into English in 1910, titled *Principal Teachings of the True Sect of Pure Land.* But here he opted instead to give his own somewhat idiosyncratic, but highly innovative, exposition of Shin Buddhism.

One motif used extensively throughout the essay is the juxtaposition of *jiriki,* self-power, and *tariki,* other-power. There is perhaps no theme more characteristic of Shin Buddhism than this. In a nutshell, it proclaims that people's enlightenment in the Pure Land occurs not as a result of their own efforts, that is, self-power, but because of the inconceivable and mysterious workings of Amida Buddha, that is, other-power. Shinran himself was a major proponent of this idea. Suzuki uses it, first of all, to contrast Shin Buddhism to the Jōdo school, founded by Shinran's master Hōnen (1133–1212). Suzuki's claim is that Shin is grounded in absolute other-power, whereas Jōdo combines self-power with other-power, a claim that the Jōdo school itself would dispute. What Suzuki seeks to highlight with this distinction is Jōdo's emphasis on regular and repeated invocation of Amida's name, the verbal nembutsu, in contrast to Shin's idealization of faith, an inner state of complete and utter reliance on Amida. It is this inner state that Suzuki identifies as the essential link between karma-ridden humans and the infinite and eternal Buddha. Despite this contrast, Suzuki acknowledges that the Jōdo and Shin schools are not really at odds, but simply emphasize different points in the Pure Land Buddhist process—engagement with Amida's name on the one hand and settling of faith on the other. It is noteworthy that in explicating Shin faith the text that Suzuki cites the most is the *Anjin ketsujō shō* (On the Final Peaceful Settlement of Mind), a work with only peripheral and occasional significance in Shin Buddhist history. His citation of it reflects the extent to which Suzuki operated outside the boundaries of traditional Shin hermeneutics. He took inspiration from whatever writings moved him, and he quoted them to make his arguments whether or not they were the most authoritative sectarian sources.

Another recurring motif in the essay is the juxtaposition of karma and akarma, or the world of causes and conditions versus Amida Buddha's world. Suzuki perceives this juxtaposition as two spheres inherent in Pure Land Buddhism. People, he argues, are inevitably locked in a world where they reap the fruit of their actions, whether good or bad. In the *jiriki* path of Buddhism humans use every means possible to maximize the good and to minimize the bad. Reason and willpower are crucial elements in this effort. But it is beyond the capacity of most humans to succeed in this path. Their sins and wrongdoings constantly surpass their virtues and good acts, thus dooming them to repeated birth, death, and rebirth in the karmic world. Amida Buddha, Suzuki maintains, abides in an akarmic state outside the structure and contingencies of this world. His vow to save all beings surpasses logic and reason, for it operates not according to karmic predictability, but is extended equally to the good and the evil alike. Humans are awakened to his vow through the other-power of Amida—that is, his mysterious workings—specifically, through their encounter with his name, the nembutsu, which he broadcasts throughout the universe. The gulf between these two worlds is thus bridged not by the effort of humans but when they remain passive. Amida's unilateral embrace of them is transmuted into the experience of faith within them. Thus, without denying the dualistic world of karma, Suzuki proposes that humans can live nondualistically because of their union with Amida inwardly.

Another line of argument in this essay is Suzuki's comparison of Shin Buddhism to Christianity. It is only natural that he would take up this topic, since Shin Buddhism is widely viewed in the West as similar to Christianity. That is, Amida Buddha is equated to God, Christian sin to karmic wrongdoing, heaven to the Pure Land paradise, and Christian faith to Shin faith. Even while acknowledging such parallels, Suzuki attempts to identify substantive differences between them and to situate Shin Buddhism in the Mahayana tradition. Suzuki points out, for instance, that the Christian God is considered a creator and a dispenser of reward and punishment, thus operating within the framework of karma, whereas Amida stands outside the karmic world and does not interfere with its operation, even though he establishes a bond with sentient beings who live amid karma. Suzuki also indicates that, although aspiration for birth in Amida's paradise after death is a traditional element in Pure Land Buddhism, the belief that one returns to this world from the Pure Land to aid others is also emphasized. Thus, Suzuki situates Pure Land concepts within the bodhisattva tradition of Mahayana and argues that faith, as an inner experience of Amida in this life, is just as important as birth in paradise after death, if not more so.

Throughout Suzuki's essay he presupposes that religious experience is at the heart of Shin Buddhism. Sometimes he expresses this in psychological terms—as a yearning of the

"Unconscious" for the "Unknown." He considers this experience, in the form of faith, to be an internal event separate from the mechanistic processes of the external world and independent of the laws of logic and reason. It occurs mysteriously, and yet it reorders a person's life and values. In explaining Shin Buddhism in this way, Suzuki helps redefine it as a modern religious worldview with a rich and fulfilling inner life instead of as an antiquated belief system centered on a mythic other-worldly paradise.

The base text for this essay is Daisetz Teitaro Suzuki, "The Shin Sect of Buddhism," in *A Miscellany on the Shin Teaching of Buddhism* (Kyoto: Shinshu Otaniha Shumusho, 1949), 1–70. It contains slight changes and augmentation to the original version, which first appeared in *The Eastern Buddhist* 7, no. 3/4 (1939): 227–284. The essay was republished with further editorial changes in Daisetz Teitarō Suzuki, *Collected Writings on Shin Buddhism* (CWSB), ed. The Eastern Buddhist Society (Kyoto: Shinshū Ōtaniha, 1973), 36–77. A Japanese translation by Sugihira Shizutoshi was published as "Shinshū kanken," in Suzuki Daisetsu, *Jōdokei shisōron* (Kyoto: Hōzōkan, 1942). See SDZ 6:7–69.

. . .

I

Of all the developments Mahayana Buddhism has achieved in the Far East, the most remarkable one is the Shin teaching of the Pure Land school. It is remarkable chiefly for the reason that geographically its birthplace is Japan, and historically it is the latest evolution of Pure Land Mahayana, and therefore the highest point it has reached.

The Pure Land idea first grew in India and the Sutras devoted to its exposition were compiled probably about three hundred years after Buddha. The school bearing its name started in China toward the end of the fifth century when the White Lotus Society was organized by Huiyuan (334–416) and his friends in 403. The idea of a Buddha-land *(buddha-kṣetra)* which is presided over by a Buddha is as old as Buddhism, but a school based upon the desire to be born in such a land in order to attain the final end of the Buddhist life did not fully materialize until Buddhism began to flourish in China as a practical religion. It took the Japanese genius of the thirteenth century to mature it further into the teaching of the Shin school. Some may wonder how the Mahayana could have expanded itself into the doctrine of pure faith which apparently stands in direct contrast to the Buddha's supposedly original teaching of self-reliance and enlightenment by means of Prajna.[1] The Shin is thus not infrequently considered altogether unbuddhistic.

What, then, is the teaching of the Shin?

Essentially, it is a teaching growing from the Original Vow *(pūrva-praṇidhāna)* of Amida, the Buddha of Infinite Light and Eternal Life. Amida has a Pure Land created out of his boundless love for all beings, and wills that whoever should cherish absolute faith in his "vows,"[2] which are the expression of his Will, would be born in his Land of Purity and Bliss. In this Land inequalities of all kinds are wiped out and those who enter are allowed equally to enjoy Enlightenment. There are thus three essential factors constituting the Shin teaching: Amida, his Vow, and Faith on the part of his devotees.

Amida is not one who quietly enjoys an infinite light and eternal life in his Land of Purity, he holds all these qualities on the condition that they are to be shared by all beings. And this sharing by all beings of his light and life is made possible by their cherishing an unconditioned faith in Amida. This faith is awakened in all beings who hear the Name *(nāmadheya)* of Amida, and sentient beings are bound to hear it sooner or later as he has made his vows to the effect that his Name be heard throughout the ten quarters of the world.

Some may ask: How is it that Amida's vows are so effective as to cause us to turn toward him for salvation or enlightenment? The Shin follower will answer: Amida is Infinite Light, and, therefore, there is no corner of the human heart where its rays do not penetrate; he is Eternal Life, and, therefore, there is not a moment in our lives when he is not urging us to rise above ourselves. His vows reflect his Will—the Will as illumined by Infinite Light and imbued with Eternal Life: they cannot be otherwise than the most efficient cause to lift us above ourselves who are limited individuals in time and space.

Amida's vows are expressions of his love for all beings, for Amida is love incarnate. Love is eternal life and emits infinite light. Each ray of light carries his Name to the farthest end of the universe and those who have ears are sure to hear it. They are indeed recipients of Amida's love whereby they are at once transferred into his Land of Purity and Bliss, for hearing is receiving and receiving is believing and believing is the condition Amida requires of his devotees.

In short, the above makes up the principal teaching of the Shin Sect.

II

The evolution of the Pure Land idea marks an epoch in the history of Mahayana Buddhism. While the latter itself is a phenomenal fact in the history of general Buddhism, the rise of the Pure Land idea illustrates the persistent and irrepressible assertion of certain aspects of our religious consciousness—the aspects somewhat neglected in the so-called primitive teaching of the Buddha.

Mahayana Buddhism is a religion which developed around the life and personality of the Buddha, rather than a religion based upon the words of his mouth. The person is greater and more real than his words; in fact words gain validity because of a person behind them; essentially is this the case with moral teachings and truths. Mere logicality has no spiritual force which will compel us to follow it. Intellectual acquiescence occupies a corner of our surface consciousness, it does not penetrate into the seat of one's inner personality. Words or letters are needed to communicate events detached partly or wholly from personality, and therefore they are more or less impersonal, and to that extent ineffective in moving the spirit itself. Religion is nonsensical unless it comes in direct contact with the spirit. This contact is only possible when a real personality stands before you or when his image or memory lives forever vividly and inspiringly in you. For this reason, the Mahayana was bound to rise soon after the passing of the Buddha, and became a form of Buddhism in which the personality of the Buddha occupied the center although this does not mean that his words were neglected or altogether set aside. Indeed his teachings were interpreted in the light of his life and personality and followed as containing the seeds which will eventually come to maturity in Buddhahood.

There is no doubt that Buddha was a wonderful personality: there must have been something in him which was superhuman impressing his immediate disciples with a supernaturally overwhelming and entirely irresistible power. While still walking among them, Buddha wielded this power over them with every syllable he uttered; in fact his mere presence was enough to inspire them to rise above themselves not only in the spiritual sense but even in the physical because some of his followers believed that his miraculous power was capable of driving away an evil spirit which would cause pestilence.

It is perfectly in accord with human nature to believe that the great personality has divine power known among the Mahayanists as *Adhiṣṭhāna*. This power goes out of its owner and moves the inmost hearts of those who come into its presence. It is a kind of personal magnetism raised to the nth power, we may say. The Buddha attained Enlightenment, that is to say, Siddhārtha Gautama of the Śākya family became the Enlightened One after so many kalpas (eons) of moral and spiritual training. Enlightenment means perfected personality—one who is perfect in Prajna ("transcendental or intuitive knowledge") and Karuna ("love"). Inasmuch as this perfection is the result of the accumulation of all kinds of spiritual merit, it cannot be something exclusively enjoyed by an individual being, that is, something which does not go out of himself in some way. When one is perfected the rest of the world must also to a certain extent share in its perfection, because the world is not a mere aggregate of units individually separated, but an organism whose units are in a most intimate way knitted together. This is the reason why the Enlightenment of the Buddha does not stay closed up in himself, in his individual personality, but is bound to step out of its spatial-temporal shell into a world encompassing all beings. The appearance of a Buddha therefore corresponds to the awakening of faith in universal enlightenment. The Buddha is creative life itself, he creates himself in innumerable forms with all the means native to him. This is called his *adhiṣṭhāna,* as it were, emanating from his personality.

The idea of *Adhiṣṭhāna* is one of the Mahayana landmarks in the history of Indian Buddhism and it is at the same time the beginning of the "other-power" (*tariki* in Japanese) school as distinguished from the "self-power" *(jiriki)*.[3] The principle of the "self-power" school is one of the characteristics of the so-called Hinayana or the earlier school of Buddhism in India. "Self-power" means "to be a lamp to yourself," it is the spirit of self-reliance, and aims at achieving one's own salvation or enlightenment by the practice of the Eightfold Noble Path or of the Six Virtues of Perfection. If this is impossible in one life, the devotee of the self-power will not relax his efforts through many lives as was exemplified by the Buddha who underwent many a rebirth in order to perfect himself for his supreme enlightenment. Recruits for the self-power school must therefore be endowed with a strong will and a high degree of intelligence. Without intelligence he will not be able to grasp the full significance of the Fourfold Noble Truth, and an intelligent grasp of this truth is most necessary for the sustained exercise of the willpower, which is essential for the performance of the various items of morality as prescribed by the Buddha.

The purport of the Fourfold Noble Truth is to acquaint us with the moral law of causation, i.e., the doctrine of karma. Karma means "What you sow, you reap," and the Noble Truth states it in a more formal way from the point of view of spiritual emancipation. The reason why Buddhists condemn Ignorance *(avidyā)* so persistently is that one who is ignorant of the Noble Truth, which is the spiritual law, will keep on forever committing evil deeds. Evil in Buddhist terminology is to ignore the law of causation and the doctrine of karma, for this ignoring involves us in an endless transmigration. Self-power, karma, and causality thus are closely correlated terms in Buddhism, and as long as this correlation continued there was no need for the idea of *Adhiṣṭhāna* to develop among the Buddhists.

There is however an innate yearning in our hearts to break up this closely knitted correlation existing between karma, causality, and self-power; there is something in the depths of our consciousness always craving to go beyond these terms of mutual limitation. This secret yearning is indeed the primal factor entering into the foundation of the Mahayana teachings. It may be regarded in a way as contradicting the views of the earlier Buddhists or even those of the Buddha. But it had already been on its way to a fuller development when the Mahayanists began to conceive the personality of the Buddha together with his teachings, as the basis of their religious life and thought.

In short, it is human desire to transcend karma, to break through the chain of causation, to take hold of a power absolutely other than "self-power." It may not be quite adequate to call this a desire; it is far stronger, more innate, more fundamental, and more enduring than any kind of desire the psychologist may analyze; it occupies the core of personality; it is awakened in the human heart with the awakening of consciousness, and really constitutes the grand paradox of human life. But it is here where we have the fundamental of the "other-power" *(tariki)* teaching.

Karma, the moral law of causation, is the principle governing human life as it endures in a world of relativity. As long as Buddhism moves in this world demanding the practice of the Eight Paths of Morality and of the Six Virtues of Perfection, the law of karma is to be most scrupulously followed, for without this law all our moral and ascetic endeavors will come to naught. But as our existence reaches out into a realm of the unconditioned, it never remains satisfied with the teachings based upon the rigid, inflexible law of karma; it demands teachings more pliable, adaptive, and mobile, that is to say, more living and creative. Such teachings are to be founded on things lying beyond the ken of karma or causality which is after all only applicable to the conditionality-phase of existence.

Human life is rigorously karma-bound, there is no denying it, and when we disregard this fact, we are a miserable sight. But at the same time one of the human legs stands in a world where karma loses its domination. It may be better to describe this state of affairs thus: while our limited consciousness urges us to conform ourselves to the working of karma, the Unconscious attracts us away to the Unknown beyond karma. The Unconscious and the Unknown are not terms to be found in the dictionary of our ordinary life, but they exercise a mysteriously irresistible power over us, to which our logic and psychology are inapplicable. This most fundamental contradiction which appears in every section of human life refuses to be reconciled in no other way than by the "other-power" teaching of Mahayana Buddhism.

To be living within the boundaries of karma and yet to transcend them—that is, to be and yet not to be—is the climax of irrationality as logic goes. "To be or not to be" is the question possible only within logic. Simultaneously to be and not to be means to occupy two contradicting points at once—and can there be anything more absurd, more nonsensical, more irrational than this?

The self-power is logical and therefore intelligible, appealing to ordinary minds, but the other-power is altogether irrational, and the fact is that this irrationality makes up human life. Hence the inevitability of Mahayana Buddhism.

We must, however, remember that the teaching of the other-power school does not mean to annihilate the karma-phase of human life in order to make it absolutely transcend itself, to live altogether away from its own life. This is an impossibility inasmuch as we are what we are; if we try to deny the present life as we live it, it will surely be suicidal, it is no transcending of the earthly life. What the other-power tries to do, indeed, what all the schools of the Mahayana try to do, is to live this life of karma and relativity and yet to live at the same time a life of transcendence, a life of spiritual freedom, a life not tied down to the chain of causation. To use the Christian expression, immanence is conceivable only with transcendence and transcendence with immanence; when the one is made to mean anything without the other, neither becomes intelligible. But to have both at the same time is altogether illogical, and this is what we are trying to do, showing that logic somehow contrives to adjust itself.

The Mahayana philosophers have a theory by which they solve the question of immanence and transcendence or which solves the relationship between *karma* and *akarma.*[4] This theory, as systematically expounded in Aśvaghoṣa's *Awakening of Faith,* starts with the idea of Suchness (*tathatā* in Sanskrit). Suchness is the limit of thought, and human consciousness cannot go any further than that; expressed in another way, without the conception of Suchness there is no bridge or background whereby the two contradictory ideas, karma and akarma, can be linked. In Suchness or Thusness, affirmation and negation and all forms of opposites find their place of reconciliation or interpenetration; for affirmation is negation and negation is affirmation, and this interpenetration is only possible in Suchness. Suchness may thus be said to be standing on two legs—birth-and-death which is the realm of karma, and no-birth-and-death which is the realm of akarma beyond the reach of causality.

Suchness is also termed "Mind" *(citta)* from the psychological point of view, and again "Being-Body" *(dharmakāya).* "Suchness" may sound too abstract and metaphysical, and the Mahayana doctors frequently substitute "Mind" for it; "Mind" is a more familiar and therefore more accessible and also acceptable term for general Buddhists, who can thus establish an intimate relation between their individual minds and Mind as final reality. When, however, even "Mind" is regarded too intellectual the Buddhists call it Dharmakaya or "Being-Body." Dharmakaya is commonly rendered "Law-Body," but *dharma* really means in this case not "law" or "regulative principle," but any object of thought abstract or concrete, universal or particular, and *kāya* is "the body," more in the moral sense of "person" or "personality." The Dharmakaya is therefore a person whose bodily or organic or material expression is this universe, Dharma. The doctrine of the Triple Body *(trikāya)* has thus evolved from the notion of Dharmakaya.[5]

There is still another term for Suchness, considered principally characterizing the teaching of the *Mahāprajñāpāramitā Sūtra.* It is Emptiness or Void *(śūnyatā)*—one of the terms most frequently misinterpreted by Buddhist critics of the West who have never been able really to get into the Buddhist way of thinking. Emptiness is Suchness in which there is nothing empty. When we speak of Emptiness, we are apt to understand it in its relative sense, that is, in contrast to fullness, concreteness, or substantiality. But the Buddhist idea of Emptiness is not gathered from the negation of individual existences but from the transcendental point of view as it were, for Emptiness unites in itself both fullness and nothingness, both karma and akarma, both determination and freedom, both immanence and transcendence, and *jiriki* ("self-power") and *tariki* ("other-power").

III

The principal sutra of the Shin sect of the Pure Land school is the *Sutra of Eternal Life*[6] in Chinese translation. The Sanskrit text still available is not in full agreement with the Chinese version which is used by Japanese and Chinese followers of the

Pure Land school. The points of disagreement are many and varied, but since it is the Chinese text translated by Kōsōgai (C. Kang Sengkai), that is, Saṃghavarman of Khotan of the third century, and not the Sanskrit text still extant, which forms the basis of the Pure Land teaching, a summary will be given here of the Chinese version. After this, we will proceed to expound the Shin school as distinguished from the Jōdo school.

The Sutra of Eternal Life consists roughly of 9000 Chinese characters and is divided into two parts. Its interlocutors are Śākyamuni, Ānanda, and Maitreya or Ajita. The scene is placed on Mount Gṛdhrakūṭa where the Buddha sits surrounded by a large number of Bhikshus and Mahayana Bodhisattvas. Ānanda, observing the Buddha's expression full of serenity, clear, and shining, asks for its reason, and the Buddha begins to tell the whole congregation the story of Dharmākara the Bhikshu who devoted himself to the work of establishing a land of happiness for all sentient beings.

It was long time ago indeed in an innumerable, immeasurable, incomprehensible kalpa before now, that Dharmākara studied and practiced the Dharma under the guidance of a Tathagata called Lokeśvararāja. His motive was to perfect a Buddha-land in which every conceivable perfection could be brought together. He asked his teacher to explain and manifest for him the perfection of all the excellent qualities of hundreds of thousands of *koṭis* of Buddha-lands, and after seeing all these excellently qualified Buddha-lands, he was absorbed in deep meditation for a period of five kalpas. When he arose from the meditation his mind was made up for the establishment of his own land of purity and happiness, in which all the inconceivable excellences he observed were to be integrated. He appeared before his teacher Lokeśvararāja and vowed in the presence not only of this Buddha but of all the celestial beings, evil spirits, Brahmā, gods, and all other beings, that unless the following forty-eight conditions were fulfilled[7] he might not attain the highest enlightenment. These vows are what is known by Amida followers as his Original Vow.

After this Dharmākara the Bhikshu devoted himself for a space of innumerable, immeasurable, incomprehensible kalpas to the practice of innumerable good deeds which were characterized with the absence of the thoughts of greed, malevolence, and cruelty. In short, he completed all the virtues belonging to the life of a Bodhisattva, which consists of the realization of Love *(karuṇā)* and Wisdom *(prajñā)*. He is now residing in the Western quarter, in the Buddha-land called Sukhāvatī, Land of Happiness, far away from this world by a hundred thousand *niyutas* of *koṭis* of Buddha-lands. He is called Amitābha, Infinite Light, because of his light the limit of which is beyond measurement. He is again called Amitāyus, Eternal Life, because the length of his life is altogether incalculable. For instance, let all beings in this world collect their thoughts on measuring the length of Amida's life for hundreds of thousands of *koṭis* of kalpas and yet they would fail to obtain a result.

The forty-eight vows enumerated in the Sutra are as follows:

(1) If in my country, after my obtaining Buddhahood, there should be hell, a realm of hungry ghosts, or brute creatures, may I not attain the Highest Enlightenment.

(2) If those who are born in my country, after my obtaining Buddhahood, should return to the three evil paths of existence, may I not attain the Highest Enlightenment.

(3) If those who are born in my country, after my obtaining Buddhahood, should not all shine in golden color, may I not attain the Highest Enlightenment.

(4) If those who are born in my country, after my obtaining Buddhahood, should not all be of one form and color, showing no difference in looks, may I not attain the Highest Enlightenment.

(5) If those who are born in my country, after my obtaining Buddhahood, should not have the remembrance of their past lives, at least of things of hundreds of thousands of *koṭi*s of kalpas ago, may I not attain the Highest Enlightenment.

(6) If those who are born in my country, after my obtaining Buddhahood, should not be endowed with the heavenly eye so as at least to be able to see hundreds of thousands of *koṭi*s of Buddha-countries, may I not attain the Highest Enlightenment.

(7) If those who are born in my country, after my obtaining Buddhahood, should not be endowed with the heavenly ear so as at least to be able to hear and retain in memory all the Buddhas' preaching in hundreds of thousands of *koṭi*s of Buddha-countries, may I not attain the Highest Enlightenment.

(8) If those who are born in my country, after my obtaining Buddhahood, should not be endowed with the mind-reading faculty so as at least to be able to perceive all the thoughts cherished by beings living in hundreds of thousands of *koṭi*s of Buddha-countries, may I not attain the Highest Enlightenment.

(9) If those who are born in my country, after my obtaining Buddhahood, should not be able to step over in the moment of one thought at least hundreds of thousands of *koṭi*s of Buddha-countries, may I not attain the Highest Enlightenment.

(10) If those who are born in my country, after my obtaining Buddhahood, should cherish any thought of the body and be attached to it, may I not attain the Highest Enlightenment.

(11) If those who are born in my country, after my obtaining Buddhahood, should not be definitely settled in the group of the faithful before their entrance into Nirvana,[8] may I not attain the Highest Enlightenment.

(12) If, after my obtaining Buddhahood, my light should be limited and not be able at least to illumine hundreds of thousands of *koṭi*s of Buddha-countries, may I not attain the Highest Enlightenment.

(13) If, after my obtaining Buddhahood, the length of my life should be limited and not be able at least to last for hundreds of thousands of *koṭi*s of kalpas, may I not attain the Highest Enlightenment.

(14) If, after my obtaining Buddhahood, the number of Sravakas in my country should be measurable by all beings in three thousand chiliocosms, who, becoming Pratyekabuddhas, should devote themselves to counting for hundreds of thousands of *koṭi*s of kalpas, may I not attain the Highest Enlightenment.

(15) If those who are born in my country, after my obtaining Buddhahood, should be limited in the length of their life, except those who because of their original vows have their life shortened or lengthened, may I not attain the Highest Enlightenment.

(16) If those who are born into my country, after my obtaining Buddhahood, should hear even the name of evil, may I not attain the Highest Enlightenment.

(17) If, after my obtaining Buddhahood, all the immeasurable Buddhas in the ten quarters do not approvingly proclaim my name, may I not attain the Highest Enlightenment.

(18) If, after my obtaining Buddhahood, all beings in the ten quarters should not desire in sincerity and trustfulness to be born in my country, and if they should not be born by only thinking of me for ten times, except those who have committed the five grave offenses and those who are abusive of the true Dharma, may I not attain the Highest Enlightenment.

(19) If, after my obtaining Buddhahood, all beings in the ten quarters awakening their thoughts to enlightenment and practicing all deeds of merit should cherish the desire in sincerity to be born in my country and if I should not, surrounded by a large company, appear before them at the time of their death, may I not attain the Highest Enlightenment.

(20) If, after my obtaining Buddhahood, all beings in the ten quarters hearing my name should cherish the thought of my country and planting all the roots of merit turn them in sincerity over to being born in my country, and if they should fail in obtaining the result of it, may I not attain the Highest Enlightenment.

(21) If those who are born in my country, after my obtaining Buddhahood, should not be complete in the thirty-two marks of a great personality, may I not attain the Highest Enlightenment.

(22) If, after my obtaining Buddhahood, all the Bodhisattvas in other Buddha-lands should desire to be born in my county and if they should not be all bound to

one birth only, excepting indeed those Bodhisattvas who, because of their original vows to convert all beings, would, fortifying themselves with the armor of universal salvation, accumulate the stock of merit, deliver all beings from misery, visit all the Buddha-countries, practice the discipline of Bodhisattvahood, pay homage to all the Buddha-Tathagatas in the ten quarters, and enlighten all beings as immeasurable as the sands of the Ganga so that all beings might establish themselves in true peerless enlightenment, and further be led on beyond the ordinary stages of Bodhisattvahood, even indeed to the virtues of Samantabhadra, may I not attain the Highest Enlightenment.

(23) If, after my obtaining Buddhahood, all the Bodhisattvas born in my country should not by virtue of the Buddha's miraculous power pay homage to all the Buddhas, and even in one meal's duration visit all the Buddha-countries numbering as many as hundreds of thousands of *koṭi*s, may I not attain the Highest Enlightenment.

(24) If, after my obtaining Buddhahood, all the Bodhisattvas born in my country should desire to cultivate all the root of merit, and if they should not be able to obtain according to their wish every possible article of worship they may require, may I not attain the Highest Enlightenment.

(25) If, after my obtaining Buddhahood, all the Bodhisattvas born in my country should not be able to preach the Dharma which is in harmony with all-knowledge, may I not attain the Highest Enlightenment.

(26) If, after my obtaining Buddhahood, all the Bodhisattvas born in my country should not be endowed with the body of Nārāyaṇa, may I not attain the Highest Enlightenment.

(27) If, after my obtaining Buddhahood, all beings born in my country should be able even with their heavenly eye to enumerate and describe precisely all the objects there which are shining in all splendor and purity in the most exquisite manner, may I not attain the Highest Enlightenment.

(28) If, after my obtaining Buddhahood, the Bodhisattvas born in my country, even those endowed with the least merit, should not perceive a Bodhi-tree most exquisitely colored and four hundred yojanas in height, may I not attain the Highest Enlightenment.

(29) If, after my obtaining Buddhahood, the Bodhisattvas in my country, who devote themselves to the reading, reciting, and expounding of the sutras, should not be in possession of perfect knowledge and eloquence, may I not attain the Highest Enlightenment.

(30) If, after my obtaining Buddhahood, the Bodhisattvas in my country should be in possession of eloquence and perfect knowledge the extent of which is measurable, may I not attain the Highest Enlightenment.

(31) If, after my obtaining Buddhahood, my country should not be so pure and spotless as to illumine, like a bright mirror reflecting images before it, all the

Buddha-worlds in the ten quarters which are in number beyond description and calculability, may I not attain to the Highest Enlightenment.

(32) If, after my obtaining Buddhahood, my country from the ground up to the sky should not be filled and ornamented most exquisitely with all kinds of vases made of jewels emitting an immeasurable variety of sweet perfume which rising above gods and men spreads over the ten quarters and if the Bodhisattvas smelling it should not be induced to practice the virtues of Buddhahood, may I not attain the Highest Enlightenment.

(33) If, after my obtaining Buddhahood, all beings in all the immeasurable and inconceivable Buddha-worlds in the ten quarters should not be enveloped in my light and if those coming in touch with it should not enjoy the softness of the body and mind beyond the reach of gods and men, may I not attain the Highest Enlightenment.

(34) If, after my obtaining Buddhahood, all beings in all the innumerable and inconceivable Buddha-worlds in the ten quarters hearing my name should not obtain the recognition of the unborn Dharma[9] and all the Dharanis belonging to Bodhisattvahood, may I not attain the Highest Enlightenment.

(35) If, after my obtaining Buddhahood, women in all the immeasurable and inconceivable Buddha-worlds in the ten quarters should not, after hearing my name, be filled with joy and trust and awaken their thoughts to enlightenment and loathe their femininity, and if in another birth they should again assume the female body, may I not attain the Highest Enlightenment.

(36) If, after my obtaining Buddhahood, all the Bodhisattvas in all the innumerable and inconceivable Buddha-worlds in the ten quarters should not, after hearing my name, always devote themselves to the practice of the holy deeds, in order to perfect the Buddha-truth, this even to the end of their lives, may I not attain the Highest Enlightenment.

(37) If, after my obtaining Buddhahood, all beings in all the innumerable and inconceivable Buddha-worlds in the ten quarters should not, hearing my name, prostrate themselves on the ground to worship me in joy and trust and devote themselves to the practice of the Bodhisattva discipline, thereby winning the reverence of all gods and men, may I not attain the Highest Enlightenment.

(38) If, after my obtaining Buddhahood, beings born in my country should not acquire whatever exquisite cloaks they wish to have which are permitted by the Buddha, and if these cloaks should not be placed upon their bodies, which require neither cleaning, nor fulling, nor dyeing, nor washing, may I not attain the Highest Enlightenment.

(39) If, after my obtaining Buddhahood, beings born in my country should not be recipients of joy as great as that enjoyed by Bhikshus thoroughly purged of their defilements, may I not attain the Highest Enlightenment.

(40) If, after my obtaining Buddhahood, Bodhisattvas born in my country should not be able to see innumerable Buddha-lands in the ten quarters produced from among the jewel-trees in the land, according to their wish and at any moment desired and so transparently as one perceives one's image in a brightly burnished mirror, may I not attain the Highest Enlightenment.

(41) If, after my obtaining Buddhahood, all the Bodhisattvas in other countries should, having heard my name, sustain any defects in their sense organs while pursuing the study of Buddhahood, may I not attain the Highest Enlightenment.

(42) If, after my obtaining Buddhahood, all the Bodhisattvas in other countries should not realize the samadhi called "pure emancipation" by hearing my name and if they even while in this samadhi should not be able to awaken a thought and pay homage to all the innumerable and inconceivable Buddha-Tathagatas and yet all the time retain their samadhi, may I not attain the Highest Enlightenment.

(43) If, after my obtaining Buddhahood, all the Bodhisattvas in other lands having heard my name should not be born after death in noble families, may I not attain the Highest Enlightenment.

(44) If, after my obtaining Buddhahood, all the Bodhisattvas in other lands should not, by hearing my name, leap with joy and devote themselves to the practice of the Bodhisattva discipline and perfect the stock of merit, may I not attain the Highest Enlightenment.

(45) If, after my obtaining Buddhahood, all the Bodhisattvas in other lands should not by hearing my name realize the samadhi called "Samantānugata" (all-arrived) and if abiding in this samadhi they should not always see until their attainment of Buddhahood all the Buddhas beyond measure and thought, may I not attain the Highest Enlightenment.

(46) If, after my obtaining Buddhahood, Bodhisattvas born in my country should not be able to hear, without any effort, whatever Dharmas they aspire to hear, may I not attain the Highest Enlightenment.

(47) If, after my obtaining Buddhahood, all the Bodhisattvas in other lands by hearing my name should not instantly reach the stage of no-turning-back,[10] may I not attain the Highest Enlightenment.

(48) If, after my obtaining Buddhahood, all the Bodhisattvas in other lands by hearing my name should not instantly realize the first, the second, and the third Recognition *(kṣānti)* of the Dharma, and if they should ever turn back in the mastery of all the Buddha-teachings, may I not attain the Highest Enlightenment.

These forty-eight separate vows were fulfilled by virtue of Dharmākara's loving and unselfish devotion to his work, and the country thus created is known as the

Land of Bliss, Sukhāvatī, presided over by him now called Amitābha, Infinite Light, and also Amitāyus, Eternal Life—the shortened form of which in Japanese is Amida and in Chinese Emituo Fo. Ten kalpas have elapsed since the establishment of this miraculous kingdom.

The Sutra then proceeds to the description of the Land of Bliss, commonly designated Jōdo (*jingtu* in Chinese), meaning Land of Purity. The description is naturally filled with terms not of this world, being altogether beyond the ordinary human understanding.

The second part of the Sutra opens with Śākyamuni's confirmation of all that has been said before regarding the birth of all beings in the Pure Land of Amida as soon as they hear his Name with joy and trust. The Buddha tells Ānanda that all those destined to be born there are those who are definitely established in the true faith even while here, that all the Buddhas in the ten quarters numbering as many as the sands of the Ganga uniformly praise the power and virtue of Amida, both of which are indeed beyond comprehension, and that if we, hearing the Name of Amida, even once turn our thought toward him, he will assure of our rebirth in his country.

(The most significant remark which may be made here is that Shinran, founder of the Shin sect, has his characteristic way of reading the Chinese passage containing the characters *shishin ekō,* "to turn toward . . . in sincerity of thought." "To turn toward whom" is the question here. Ordinarily it is for all beings to turn toward Amida and direct all their stocks of merit toward their rebirth in his country, and no doubt, from the literary point of view too, this is the correct reading. But Shinran reverses the customary way of reading and makes Amida turn all his accumulated merit toward opening the passage for all beings to his Pure Land—where lies the essence of the *tariki* teaching. That we are assured of our rebirth in Amida's land is not by any means due to our own merit but to Amida's unqualified love for us who in no circumstances by ourselves can work out our own salvation.)[11]

The rest of the Sutra is largely devoted to the narration of the state of things as they are in this world compared with the Pure Land of Amida. The contrast is appalling and the reader would naturally turn away from those disgusting scenes taking place not only in his surroundings but in fact in his own heart day in day out. This depictment is no doubt an annotation added by a commentator, although it now forms an integral part of the Sutra itself.

After this Ānanda expresses his desire to see Amida's Pure Land, and the entire scene reveals itself at once before Ānanda and the whole congregation. The one statement which strikes us here most significantly is: "The four groups of beings on this side at once perceived all that was [on the other side], and those on the other side in turn saw this world in the same way." One may almost feel like making the remark that the Pure Land is the reflection of this world as this world is the reflection of the Pure Land and that if this be the case various inferences may be drawn from this, among which we can point out some theories going directly against the orthodox teaching of Shin.

After this the Sutra ends with the Buddha's usual exhortation to his assembly as to the continuance of the Buddhist teaching and the upholding of the Buddhist faith especially as expounded in the present Sutra.

IV

Both Jōdo and Shin belong to the Pure Land school. Jōdo means the "Pure Land" and the official title of the Shin is Jōdo Shin and not just Shin. *Shin* means "true" and its devotees claim that their teaching is truly *tariki* whereas the Jōdo is not quite so, being mixed with the *jiriki* idea: hence *Shin* "true" added to *Jōdo.*

The main points of difference between the Jōdo and the Shin teaching are essentially two: 1. Jōdo fully believes with Shin in the efficacy of Amida's Vow but thinks that Amida's Name is to be repeatedly recited; whereas Shin places its emphasis upon faith and not necessarily upon the nembutsu,[12] which is the repeated recitation of the Name. 2. Jōdo encourages good works as helpful for the devotee being born in the Pure Land; whereas Shin finds here a residue of the *jiriki* ("self-power") and insists that as long as the devotee awakens his whole-hearted faith in Amida, Amida will take care of him unconditionally, absolutely assuring his entrance into the Pure Land. Whatever nembutsu he may offer to Amida it is no more than the grateful appreciation of the favor of the Buddha.

The fundamental idea underlying the Shin faith is that we as individual existences are karma-bound and therefore sinful, for karma is inevitably connected with sin; that as no karma-bound beings are capable of effecting their own emancipation, they have to take refuge in Amida who out of his infinite love for all beings is ever extending his helping arms; and that all that is needed of us is to remain altogether passive toward Amida, for he awakens in our hearts, when they are thoroughly purged of all the ideas of self and self-reliance, a faith which at once joins us to Amida and makes us entirely his. This being so, we as creatures subject to the law of moral causation can accomplish nothing worthy of the Pure Land; all good works so-called are not all good from the viewpoint of absolute value, for they are always found deeply tinged with the idea of selfhood which no relatively-conditioned beings are able to shake off. Amida, in his capacity of Infinite Light and Eternal Life, stands against us, ever beckoning us to cross the stream of birth-and-death. Faith is the act of response on our part, and its practical result is our crossing the stream.

One difference at least between Jōdo and Shin or between *jiriki* and *tariki* as regards their attitude toward the nembutsu is, according to the author of the *Anjin ketsujō shō,*[13] that

The nembutsu as practiced by the *jiriki* followers puts the Buddha away from themselves far in the West, and thinking that they are worthless beings they would now and then recollect the Original Vow of the Buddha and pronounce his Name *(shōmyō)*. This being so the most intimate relationship between the Buddha and all beings fails to establish itself here. When a pious feeling however slight moves in their hearts, they may be persuaded to think that their rebirth is approaching. But when they are not too anxious to say the nembutsu and whatever pious feeling they have grows weaker, the assurance of their rebirth wavers. Inasmuch as they are common mortals, it is only on exceptional occasions that they cherish pious feelings; and they thus naturally have an uncertain outlook in regard to their rebirth [in the Pure Land]. They may have to wait in this uncertain state of mind until the time actually comes for them to depart from this life. While they occasionally pronounce the Name with their mouth, they have no definite assurance for the Pure Land. This position is like that of a feudal retainer who only occasionally comes out in the presence of the lord. [His relationship with the latter can never be intimate and trustful.] Such a devotee is all the time in an unsettled state of mind as to how to court the favor of the Buddha, how to be reconciled to him, how to win his loving consideration, and this very fact of his uncertainties alienates him from Buddha, resulting in the unharmonious relationship between the devotee's unsettled mind and Buddha's great compassionate heart. The *[jiriki]* devotee thus puts himself at a distance from Buddha. As long as he keeps up this attitude of mind his rebirth in the Pure Land is indeed extremely uncertain. . . .

From this, we see that the *jiriki* followers' relation to Buddha is not so intimate and trustful as that of the *tariki*. They endeavor to court the favor of Amida by doing something meritorious, including the recitation of his Name, but this attitude indicates a certain fundamental separation and irreconcilability as existing between Buddha and his devotees. The *jiriki* thus tends to create an unnecessary gap where according to the *tariki* there has never been any from the very first. The being conscious of a gap interferes with the assurance of rebirth and peace of mind is lost. The *tariki* on the other hand places great stress on the significance of the eighteenth vow made by Amida, and teaches that when the significance of this vow is fully realized, rebirth is assured and the devotee is released from all worries arising from the sense of separation.

What, then, is the significance of Amida's Vow?

According to the *Anjin ketsujō shō* it is this.[14]

The purport of all the three Sutras of the Jōdo school is to manifest the significance of the Original Vow. To understand the Vow means to understand the Name, and to understand the Name is to understand that Amida, by bringing to maturity his Vow and Virtue (or Deed) in the stead of all beings, effected their rebirth even prior to their actual attainment. What made up the substance of his Enlightenment was no other than the rebirth of all beings in the ten quarters of the world. For this reason, devotees of the nembutsu, that is, of the *tariki*, are to realize this truth each time they hear Amida's Name pronounced that their rebirth is indeed already effected, because the Name stands for the Enlightenment attained by Hōzō the Bodhisattva[15] who vowed that he would not attain enlightenment until all beings in the ten quarters of the world were assured of their rebirth in his Pure Land. The same realization must also be awakened in the minds of the *tariki* devotees when they bow before the holy statue of Amida Buddha, for it represents him in the state of Enlightenment which he attained by vowing that he would not have it until all beings were assured of their rebirth. When any reference is made to the Pure Land, they should cherish the thought that it is the realm established by Hōzō the Bodhisattva for the sake of all beings whose rebirth there was assured by his Vow and Enlightenment. As far as the devotees themselves are concerned they have nothing in their nature which will enable them to practice any form of good either worldly or unworldly since they only know how to commit evil deeds; but because of Amida's having completed an immeasurable amount of meritorious deeds, which constitutes the substance of Buddhahood, even we who are ignorant and addicted to wrong views are now destined for the Land of Purity and Happiness. What a blessing it is then for us all! We may believe in Amida's Original Vow and pronounce his Name; but if we, failing to perceive that Amida's meritorious deeds are our own, stress the merit of the Name in order to assure ourselves of rebirth, we would indeed be committing a grievous fault.

When the belief is once definitely awakened that *Namu-amida-butsu* symbolizes the truth of our rebirth assured by Amida's Enlightenment, we see that the substance of Buddhahood is the act [or fact] of our rebirth, and consequently that one utterance of the Name means the assurance of rebirth. When, again, the Name, *Namu-amida-butsu,* is heard, we see that the time is come for our rebirth and that our rebirth is no other than the Enlightenment attained by Amida. We may cherish a doubt, if we choose, whether Amida has already attained his Enlightenment or whether he has not yet attained it; but we should never have a doubt as to our rebirth being an accomplished fact. Amida has vowed not to attain his Enlightenment as long as there is one single being whose rebirth has not yet been assured. To understand all this is said to understand what is meant by Amida's Original Vow.

While the *jiriki* teaches us that it is on our side to make vows and to practice good deeds if we wish to be assured of our rebirth, the *tariki* teaches just the reverse: it is on the side of Amida who makes vows and practices good deeds while the effect of all this is matured on our side—the fact which altogether goes beyond the reason of causation as we see in this world or anywhere else.

It is thus evident that for the *tariki* devotees the Buddha is not very far away from them, indeed that they are living with him, in him, "rising with him in the morning and retiring at night again with him." Amida to them is not an object of worship or thought which stands against them, although as far as logical knowledge goes, which is good for the world of karma and birth-and-death, Amida is a being quite apart from us who are nothing but ignorant and sinful beings. It is by faith that we transcend the logic of dualism, and then, in Shin terminology, we are assured of our rebirth in the Pure Land of Amida. Faith is an eternal mystery, and the truth and vitality of Shin faith is rooted in this mystery.

To quote further the author of the *Anjin ketsujō shō:*

> Generally speaking, the nembutsu means to think of the Buddha, and to think of the Buddha means that the Buddha has by the karmic power inherent in his Great Vow cut asunder for all beings the bonds whereby they are tied to birth-and-death, and that he has thus matured the condition for their rebirth in the Land of Recompense[16] where once entered they would never retrograde, and further that when thinking of this merit accomplished by the Buddha they take advantage of his Original Vow and give themselves up to it, their threefold activity [of body, mouth, and mind] is supported by the Buddha-substance and raised up to the state of enlightenment which constitutes Buddhahood. For this reason, by being thorough in the nembutsu we are to understand that our pronouncing the Buddha's Name, or our paying him homage, or our thinking of him is not an act originating in ourselves but doing the act of Amida Buddha himself. (Or shall we say "living the life of Amida," or "living in Christ and not in Adam"?)

What the Shin devotees object to in the way cherished by their fellow believers of the Jōdo teaching is that the latter are a mixture of *jiriki* and *tariki* and not *tariki* pure and simple, that if one at all advocates *tariki,* this must he thoroughly purged of the *jiriki* element, and that *tariki* even to the slightest decree tainted with *jiriki* is not only logically untenable but is a revolt against the universal love of Amida which he entertains for all sentient beings. As long as one puts a wholehearted trust in the Original Vow of Amida, one ought not to harbor even an iota of *jiriki* idea against it; when this is done the entire scheme collapses. *Jiriki* means literally "self-power," that is, self-will, and what self-will is needed in the work of transcending the karmic law of causation which binds us to this world of relativity? The self-will is useful and means something while we stay in the realm of birth-and-death, but what is to be achieved by the Buddhists is the realization of things of eternal value. The self-will is called *hakarai* by Shinran, founder of the Shin school of the Jōdo (Pure Land) teaching. *Hakarai* is "to contrive," "to calculate," "to lay down a plan," "to have an intention," for one's rebirth in the Land of Amida. Shinran has consistently disavowed this *hakarai* as the essence of *jiriki* lying in the way of absolute faith in which all the Jōdo followers are to accept the Original Vow of Amida. So we have the following in one of his epistles given to his disciples:

> By *jiriki* is meant that the devotees, each according to his karmic condition, think of a Buddha other [than Amida], recite his Name, and practice good deeds relying on their own judgments, that they plan out their own ideas as regards how properly and felicitously to adjust their activities of the body, mouth, and mind for the rebirth in the Pure Land. By *tariki* is meant wholeheartedly to accept and believe the Original Vow of Amida whereby he assures those who pronounce his Name that they will be reborn in his Pure Land. As this is the Vow made by Amida, it has a sense which

> cannot be prescribed by any common measure of judgment—a sense which is beyond sense, as has been taught by my holy master. Sense is contrivance, that is, intention. The devotees have an intention to move in accordance with their own ideas, and thus their doings have sense.
>
> The *tariki* devotees, however, have placed their faith wholeheartedly in Amida's Original Vow and are assured of their rebirth in the Pure Land—hence they are free from sense [or from intention of their own]. This being so, you are not to imagine that you would not be greeted by Amida in his Land because of your sinfulness. As ordinary beings you are endowed with all kinds of evil passions and destined to be sinful. Nor are you to imagine that you are assured of rebirth in the Pure Land because of your goodness. As long as your *jiriki* sense is holding you, you would never be welcomed to Amida's True Land of Recompense.

To begin with, according to Shinran, Amida's Original Vow is a mysterious deed altogether beyond human comprehension, and now that you have awakened faith in it, what worries could ever harass you? What contrivances could ever save you from sinfulness so completely that you would be worthy residents of the Pure Land? You just give yourselves up absolutely to the mysterious workings of the Original Vow and, instead of growing anxious about or being vexed by anything of this world, be satisfied with yourselves, be free as the wind blows, as the flowers blossom, in the unimpeded light of Amida. Shinran frequently advises not to think of good, nor of evil, but just to give oneself up into the mysterious Original Vow and be "natural."

To be "natural" *(jinen)* means to be free from self-willed intention, to be altogether trusting in the Original Vow, to be absolutely passive in the hands of Amida who has prepared for you the way to his Pure Land. We humans are supposed to be intelligent beings but when we reflect at all on things claiming our attention and try to carry out the thinking to the furthest end, we find that our intelligence is not adequate for the task and that we are surrounded on all sides by thick clouds of mysteries. It makes no difference in which direction our thinking turns, inwardly or outwardly, it always confronts a mystery, for it is in its nature that it can never solve the questions it raises for itself. We have thus no other way but to give ourselves up to this mystery, which, from the Shin point of view, is known as the mystery of the Original Vow or the mystery of the Name. When this mystery is reached which is the limit of intellectual reflection, it is comprehended, not indeed intellectually but intuitively, that is to say, it is accepted unconditionally—which is another way of describing faith. In terms of the Shin teaching, the faith thus awakened is the assurance of rebirth in Amida's Pure Land, and those who have this faith are said to be already walking in the Pure Land in company with all the Tathagatas. That the Shin devotees of true and never-relapsing faith are the equals of Maitreya Bodhisattva is a most significant declaration on the part of the Shin teachers. It is evident that the faith advocated by them is an identical state of mind with Enlightenment realized by all the Buddhas. As for the real supreme Enlightenment the devotees are to wait until they reach the Pure Land itself. Insofar as they still belong to this world, the body may commit acts of impurity, but the mind is already where all the Tathagatas are, that is, in the Pure Land. To live this mystery is known as being "natural," following the course of things, especially of things of the spirit, as arranged by the Original Vow of Amida.

To have the body in this world of time and space with the mind somewhere else, to let the body live a life of evils since it cannot do anything different and yet to keep the mind in the Land of Purity in the most friendly relationship with all the Buddhas—how can this be possible? Apart from the psychological and philosophical question of body and mind, how can one individual totality be at two points at the same time? Logically stated, the Shin expressions such as above referred to are full of difficulties, in fact impossible for intellectual solution. But one thing we can say about the statements made by the Shin teachers is that, generally speaking, religious intuition consists in consciously coming into contact with a realm of absolute values, which stands in no spatial or temporal relationship to this world of senses and ratiocination, but which forms the basis of it, gives it its meaning, and without which it is like a dream, like a dewdrop, like a flash of lightning. The relation of the body and the mind, of this world and the Pure Land, of sinfulness and enlightenment, and of many other forms of opposition is an inscrutable mystery so long as it is viewed from this world, but it becomes at once natural and acceptable when we become conscious of another world which Christians may call supernatural, and the truth thus dawned upon one is "revealed" truth. Here also lies the mystery of the Original Vow and of the Name, which is indeed the mystery of *tariki.*

V

A comparison with Christianity may help us to understand the characteristic teaching of Shin as a development of the Pure Land doctrine and also as a school of Mahayana Buddhism however strangely formed at first sight it may appear. The following points of difference may be observed as existing between Buddhism and Christianity:

1. Amida to all appearances may be regarded as corresponding to the Christian notion of God. Amida however is not the creator, nor is he to be considered the author of evil in this world, which inevitably follows from the notion of creatorship.

Whatever evils there are in this world, they are all our own doings, for everything karma-conditioned individuals can do is necessarily evil and has no merit entitling them to appear before Amida. This polarization of Amida and individual beings *(sarvasattva)* is one of the specific features of Shin thought. In this respect its followers may be said to be transcendentalists or dualists.

Amida is the pure embodiment of love. Whoever believes in him as savior is sure of being taken up by Amida and sent to his Pure Land. Amida's love makes no distinction between evildoers and good men, because as Shinran says there is no evil strong enough to prevent one's being embraced in Amida's infinite love, nor is there any good in this world which is so perfect and pure as to permit its agent into the Land of Purity without resorting to the Original Vow. We who belong to this world of relativity are always conscious of what we are doing, for we are so constituted and cannot be otherwise. When we do something good, we become conscious of it, and this very consciousness it is that destroys the merit of goodness. The being conscious of something comes out of the idea of selfhood, and there is nothing more effective than the idea of selfhood which will disqualify one as candidate for the Pure Land of Amida. The unqualified acceptance of the *tariki* is what leads to the presence of the infinitely loving one. For this reason, as long as we are creatures of the world conscious of its relative values, we lose the right to be with Amida and his hosts. Good men cease to be good as soon as they become conscious of their goodness and attempt to make something out of it; evildoers have their sins eradicated and become worthy of the Pure Land at the very moment they are illumined by Amida's light: for Amida is a kind of melting pot of good and evil, in which faith alone retains its absolute value. Not being the creator, Amida has no idea to discipline beings. He is the Light of Love shared universally by all beings. However bad they are, Amida knows that it is due to their karma and that this never proves to be a hindrance to their entering into the Pure Land. What he demands of them is faith. This keeping Amida away from responsibilities and relativities of this dualistic world marks out Shin as a unique religious teaching.

2. In Christianity, God requires a mediator to communicate with his creatures and this mediator is sacrificed for the sake of the latter whose sin is too dark to be wiped off by their own efforts. God demands an innocent victim in order to save souls who are not necessarily responsible for their unrighteousness because they are born so. This proceeding does not seem to be quite fair on the part of God, but the Christian experience has demonstrated at least its pragmatic value. In Shin Amida performs in a sense the office of God and also that of Christ. Amida with Amidists is Light *(ābha)* and Life *(āyus)* and Love *(karuṇā)*, and from his Love and Life issue his vows, and it is through these vows that Amida is connected with us. The Vow is mediator, and as it emanates from Amida's Love, it is just as efficient as Christ in its office of mediatorship. One thing we must observe here is that in Christianity concrete images are made use of while in Shin words and phrases, more or less abstract in a sense, are given out to do the work of a mediating agent, as is exemplified in *Namu-amida-butsu.*

3. The Christians like to think that their religion is based on historical facts while Buddhism especially Shin is a metaphysical reconstruction, so to speak, of the ideas and aspirations which generally make up a religion. For this reason,

Christianity to its followers is more solidly and objectively constituted. Here is one of the fundamental differences—indeed the fundamental difference—between Christianity and Shin. Shin in accordance with the general makeup of Buddhism is not dualistically minded, however much it may so appear superficially; moreover it does not take very kindly to the idea that objectivity is more real than subjectivity. Truth is neither subjective nor objective, there is no more reality in what is known as historical fact than in what is considered psychological or metaphysical. In some cases historicity is mere fiction. History takes place in time, and time as much as space depends upon our intellectual reconstruction. Religious faith, however, wants to grasp what is not conditioned by time and space, it wishes to take hold of what is behind historical facts. And this must be Reality transcending the polarization of subject and object. History is karmic, and Shin aspires after the akarmic or that which is not historical.

Amida is above karma, he is not of history, he is akarmic; that is to say, all historical facts, all karmic events have their origin in Amida and return to him, he is the alpha and omega of all things. From him, therefore, are all his vows taking effect in the world of karma where we sentient beings have our temporal and spatial abode. Some may say that Amida is too metaphysical to be an object of religious consciousness which requires a concrete and tangible historical person. To this Shin would answer: As long as we are on the time-plane of relativity, we may distinguish between metaphysical and historical, between abstract ideas and concrete events; but in genuine religious faith once realized, there are no such discriminations to be made, for faith is attained only when there is the going-beyond of a world of contrasts, which is the leaping over the gap of dualism.

4. There is no crucifixion in Shin, which is significant in more ways than one. I presume that the crucified Christ is the symbol of self-sacrifice for the Christians, but at the same time to see the figure of crucifixion on the altar or by the country roadside is not a very pleasant sight, at least to the Buddhists. The sight, to tell the truth, is almost the symbol of cruelty or of inhumanity. The idea of washing sin with the blood of Christ crucified reminds us of the primitive barbarism of victim-offering to the gods. The association of sin and blood is not at all Buddhistic.

I am saved by the blood
Of the Crucified One.

This will never awaken in the Buddhist heart a sacred exalted feeling as in the Christian. The agony of crucifixion, death, and resurrection making up the contents of Christian faith have significance only when the background impregnating old tradition is taken into consideration, and thus background is wholly wanting in Buddhists who have been reared in an atmosphere different not only historically but intellectually and emotionally. Buddhists do not wish to have the idea of self-sacrifice brought before their eyes in such a bloody imagery. It is a Jewish sentiment.

The Buddhist idea of death is rest and peace, and not agony. The Buddha at his Nirvana lies quietly on his bed surrounded by all beings including the birds of the air and the beasts of the field. His horizontal posture is a great contrast to Christ on the cross. The Buddha is again represented as sitting in meditation, symbol of eternal tranquility.

5. The Christian notion of vicarious atonement may be considered corresponding to the Buddhist notion of merit-transference *(pariṇāmana),* but the difference is that somebody in one case is to be sacrificed for the fault of others, while in the other case it is merit accumulated by the Bodhisattva that is desired to be transferred to other beings. As far as the fact of transference is concerned, there is an analogy between the Christian and the Buddhist, but the analogy stops here. In Buddhism, naturally including Shin, the idea is positive and creative in the sense that value produced in one quarter of the universe is made to spread all over it so that the whole creation may advance toward Enlightenment. Strictly speaking, there is no idea of atonement in Buddhism, especially in Shin—which makes indeed the position of Shin unique in the various systems of Mahayana Buddhist philosophy.

Amida, according to the teaching of Shin, has no intention to interfere with the working of karma, for it has to run its course in this world, the debt incurred by one person is to be paid by him and not by another. But the mysterious power of Amida's Name and Vow—which is the mystery of life to be simply accepted as such, all the logical contradictions notwithstanding—lifts the offender from the curse of karma and carries him to the Land of Purity and Happiness, where he attains his supreme enlightenment. While karma is left to itself, what is beyond the reach of karma, which may be termed the akarmic power of Buddha, is working quite unknowingly to the karma-bearer himself. But he begins to realize this fact as soon as faith in Amida is awakened in him. Faith works this miracle in his consciousness. Although he knows that he is subject to the law of karma and may have to go on in spite of himself committing deeds of karma, his inmost consciousness, once his faith is established, tells him that he is bound for Amida's land at the end of his karmic life on this earth. It is by this inmost consciousness in the Shin devotee that the truth of merit-transference *(pariṇāmana)* is demonstrated. In a similar way Christians feel assured of vicarious atonement when their faith is confirmed in Christ. Whatever theological and ethical interpretation may be given to this, the truth or fact, psychologically speaking, remains the same with Christians and Buddhists: it is the experience of a leap from the relative plane of consciousness to the Unconscious.

Crucifixion, death, resurrection, and ascension—these are really the contents of individual religious experience regardless of difference in philosophical reconstruction. Different religions may use different terminology which is the product mainly of intellectual antecedents. To the Shin Buddhists, resurrection and ascension will mean rebirth in the Pure Land and Enlightenment while crucifixion and death will correspond to the death, that is, abandoning of "self-power" *(jiriki).* That the abandoning of self-power is death is a well-known experience with the Shin followers, and it is at this moment that they utter from the depths of their being the *Namu-amida-butsu.* This utterance, given just once, of Amida's Name puts an end to all their sufferings and agonies of the beginningless past and they are born in Amida's Pure Land. Their bodily existence as far as they are conscious of it will continue in the world of karma, but as their faith tells them, they already belong to another world. The Christians may not agree with this form of interpretation, they may like to ascribe all such experiences to Christ himself while their individual human salvation is regarded to come from believing in supernatural events. This is quite natural with the Jewish genius and Jewish tradition. Even when they say "to die in Adam and to live in Christ," I wonder if by this they mean our going through all the spiritual experiences individually and personally of Christ himself, instead of our merely believing in Christ as divine mediator.

6. The Christian relation of man to God is, so to speak, individualistic. By this I mean: Christian salvation consists in saving oneself through God's discriminative favor conferred upon one particular being, and this particular being has no power to extend his favor over his fellow beings for the reason that this power belongs to the giver and not to the recipient; all that the latter can do is to go on preaching, i.e., to talk about his experience, and to let others awaken interest in him. With the Buddhists everything they do is dedicated to the spread of Enlightenment among their fellow beings; in fact, the motive which urges devoted Buddhists to the understanding of the Dharma and to the practice of the Buddhist virtues is said to lead all sentient beings to Enlightenment, and all their self-improvement is to this purpose. Thus it may be said that the Buddhists work for salvation of their fellow beings including themselves whereas the Christians are busy with their self-salvation and that the former are socialistically motivated and the latter individualistically.

Superficially, Shin, like Christianity, aims at self-salvation; the relation of Shin followers to their Amida may support individualism; for they are concerned with themselves only and Amida is supposed to be the only helping agency. But when we examine more closely its teaching, we discover that Shin is after all Buddhistic in its socialistically-mindedness. Its route of merit-transference *(pariṇāmana)* is double and not single. One route is the way to the Pure Land, the steps of all Shin devotees are directed naturally toward Amida and his country; but as soon as they are born there, they come back to this world of karma and work for their fellow beings. This way is known as the "return route." The Pure Land is therefore not the place of self-enjoyment but a kind of railway station where passengers stay for a while but never for any length of time. It will be a great mistake to regard the Pure Land as the permanent house for Shin people. Indeed, if they were to stay there even for a few days, they would be bored to death, for if every desire of theirs is granted as soon as it rises in their hearts, they are thoroughly deprived of the feeling of strife or effort or resistance, and this deprivation would surely result in altogether eradicating the sense of living in the inhabitants of the Land of Happiness—which is the same thing as death. And Shin followers do not decidedly wish to be buried alive in the land where they have coveted to live and enjoy themselves to the fullness of their being. They surely want to be born there, but not to live like corpses. If they are to live at all, they must come back among us once more and work with us and for us. There must be a return route in the Pure Land to this world of karma and relativity. All those therefore who are bound for Amida's country are those who are desirous to be back in the world they used to live in, and here again to experience all resistance that is in the way to Enlightenment for the sake of their fellow beings. The Christians once in Heaven show no desire to come back to their former home, although they may not know what to do up there in company with Christ and the angels. Swedenborg gives a detailed account of heavenly life, but as far as our earthly viewpoint goes, there does not seem to be very much there that will make us envious of a life in Heaven. It is for this reason I believe that some Christians of modern days bring the kingdom of God down on earth, the realization of which being their aim while here.

7. Here we have to dwell for a while upon the distinction between salvation and enlightenment, for what Shin followers desire is after all enlightenment and not salvation. Enlightenment is the objective of the Buddhist life irrespective of schools and creeds, and in this Shin with all its Bhakti formulas is no exception. In this it is Buddhistic as much as Zen or Tendai (C. Tiantai). I have sometimes used the word salvation in connection with Shin faith, but, to be exact, it is not at all proper to designate Shin experience as salvation in the Christian fashion.

True Christians aim at salvation and not at enlightenment. To save one's soul from damnation is what constitutes Christian piety. But Buddhists desire to be enlightened, to get rid of ignorance, which will emancipate them from the bondage of birth-and-death. Shin however seems to want to be saved from karma which corresponds to sin in the Christian sense; but in truth Shin followers know the impossibility, as long as they are living in this world of relativity, of escaping karma; however much they endeavor with all their intellectual and ethical strength which they have in them, there is no way for them to be emancipated from the inevitability of karma. For this reason, they submit themselves to it, and seek another method of transcending it whereby they can go back to their original freedom: the method consists in throwing themselves before the Buddha of Infinite Light and Eternal Life, who is in charge of a Land of Purity and Happiness well provided with all the necessary conditions for attaining Supreme Enlightenment. Thus the first objective of the Shin followers is to be born there, which means instantly to realize enlightenment. Indeed, being born in Amida's Land means no more than attaining enlightenment—the two terms are entirely synonymous. The ultimate end of the

Shin life is enlightenment and not salvation. This world of karma and relativity does not furnish them with an environment favorable for the realization of supreme wisdom, and it was for this reason that Amida established a special Buddha-land for the sake of his devotees where things are so conditioned as to make them instantly come to the realization. And when this realization comes to them, they hurry back to this world and work for their fellow beings. Even Shin people, though unknowingly, are living for the enhancing of enlightenment in the world at large. With all their consciousness of sin or a karma-bound life, they are striving after enlightenment and not for individualistic salvation.

Popularly, Shin is understood to teach the doctrine of "Nembutsu *Ōjō*," literally "to go and be born by thinking of the Buddha." By this it is meant that when one thinks of the Buddha, i.e., Amida, with singleness of heart and in all earnestness, one after death will go to and be reborn in the Pure Land. In practice, "thinking of Amida" is pronouncing his Name one or more times. According to Shin, once is enough if it comes from absolute faith in Amida, but Jōdo tells us to say *Namu-amida-butsu* repeatedly; and here lies one of the essential differences between Shin and Jōdo, to which reference has already been made. At any rate, the "Nembutsu *Ōjō*" sums up to popular minds the teaching of both Jōdo and Shin. But a closer analysis shows that merely being born in the Pure Land is not what is really promised in the Sutras. As was stated before, rebirth is advised because of the Pure Land being the most favorably conditioned environment for enlightenment which is the aim of the Buddhist life, both of *tariki* and of *jiriki*. The practical outcome of this is the identification of rebirth and enlightenment, and being assured of rebirth means the foretasting of enlightenment. It is for Buddhas alone, the most highly perfected beings, to enjoy Supreme Enlightenment, while what is granted to us, ordinary mortals, is to experience something of enlightenment and thereby to orient ourselves—this orientation is the foretasting and the assurance of rebirth.

From the general point of view of Buddhism, however, what is most essential in the life of every Buddhist is to come back to this world of karma and work for others like Śākyamuni himself in the enhancement and realization and prevalence of Enlightenment. Although the "Nembutsu *Ōjō*" appears to be the sole concern for Shin followers, we must not forget that Shin is also one of the Buddhist schools however superficially its Bhakti construction may suggest its alien associations.

8. "Where is the Pure Land?" we may ask. This is not at all a difficult question when we know what Amida is and when our faith is established in him; but to the outsider who has never delved into the mystery of Shin it presents insurmountable difficulties and contradictions. In fact, the question of the Pure Land is the fundamental problem of religion and wherever the objective validity of faith is inquired into the question inevitably comes up. The Shin doctors have exhausted their philosophical ingenuity upon its solution. As the Christian conception of Heaven is

not so definitely and concretely described as the Buddhist Pure Land is, the Christians do not seem to be so troubled with the whereabouts of Heaven.

According to Shin, the Pure Land is located in the West. Is this a symbolical expression? Or is it to be taken literally, i.e., spatially? Either way, there is no satisfactory reasonable solution of it. The orthodox Shin interpretation is spatial and Shin followers are persuaded to believe in the realistic existence of the Pure Land somewhere away in the West, at the distance of an infinite number of miles from this earthly habitation of ours. Those who try to give different constructions to the statements in the Sutras are denounced as heretical. The scientifically inclined followers of Shin are sometimes too honest and simpleminded and take the orthodox teaching too logically, condemning it as altogether unscientific. But the truth is that the conception of Amida and his Pure Land is in one way too complicated and in another way altogether too simple. Too simple because when the relative plane of consciousness is abruptly transcended, an unexpected view opens before the devotee and all that has been annoying him emotionally as well as intellectually vanishes away—nothing can be simpler than this. But the problem becomes too complicated when it is approached from the logical and metaphysical point of view because it leads to many another problem involving the whole field of the philosophy of religion—which is the task to be undertaken by the specialists only. For the plain average man in the street the most practical and ready approach to Shin will be to take everything told him by its teachers as gospel truth, and by blindly following it one day he will awake to its truth and understand it in his own light. The will to believe will naturally take him where he ought to be. It is therefore said that "Do not ask questions, for their solution is in you and not from the mouth of the teachers." So with the most essential question of Shin including that of the Pure Land, one's personal experience is the sole key to its solution. Once a Shin devotee called Shōma was asked whether or not Amida is capable of helping you out of karma, Shōma immediately answered, "You are not helped by him!" Being solely a matter of intimate personal experience, a discussion of the matter here is an idle business, one may declare. The Christians are no doubt similarly disposed toward questions such as are raised here. To those who have really got into the experience of Shin or in fact of any genuine religious faith, all those discussions are much ado about nothing,

9. One of the most remarkable features of the teaching of Shin or Jōdo generally concerns Amida's Name and Vow. Christianity has nothing corresponding to it.

When Amida was to attain Enlightenment, he vowed that his Name should be heard throughout the universe so that those who hear it may come to him. Thus his Name came to possess the mysterious power of awakening the soul of his devotee in the faith of Shin. The significance of a name is a historical fact: when you know the name of an evil spirit you can call him up and bring him to your service in any way you like. When an initiation ceremony takes place among some primitive people, the first thing for the initiate to be informed of is the name of the god to whom they are to offer their prayers. To know the name of an object is the same as naming an object and bringing it to existence. Naming in a sense is creating, and creation is the most wonderful event and a mysterious power. When Amida willed to have his Name fill the world, his idea was to rouse his own image in the heart of every being. When this individual Amida devotee responds to the call of Amida who is the Buddha of Infinite Light and Eternal Life, his faith is confirmed and the assurance of rebirth in Amida's land is attained. This is deep calling unto deep. Although the orthodox Shin followers do not like this way of expressing the idea, the truth when it is logically presented ultimately comes to it. Amida's Name is heard because the devotee has something to respond to it, and this something must be of the same order as Amida himself, otherwise there cannot be any response in any sense. The Name goes out from Amida riding upon the ether-waves to the farthest end of the universe, and every substance there so organized as to feel the vibrations echoes the sound back to the originating source; the communication thus established is no other than faith and he is said to have entered upon the order of steadfastness. Faith which is the assurance of rebirth comes into being only when this echoing is mutual between Amida and his devotee. To be more exact, the pronouncing of the Name is possible only when the devotee's own inner Amida so to speak is awakened from the darkness of Ignorance, or, we might again say, released from the bondage of karma. When the latter event does not take place, the pronouncing of the Name is mere shadow with nothing really backing it; there is no correspondence between reality and expression, between content and form, between heart and lips. When Shin states that the pronouncing for once is enough, it refers to this fact, while the reason why Jōdo insists on repetition is based upon what may be termed the psychological law of imitation and of reproduction. By this I mean that when a certain motion is imitated say even for a few times the very fact of repetition sets up the whole mechanism corresponding to it. When this is repeated for a sufficient number of times it ceases to be mechanical and finally evokes the original impulse, and then the mind will come to consider it its own spontaneous creation. The repeated pronouncing of Amida's Name advised by Jōdo, however mechanical and contentless in the beginning, so gradually sets up a process of rearrangement in the consciousness of the practicer who becomes thus unwittingly conscious of the presence of Amida in his own inner being. When this moment is realized he utters for the first time from the depths of his soul the Name of Amida as the power lifting him from the burden of karma. Philosophically, then, Jōdo and Shin may be said to be speaking about the same psychological truth; but from the point of view of practical method of teaching, Shin tends to emphasize the critical moment itself whereas Jōdo is more for the process of education.

When both Jōdo and Shin talk so much about the nembutsu which means "thinking of the Buddha," how is it that they refer to the Name *(myōgō)* at all?

Strictly speaking, thinking and reciting or pronouncing are not the same; you think of an object but may not pronounce its name, while a name may be thought of or pronounced independently by itself, apart from the object to which it is attached. How did the pronouncing of the Name come to such a prominence as at present it does in the Jōdo teaching?

In the beginning of the history of the Pure Land school, the nembutsu was practiced in its literal sense, the followers thought of the Buddha in their minds, formed his images before their eyes, and perhaps recounted all the excellent virtues belonging to him. This is thinking of the Buddha. It demands a great deal of mental concentration, it is quite an exacting exercise, and requires a long arduous training in meditation before one can absorb even a small portion of the Buddha's excellent personality into his own spiritual system. Most of us will soon grow tired of the exercise and may discontinue it though unwillingly. There must be some easier method to educate ourselves to be good Buddhists.

The object of the *nembutsu*, "thinking of the Buddha," was to see him face to face so that the devotee could advance in his spiritual life and finally even come to the attainment of Buddhahood. But as the exercise involves so much application of the psychological energy, it cannot be practiced by every Buddhist however devotionally minded he may be. He must be given a new method much easier than the "thinking of the Buddha," and this was found in repeatedly pronouncing the Name of the Buddha.

A name as was stated before contains in it the mysterious power to recall everything associated with it, i.e., the object with all its details. It is true that a name can be detached from its object and itself treated as an object. But when a devotional mind pronounces the name of its object of worship, the name will inevitably bring up in it things connected with the Buddha. The devotee while pronouncing the Name may not necessarily meditate on the Buddha with any degree of mental concentration, but the recitation at least directs his attention toward Buddha with all that follows from it. Thus when the Buddha's Name is repeatedly, steadily, single-heartedly pronounced, it is not an impossible event that he appear before the devotee or in his mind with all his characteristic marks, major and minor, although these may not be in full detail. The *shōmyō,* "pronouncing the name," thus came to help the *nembutsu,* "thinking of the Buddha."

Instead of trying to invoke the Buddha-images in silent meditation, the devotee will now recite his name and make psychology do the rest of the work. It goes without saying that he is not merely to practice the *shōmyō,* but he must make it go along with the *nembutsu,* the thought of the Buddha. The *shōmyō* is a great aid to the *nembutsu* exercise. While the *shōmyō* is not the *nembutsu*, the former, as time went on, came to be identified with the latter, and nowadays when we talk of the nembutsu, it may not mean "thinking of the Buddha" or "invoking the Buddha-image," but in fact the *shōmyō,* "pronouncing or reciting the name," unless a reservation is made. It may be said that the mystery of the name has usurped the original office of memory.

Historically, the *shōmyō* practice is related to the kōan exercise in Zen Buddhism. Of this the reader is asked to consult my *Zen Essays (Series II),* pp. 115ff. The only point on which I should like to make a remark here is the shifting of psychological attitudes. In the *nembutsu* proper, the thought was essentially directed toward the Buddha which was quite the natural thing, but in the *shōmyō* identified with the nembutsu the attention, not necessarily deliberate and fully intentional, is more concentrated on the mechanism of repetition. Naturally, the devotee's mind is on the Buddha as his Name is pronounced, but not, as in the case of the *nembutsu,* on reproducing the Buddha-image before his mental eye. While there is every opportunity of the *shōmyō* turning into mere repetition of the sounds *na-mu-a-mi-da-bu-tsu,* the psychological tone of consciousness created by a monotonous recitation will one day, when time matures, prepare the way for the devotee to the awakening of faith in Amida. The Jōdo's advice to say the nembutsu aims in all probability at creating this psychological crisis, although I am inclined to think that the Jōdo leaders may have some subtle philosophy to interpret the meaning of the Nembutsu *Shōmyō.*

In this connection it will be of great interest to recall what Hōnen, the founder of the Jōdo school of Buddhism in Japan, has to say about the significance of the *shōmyō,* the pronouncing of the Name of Amida, in the cultivation of the Jōdo faith. He advises in the paper known as *Nimai kishōmon,* "the double-sheet document":

> Generally stated, to trust in Buddha does not mean to think of him mentally, it is simply to pronounce his Name, which is to trust in his Original Vow. Let not those followers of the nembutsu stop at merely thinking of him, let them audibly pronounce his Name. For besides this pronouncing the Name there is no right cause that will definitely determine our rebirth; besides this pronouncing the Name there is no right act that will definitely determine our rebirth; besides this pronouncing the Name there is no right karma that will definitely determine our rebirth; besides this pronouncing the Name there is no thinking of Buddha that will definitely determine our rebirth; besides this pronouncing the Name there is no transcendental wisdom that will definitely determine our rebirth. Further, there is no threefold mind apart from the pronouncing of the Name; there is no fourfold discipline apart from the pronouncing of the Name; nor is there the fivefold recollection possible without the pronouncing of the Name. Amida's Original Vow is no other than the pronouncing of his Name; the mind that loathes the defiled land lies at the bottom of this pronouncing the Name.

10. We now come to the consideration of the Original Vow made by Amida, relying upon which all the followers of Jōdo believe in being reborn in the Land of Purity and Happiness. This idea is unique to this school of Buddhism. It is true

that every Bodhisattva in the beginning of his spiritual career makes a number of vows and bends all his efforts to their fulfillment. Amida's case is no exception, but so far Amidism is the only religion that developing out of this idea has most successfully maintained its moral and spiritual vitality.

The Original Vow (*hongan* in Japanese and *pūrva-praṇidhāna* in Sanskrit) is the expression of Amida's Will or Karuna ("love" or "compassion") which he cherishes over all beings. Karuna constitutes with Prajna the personality of every Buddha; with Prajna, "transcendental wisdom," he contemplates the world and perceives that it is of Suchness; while by Karuna he comes out of his meditation to live among us, and this coming out is the utterance of his vows known as Original Vow.

"Original," i.e., *pūrva,* literally means "before" spatially and temporarily, and "vow," i.e., *praṇidhāna* = *pra* + *nidhāna* means originally or rather ordinarily "application," "attention," "intense energy," and in Buddhism "wish," "will," or "prayer." So the Original Vow is Amida's Willpower, in this case Amida's compassionate heart, which is with him from the beginningless past; in other words, the Original Vow is Amida himself expressed in human terms. As long as Amida abides in his meditation, as long as he is with himself as Prajna, he is not at all accessible to beings or to the plane of relativity. But he is also the embodiment of Karuna by which he feels for beings other than himself and knows how to express this feeling in terms of the Original Vow. In the Original Vow, therefore, Amida communicates with us karma-bound beings and we in turn come thereby in touch with Amida. Relatively speaking, Amida's Original Vow awakens in us what corresponds to it but what lies in us quite latently. To express the idea more intelligently, for general Buddhists Amida's will to help us out of the ocean of birth-and-death is no other than our faith in Amida. In Amida faith is the will to help and in us this will becomes faith; his will and our faith are consubstantial as it were, hence a perfect correspondence between the two terms of Reality. The mysterious power abiding in the Original Vow is the mystery of Amida himself who, in the terminology of Shin, is Infinite Light and Eternal Life. In Christianity God's will or love of humanity, I may say, is expressed in the crucifixion of his only son, i.e., as a concrete event in the history of karma-bound beings; whereas in Shin Buddhism Amida's will takes the form of intense determination and its solemn declaration. The latter may seem insipid, inane, and evaporating compared to the Christian realism. But in point of fact the Shin together with its parental Jōdo has been the most irresistingly inspiring power in the history of Far Eastern Buddhism, and this power has been exercised without ever shedding blood, without committing cruelties, without persecuting heresies.

VI

There is another and last consideration I would like to make about Shin, which concerns the practical life of its followers. Strictly speaking, Shin is not to have any professional priest class corresponding to those we see in the other schools of Buddhism. The Buddhist priests are generally supposed to practice asceticism, leading a life quite dissimilar to that of the laity. They live in specially constructed buildings and under regulations specially meant for the enhancement of their moral and spiritual life, they are devoted to the study of the Buddhist texts, they read and recite the Sutras, they sing the hymns, they conduct various ceremonies on various occasions, they give sermons, they perform burial rites, they are invited out to laymen's houses to hold the customary religious services for the commemoration of the dead, in short they lead a life apart from that of the secular people. The idea is that the priestly classes are those Buddhists who are exclusively devoting themselves to the study and propagation of the religion they profess. As they are specialists, their daily lives are supposed to be exemplary and models for the laity. They have their reason of existence when the rest of the world is engaged in wars of greed, anger, and folly; it is so refreshing and inspiring to see a group of souls given up to the cultivation of the various Buddhist virtues. In spite of the economic questions involved in their way of living, it does good to society in more ways than its members realize, and they are not to be treated with indifference, much less with disdain or antagonism.

However this may be, from the purely theoretical point of view, Shin is the religion of the laity and for the laity. No special form of discipline is demanded of its followers; no distinct curriculum of study is prescribed; no accumulation of merit just for the sake of rebirth is required; and by just having faith in Amida as the author of the Original Vow the devotee is assured of his entrance into the Pure Land after his departure from earthly life. Such a simple and easy religion—this is what is claimed for Shin uniformly by its founder and his successors—does not necessitate the establishment of any institution exclusively devoted to the maintenance and propagation of its teaching. But in point of fact we are all historical beings, we cannot live away from our past, indeed the present has no meaning whatever without its past. So, Shin too could not escape its history, its environment, i.e., its karma; its present status is that of a hybrid between the old schools of Buddhism and a pure religion of the laity. Shin teaches *tariki* but practices half *jiriki*—which is indeed from the practical point of view wholly inevitable.

As all is the work of the "other-power" and to be left to the functioning of Amida's Original Vow and the only thing needed on this side is to have "a steadfast faith," the Shin followers do not practice asceticism as the means of courting Amida's favor. What distinguishes the *jiriki* school from the *tariki* is essentially their life of asceticism, and when this is no more demanded of the Buddhists, all the differentia marking out the priesthood disappear. And this was exactly the teaching and life of Shinran Shōnin, the founder of Shin Buddhism. In fact, the secularizing movement has been going on ever since the time of the Buddha; the rise of the Mahayana really opens the inchoate stage of this movement. The secularization of the Sangha institution or rather its abolishment means doing away with the Arhatship ideal of Buddhism, which in turn means the democratization of the whole system of Buddhism. And, we can say, this movement of secularization and democratization has culminated in the evolution of Shin Buddhism in Japan. I add that if another about-face is needed of Japanese Buddhists, it would be to make a backward movement without losing all the experiences which were gained during its long history in India, China, and Japan.

By a backward movement I mean that the Buddhists must go back to their primitive ideals: let them practice asceticism, let them devote themselves to a life of unselfishness in all its possible forms; let them aspire to carry out the Bodhisattva ideals *(bodhisattva-caryā);* let them form a colony of Arhats to demonstrate the possibility of a society free from greed, anger, and folly; let them see to it that all our sciences and philosophies can be utilized for the welfare of all mankind, and that all our economic systems are not to be established on the basis of materialism but on the principle of interpenetration as expounded in the Buddhist Sutras.

VII

There are some more points to consider as regards the teaching of Shin Buddhism than these already dwelt upon, which I will now try to elucidate briefly in the following pages.[17] The points concern (1) Merit-transference, (2) Karma and Love, (3) The Mystery of the Name, (4) Prayer, and (5) This World and the Pure Land.

These subjects are in fact interrelated, and when one of them is taken up for a thorough treatment, it will naturally cover the other fields. For instance, "the mystery of the Name" is the great religious problem on which all the other mysteries may be said to hang. The gist of the Shin teaching is to hear Amida's Name or his call. When this is experienced, it is said that a new lotus blooms in the Pure Land to afford a seat for the devotee.

One may ask here: What is meant by Amida's Name? How is it possible for us to hear Amida's Name? What relationship has the Name with our rebirth in the Pure Land? These and other cognate questions that may come up in connection with the Name will be understood when the Name itself is heard. No mere conceptual interpretation will suffice, probably it will involve the reader in more difficulties. But I have to do it anyway, for everything we experience is to be brought out in the field of thought.

The Name is the bridge spanning the chasm between Amida and us sentient beings. The chasm is ordinarily impassable, we have no means to cross it by our own efforts, moral or intellectual. We just stand before it helplessly, we even do not know what it is that lies before us, it is a namelessness. The trouble is that something within urges us to plunge ourselves into it; in other words, we cannot have peace of mind until we do. But this plunging or the leaping over we cannot somehow do.

If this urge is an absolute necessity, there is no choice, we just plunge and let fate take care of itself. It is in the nature of the urge, however, that we hesitate no matter how pressing it is. Here we face a dilemma, and we have to make a final decision. A mystery takes place: a call is heard from nowhere, which we later intellectually designate as "the other end," or the Beyond, or Amida. The call is no other than Amida's Name. To say that the call is heard is to say that Amida's Name is uttered. Because it is not we that utter the Name but Amida himself. Amida uttering his own Name is interpreted, when brought down onto the plane of the human understanding, as a call reaching us from the other side of the stream of birth-and-death.

This is an *acintya,* an unthinkability, a mystery beyond ratiocination—this bridging the impassable chasm which gapes between a realm of relativity and the absolute.

When this bridge is spanned from the other end, all forms of logical impossibility become facts of experience. Questions are no more asked, and we feel quite at home with the world as well as with ourselves.

1. The Shin idea of "merit-transference" *(pariṇāmana)*[18] is in direct opposition to the general Mahayana idea of it. In the latter merit created anywhere by any being may be turned over to any other being desired or toward the enhancement and prevalence of Enlightenment in the whole world. A Bodhisattva practices asceticism not only for the perfection of his own moral and spiritual qualities but for the increase of such qualities among his fellow beings. Or he suffers pains in order to save others from them and at the same time to make them aspire for Enlightenment. Merit-transference has thus also the nature of vicarious atonement. The idea is based on the principle of interpenetration as advocated by the philosophy of Kegon *(Avataṃsaka),* which is to say that one grain of sand holds in it the entire cosmos not only as a totality but individually.[19] With the Shin, however, the source of this activity lies with Amida, and from Amida alone as the center starts the spiritual vibration known as merit-transference. This is the fulfillment of his Original Vow. Reference has already been made [above (JCD)] to one famous passage in the *Sutra of Eternal Life*, the regular reading of which is revised by Shinran Shōnin. According to him, the transference starts from Amida to all beings and not from all beings to the realization of enlightenment.

When this merit-transference is made to originate exclusively from Amida, we see where the idea of *tariki* comes from. We can almost say that the entire structure of the Shin teaching is dependent upon Shinran's interpretation of the principle of merit-transference.

The doctrine of merit-transference is really one of the significant features of Mahayana Buddhism and its development marks the start of a new era in the history of Buddhist philosophy. Before this, the accumulation of merit or the practice of good deeds was something which exclusively concerned the individual himself;

the doer was responsible for all that he did, good or bad; as long as he was satisfied with the karma of his work, to enjoy happiness or to suffer disaster was his own business and nothing further was to be said or done about it. But now we have come to deal with a different state of affairs. We are no more by ourselves alone, each is not living just for himself, everything is so intimately related that anything done by anybody is sure to affect others in one way or another. The individualistic Hinayana has now become the communistic Mahayana. This was really a great turning point in the evolution of Buddhist thought. When it was joined to the Original Vow of Amida, Shin naturally made Amida the source of all the activities belonging to merit-transference. Here we find ourselves confronted with still another advance or movement effected in the history of Mahayana Buddhism. Instead of a mutual transference of merit we have now all such activities issuing from one source which is according to Shin Amida Buddha. Individual beings cease to send out transference-waves from themselves, they are no more self-creative, they are now made to be passive recipients owing all that they are or do to the "other-power" who is a being of great wisdom *(prajñā)* and love *(karuṇā).*

This movement on the part of the founder of the Shin school of Buddhism was indeed a leap—technically known as "crosswise leap." Instead of making one continuous progress ahead which has no end or rather which is a never-ending course, he abruptly turns toward Amida and throws himself up into his arms. The Mahayana way of thinking hitherto pursued by the *jiriki* doctors is here completely reversed.

2. In one sense the Shin conception of the religious life may be said to be dualistic, probably all religions belonging to the Bhakti group are dualistic, and it is on account of this that we generally encounter terms of paradoxical relationship in the course of religious philosophy. Shin tries to reconcile them in accordance with the Mahayana system of thought but the old traces are recognizable.

Amida always stands against karma which works independent of him. Karma is the world of all sentient beings, and their object of following Shin is to understand this world, i.e., to transcend karma and break through the bondage of birth and death. What Amida does for them is to embrace them in his love and take them to his Land of Purity and Happiness. The karma world is left to itself, as long as beings are still here, they allow themselves to be ruled by karma, for there is no other way of living. Death however puts an end to this relativity-bound existence, and one is free to go to Amida's world. This opposition between karma and akarma which is Amida runs through the system of Shin thought.

This form of dualism is also observable in the Christian notion of sinner and savior. But what differentiates Shin from Christianity in this respect is that Amida is not the dispenser of reward or punishment, he does not interfere with the working of karma in any particular case; but in Christianity God chastises sinners and rewards those who behave. Amida lets karma alone, with him there is no rewarding, no punishing. If a sinner feels he is punished, it is his own construing of the event; as far as Amida is concerned, he is all love, there is no thought in him of punishing anybody, such discriminative judgments are not in him. He is like the sun in this respect shining on the unjust as well as the just. A sinner comes to the Pure Land with all his sins, or rather, he leaves them in the world where they belong, and when he arrives in the Pure Land he is in his nakedness, with no sinful raiments about him. Karma does not pursue him up to the Pure Land. Amida's dealing with karma is in its generality. He is akarma itself and has nothing pertaining to the other term.

The idea of punishment belongs to human society which is governed by hate and love, and which therefore cannot transcend human psychology. To conceive God as judge and executor is Jewish-Christian and not Buddhist and brings him down to the world of karma. While the Shin conception of Amida is quite personal, he is above human frailties, his light has no shadow, his love is absolute, and whoever listens to his call ready to run into his extended arms will be embraced by him regardless of the devotee's past life, i.e., of his karma. Karma naturally follows its own course, but the devotee no more feels its burden however heavy and ordinarily unbearable and often unreasonable it may be. Karma is not wiped out, it is there all the time, but it has lost its effect on him; as far as he himself is concerned, karma is altogether vanished, his intellectualism may have to recognize the objectivity of karma, but his spiritual life is filled with the love of Amida. So says Shinran in the *Tannishō:* "While my body is in the world of karma my mind is in the Pure Land of Amida." Again, "When Amida's Name is heard, all the evil karma of so many kalpas is wiped off." This does not mean that karma as a sequence of objective events is eradicated, but that its effect on the devotee is nil—which amounts to the same thing as the non-existence of karma or the cancellation of sin. He is living in the world as if not in it. Insofar as the intellect divides and does not integrate, a form of dualism always goes on in the philosophy of religion. It is only in the religious life itself that all the paradoxes raised by the intellect vanish without giving the devotee any inconvenience. Hence Shin's advice: Give up your "self-power," morally and intellectually, accept Amida's call without questioning, and live a life of absolute passivity, i.e., of "other-power." A life of absolute passivity, a life entirely given up to "other-power" is a life of the love of God—of the love wherewith God loves himself.

3. The life of *tariki* is a life of passivity, when *jiriki* is all abandoned, Amida occupies the devotee's heart; while his relative existence chained to birth and death has to suffer karma, he lives a life of Amida as he is now possessed by Amida. This living a life of Amida is known as the responding to his call, the hearing of his voice, the taking refuge in his Name. The mysterious power of the Name which is the foundation of the Pure Land teaching comes from living this kind of life. The Name is, in other words, the voice of Amida; when he vowed that his Name should reach the ten quarters of the world so that all beings would hear it, it meant that all

beings, if they quietly but intently listened by purging out everything from their minds, could receive the voice of Amida. This purging must be complete, otherwise the voice cannot be heard. Shin therefore insists on the purging and listening, perhaps more positively on the listening, because the listening is effected only when the purging is complete. Shin is always more positive than negative. "Listen and believe!" This is Shin's constant advice given to its followers. No learning is needed, no logical acuity, no accumulation of knowledge, secular or spiritual, is recommended, but just listening with a mind emptied of self-power will put it in tune with the voice of Amida, and with it a new life begins.

4. The Shin followers are generally bitterly against offering prayers for any special favors, thinking that it is the direct violation of the principle of *tariki;* for as long as Amida takes care of you and karma has its own course to follow, what use is there to make petitions to any higher powers? Not exactly fatalistic, but more in a scientific spirit, they are joyous sufferers of all kinds of events of this world. This may be in general accord with the Mahayana attitude toward prayers.

When Myōe Shōnin (1163–1232) was asked by someone to offer a special prayer to the Buddha for his own benefit, the Shōnin said:

> I pray every morning and every evening for the sake of all beings and I am sure you are also included among them as one of sentient beings. There is no special need to offer a prayer for one single particular person. If your wish were something to be granted in the general scheme of things it would most assuredly be granted; but if not, even with the power of the Buddha, nothing could be done for you.

The Shin people are consistent as far as their conception of Amida is concerned in rejecting individual favoritism, so to speak. But they often forget that there are other kinds of prayer besides mere asking for a favor or an intercession. When, for instance, prayer is the utterance of the suffering soul to emancipate itself from the bondage of karma or to be helped out of being hopelessly drowned in the ocean of its own sin, it is really of religious significance and in full accord with the spirit of the Shin teaching.

Shin makes a sharp distinction between karma and akarma, a world of defilement and the Land of Purity, sinful beings and the Buddha of Infinite Light and Eternal Life. This dualism, as I stated before, runs through the teachings of Shin, making up indeed the chief one of its characteristic features. It therefore insists that its followers should realize the fact to its fullest extent that this is an evil world and they have nothing in their being but evil, actual and potential, and for this reason and solely for this reason that they are to give themselves up to the loving help of Amida and to be reborn in his Land of Purity where they become thoroughly purged of their evils and defilements and are made fit for final enlightenment. This is really the principle by which all the schools of Jōdo are made possible, and without which Amida with his Land of Purity is of no avail. Amida and his

Land belong to the realm of pure consciousness whereas sentient beings with their evil karma are inevitably of the world of sense-experiences. These two worlds, Amida and sentient beings, are diametrically opposed. To enter into the one, the other is to be abandoned unconditionally, for there is no halfway, you cannot have one leg in the one and the other in the other, except by means of prayer, which, translated into Jōdo terminology, is to realize the sinfulness of the karmic life. This realization is the moment of absolute faith secured in Amida. The reason why Shin puts great stress on the sinful life of relative beings is to make them thus turn toward Amida and his Land.

Whatever the Shin followers may say, prayer to my mind corresponds to their "white road" which crosses the river of birth and death or of fire and water. Driven by the wild beasts and highway robbers who are found inhabiting everywhere in this world of defilement, sinners come to the shore and are about to be drowned in the waves of fire and water; they are desperate, they are completely at a loss what to do; if they go back they are sure to be devoured by the beasts, and proceed they cannot, for the waves are too high to ford; they have not yet descried the narrow white road which spans the stream; but finally they come to detect it which however does not seem for them secure enough to cross. Then for the first time they hear the voice of the Buddha standing on the other shore and calling them to come to him without cherishing a doubt as to the security of the road which leads to him. With a bound they cross, and they are safely taken up in the arms of Amida. This hearing or the recognizing of Amida's voice at the moment of despair is, on the part of the sinner, prayer, that is to say, the utterance of *Namu-amida-butsu*. By this Shin followers effect a successful bridging of the world of karma-experience and the Land of Purity. They are not yet actually in Amida's Land for they are still in this world, but, as Shinran declares, they are in their minds walking about in the Pure Land.

5. The interrelationship of the karma world of sense-experiences and of Amida's transcendental world of values is very difficult to explain logically, and it has been a subject of heated discussion of the Jōdo teaching inclusive of Shin. The Pure Land is said to be so many hundreds of thousands of *koṭis* of lands in the West, which however has never been visited by inhabitants of this world, has never been an object of experience, and can never be made accessible to our sense-experiences. And yet what a power of allurement the idea has had on all the followers of the Jōdo! An intellectually and empirically impossible thing has an absolute value irresistibly to turn our minds toward it. This cannot be laid aside as an utter absurdity. Somehow Amida's shadow must be hovering about us.

To follow the Shin way of thinking, is it not after all an illogical attitude on our part to take the sense-world as the starting point of all our ratiocination and to build up our intellectual structure of reality on it? Would it not rather be more logical and sure of results if we try to interpret this world as experienced by our senses by the aid of ideas growing out of our inmost perceptions? As far as certainty and demanding acceptance are concerned, these inner perceptions are just as persuasive and compelling as sense-perceptions; indeed the former are more so than the latter in the sense that the inner experiences have a controlling power over the empirical world. In other words, the world of karma loses its baneful effects as Amida's Land of Purity is envisaged. Instead of Amida being defined in terms of the sense-world, he fills the latter with his Vow and makes it shine in his own Light. This is known by Shin followers as Amida illumining the world with his infinite light. The individual devotees vanish and become parts of "adornment" *(vyūha)* as set up by Amida. Have this order reversed: instead of Amida interpreting our lives, we try to paint Amida in our own worldly light and Amida is never taken hold of, he is lost in the multiplicities of things, he ceases to shine over us and our lives become meaningless. This is the reason why when some Shin philosophers attempt an empirical description of Amida and his Land, they invariably flounder. As long as they proceed from experiences of this world, the so-called doctrine of localization falls flat and fails to lure the more really religious-minded people.

It is for this reason that Shinran explains this world of relative values to be altogether a falsehood and there is nothing real in it to be trusted.

5

Selections from Japanese Spirituality

This collection of excerpts, translated and updated by Norman Waddell (NW), is from Suzuki's book *Nihon teki reisei* (Japanese Spirituality). The book is a highly speculative, conceptual work dealing with the nature of religious awareness—specifically, what Suzuki proposes as its highest and most sophisticated expression, which he calls *reisei,* translated here as "spirituality." The ideas in this text are rather abstruse and difficult to understand, both in their Japanese original and in translation. Suzuki first propounds his concept of *reisei* and then attempts to explain it through a wide variety of examples, which he explicates in a somewhat subjective way. He makes sweeping claims here and there that other scholars may or may not agree with. *Reisei,* according to Suzuki, is found in its truest form in the Zen and Pure Land traditions of Japan. Though Suzuki is best known for championing Zen, this work surprisingly dwells more on Pure Land Buddhism as a paradigm for *reisei,* specifically on Shinran (1173–1262) and the Shin teachings. These excerpts thus exemplify both the theoretical meanings that Suzuki read into Pure Land Buddhism and the distinctive way he interpreted Shinran and Shin Buddhism apart from mainstream sectarian dogmatics.

Suzuki defines *reisei* as a spiritual outlook, awareness, or realization in which the contradictory aspects of the world—between the material and the spiritual, the self and the other, the worldly and the other-worldly, the unenlightened and the Buddha, and Samsara and Nirvana—are reconciled without obliterating their differences. He construes *reisei* to be a nondualistic awareness that simultaneously recognizes the dualisms of the world. In that sense, it is a mindset that defies rational thought. Expanding on *reisei,* Suzuki proposes a corollary known as "the logic of simultaneous identification and differentiation," the so-called *sokuhi no ronri* theory. It indicates a mode of thought in which things are considered both the same and different from one another. When Suzuki first propounded these ideas, he perhaps thought that *reisei* would be his great contribution to Japanese Buddhist philosophy. But over time *sokuhi no ronri* has had more prominence and staying power. Suzuki argues that *reisei,* the nondualistic consciousness of the world's dualities, is the defining characteristic of both Zen enlightenment and Shin Buddhist faith.

Reisei is an extremely rare word in Japanese, so it is surprising that Suzuki selected it to express his ideas instead of the more conventional term *seishin,* meaning spirit. But by the time Suzuki published this book, Japan had entered the darkest days of World War II, and the word *seishin* was strongly associated with a nationalistic ideology emphasizing the Japanese spirit, fueling a sense of cultural chauvinism toward other countries. In this politically charged environment, Suzuki's idea of *Nihon teki reisei* (Japanese spirituality) was no doubt conflated in the minds of most ordinary readers with this nationalistic discourse. After the war, though, Suzuki claimed in a new introduction to this work that he wrote it as a muted critique of the wartime portrayal of the Japanese spirit. What is ambiguous in the book, however, is whether Suzuki ties the ideal of *reisei* exclusively to Japanese consciousness. Some passages indicate that every country and culture has a *reisei* inherent in it. But other passages suggest that the particular *reisei* Suzuki extols as the highest is distinctly Japanese or arises out of a Japanese mentality. Whatever the case, it is fair to say that Japan's spiritual evolution and consciousness are at the heart of Suzuki's exposition here.

Suzuki's book comes across as a sophisticated intellectual exercise, but he in no way treats intellectualism as a spiritual expression. Rather, he considers *reisei* to be grounded in something less cerebral and more elemental to human beings. Specifically, he identifies one's connection to the earth—tilling it, living off of it, interacting with it, adapting to its cycles—as the source and inspiration of *reisei.* The farther people are from the earth, the less spiritual they become. For that reason Suzuki's feels that the peasants and samurai of Japan's Kamakura period (1185–1333) better manifested the *reisei* of Japanese Buddhism than did the cultured aristocrats of the Heian period (794–1185). In short, he ascribes the nondualistic consciousness of *reisei* more to lowly Buddhist believers than to scholarly priests. Suzuki's critique of scholasticism is consistent with both the anti-intellectual rhetoric of historical Zen and the modern Western treatment of religion as a nonrational experience, both of which influenced Suzuki heavily. This antipathy toward intellectualism has shaped Suzuki's assessment of Japanese Buddhist history—its ideas, texts, practices, and personages—in ways that separate him from the views of some Buddhist historians and scholars.

The various presuppositions associated with Suzuki's concept of *reisei* provide the framework for his innovative interpretation of Pure Land Buddhism in the book. He believes that the traditional view of the Pure Land as an other-worldly paradise after death represents a mechanical and imperfect understanding, characteristic of Chinese and Japanese Buddhism prior to Hōnen (1133–1212) and Shinran. Though Suzuki cites Hōnen extensively, he does not treat him as independent from Shinran, but rather as a precursor to him, and thus as an incomplete model of *reisei* in Pure Land Buddhism. Shinran, on the other hand, is presented as the consummate and fully formed exemplar of *reisei.* According to Suzuki, he was awakened to *reisei* because of his banishment from Japan's effete culture in Kyoto and his long sojourn in the countryside close to the peasants and the earth. With them as a catalyst, Shinran came to comprehend Pure Land Buddhism as a nondualistic experience of this world even amid its conflicts and contradictions. Suzuki sees this as the true meaning of faith and the nembutsu in Shin Buddhism. To demonstrate that, he cites a passage from the *Tannishō*, a collection of Shinran's sayings that Suzuki treasured throughout his career. In it Shinran declared that he would practice the nembutsu, which Hōnen had imparted to him, even if it led him to hell. Suzuki takes this to mean that the crux of Shinran's spirituality was not the aspiration for birth in the Pure Land after death but the immediate experience of the nembutsu—impregnated with Amida's vow (or prayer) to awaken all living beings to enlightenment, and inseparable from the faith of relying on the Buddha's other-power, *tariki*. This, Suzuki maintains, is the true expression of *reisei* in the life and experience of Shinran.

This unconventional interpretation of Shinran sets Suzuki apart from the established Shin tradition in several ways. One difference is Suzuki's critique of the *Kyōgyōshinshō* (Teaching, Practice, Faith, and Attainment), Shinran's longest and most complex writing, on which mainstream Shin Buddhist doctrine is based. In it Shinran cited and explicated the foremost Pure Land texts and thinkers of India, China, and Japan. According to Suzuki, this work is an unreliable source for understanding Shinran's true teachings. He treats it as an arid expression of Buddhist scholasticism lacking the earthy spirit of Shinran's *reisei*. Suzuki points instead to collections of Shinran's sayings such as the *Tannishō* and to his letters as a more accurate reflection of his spiritual outlook. These are the sources that Suzuki cites the most in his writings on Shinran. It is noteworthy that, years after the publication of *Nihon teki reisei*, Suzuki was persuaded by Shin sectarian officials to translate the *Kyōgyōshinshō* into English. Many believe that he came to have a great appreciation of it late in life.

Another difference from the mainstream Shin tradition is Suzuki's dismissal of the doctrine of *masse* or *mappō* as inconsequential to Shinran's spirituality. This is the belief, which was widespread in medieval Japan, that Buddhism had entered a state of decline, a Latter-Day period, in which enlightenment in this world was no longer possible. In the context of Pure Land Buddhism, this doctrine inspired people to yearn for birth in Amida's paradise after death, where enlightenment is assured. Shinran's writings, both doctrinal and vernacular ones, are filled with references to Buddhism's Latter-Day, so the prevailing view is that it was a pivotal idea in his understanding of religion. Despite this evidence, Suzuki maintains that the belief was a product of elite, scholastic Buddhism with no credibility among Buddhists living close to the earth. As a historical argument, Suzuki's claim seems tenuous. But as an existential argument, it coalesces well with his idea of Japanese spirituality. To the extent that the Latter-Day doctrine fits better with an other-worldly understanding of the Pure Land, it is less compatible with Suzuki's ideal of spiritual fulfillment in this life. By purging Shinran's spirituality of Latter-Day thought, Suzuki portrays him as a religious figure well suited to and consistent with modern religious sensibilities.

The base text for these excerpts is *Japanese Spirituality*, trans. Norman Waddell (Tokyo: Japanese Society for the Promotion of Science, 1972), 14–16, 17–18, 19–21, 48–54, 78–82. (The translation of these excerpts has been extensively revised and updated by Waddell.) The work was originally published in Japanese as Suzuki Daisetsu, *Nihon teki reisei* (Tokyo: Daitō Shuppansha, 1944). The book was republished in 1946 with chapter 5 omitted. See SDZ 8:21–23, 24–26, 27–28, 53–59, 82–87.

. . .

THE MEANING OF *REISEI*

It is now perhaps time to explain what I mean by *reisei,*[1] translated here as "spirituality," a term rarely encountered outside of old Buddhist texts. I would like to have it encompass areas not normally included in the more common Japanese words *seishin,* often translated "spirit," and *kokoro,* whose various translations include "mind," "heart," and "spirit."

Within the notion of *seishin* (or *kokoro*) as standing in opposition to things, materiality, or substance, they cannot be included within the material, and vice versa. I believe something more must be seen at the depths of both these concepts. As long as two things oppose each other, contradiction, rivalry, mutual suppression, and annihilation cannot be averted. In such situations, it will become impossible for human beings to carry on. What is needed is something that can encompass both of them and understand that the two are really not two, but one, and that the one is, as it is, two. *Reisei* accomplishes this. If we want the rivalries of the existing dualistic worldview to cease and become conciliatory and fraternal, and mutual interpenetration and self-identity to prevail, we have no choice but to await the awakening of man's religious consciousness, *reisei.* It can be said that another world beyond the realms of *seishin* and materiality opens up, where the two exist in harmony though still remaining mutually contradictory. This is possible through the insight, or self-awakening, of religious consciousness.

Reisei can be used more or less synonymously with "religious consciousness," though I hesitate to use that term because in Japan misconceptions arise when the word religion or religious is used. Japanese do not seem to have a very profound understanding of religious matters. They tend to think of religion as just another name for superstition, or that religious belief is to be used to support something that has nothing to do with religion or anything else of any consequence. That is why I prefer to use the word *reisei.*

But essentially, as long as a consciousness is not awakened regarding religion, it is not really comprehensible. This might be said about most other things as well, and when it is a case of phenomena appearing to the ordinary consciousness, a certain degree of speculation, conjecture, and sympathy is permissible. But when it comes to religion, it is absolutely essential for the operation of the religious consciousness, which I call *reisei,* to come into play. In other words, religion cannot be understood without the awakening of *reisei.* I do not want to suggest that *reisei* possesses the ability to perform some special activity or function, merely that its working is different from that of *seishin. Seishin* has an ethical character that *reisei* transcends, although this transcendence does not imply negation or denial. Whereas *seishin* is based in the discriminatory consciousness, *reisei* is nondiscriminatory wisdom. Again, this does not mean that *reisei* appears by discarding or ignoring intellectual discrimination. *Seishin* does not necessarily function as an agent in thought or logic; it sometimes presses on by means of willpower and intuition, in which case it may bear a close resemblance to *reisei.* Yet the direct intuitive power of *reisei* operates on a higher level than that of *seishin.* The willpower of *seishin* is only able to transcend the self by relying on the support of *reisei.* What is called "strength of *seishin*" or "*seishin* power" contains an impure residue—the self, or the various forms the self assumes. So long as this remains, it is impossible for it to penetrate to the true meaning of Prince Shōtoku's words, "the spirit of harmony is the most precious of all things," which has been called the ideal of the Japanese people.

JAPANESE SPIRITUALITY

I believe readers will now have generally grasped what I mean by spiritual awakening *(reisei).* Clearer also, I hope, is the conceptual sphere that surrounds spirituality and *seishin.* It should be clear that the awakening of religious consciousness is the awakening of spirituality, and that this means *seishin* itself has started to move at its deepest roots. Because of this, spirituality can be understood to possess a universality and is not limited to any particular people or nation. Inasmuch as the Chinese, Europeans, and Japanese all possess spiritual consciousness, *reisei,* they are the same. However, once the religious consciousness awakens, each of them has differences in the patterns or forms in which the phenomena of *seishin*'s activity are manifested.

What are the Japanese characteristics of religious consciousness? I personally believe that they are found in their purest form in Zen and in the thought of the Jōdo or Pure Land schools. My reasons for saying this can be stated simply: Jōdo and Zen are schools of Buddhism, which is an imported religion that might be considered dubious in playing a role in either the awakening of a purely Japanese religious consciousness or in the expression of that consciousness. As I do not consider Buddhism a foreign religion, however, I regard neither Zen nor Pure Land as having a borrowed nature.

It is true that Buddhism came from the continent, probably during the reign of the Emperor Kinmei (539–571), but what entered was Buddhist ritual and manners and its trappings. Its importation did not give rise to any quickening of Japanese spirituality. Though it is said that opposition arose to its adoption, this was of a political nature and had nothing to do with the religion itself. Buddhism went on to make its presence felt in the realm of architecture and in the other arts and sciences, yet this was again rather the assimilation of various spheres of continental culture, not a matter of the Japanese religious consciousness. At this point, it had not yet begun to function, having still no vital connection with Buddhism. When a genuine religious consciousness did begin to raise its head through the influence of Buddhism, even though it assumed Buddhist form, that was merely an historical coincidence. We must go beneath these fortuitous circumstances to discover the true substance of Japanese religious consciousness lying beneath them.

Although the various sects of Shinto might be regarded as transmitters of Japanese religious consciousness, it does not appear in Shinto in a pure form. Shrine Shinto, or Ancient Shinto, is the fixed accumulation of the manners and customs of the ancient Japanese, but they could not develop this spiritual consciousness *(reisei)* itself. Of Japanese elements they had more than enough, but from them the light of religious insight did not emerge. No doubt others would assert that spiritual insight was there in abundance, but I cannot concur with that view. In certain areas the question of spiritual awakening allows little room for discussion, for the matter would only end in futile argument. . . .

JŌDO (PURE LAND) THOUGHT

To gain a thorough understanding of Japanese religious consciousness in Pure Land thought, and especially in the beliefs of the Shin sect, it is necessary to distinguish distinctly between Shin as a sect, which is a group entity, and Shin experience on which it is based. Unless this distinction is sufficiently understood, it would not be difficult to conclude that there is nothing less Japanese than Shin belief, because the thought of all the Pure Land schools is based on accounts in the Three Pure Land Sutras, which are decidedly Indian in nature as well as in fact. Yet such a notion is extremely superficial and cannot penetrate beyond even the thin surface of things.

Of course, Shin followers give these three sutras scriptural authority. But then why did something like the Shin sect not evolve in India or China? Pure Land Buddhism emerged in China during the Six Dynasties period (222–589), yet even after the elapse of fifteen hundred years, the Chinese Pure Land school of today is the same as it was then. It did not give rise to the *ōchō* (leaping sideways)[2] experience of the Shin sect or an absolute *tariki* (other-power) view of Amida's salvation. In Japan, Hōnen made the Jōdo sect independent of Tendai teachings and attempted to clarify its significance as a separate sect. Before he even finished doing this, Shinran appeared from among his disciples and proceeded to greatly and rapidly advance his teacher's Pure Land thought. The working of Japanese religious awakening during the Kamakura period was unable to stop even when it had engendered Hōnen's Pure Land thought; it had to continue until it had produced Shinran. This is not to be regarded as fortuitous. Had it not been for Japanese religious awakening, such an experience could not have so swiftly evolved within Pure Land thought. Pure Land thought had existed in India as well as China. The fact that it was in Japan alone that, passing from Hōnen to Shinran, it came to assume the form we see in the Shin sect is an occurrence that must have been dependent upon the active participation of Japanese spirituality—Japanese religious consciousness. Had Japanese spirituality merely been a passive player in this development, such an achievement would not have been possible, and Pure Land thought would doubtless have merely been accepted just as it was, foreign importation or whatever.

The self-awakening of the Japanese religious consciousness, and the external means that provided the opportunity for that self-awakening, must be considered separately. Even passiveness that does nothing but receive must contain active elements of some kind; but in this case active elements alone—the *ōchō* experience of Shin faith—would not have been enough. It was absolutely essential for it to have received the great and powerful influence emerging from within Japanese spirituality. When this influence was expressed through Pure Land thought, the Pure Land Shin sect was born.

Shin experience is really none other than the working of the Japanese religious consciousness. That it emerged within a Buddhist context was, as I have said, historically fortuitous, and does nothing to prevent the essential quality of the Shin sect from being identified with what I call Japanese spirituality.

THE AWAKENING OF JAPANESE SPIRITUALITY

. . . In the Kamakura period, religious thought and faith and sentiment—religious consciousness in the true sense—developed in many directions. When Pure Land thought is discussed in Japan, scholars usually relate it to *masse* (Latter-Day or *mappō*) thought. I do not necessarily agree with this approach. To begin with, Latter-Day thought must be examined to discover whether or not it was prevalent among the Japanese people as the scholars contend. Since the time of Dengyō Daishi [Saichō (JCD)] Latter-Day thought probably circulated among Buddhist scholars, but Buddhist scholars do not represent all Buddhists and certainly not all of the people. What level of competence in the Chinese-language Buddhist canon did ordinary Buddhists generally have at that time? To what degree did missionaries spread Buddhist consciousness throughout the general populace? There were temple buildings and Buddhist priests (there were, and still are, shameless priests who break the Buddhist commandments as there have been at all times in all Buddhist countries), but to what extent did the average person have to do with Buddhism? How many of them came to believe in Latter-Day thought? Throughout the Heian period, Buddhist attainment—granting its existence at all—was limited to a few Buddhist scholars. The nobles who visited the temples for memorial services with offerings for the monks had no understanding at all of Buddhism, much less did they believe in it. They regarded Buddhism as another of their pastimes, a social activity of some kind, and the priests generally did not demand anything more from them. Even when the government became corrupt, and the peace of society and the lives and property of the populace were all under threat, that was not the world of the degenerate Latter-Day *(masse)*. I do not think Buddhism had spread widely enough for people to be conscious of such things. At that time, and today as well for that matter, Buddhism had virtually no connection to the political and social life. If the advocacy and acceptance of Pure Land teaching owed anything at all to the increasing influence of Latter-Day thought, it was only among a part of the priesthood and was probably never widespread. What I would stress is that, even granting that Pure Land thought was generally accepted by the populace, it would not have been the result of Latter-Day thought, but because ordinary people were brought by the degeneracy of the times to contemplate the meaning of their own existence. It was from this that the awakening of Japanese spirituality came about.

Calls of the Latter-Day are not limited to Buddhism. They have been heard in all periods of history: laments that the world is at an end, cries of decadence. They were heard in China from remote antiquity. I am not familiar with the circumstances that surrounded Japan's transition from the "age of the gods" to the "age of man," nor do I know whether it represented a progression or a regression. In any case, the idea that the times are degenerate, that the Latter-Day has come, would seem to be a universal phenomenon. In Japan, such references appear in the tales *(monogatari)* and diaries of the period, but only as hackneyed expressions voiced by those of the population who were able to read and write. Somehow, the idea of the Latter-Day becomes just one of the various complaints heard from the effete, tear-drenched Heian nobility. I do not believe it is possible that Pure Land thought could have spread among the ordinary people in such a manner (though I will not attempt to document this contention). The ways in which Buddhism was transmitted to the common people during Heian times are not very well understood, and there is a need for detailed and accurate studies regarding the extent to which the general populace comprehended Buddhist faith and such. Inasmuch as this has not yet been done, I will assume that, even though priests talked of the Latter-Day and the intelligentsia followed them, it had no relation to the ongoing propagation of Pure Land thought.

In view of their own decadence, there was some meaning to the priests' and intellectuals' talk of a degenerate Latter-Day, but because the lot of the common man never improved, there was no need for him to feel the coming of a Latter-Day at this particular time, in the final years of the Heian period.

Why was it, then, that the Pure Land teaching, especially Shin teaching, spread among the common people? I believe that a simultaneous mutual response occurred between the fundamental religious truths found in the special characteristics of absolute *tariki* faith and the awakening of the Japanese religious consciousness that began at this time—what I call the awakening of Japanese spirituality.

There is something in the Shin teaching that can work its way straight into the heart of the average Japanese. This something is the pure other-power and the power of great compassion. Here is where the doors of religious consciousness open. Here is where the ultimate ground of Pure Land faith must be found. The Shin sect, being fully aware of this, was able to become the faith of the common man. If Pure Land faith does not go this far, it cannot fulfill its original and primary mission. The true essence of the Pure Land teaching is found in absolute *tariki,* rather than in the teaching of a Pure Land of Infinite Bliss. Its fundamental meaning does not consist in saying that, because "this land" is impure, we should go to "that land" and enjoy a life of purity. Pure Land schools preach about the Pure Land because in it one is able to free oneself from karmic entanglements and enter the path of enlightenment. *Ōjō,* or birth in the Pure Land, is the means; enlightenment is the end. And entering the Pure Land is possible owing to the other-power of Amida, something that would be impossible for a person bound in his own karma. Through the absolute other-power one must achieve an understanding based on experience of the world that transcends karma. It is thought that the teaching of the Pure Land has as its objective attainment of the Pure Land, but in fact the true Pure Land is no such place. It is something like the waiting room of a station, where one stops briefly in transit.

The world of the Latter-Day and the Pure Land should not be considered as polar opposites. If a contrast is to be made, it would have to be between the karmic causation that enthralls man and the life of enlightenment that transcends karma. In theoretical terms, to be freed from the chains of karma is, according to the logic of *sokuhi,*[3] to acquire the transcendental intuition of prajna wisdom. In terms of religious belief, it refers to great nondiscriminating compassion, the salvation that comes from Amida's Original Prayer (or Vow).[4]

Attempts to link the Pure Land to the concept of a Latter-Day, making it an extension of the present world, have nothing at all to do with religion. It is nothing more than an easy materialism, a product of individualism of an extremely inferior class. Since in doing this, short shrift is given to the earth's spiritual strength, materialists can then call religion an opiate. A man who has achieved a penetrating insight into the depths of spirituality—the true essence of Buddhism—would never consider such an idea.

With a genuine *tariki* faith it does not matter whether the future world is hell or heaven. This is what Shinran stated in the *Tannishō.* This is genuine religion. Naturally, Pure Land teaching did not come this far overnight. The Pure Land view of the Heian period was unquestionably influenced by an aristocratic culture that saw it as an extension of the present world. Nembutsu was debated as a device for entering the Pure Land. The Pure Land of Eshin Sōzu [Genshin, 942–1017 (NW)] still seems very rich in actuality, and the paintings of the time depicting bodhisattvas descending to welcome the spirits of believers are certainly charged with the qualities of Heian culture. When we come to Hōnen, we feel that he is in full contact with the essence of religion. Yet even he gets caught up, as when he discusses the subject of *raigō,* the idea of bodhisattvas arriving at death to show you the way to the Pure Land. In giving the following explanation to one Amakasu no Tarō Tadatsuna, he says:

> Amida's Original Prayer (or Vow) does not speak of good and evil, does not consider the abundance or lack of good deeds, does not choose between a pure and an impure body. Since it takes no account of time, place, or other relationships, it isn't concerned with how one dies. A sinner is a sinner, yet if he calls the Name, he attains the Pure Land—this is the wonder of the Original Prayer. A person born to a samurai family, even though he engages in combat and falls in battle, if he says the Nembutsu, he shares in the Original Prayer. He must never have the least doubt that he will be met by the coming of the bodhisattvas. *(Chokushū goden,* vol. 26, also known as *Hōnen Shōnin gyōjō* and *Chokushū Hōnen Shōnin den)*

With the words "A sinner is a sinner, yet if he calls the Name, he attains the Pure Land; this is the wonder of the Original Prayer," Hōnen strikes home to the true and wonderful meaning possessed by the *tariki* sects, but his mention of *raigō* (the descent of the bodhisattvas) seems somehow a remnant of Heian times. The real office that Hōnen performed was to erect a bridge between Heian and Kamakura times, and as such he is one of the brightest luminaries in Japanese spiritual history.

It was Shinran who exemplified almost perfectly the life of the earth and the true spirit of Kamakura times. Under Hōnen, Shinran achieved self-realization of the great meaning of *tariki* (other-power), but it was his period of exile in the northern provinces and later his wanderings around the Kantō region that brought this great awakening into contact with the earth. Had he remained in Kyoto, Shinran would never, no matter what he did, have been able to extricate himself from the ideals and conceptions of Heian culture.

What is more, if Hōnen had spent much more of his life in the countryside—the areas away from Kyoto—in all probability his spirituality would have achieved an even greater brilliance. Owing to his advanced age, this was not possible. But Shinran was young and was able to assume his teacher's mantle. The two men's personalities cannot be separated; one follows right after the other, like two beads on a rosary string.

Had Shinran not spent many years of exile and wandering in remote rural areas, he would have been unable to penetrate to the realization of pure *tariki.* His exile provided him with the chance to propagate Buddhism among the people in remote areas of the country. This was a blessing for them, yet Shinran himself would have been the first to admit that it was a blessing for himself as well. Living among such people gave his religious experience an added profundity. Not being a specialist in Shin history, I do not know the reasons why Shinran did not return directly to Kyoto after he was released from exile. But viewing him in terms of his inner, spiritual life, there is no doubt in my mind that living in the country, close to the earth, gave him an increasingly deep existential understanding of Amida's great compassion.

I like to think that the collection of letters, *Shōsokushū,* that Shinran wrote to people who lived in close proximity to the earth is a reflection of the new cultural spirit of the Kamakura period. Shinran's twenty years in the eastern provinces must not be viewed simply as a historical coincidence. It is not difficult to imagine what a profound effect this long period in Shinran's life has had on the development of Shin sect thought. The Shin sect never forgot the country, and one can easily understand that the reason its foundations exist in the country even today is due more to the fact that its faith emanates from the earth than to doctrinal considerations. Japanese spirituality cannot be separated from the earth.

To make Nembutsu the primary consideration of the Shin sect, or to say that Shin teaches birth in the Pure Land *(Ōjō),* or words to similar effect, does not penetrate to the essence of Shin faith. The base and center of Shin Buddhism is belief in Amida's Original Prayer (or Vow), which means reliance upon Amida's boundless compassion. I myself believe that the essential religious life in Shin Buddhism consists in throwing yourself into the unobstructed light of compassion, whose working transcends karma, is free of its effects, and shunts all such things to the side. When you do, then it no longer matters whether rebirth in the Pure Land as an extension of this world exists or not. If you attain the self-realization that you are embraced within the Light, that is enough. The Nembutsu appears from within this realization. To say that the realization appears from the Nembutsu is mistaken. You must first once be embraced within boundless great compassion. And this can be experienced when you yourself realize that you originate, profoundly, from the earth. You must perceive the truth that both the sorrows and hardships of the world come from attempting to live by yourself, cut off from the earth. The desire to go to some "Pure Land" because this world is difficult does not accord with the true faith of Shin Buddhism, nor is it a characteristic of Japanese spirituality. It is the popularization of religious faith, the faith of *Weltschmerz,* and is not the true form of *tariki.* It is a vestige of aristocratic culture.

The "certain" or "inevitable" hell often spoken of by followers of the Pure Land is not something that exists apart from life and death. It should not be thought that hell is located at some distant point beyond innumerable Buddha-lands, like the Pure Land, with the Pure Land lying to the west and hell to the east. That implausible notion is a hand-down from Heian culture. I am not saying that both heaven and hell exist in this world, a notion that comes from an insufficient understanding of this world. If our thoughts progress in a direction that isolates us from the earth, both heaven and hell exist in this world. But if we are conscious of our self-identity with the earth, this world is, straightaway, the Pure Land of Bliss. Our thoughts themselves become the earth, the earth our thoughts, and the light of great compassion shines forth. Where this great compassion exists is the Pure Land of Bliss. Where it does not exist is "certain, inevitable hell."

Here is the culmination of Shin faith, and here, I believe, it must be. And here is the self-awakening of Japanese religious faith, what I call the awakening of Japanese spirituality. The cultural process up until this point had been a period of preparation. Once genuine religious awakening occurred, it was possible for Japanese spiritual history to evolve in a steady forward development. . . .

To summarize: upon reaching the Kamakura period, the Japanese spiritual consciousness for the first time in its history displayed its true significance. The genuine nature of Buddhism also at that time came into contact with the vital religiosity emanating from the earth. Boundless great compassion was opened up on the one hand and, on the other, intellectual insight, fusing into the Japanese character, brought about unique expressions in the artistic life of the country. These two manifestations were absolute *tariki* [of Shin Buddhism (JCD)] and Zen's "transmission beyond the teachings."

JAPANESE SPIRITUALITY

That Japanese spirituality possesses something that is brought to bear in the emotions of the individual self can be discerned in the fact that the development of imported Chinese Pure Land thought soon advanced along such lines. Not long after Hōnen declared his intention to establish a new Pure Land sect, Shinran began consciously extracting elements from within it. As long as Amida's Original Prayer (or Vow) did not go beyond the confines of generality, Japanese spirituality did not fully respond to it.

Japanese religious consciousness had not yet broken open its shell and emerged from within, because its most primordial and concrete element (what I call its "one by one" character) was not yet at work. "Primordial" may suggest something abstract, general, or conceptual, but that is only because it is considered objectively. When it is a matter of the feelings or emotions—the individual self—there is nothing more concrete. That is what is meant by "one by one," as when Shinran says in the *Tannishō* that Amida issued his Original Prayer "solely for the sake of this one individual person." It is significant that someone like Shinran did not appear in China but in Japan; also significant is the fact that his emergence followed closely upon Hōnen's. In fact, I think it is proper to view them as a single individual.

There must be some meaning in the fact that Shinran did not have a thousand years of Chinese Pure Land thought behind him but did have the thousand-year development of Japanese spirituality. We are obliged to discover the significance of the fact that it was the Kamakura period when this religious consciousness was manifested, and also the meaning that this has in the spiritual history of that period.

Had Shinran's appearance in Japan paralleled that of Buddhist teachers such as Zhiyi and Fazang in China, his teaching would probably have died out like those of the Tiantai and Huayan traditions. Though we in East Asia may well be proud of Zhiyi and Fazang as great religious thinkers, they had not completely shed their Indian mantle. I believe it can be said that their thought was not an indigenous growth from the psyche of the Chinese people themselves. Because Shinran's experience of "one by one" came from the spiritual life of the Japanese people—from spirituality itself—it began to work deeply within the Japanese mentality, and is working there even today.

Because the religious consciousness of both Hōnen and Shinran was derived from the earth, we may say that its absolute value is to be found there. And the working of this religious consciousness first became possible in the Kamakura period. There is little question that we can see the initial stirrings of Japanese spirituality in the religious genius of men like Dengyō Daishi [Saichō (NW)] and Kōbō Daishi [Kūkai (NW)]. But because its relation to the earth was still limited, it lacked concreteness. The individual self *(koonore)* had not awakened to the primordial origin of its existence through contact and union with the supra-individual self *(chō koonore)*.

This first was possible in the world in which Shinran lived. Although he was to some degree the product of Kyoto's aristocratic culture, his individual self awakened to its original ground when he was living in remote Echigo. Although he had received his initial baptism from Hōnen in Kyoto, it did not bring him into contact with the "Person" of the supra-individual self. That began to emerge only after he had taken up life in an area untouched by Kyoto culture. Dwelling among the rural people of Echigo in northern Japan, for whom the earth was a daily, concrete reality, and coming into contact with their spirituality, he experienced through his individual self the supra-individual self that transcended it. No matter how much faith might have been instilled in him by Hōnen, had Shinran not had the opportunity to separate himself from the cultural influence of the capital, it is extremely doubtful whether the Shinran of the *tariki* Original Prayer (or Vow) would have surpassed Dengyō or Kōbō. I do not believe Shinran would have been able to reach full spiritual maturity in Kyoto, for although Buddhism did exist there, it lacked the experience of Japanese spirituality.

JAPANESE SPIRITUAL AWAKENING IN THE *TANNISHŌ*

I believe it can be seen from what has been said that the fundamental nature of Shinran's sect is not to be found in his *Kyōgyōshinshō,* but in his letters, his *Wasan* (Buddhist hymns), and above all in the *Tannishō* [collection of his sayings (JCD)]. Although it is quite understandable that Shin scholars regard his *Kyōgyōshinshō* as a supreme sacred book, Shinran's true essence appears elsewhere. It is something that can be grasped intuitively in the spontaneous words he uttered, which are recorded in his other works. *Kyōgyōshinshō* exhibits traces of aristocratic culture, sectarian philosophy, and it is scholarly in tone. It is not constituted of Shinran's true substance. Compelled to judge him by this work alone, it would be difficult to refrain from concluding that his spiritual awakening was still incomplete.

Now let us look at the following excerpt from the *Tannishō:*

> Your intention in coming here, after a long journey through more than ten different provinces even at the risk of your lives, was for no other reason than to hear me explain the way of rebirth in the Pure Land. But you are greatly mistaken if you think that I have any knowledge for attaining rebirth in the Pure Land other than saying the Nembutsu, or that I possess knowledge of some secret religious texts, and envy me on that account. If that is what you believe, you would be better off traveling to Nara or to Mount Hiei, where you will find many learned scholars of Buddhism, and learning from them the essential means of being reborn in the Pure Land. As far as I, Shinran, am concerned, the only reason I say the Nembutsu is because of the instruction I received from my good teacher [Hōnen (NW)], who made me realize that the only condition for receiving Amida's salvation is reciting the Nembutsu. I do not even know whether the calling of the Name will take me to the Pure Land or to hell. Even if my teacher has deceived me and I am sent to hell for calling the Name of Amida Buddha, I shall never regret doing it. Those who have engaged in sufficient practice to attain Buddhahood may regret calling his Name when they are sent to hell and find that they were deceived. But I am far from accumulating sufficient merit to attain Buddhahood. Hell may be my proper residence. If the Original Prayer (or Vow) is true, the teaching of Śākyamuni cannot be untrue; if the teaching of Śākyamuni is true, the commentaries of Shandao cannot be untrue; if Shandao's commentaries are true, the teaching of Hōnen cannot be untrue; if the teaching of Hōnen is true, how is it possible for me, Shinran, to utter untruths? Such, in short, is my faith. Beyond this, you must decide for yourselves whether to believe in the Nembutsu or discard it altogether.

We can see first of all that the concrete foundation of Shinran's sect is situated in the earth. The earth means the countryside, the farmers and peasants—the polar opposite of intellectual discrimination. The political and economic importance of the earth goes without saying, and it can also be understood that because of this, the earth is our flesh and blood itself. But in Shinran's sect, the earth has its own religious significance, its own spiritual value. This did not and could not emerge in a superficial, Kyoto-bound aristocratic culture. The opening sentence of the *Tannishō,* "Your intention in coming here, after a long journey through more than ten different provinces even at the risk of your lives," is not merely words. If we can imagine these country folk, traveling enormous distances from homes in far-off Hitachi [north of present-day Tokyo (NW)] all the way to Kyoto, we can grasp that their relation to Shinran was not in the least conceptual or metaphysical, and it had nothing to do with words or letters. It was a relation forged in the earth. It can be said that what is not found among the Buddhist scholars of Nara and Mount Hiei exists here. And if Shinran had not had the opportunity to leave

Kyoto, the earth would never have been able to work its way so deeply into his being.

I often wonder what kind of life Shinran led after he was exiled and found himself away from the capital for the first time. Surely he did not reside in local Tendai or Shingon temples, and he probably did not even have a small hermitage. We may suppose he lived as a layman. To earn his livelihood during this period, there could not have been much available to him besides farming. At any rate, he did not just continue life as a monk, begging alms from the farmers. It is not difficult to imagine him attempting to polish and refine in this very practical life the faith he had acquired thanks to Hōnen. It is not likely that he tried to examine his faith in books and writings as he had done before as a young monk living and studying on Mount Hiei. He probably did not have the least ambition to compile writings such as *Kyōgyōshinshō*.

Possessing only the way of Pure Land *Ōjō* through practice of the Nembutsu, did not Shinran endeavor to put this into practice in his daily life, in direct contact with the earth, using the plow and hoe, living as a Buddhist layman, eating meat and taking a wife? I do not think he was capable of engaging in a life of trade, or of being a hunter or a fisherman. I do not think that he had the temperament to become a craftsman. He probably did not even have an opportunity to teach villagers to read and write, as might have been the case had he been a *rōnin,* or lordless samurai, in Edo times. Villagers in Kamakura Japan would have had little need for such things.

Moreover, there is no evidence that Shinran had any contact or dealings with regional authorities or local samurai. The best way to interpret this is probably to say that he attempted to live quietly as a farmer, saying the Nembutsu as one common man among others. It must be recalled that those who previously had come to visit him in Kyoto from the Kanto region were not from the intellectual classes, but people with no influence or power whatever. In this remote rural area of Echigo province, Shinran took his first steps in a lay Buddhist life, living as a *gutoku,* a bald-headed, simple-hearted man. He continued this existence during the time he spent in the Kanto as well, a course that is said to have been suggested to him by the example of a Pure Land devotee of the late Heian period named Kyōshin. . . .

6

Sayings of a Modern Tariki Mystic

One of Suzuki's contributions to Buddhist Studies was the introduction of the *myōkōnin* into scholarly discourse. *Myōkōnin,* which Suzuki once translated as "the wondrous good man," is a term used for pious Shin Buddhists of very humble origins who display in word and deed a deep and inspiring faith even though they are often illiterate. They stand in contrast to learned and highly trained priests who are respected for their erudition and mastery of Buddhist texts. Stories and sayings of *myōkōnin* circulated in Shin Buddhist circles in the Tokugawa period (1603–1867), and they gradually came to be viewed as one archetype of Shin religiosity. But their appeal was largely confined to the realm of popular piety and sermonizing, and they were not the subject of scholarly examination until Suzuki took an interest in them. Suzuki, though an intellectual himself, was always captivated by stories of colorful and earthy religious figures who expressed insight through pithy sayings and folk wisdom. His fascination with the paradoxes and outrageous behavior of Tang Chinese Zen masters is one example, and his attraction to the sayings of *myōkōnin* is another. Their stories struck a resonant chord in Suzuki perhaps because they reminded him of Shin Buddhist sermons he may have heard as a child. His primary studies of *myōkōnin* were published in the 1940s, 1950s, and 1960s, but as this essay demonstrates, he became interested in them as early as the 1920s, when he began his career as a professor at Otani University.

This essay has two purposes. One is to introduce the *myōkōnin* named Shichiri Gōjun (1835–1900), whom Suzuki learned about from Akanuma Chizen (1884–1937), his Shin Buddhist colleague at Otani, who published a collection of Shichiri's sayings in 1912. Actually, Shichiri was not illiterate, but rather a well-educated scholar-priest. But he had a knack for catchy aphorisms and expressing religious truths in down-to-earth similes. Suzuki presents here thirty-eight sayings attributed to Shichiri in loose translation or paraphrase. He highlights, among other things, Shichiri's use of the parent-child relationship as a metaphor for the bond between Amida Buddha and humans. Shichiri conveys with folksy wisdom the sublime and satisfying life of Shin believers who find repose in Amida and his vow.

Anguish over wrongdoings and anxiety about birth in the Pure Land after death all melt away into a state of ease and acceptance within Amida's loving embrace.

The second purpose of this essay—which actually comprises the first half of the text—is to present Shichiri as a classic example of mysticism. That is why Suzuki calls him a "*tariki* mystic." Over the course of his career Suzuki applied the concepts of religious experience, mysticism, and spirituality to various forms of Buddhism. These concepts were inspired in part by Western scholarship on religion. For instance, Suzuki's emphasis in this essay on passivity in the *tariki* mystic and on absolute dependence on "The Other" after much inner struggle is reminiscent of the ideas of passivity in mysticism and of self-surrender conversion articulated by William James in *The Varieties of Religious Experience* (1902). Suzuki thus treats *myōkōnin* as exemplars of religious experience as a universal human phenomenon. This attempt to identify and explicate universal aspects of religion was a common enterprise in twentieth-century scholarship. A later book by Suzuki that attempts to do so in greater depth is *Shūkyō keiken no jijitsu* (*The Actual Facts of Religious Experience,* 1943, SDZ 10:1–124), in which he uses another *myōkōnin,* Shōma (or Shōmatsu, 1799–1871) of Sanuki, as his case study. The characteristics of religion that Suzuki seeks to highlight in these studies—specifically, mystical or experiential qualities rather than ethics or the afterlife—are sometimes borne out in the sayings of Shichiri, but not always. That is, some sayings seem to affirm the traditional Shin Buddhist view of birth in the Pure Land after death and also emphasize conventional morality as an extension of religious life.

The base text for this essay is "Sayings of a Modern Tariki Mystic," *The Eastern Buddhist* 3, no. 2 (1924): 93–116. It was republished in Daisetz Teitaro Suzuki, *A Miscellany on the Shin Teaching of Buddhism* (Kyoto: Shinshu Otaniha Shumusho, 1949), 92–121; and republished again under the title "A Tariki Mystic," in Daisetz Teitarō Suzuki, *Collected Writings on Shin Buddhism* (CWSB), ed. The Eastern Buddhist Society (Kyoto: Shinshū Ōtaniha, 1973), 92–110. A Japanese translation by Kusunoki Kyō was published as "Gakusō no mita Shinshū," in Suzuki Daisetsu, *Nihon Bukkyō no soko o nagareru mono* (Kyoto: Ōtani Shuppansha, 1950), 139–173. See SDZ 11:401–423.

. . .

I

Japanese Buddhism may be divided into two groups: *jiriki* and *tariki,* or "Self-power" and "Other-power." The Self-power School teaches the doctrine of individual salvation, according to which moral purity and enlightenment are the necessary conditions of emancipation; while the Other-power School teaches an absolute reliance on the grace of Amitābha Buddha; for finite beings are not by themselves able to attain to a state of perfect freedom and saintliness. What is needed of a *tariki* devotee is therefore an unqualified and wholehearted faith in the love of the Buddha, and in the absolute efficacy of his Original Vows.[1] He may be full of moral shortcomings and cherish evil passions *(kleśa)* which he has not brought under control, but he need not worry about this if only his heart overflows with joy and gratitude for the merciful care of Amitābha; for such a heart, which is above morality and intellection, will not be bothered by its moral imperfections, as it knows that the latter are no hindrance to one's rebirth in the Pure Land.

Amida's[2] love for finite beings and the latter's absolute confidence in his love are often compared to the relations between mother and child and have been specified by one[3] of the recent Shinshū scholars as follows:

1. As the child makes no judgments, just so should the followers of *tariki* be free from thoughts of self-assertion *(jiriki).*
2. As the child knows nothing of impurities, so should the *tariki* followers never have an eye to evil thoughts and evil deeds.
3. As the child knows nothing of purities, so should the *tariki* followers be unconscious of any good thoughts they may cherish.
4. As the child has no desire to court its mother's special favor by making her offerings, so should the *tariki* devotees be free from the idea of being rewarded for something given.
5. As the child does not go after any other person than its own mother, so should the *tariki* devotees not run after other Buddhas or Bodhisattvas than Amitābha himself.
6. As the child ever longs for its mother, so should the *tariki* followers think of just one Buddha, the Buddha of Infinite Light.
7. As the child ever cherishes the memory of its own mother, so should the *tariki* followers cherish the thought of one Buddha, Amida.
8. As the child cries after its mother, so should the *tariki* followers invoke the name of Amida.
9. As the child, thinking of its mother as the only person whom it could absolutely rely on, wishes to be embraced by her on all occasions, so should the *tariki* followers have no thought but to be embraced by Amida alone even when in peril.
10. They should have no fears, no doubts, as to the infinite love of Amida, the One Buddha, whose vows are not to forsake any beings in his embrace. When once embraced in his light, no beings need entertain the idea of being deserted by him.

Though somewhat repetitious, the above sums up what the Shinshū faith is, and why it is called "Other-power" in contradistinction to "Self-power." While Amida or God or The Other stands all by himself asserting his absolute independence, the "I" symbolizing all that is mortal, finite, imperfect, sinful, and bound for *naraka* [hell (JCD)][4] or eternal annihilation is made to find the meaning of its existence in The Other only. Gōjun Shichiri,[5] the author of the sayings reproduced below, belonged to this sect of *tariki.* He lived at Hakata, a city in the southwestern part of Japan, and was sixty-six years old when he died in 1900. He had a large following, and his spiritual influence was great among all classes of people. A burglar once broke into his house and demanded of him to give up his valuables. The way however the intruder was treated by the follower of the all-merciful Amida moved him greatly. When he was later arrested, he confessed everything and told the police how he came to be an entirely new man after his encounter with Shichiri. Shichiri was also a great scholar and left quite a few learned writings; but what interests us here is his practical faith and not his scholarly discourses filled with technicalities, which generally marks those of the learned followers of the Shin sect. The following passages in this section of the article are principally culled from a small book entitled "Sayings of Reverend Shichiri" *(Shichiri Rōshi goroku)* which was compiled by Chizen Akanuma, 1912; the translations made from its eighth edition are somewhat free.

As the *tariki* doctrine denies the efficacy of "self-power" as the means of salvation, it naturally cultivates the feeling of absolute dependence as the one thing that is needed. Negatively, or from the devotee's subjective point of view, this feeling may best be cherished by abandoning all thoughts of selfhood and filling his consciousness with the infinite love of Amida, who does not ask for moral perfection as the condition of rebirth in his Pure Land. This simple faith unadulterated by reflection or self-criticism is all that is demanded of a *tariki* follower. Therefore says Gōjun Shichiri:

> Even when you understand that the Nembutsu[6] is the only way to salvation, you often hesitate reflecting within yourselves, "Am I all right now? Is there something more to be done?" This is not quite right. Better be fully confirmed in the thought that your karma has no other destination but that for *naraka*. When you are fully confirmed in this, nothing will be left for you but to hasten forward and take hold of Amida's helping hands. You may then be assured of your rebirth in his Pure Land. Have no scruples in your minds thinking how to curry favor with Amida or whether you are really to be embraced by him. These scruples come from not having fully abandoned the thought of selfhood. Resign yourselves to the grace of Amida and let him do what he chooses with you; whether you are to be saved after or before all your sins are wiped clean is the business of Amida and not yours.
>
> Here is a blind man going along the mountain pass. He is about to cross a log bridge over a river. Being a self-confident man, he walks straight ahead beating his way with a stick. When he comes halfway the bridge turns over. Quickly throwing the stick, he holds on to the log with both hands. The realization of his impending fall down in the rapids and the consequent sure loss of life frightens him terribly. A merciful man with a boat happens at this moment to be waiting just below the bridge ready to receive the poor blind venturer. "Let go!" cries the boatsman, "let go your hold on the log. I am ready to get you down here." The blind man however refuses to listen to him, saying, "I cannot. If I let go my hold, I shall surely be swept down in the rapids." The boatsman is insistent and urges him to come down. Being still undecided and wavering, he tries to release one hand. Finally, the impatient boatsman tells him that if he does not do what he tells him to do, he will not be bothered any longer. In utmost

> despair and with the thought of certain death either way, he lets both hands off the log, and to his greatest joy finds himself safely and comfortable in the boat below.
>
> In a similar way, people at first wander from one god to another sounding their way in vain with the stick of "self-power," until they come to Amida's one passageway. But they tenaciously hold on to this passageway and refuse to leave it. Amida, who is waiting underneath with his boat of Original Vows ready to take them in with him, tells them to give themselves up to his embrace. But they cling to the Nembutsu believing in its efficacy. When they are told again that the Nembutsu in itself has nothing to do with their salvation, they now cling to the thought that they have a faith. This is like holding on to the log bridge with one hand. When however even this last string of self-justification is cut off, they are truly embraced in the boat of the Original Vows and assured of their rebirth in the Pure Land of Amida, when they have a feeling of complete relaxation and indescribable happiness.

Therefore, according to this *tariki* mystic, "to believe truly means absolutely to rely on Amida, or to embrace him unreservedly and unconditionally, or to abandon all thought of selfhood and self-assertion." More technically expressed,

> . . . to believe is not to have a shadow of doubt concerning the Original Vows of Amida in which he most definitely assures us of our rebirth in his Land of Eternal Bliss. This assurance being absolute, Amida does not lay down any conditions, nor does he expect of us any self-sacrificing and merit-accumulating practice. For where faith is once established, our life will be entirely at Amida's disposal. It is like giving up all our possessions in his hand which distributes them in the way he thinks best. We receive from him what we need, and we are perfectly satisfied with him as well as with ourselves. Here lies the ultimate signification of *tariki* faith.

Theologically, Christian faith and the *tariki* seem to be irreconcilably opposed, but psychologically I am inclined to think that the *tariki* Buddhist will not hesitate to accept wholeheartedly everything that is quoted below from one of the sermons delivered by the German mystic Gerhard Tersteegen.[7] Even the terminology may not stand in the way.

> "Place no confidence whatever," says Tersteegen, "in your own hearts, your courage, your strength, your light, your virtues, or your faithfulness; but, like myself, be as little children who must perish without a mother's care. All that is our own is worthless, and everything else is free grace, for which we must every moment wait and receive. But we can never trust too much to our gracious Redeemer; to Him, the most miserable may approach on the footing of free grace, cordially seek His favor and friendship, pray to Him without ceasing, filially depend upon Him, and then boldly venture all upon Him. Oh, He is faithful, and will perform that in us and through us which neither we nor any other mortal would be able of himself to accomplish."

The *tariki* devotees thus come to Amida not only with their feeling of absolute dependence but with all their troubles, passions, and moral imperfections whatever they may be. They have thrown themselves down, body and soul, at the feet of their Lord, with the most unselfish faith that Amida will dispose of them in whichever way he likes. They accept everything and anything from Amida. According to Shinran, the founder of the *Tariki* School, he is willing even to go to *naraka* because of his faith in Amida. Affirmation, "Everlasting Yea," marks the life of the *tariki* followers.

This "Yes" attitude toward the world, accepting everything, good or bad, pleasant or painful, and viewing life sub specie aeternitatis, is one of the characteristics of all genuine mystics, and we read the same general attitude of mind in the sayings of Shichiri, who has this: "To hear the call of Amida, or believe in his Original Vows, ultimately comes to utter this one word, 'Yes,' in response. Don't say 'but,' and get away from the embrace of merciful Amida." Again,

> To trust or to place reliance upon the Original Vows of Amida means to understand or to nod assent to what is given to you—and this without any thinking or reflection or deliberation. As soon as you hear the call, you respond at once, saying, "Yes, I come." In the teaching of *tariki,* nothing more is needed, for we just let the Original Vows work by themselves.
>
> It is like the moon reflected in the tub. When we try to take hold of it, the harder we try the more turbulent grows the water and the more disturbed the shadow. But by letting them alone, the full moon serenely shines on the water. Just so, when we are too anxious to feel joyful, this defeats its own end. Better have no such anxieties, but simply believe in the efficacy of the Original Vows, and all that is needed for your happiness will follow by itself.

Zen is generally regarded as the *jiriki* end ("self-power") of Buddhism, standing in diagonal opposition to the *tariki.* But extremes meet, for Zen is one with Shin in saying "yes," "yes," in response to the kaleidoscopic changes of the objective world. When Huizhong, the National Master of Nanyang (Nanyang Huizhong Guoshi), called his attendant, the latter responded. When this was repeated three times without the disciple's awakening to the knowledge of Zen, said the master: "Until now I thought I was not worthy of you, but I find that you have not been worthy of me all this time." This may sound unintelligible as it stands, but what Zen wants us to see here is to have us realize the "yes" attitude of mind in its simplest and most original type. There is however a difference metaphysically between Zen and Shin in this respect. While Shin regards the one who responds to the call of Amida and says "Yes" unconditionally as Amida himself in you, that is, The Other standing in opposition to "I," Zen merges the "I" in The Other, and this synthetic merging forms the basis for the Zen psychology of affirmation. In Zen this consciousness of identification is read in terms of the enlightened "I," whereas in Shin The Other always stands out prominently and the "I" is considered to have been embraced in the wholeness of The Other. Zen is therefore richer in the intellectual elements and

Shin in the affective or emotional. Isolation is one of the features of Zen, and sociability of Shin.

The doctrine of identification which is characteristic of all schools of Buddhism as distinguished from Christianity is also taught by the Shin mystic: "When the founder tells us to place reliance upon Amida, it means to make his power my own. It is like a child being carried on the back of its parent. The strength of the latter is the strength of the former." "When we speak of Amida and sentient beings, they appear to be different one from the other; but when in one thought beings are thrown into the fire of mercy, they are one even with Amida himself. Like a piece of live charcoal, fire is charcoal and charcoal is fire, they cannot be separated." Further, writes the Shin mystic Shichiri, "If I say I have sins of one thousand kalpas, there is Amida on the other side with merits of ten thousand kalpas. But when all is told, these imperfections, those merits—they both belong to Amida as well as to myself. When we understand this, we realize the state of absolute freedom. In a poor family, there is but one coat for both father and son." Again, "it is like throwing a handful of snow into boiling water, no trace of it will be visible in the cauldron. Let all the faith, all the joy, all the Nembutsu that you can find in your heart be thrown into the pot of the Original Vows, and you will find yourself in one water of identification."

We must not however forget that with the Shin devotees this one water of identification is always described in terms of The Other and not "I."

> Look into the tub filled with water: how deep it looks! and how gleaming is the crystal at the bottom! But, halt, do not rush to the conclusion, as in the other schools of Buddhism, that the Buddha-Nature is in me, that Amida is an idealistic creation, and that the Pure Land lies nowhere else but in my Mind. But really there is no depth in the tub-water, the depth is the reflection of the sky; there is no crystal at the bottom of the tub, it is the shadow of the moon which shines far above. Therefore, says the founder of the Shin faith: The water looks deep because of the unfathomability of Amida's love, and the crystal shines because of the moonlight of his Buddha-Nature. I therefore tell you, put your reliance upon Amida.

This putting everything upon the shoulders of Amida may seem to encourage moral irresponsibility and to create the habit of utter indifference to social welfare and advancement. But we must remember that religion has its transcendental domain of activity where facts and events are judged and valued by a standard of its own. It does not teach mere passivity as we may superficially infer. For before one comes to the realization of absolute dependence one has to go through much of inner struggle; the *tariki* realization is never attained until the last straw of self-assertion is given up. Passivity marks the end of the utmost strenuosity and tension. Without the latter no *tariki* experience will take place in anybody's spiritual life. As the Egyptians would have it, "the archer hitteth the target, partly by pulling, partly by letting go; the boatsman reacheth the landing, partly by pulling, partly by letting go." There is something in the mechanism of the human soul that cannot be worked by self-consciousness and critical philosophy.

> To be delivered does not mean to run after Amida while he flees away from you, but it means to pick up the drowning persons on to the boat and save them from death. When the boatsman says he will save you from being drowned, will you try to swim up to him by yourself? Have you strength enough to do so? Understanding, as you do, how sure your death is and how merciful The Other is, why do you hesitate? The only thing you may do in this case is to let your lifesaver do whatever he knows best for your welfare. There is no need for you to look backward and forward and to carry along such old stuff as Nembutsu or faith or joyful heart. As soon as you realize the destiny of your sinful existence and the infinite, unconditional love of The Other, be gone with the last trace of self-assertion in whatever form, and abandon yourself, heart and soul, at the feet of the savior.

The giving up of everything of mine and the embracing of The Other unconditionally is to be preceded by humiliation and helplessness. Without the latter no salvation will be possible. Humiliation comes from the sense of unworthiness, and helplessness is the consciousness of finitude and limitation. Being finite and limited on all sides and in every way, we do not know how to get out of this, how to realize the state of freedom. When reflection turns upon the infinite perfectibility of moral character, that is, on the impossibility of attaining to a state of self-perfection in which all sinfulness has been thoroughly purgated, we are placed at the last stage of despair and hopelessness. If The Other demanded purity, perfection, and strength as the conditions of rebirth in the Pure Land, who on earth could ever hope for salvation? All is destined for *naraka,* every one of us, and the world will be the valley of the utmost misery. Thus, we can see that the background of *tariki* mysticism is deeply stained with blood and tears and that the doctrine of absolute passivity is heavily lined with the ugly wounds of merciless self-criticism. "Let go and you come up to the surface" is the Japanese saying. Renunciation is however the last resort we can come to and means so many vain efforts previously made for our own salvation. We clung to one thing after another always connected with the "I," we could not renounce this last possession, we failed to come up to Amida all naked, all shorn of selfhood. The last possession was the hardest to give up. Riches, fame, honor, and worldly pleasures were abandoned, but the self-consciousness or self-conceit that "I" have abandoned, that "I" have faith, still clings to us. As long as this "I" is still with us, we cannot rise to the surface, we cannot be born in the Pure Land; for we are not yet in the state of absolute passivity, that is, perfectly ready to receive the Original Vows of Amida. The giving up which is the mystic's ambition is by no means an easy task. But when this once takes place in its liveliest form, the infinite light of Amida fills up the darkest corners of our minds, and all the imperfections, weaknesses, and turbulences turn into so many rays of the Infinite Light.

> When the stalks are burned, not only their form disappears but they turn into fire. So when the virtues of Amida fill us not only the stalks of our evil passions disappear, but they are transformed into virtues. In the Psalms [*Wasan* (JCD)] we read: "As the more ice produces the more water, so do the more karma-hindrances the more virtues. This is because Amida's virtues are boundless and know no hindrances."

Renunciation is effected when we make a sudden turn in the course of a march which has come to its end. Believing that the thing we seek lies in a certain direction, we make steady efforts toward it; we come to the terminus, there is no way to go further, it is a blind alley, we beat against the wall, when suddenly we turn backward and lo! there lies an open field with an ever-receding horizon and with nothing to hinder one's freest movements. This is the occasion when the *tariki* mystic feels as if every piece of luggage he has been carrying was suddenly transferred on the shoulders of Amida. A monk came to a Zen master and asked, "What would you say when I have nothing on my back?" "Throw it down!" said the master. "But, sir, did I not say I carry nothing on my back?" "If so," roared the master, "carry it on." The monk was not yet free from selfhood, of his individual and self-assertive will, he was not walking in the open field empty-handed. Even when he said he had nothing on his back, his "I" was still at the tip of his shoulder, which was at once detected by the master's trained eye.

Shichiri writes:

> When Shenzan, a Zen adept of the Tang dynasty, was one day sitting in his room he saw a fly trying hard to pass through the paper-screen. It buzzed and fluttered its little wings violently but to no purpose. Shenzan composed a poem:
>
> Why dost thou not fly away through the empty door?
> How so very strangely thy thought moveth!
> For a hundred years thou mayest strike against the old paper-screen,
> But no time will ever come to thee when thou canst get thy head through.

The master here means to say this: "However self-confident a man may be in his power to go ahead, it is in vain. It is best for him to turn backward where he will see an extensive field. Learning, memory, or intellect is of no help as far as salvation is concerned. Abandon the course of your *jiriki* efforts and turn round to the *tariki* way where Amida awaits you with his Original Vows and infinite love."

Here is a kind of Shin catechism summing up the gist of its teaching:

Q. What is the Shin faith?

A. The easiest of all faiths. You have been in it for the last ten years only that you are not conscious of it yourself.

Q. What shall I do to have the faith?

A. Nothing much but to hear.

Q. How shall I hear?

A. Just as The Other wills. When you hear a storyteller, you just hear him. All the labor is on his side. As he talks you hear him. There is no special way of hearing. When you have heard, that is the time when *Namu-amida-butsu* has entered into your heart.

Q. If so, is just hearing enough?

A. Yes.

Q. Even then, I have fears as to my really hearing it: Did I hear or not? What shall I do with this?

A. That is not hearing but thinking. No thinking is needed here. Faith is awakened by hearing. Don't be caught here. If you reflect and begin to ask yourself whether you have faith or not, you turn your back toward Amida.

II

The second section of this paper will consist of thirty-eight sayings by Gōjun Shichiri culled from Akanuma's aforementioned work as well as from Ryōtai Koizumi's compilation, whose fifth edition appeared in 1920. While writing this paper the author has come into possession of another work on Shichiri entitled, "Anecdotes and Sayings of Shichiri Wajō" *(Shichiri Wajō genkōroku),* by Eshō Hamaguchi, in two volumes. It first appeared in 1912 and is published by Kōkyō Shoin, Kyoto. It saw its fifth edition last year.

(1) According to the other schools of Buddhism, good is practicable only after the eradication of evil. This is like trying to dispel darkness first in order to let the light in. It is not so with us, followers of *tariki:* if you have some worldly occupations such as shopkeeping, etc., just begin saying the Nembutsu even with your mind busily engaged in the work. It is said that where the dragon goes there follow clouds. With faith, with your thought directed toward the West, invoke the name of Amida with your mouth, and good actions will follow of themselves. You fail to hit the mark just because you try to catch the clouds instead of looking for the dragon itself.

(2) You cannot stop evil thoughts asserting themselves because they belong to the nature of common mortals. In the "Sayings of Yokogawa" we read that if we recite the Nembutsu we shall be quite certain of our rebirth in the Pure Land like the lotus blooming above the muddy water. The founder of our sect preaches that if we, instead of waiting vainly for the water to recede, start at once to wade through it, the water will recede by itself from under our own feet. Now when the heart is gladdened in the faith of *tariki,* there are in it no waters of greed, anger, etc.

(3) Dedicate your mouth to the Nembutsu. When you regard the mouth as belonging to yourself, it always tends to foster the cause of your fall into *naraka.*

(4) After enumerating the sins of common mortals, the reverend master said: It is thus that, in spite of our wish to attain the Pure Land, we find ourselves destined

for *naraka*. Therefore, let us realize that *naraka* is, after all our efforts, our destination. As far as our ignorant past is concerned there is no help for it; but as we have now come to the realization of our own situation, nothing is left for us but to embrace the way of salvation; for herein lies the purport of the Original Vows.

(5) There are some people who think that they understand what is meant by absolute devotion to the Nembutsu, but who are still doubtful as to their possession of the faith and inquire within themselves whether they are really all right. To such I would say: Give up your self-inquisition and have your minds made up as to the inevitableness of your fates for *naraka*. When you come to this decision, you will be serener in mind, ready to submit yourselves to the savior's will. To express the idea in a popular way, such people are like those wives whom their husbands do not seem to care for; they are in constant fear of being divorced. Being uncertain about Amida's love, they are anxious to court his favor. This is because they have not yet altogether given up their selves. When we know that *naraka* is inevitable for common mortals filled with evil thoughts and passions—and in fact we all are such mortals—there is nothing left for us but to be cheerfully grateful for Amida's promise of salvation. Whether we should be saved after or before our sins are expiated is the business of The Other and not ours.

(6) What? Is it so hard for you to surrender yourself? For, you say, when my advice is literally observed, you cannot carry on your business. Well, if you cannot, why would you keep it up? "If I don't I shall starve to death," you may say. Well, but is it after all such a bad thing as you think, this dying? When I say this you may regard me as inhuman and heartless, but is not your real aim to be reborn in the Pure Land of Amida? If so, when you die your wish is fulfilled. If this was not your original wish, what was it? What made you come here to listen to my sermons? You are inconsistent.

(7) Some people are not quite sure of their state of faith. They seem to put their faith on the scale against Amida's miraculous way of salvation, and try to weigh the latter with their own understanding, while salvation is altogether in the hands of The Other. To think that our attainment of the Pure Land is conditioned by our understanding of Amida's plans so that we cease to harbor any doubt as to the wonderful wisdom of the Buddha—this is relying on the strength of our faith and setting Amida's mercy away from us. When his mercy is not taken into our own hearts and we only ask whether our doubt is cleared and faith is gained, this faith becomes a thing apart from mercy and the one is set against the other. This we call a state of confusion.

(8) The great Original Vows of Amida are his Will, and the ten powers and four fearlessnesses are his Virtues. Both cause and effect are sealed up in the one name of Amida. A paper parcel superscribed as containing one thousand yen may consist, when counted in detail, of so many ten-sen notes and so many fifty-sen notes, but all the same the total is one thousand yen. Whether we know the contents in

detail or not, we are the owner of the one thousand yen as we have the parcel in our hands. Similarly, in whichever way we may embrace Amida, whether knowingly or unknowingly as to his Original Vows and manifold Virtues, we are, as soon as we accept him, the master of *Namu-amida-butsu*. So says Rennyo, "One is the master of *Namu-amida-butsu* when one accepts Amida." When his name resounds in your mind you have faith, and when it is expressed on your lips it is the Nembutsu. Oh, how grateful I feel for the grace of Amida! The Pure Land is drawing nigh day by day!

(9) In case we are depending on others, for instance, if we are working as servants we must first win the confidence of the master by showing our loyalty; for otherwise we can never serve him for any length of time. When a poor man wants to borrow money from a rich man he must prove first how honest he is; for otherwise the latter will never have enough confidence in the debtor. The faithfulness of the debtor must be recognized by the creditor. So in the other sects of Buddhism people are encouraged to rely on their own sincere desire to be saved, which they would have Amida accept for the price of his grace. But "reliance" or "dependence" is differently understood in the teaching of *tariki*. The feeling of dependence the child has for its mother has not been bought by its own filiality. When the sincerely loving heart of the parent is taken into its own little heart and when these hearts are made into one heart, the child is truly said to be filial. "Think of your parents with even half as much of the love as is entertained for yourself by the parental hearts"—so goes the old saying. If you had even one-tenth of such love, you would be the most filial child in the world. In like manner we can't come to Amida and ask him to accept us as the reward of our sincere desire to be saved. [From Amida's infinite point of view our sincerity is not worth being taken notice of by him.] What we can do is to accept his own sincere desire to save us and rest assured of the fulfillment of his Vows. This is the adamantine faith of *tariki*.

(10) You say that you never count on the Nembutsu as the efficient cause of your rebirth in the Pure Land because it is only the expression of your grateful heart, but you feel uneasy when you find that you do not say it well. As long as an old lady has a stick in her hand she may not be conscious of its utility, but she would feel unsteady with her feet if she should leave it altogether. In like manner while you can say the Nembutsu you feel all right, but as soon as your Nembutsu becomes rarer you are uneasy. Then you come to think that the Nembutsu has nothing to do with your rebirth in the Pure Land. So far so good, but still feeling that faith is somehow necessary you try firmly to take hold of it after all. While getting out of a boat one sometimes falls into water because one kicks off the boat in the effort to jump over to the bank. You fall into the fault of self-power because you jump at faith just as you let go the Nembutsu. Viewed in this light, this is also a sort of self-power, a self-power of mind if not of mouth. If you say that the Nembutsu is not the efficient cause of rebirth in the Pure Land, why should you not advance another

step in your way and also quit the faith itself? Then there will be but one mercy of the Buddha that works, and indeed there is nothing to surpass this state of mind.

(11) Referring to children the reverend master said, "Carried on the back of Amida as they are on the mother's, even the wanton, capricious ones will attain the Pure Land."

(12) "To hear" is the whole thing in the teaching of *tariki.* Says the sutra, "Hear the name of Amida!" The Buddha, let us observe, does not tell us to *think,* for hearing is believing, and not thinking. How do we hear then? No special contrivance is needed; in thinking we may need some method to go along, but hearing is just to receive what is given, and there is no deliberation here.

(13) We should live in this world as in a branch office of the Pure Land.

(14) We feel serene in mind, not because we are assured of attaining the Pure Land, but because we believe the words of Amida who promises to embrace us, to save us in his love.

(15) When holes are stopped in the broken paper screen, no draft will pass through: when we say the Nembutsu continually with our mouth, no evil language will have a chance to be uttered. Be therefore watchful.

(16) We read in the sutra, "It is ten kalpas now since the Enlightenment of Bhikshu Dharmākara." This means that family-fortune of father and children is merged in one; that is to say, the merits of Amida are now those of all sentient beings and the sins of all sentient beings are those of Amida. Here lies the uniqueness of the Enlightenment of Amida which distinguishes itself from Enlightenment attained by other Buddhas. According to the latter, thousands of virtues and merits are the sole possessions of the Buddhas themselves, whereas we poor creatures are altogether meritless. There are therefore in this case two independent family legacies; the one rich in endowments and the other next to nothing: while in the Enlightenment of Amida all is merged in one, for in him there is the virtue of perfect interpenetration. When bundles of hemp are burned, not only their original shape is transformed, but they all turn into fire. In like manner, when the merits of Amida enter into our hearts and fill them up, not only the evil passions we have are consumed like bundles of hemp, but they themselves turn into merits. We read in the *Wasan:* "The greater the obstacles the greater the merits just as there is more water in more ice. The merits of Amida know no boundaries."

(17) The lamp itself has no light until it is lighted, it shines out only when a light is put in. As Amida is in possession of this light of virtue, eighty-four thousand rays shine out of him; broadly speaking, his light knows no impediments and fills all the ten quarters. "Long have I been in possession in myself of the Original Vows made by the other-power and also their fulfillment! and yet how vainly I have wandered about deceived by the self-power's tenacious hold on me!" Again, "There is in the light of the Buddha of Unimpeded Light the light of purity, joy, and wisdom, and its miraculous virtues are benefiting all beings in the ten quarters."

Again, "As this is the teaching of Amida who turns all his merits toward the salvation of all beings, his virtues fill the ten quarters." It is thus evident that Amida is surcharging us with his merits.

(18) Certain *tariki* followers imagine that as Amida attained his Enlightenment ten kalpas ago, which determined the status of sentient beings as ultimately destined for the Pure Land, all that they have to do on their part for salvation is but to remember the fact of Amida's Enlightenment, and that as to their understanding of the meaning of *tariki* nothing is needed, for the remembrance is enough. This however is not the orthodox teaching. If we have no inner sense of acceptance as to Amida's infinite grace, it is like listening to the sound of rice-pounding at the next-door neighbor's, which will never appease our own feeling of hunger. The ancient saying is "A distant water cannot put out a near fire." A man comes into town from a faraway frontier district; while staying in an inn, fire breaks out in the neighborhood and confusion ensues. The traveler quietly remarks: "In my country there is a big river running in front of my house, and there is a great waterfall behind, besides the canals are open on all sides: you need not be afraid of the fire's getting ahead of you." But all the waters thousands of miles away will not extinguish the fire at hand. The inn is reduced to ashes in no time. You may imagine that in your native country of Amida's Enlightenment there securely lies the assurance of your rebirth in the Pure Land ten kalpas ago and also that there runs the great river of oneness in which are merged subject and object, Buddha and sentient beings; and you may nonchalantly say that you have no fear for hellfire; but inasmuch as you have no inner sense of absolute dependence your house is sure to be consumed by the flames.

(19) Such old Chinese remedies as *kakkontō* (arrowroot infusion) may do us neither harm nor good, but with a strong effective medicine there is something we may call toxic aftereffect. The grace of Amida as is taught by the other-power school is so vast and overwhelming that its recipients may turn into antinomians. This is the danger one has to be on guard against. Such *tariki* followers are inferior to the *jiriki,* who cherish a feeling of compunction even in innocently destroying the life of an ant. Whatever the Buddha-Dharma may teach, we as human beings ought to have a certain amount of conscience and the feeling of compassion; when these are missing, there will be no choice between ourselves and the lower animals.

(20) Some say that Buddhism is pessimism and does not produce beneficial results on our lives. But could Buddhists be induced to love this world so full of evils? If they were addicted to saké-drinking, a life of wanton pleasures, an insatiable thirst for fame and gain, how would they ever be expected to see into the true signification of this life? As they are detached from all these evils, they really know how to benefit the world. Since olden days there has been no one who truly worked for our welfare by leading a life of dissipation.

(21) The lower grow the mountains as the further we recede from them, but the nearer we approach the higher they are: so with the grace of Amida.

(22) When they are told this, "If you are going to take refuge in the teaching of *tariki,* you must refrain from committing evil deeds such as drinking, smoking, etc.," they are apt to hesitate. Well, let them drink then, let them wander away from the ordinary moral walks, if they are positively so inclined, but let them at the same time only believe in Amida, believe in the Original Vows of the Buddha. When the faith gradually takes possession of their hearts, they will naturally cease from evildoings. Through the grace of Amida their lives will be made easier and happier.

(23) Knowledge is good, its spread is something we have to be grateful for. But it is like fire or water without which we cannot live even for a day. But what a terrible thing fire is and water too, when we fail to make good use of them! How many human lives and how much property, we cannot begin to estimate, were lost in fire and flood! In proportion to its importance to life, knowledge is to be most cautiously handled. Especially in the understanding of *tariki* faith, knowledge proves to be a great hindrance.

(24) Knowledge is the outcome of reasoning and knows no limits; faith is the truth of personality. Faith and knowledge are not to be confused.

(25) Knowledge grows as we reason, but love stands outside of reasoning. In the education of children the mother ought to know how to reason about their future welfare and not to give way to her momentary sentiment. Love is the string that binds the two.

(26) Amida holds in his hands both love and knowledge for the salvation of sentient beings. So we read: "In the depths of Amida's love there lies his wisdom beyond calculation." *Namu-amida-butsu* signifies the union of love and wisdom and is the free gift of Amida to us sentient beings.

(27) Doubt is impossible when our salvation by Amida is so positive; and when salvation is so positive we cannot but help saying the Nembutsu.

(28) According to the *tariki* teaching, all that we sentient beings have to do in the way of salvation is to accept and believe. Have you ever seen a puppet-show? The marionettes are worked from behind, somebody is pulling the strings. We are all likewise moving through the absolute power of Amida.

(29) While Amida's Original Vows are meant universally for the salvation of all sentient beings in the ten quarters, we may not experience real joy if we are to receive only portions of Amida's grace as our shares. According to Shinran, Amida's meditation for five kalpas was only for his own sake, for himself alone; why then should not each of us take the whole share of Amida's grace upon himself? There is but one sun in the world, yet wherever we move does it not follow each of us?

(30) "To return to the great treasure-ocean of merits" means throwing oneself into it, that is, throwing oneself into a mass of wisdom, into the midst of Light.

I read somewhere a fine story about a rabbit. As it ran into a heath of scouring rush *(tokusa),* the hunter followed it but could not find any trace of the animal.

When he closely searched for it, he noticed that it has been rubbed off by the rush into a nonentity. In a similar way when we throw ourselves into the Light of Amida, all the evil karma and evil thoughts we may be in possession of altogether disappear. When flakes of snow fall into the boiling water they all at once melt away. When we have returned into the great ocean of Merits, that is, when we have thrown ourselves into the midst of Light and Wisdom, nothing of evil deeds and thoughts will be left behind. Think of it, O you, my brethren in faith, while enlightenment is impossible for us unless we reach the forty-first grade, or realize the first stage, we common mortals possessed of ignorance are now firmly established in the faith that we are to be born in the Pure Land of Amida when we have thrown ourselves into his Light where the boiling water of Wisdom melts all our evil karma and evil thought without even leaving a trace of them. This being proved, have we not every cause to be joyous?

(31) We are told to believe deeply in the mercy of Amida, but if you are too concerned with your state of mind the very mercy of Amida may prove to be a hindrance to the growth of your faith. If you strive to grow in faith thinking this must be accomplished for your salvation, the very effort will smother it. For faith means unconditionally to submit oneself to The Other, and the straining is the outcome of self-power; the heavier you step the deeper you go into the mud of self-power, and the further you stand away from other-power. In this case a step forward means a step backward, and when you think you are deep in it, that is the very time you are receding from Amida.

(32) "To have faith" means not to have any doubt about the Original Vows of Amida; when there is not the least shadow of doubt about the Vows, other things will take care of themselves.

(33) The principle of the *tariki* teaching is: "Just ask and you will be saved," and not "You do this and salvation will be its reward." Nothing is imposed upon you as the price of salvation. When you give sweets to your children you do not tell them to do this or that, you simply give them away; nothing is expected of them, for it is a free gift. With Amida, his gift has no conditions attached to it. Let your mortal weaknesses remain what they are, and be absorbed in the infinite grace of Amida.

(34) Saké cannot be poured into an overturned cup, but when it stands in its natural position, anybody can pour saké into it and as fully as it can hold. Therefore, have the cup of your heart upright ready to receive, and hear; it will surely be filled with Amida's mercy.

(35) There are some people who have heard of the Original Vows and say that they believe in them, but somehow they feel uneasy when they think of their last moments. They are like those who, feeling dizzy at the surging billows, are not at all sure of their safely sailing over the ocean. If they are too frightened at the evil passions that are stirring in their hearts, which they think will assuredly interfere with their ultimate salvation, there will be no end to their vexations. Look at the

spacious boat instead of the billows; for the boat is large enough and safe enough for every one of us, however sinful and numerous we are, and there will be no feeling of uneasiness left in us. When you think of the mighty power of Amida, you cannot have any fear as to your salvation.

(36) We must pay fair prices for things that belong to others. But when they are our own parent's they are justly ours too and we do not have to pay for them. This is because of the parental love that we are allowed to inherit all that belongs to him regardless of our mental capacities. So with Amida, he bestows upon us freely all that he has—and here is the secret of the *tariki* teaching.

(37) There are two ways to get rid of illusions and be enlightened. The one way is to accumulate our own merits and thereby gain enlightenment. The other way is to gain enlightenment depending upon the promise of the Original Vows of Amida; we are then admitted to the Pure Land, not indeed on account of our own wisdom or merit, but solely through the grace of The Other, who is the father of all beings. When we seek the Pure Land, we feel uneasy reflecting on our moral imperfections and the lack of a yielding, believing heart. But this is a state of mind not in accord with the spirit of *tariki,* for our attitude here is that of the one who would receive things from strangers and not from his own parent. As we followers of *tariki* are all naked with no outward vestments such as virtues or merits, we jump right into the water of the Original Vows of Amida where good men do not stand out any higher than wicked ones; for Amida's grace makes no preference between the two sets of beings.

(38) According to the old Chinese legend, the jellyfish has no eye and relies upon the crab for its sight. Supposing this true, we are all like the jellyfish, for we have no wisdom-eye to see through the triple world; and it is only when we are given Amida's own Light of Wisdom that we are really relieved of worry and can see the truth as the one who is destined for the Pure Land.

7

The Myōkōnin

This essay, translated and updated by Norman Waddell (NW), comprises chapter 4 of Suzuki's book *Nihon teki reisei* (Japanese Spirituality). In it he examines the sayings of two Shin Buddhist believers, Dōshū (d. 1516) of Akao and Asahara Saichi (1850–1932), both presented as *myōkōnin,* simple but inspiring examples of Shin piety. Suzuki's purpose in considering them is to illustrate and expand upon his idea of Japanese spirituality. He treats Dōshū and Saichi as models of the *reisei* spiritual outlook. Both were from humble origins and were only marginally literate. But they lived a rich and satisfying religious life. Each left a body of sayings that expressed his understanding and experience of Shin Buddhism. Suzuki explores them as an expression of *reisei teki jikaku* or *chokkaku,* "spiritual self-awakening." Implicit in their sayings, Suzuki argues, are the characteristics of Japanese spirituality—specifically, a nondualistic understanding of the world and a reconciliation with its dichotomies and contradictions. Suzuki's assumption is that this awareness arises from a closeness to the earth and the elemental aspects of human existence, rather than from learning and rational discourse. That is one reason he finds Dōshū and Saichi to be good examples of Japanese spirituality.

Though presented as sharing a common spiritual outlook, Dōshū and Saichi are in fact a study in contrasts. They arose at opposite ends of the Tokugawa period (1603–1867) when the *myōkōnin* paragon was popularized. Dōshū lived in the sixteenth century and could thus be described as a precursor to the *myōkōnin* ideal, whereas Saichi, who was only twenty years older than Suzuki, might be classified as a latter-day example. Dōshū was well known as the personal attendant of Rennyo (1415–1499), the most illustrious figure in Shin Buddhist history after Shinran, and was widely revered as a role model for Shin piety, whereas Saichi was virtually unknown until Suzuki's writings made him famous. Dōshū's sayings have a pragmatic flavor to them, focusing on conventional Shin beliefs and lifestyle, whereas Saichi's are quite subjective and personal, expressing his religious feelings through poetry. It is thus interesting that Suzuki brings these figures together as twin exemplars of the *myōkōnin* ideal.

Suzuki dedicates only a brief portion of the essay to Dōshū. He describes his simple and austere way of life and recounts anecdotes about his physical fortitude and stoic religious devotion. Suzuki then records twenty-one resolutions in which Dōshū offered advice to his fellow believers. What is noteworthy about them—and Suzuki himself points this out—is that hardly any statement reflects the nondualistic outlook of *reisei*. They dwell instead on "the One Great Matter" *(ichidaiji),* Shin code language for birth in the Pure Land after death, or on earnest and upright behavior and commitment to the Dharma. The one place where Suzuki obliquely identifies the *reisei* outlook is in the term "one thought" *(ichinen)* found in Dōshū's last resolution. In Shin teachings this word refers variously to the single moment when faith arises, the single thought of faith, and the single nembutsu accompanying faith.

Unlike Dōshū's sayings, Saichi's provide a multitude of examples of the nondualistic outlook that Suzuki highlights in his concept of Japanese spirituality. Suzuki's affinity to Saichi is reflected in the fact that he dedicates over three-quarters of this essay to him even though Dōshū was by far the more prominent figure in the minds of Shin Buddhists. Writing simple but touching poems expressing his religious feelings, Saichi reveals the words of the nembutsu, *Namu-amida-butsu,* to be the single unitary point where all the complexities and tensions of life are reconciled and resolved—between the evil person and the Buddha, between the flawed *shaba* world and the Pure Land, and between Saichi himself and Amida. In the nembutsu Saichi feels embraced by Amida as *Oya-sama,* "the loving parent," and hence the words of the nembutsu flow out of him as a spontaneous and unaffected expression, without guile or premeditation. Saichi's description of the nembutsu fits Suzuki's concept of spirituality perfectly, and hence his poems became reference material in Suzuki's Pure Land writings for the rest of his career. This essay, the earliest of Suzuki's in-depth expositions on Saichi, offers a good balance of Saichi's own words and Suzuki's elucidation of them.

The base text for this essay is chapter 4 of *Japanese Spirituality,* trans. Norman Waddell (Tokyo: Japanese Society for the Promotion of Science, 1972), 167–215. (The translation of this chapter has been extensively updated by Waddell.) This work was originally published in Japanese as Suzuki Daisetsu, *Nihon teki reisei* (Tokyo: Daitō Shuppansha, 1944). The book was republished in 1946 with chapter 5 omitted. See SDZ 6:171–223.

• • •

I. DŌSHŪ

1. His Life and Relation to Rennyo

Among Pure Land believers those particularly rich in faith and goodness are called *myōkōnin,* literally, "wondrous good people." A *myōkōnin* does not excel in scholarship or in discussing fine points of religious doctrine. He experiences in himself the thought of the Pure Land tradition, which lives in and through him. Although this should be true of all followers of the Pure Land, scholars included, it is the *myōkōnin* who are especially blessed in this regard. Being rare individuals, the term *myōkōnin* can properly be applied to very few people. Compilations have been made titled *Accounts of the Myōkōnin (Myōkōnin den)* that consist of the individual life histories of these devout people.

The first of the *myōkōnin* was Dōshū from Akao in Etchū Province (present Toyama Prefecture), a man of deep faith who served as an escort-guard of the Shin teacher Rennyo Shōnin (1415–1499). Not a great deal is known about his life, but he is mentioned or quoted several times in Rennyo's *Goichidaiki kikigaki,* and there are also references to him in the *Zoku Shinshū taikei.*

The *Accounts of the Myōkōnin* are a rich source of material for anyone tracing the historical development of Japanese spirituality. One can sift through the accounts and carefully examine the faith of the figures whose lives are recorded in it. As a start in that direction, I will now devote a few pages to these *myōkōnin.* My observations, random and disorganized as they are, I offer only as suggestions. I will begin with a discussion of Dōshū, and then turn to a *myōkōnin* named Asahara Saichi. I think that this will give the reader a general idea of how I view Japanese spirituality, as well as the manner in which I seek evidence of its development.

Dōshū, even with our limited knowledge of his life, emerges as a genuine seeker, a man who pursued his religious quest with a powerful and tenacious spiritual strength. The precise content of Dōshū's faith is not entirely clear, but there is no doubt that he devoted himself wholly to serving his teacher Rennyo, and he seems to have done this as a means of "repaying his debt of gratitude" to Amida Buddha. Dōshū compiled a collection he titled "Twenty-One Resolutions," guides and admonitions for religious conduct. While they do not disclose the essence of his faith, they do afford some valuable glimpses into it. . . .

Dōshū was born in the small village of Akao at the upper reaches of the Shō River in Etchū Province. His birth date is unknown. It is a twenty-mile journey to Akao from the Honganji branch temple at Jōgahana. The mountain path is said to be extremely dangerous, threading through deep valleys and crossing high mountain passes. Today one can travel by bus, but the mountain roads, snaking along precipitous cliffs a thousand feet high, are still perilous, especially in winter, when the entire region is covered with more than twenty feet of snow.

Legend has it that Dōshū's ancestors had served as retainers of Emperor Go-Daigo at the Southern Court. If true, it would mean Dōshū had samurai blood in his veins. Apparently, he accompanied Rennyo on his trips around the country during the conflict and upheaval of the Sengoku period. One of Dōshū's main duties seems to have been that of bodyguard, so he was probably well versed in the martial arts. According to Iwakura Seiji, who will soon be publishing a book on Dōshū, Dōshū's calligraphy closely resembles his teacher Rennyo's, but it is even stronger and more skillful. This in itself tells us something about the man.

Dōshū's secular name was Yashichi. After losing his parents when he was still very young, he was raised by his uncle Jōtoku. On once expressing a desire to find someone who resembled his parents, who had been very dear to him, he was told to go to the Temple of the Five Hundred Arhats in Tsukushi, on the island of Kyushu. There, he was told, one of the arhats would surely resemble his parents, and when the arhat saw Yashichi, he would smile in secret understanding. Yashichi made up his mind to travel to Kyushu, but he got no farther than Asōzu in Echizen province where, according to tradition, he met a priest who introduced him to Rennyo Shōnin, whose follower he became.

That Dōshū possessed spiritual insight is clearly seen from Rennyo's testimony in the *Goichidaiki kikigaki:* "Dōshū said that, though he heard a certain saying constantly, he always felt as grateful as if he had heard it for the first time." This continues from the previous section, with Rennyo, using Dōshū as an example, explaining why spiritual self-awakening is always a new and fresh experience, like hearing the first call of the *uguisu* bird in springtime: "Most people wish to hear something new or different, but a person of faith feels each thing as fresh and unique, even though he might have heard the same thing many times before. No matter how many times you hear something, it should be heard as fresh and as new as if hearing it for the first time."

A person who has experienced the self-awakening of genuine spiritual insight invariably experiences each thing as if for the first time. No matter how many times it appears, it is always fresh and new. As Dōshū had achieved this level of spiritual awakening *(reisei teki chokkaku),* his words are transmitted in Rennyo's *Goichidaiki kikigaki* as those of a saint.

> Dōshū of Akao has said, "As a matter of daily concern, you should never neglect the morning service at the family altar; you should make monthly visits to the nearest branch temple to worship the sect founder, Shinran; and each year you should make a pilgrimage to the Head Temple. . . . "

Here Dōshū shows that he was "a true gentleman *(kunshi),* striving every day from morning until night with all his might, and never slackening his efforts" *(Book of Changes).* Dōshū sought the Way and practiced it with a truly fierce determination. His spirit reminds us somehow of the warriors in the Sengoku period of fifteenth- and sixteenth-century Japan. When in his native place, he never missed the early morning services at the Inami branch temple. The path from his residence in Akao to Inami led through extremely rugged terrain, with mountains towering one behind the other. Only a person with tremendous endurance would be able to make such a daily round trip, especially in the winter months when snowdrifts were twenty- or thirty-feet deep and a single misstep would send him falling thousands of feet to his death. This did not deter him in the least. One wonders how long he continued performing this astonishing ascetic practice. It gained Dōshū the respect and admiration of all who knew him. He would also make two or three trips to the capital Kyoto each year, paying no heed when his teacher Rennyo told him it was not necessary to make the long trip so often. Dōshū apparently considered Rennyo an incarnation of Amida Buddha. Legend even tells of him worshiping a ray of light he saw shining from Rennyo's body. He once said that if ordered to by Rennyo, he would fill up great Lake Biwa with earth all by himself. In its religious fervor this exclamation shares a common spiritual ground with Shinran's avowal that he would gladly go to hell together with Hōnen.

Dōshū's life and actions are imbued with a strong element of asceticism. I sometimes feel that this attention to self-imposed discipline is something that many Jōdo followers lack. It is probably because they have a tendency on the one hand to rely completely on the power of Amida Buddha and a desire on the other hand to refrain from any tendency toward self-control that would keep a tight rein on the passions. But Dōshū applied himself to his practice with great austerity, always attempting to give a sharper edge to his religious faith. Of course he was not doing that to gain passage to birth in Amida's Pure Land. He strove diligently at his religious practice in order to remain mindful of his gratitude to the sect patriarchs and to caution himself continuously against any laxity or backsliding. Ascetic practice was not performed for its own sake. At home in Akao he would lay out forty-eight sticks of wood, representing Amida's forty-eight Prayers (or Vows), and sleep upon them to keep himself from sleeping soundly and to enable him to retain clearly in his mind the numberless eons of practice that Amida had accumulated for the sake of sentient beings. Another legend has him hanging down from the branch of a zelkova tree that grew out over a swiftly flowing river, cautioning himself against negligence by repeating to himself, "Below lies the torrent of the three evil courses, should I be irresolute . . . " In this concrete way he was able to bring his self-admonitions into sharp relief before his very eyes. While traveling, he slept on grain husks that he spread on the floor of his shelter.

Dōshū made a great effort to collect and make transcriptions of the letters that Rennyo had written to his followers, not merely for his own sake, as a means of strengthening his faith, but to show to the villagers of Akao as well, to instruct them in the Way. Section 281 in Rennyo's *Goichidaiki kikigaki* states: "When Dōshū begged Rennyo to give him some written instructions, he was told: 'You may lose a letter, but faith kept in the heart can never be lost.' Nevertheless, the following year he acceded to Dōshū's request."

Once when Dōshū was setting out for Kyoto, his wife asked him to obtain for her some instructions from Rennyo concerning the acquiring of faith. After the long and arduous return trip from Kyoto, before even stopping to take off his straw sandals, he produced a piece of paper on which was written the six characters, *na-mu-a-mi-da-butsu*. On seeing his wife's disappointment—she had obviously expected some more detailed instruction—and still without having taken off his footwear, he said, "All right," and set off for Kyoto once again, many miles, days, and hardships distant. Although he had that very moment returned from a trip of more than ten days through the mountains, he began the same journey once more. I think this story—even if it is legendary—helps us to understand the extent of Dōshū's purity and honesty. It was such that hardship and privation could make no inroad. There are preserved in Dōshū's temple three handscrolls in his own hand, containing copies of twenty-three of Rennyo's letters. This, together with the fact that Dōshū's descendants have maintained the temple in Akao to the present day, clearly reveals the great influence that Dōshū's teaching has had among the people. In any case, he became a figure of deep veneration in his village, and has remained so to the present day.

At a time when Dōshū's goodness and compassion had become widely known, a Tendai priest from a neighboring village came to Akao, thinking to test this man about whom he had heard so much. Finding Dōshū bent over weeding in the fields, the priest came up behind him and kicked him over. Without even changing his expression, Dōshū got up and resumed his weeding. The priest kicked him over again. Dōshū's reaction was the same. This was more than the priest could stand. "For no reason at all someone comes up and kicks you down, yet you don't show any anger," he exclaimed. "In what region do you exist?" Dōshū, his smile never leaving his face, answered, "I do it to pay the debts of my former existence. I probably have many more still to pay."

The idea that human beings bear a debt from a former existence derives from the theory of karmic retribution in the three periods of past, present, and future *(sanze inga)*. But I believe that this particular form—paying a debt from a former existence—originated in China. It is found in the sayings of the second Chinese Zen patriarch Huike. Zen places great store in the assertions of the *Diamond Sutra,* and in the Zen records we find priests and others frequently using the expression "using up karma." In the *Diamond Sutra* we read:

> Furthermore, Subhūti, if a good man or good woman who is about to fall into evil ways due to evil karma from former existences is belittled by others, the evil karma from his former existences will be exhausted and he will attain Supreme Enlightenment.

We all shoulder the burden of this debt, and it must at some point be paid. The debt is this present existence—the individual self. Therefore, this existence must be overturned and penetrated to its core. We must at some point succeed in leaping from the individual self *(koonore)* to the supra-individual self *(chō koonore)*. In Shin Buddhism this is called *ōsō-ekō,* receiving the blessing of birth in the Land of Bliss. When it is achieved, *gensō-ekō,* the "return and transfer," occurs, the return to this life to dedicate all our merit toward the salvation of our fellow beings. However, the process is not one of first achieving rebirth and then transferring one's merit. Rebirth itself is the returning and transferring. Rebirth in the Pure Land is itself the return to this life to help other beings. The words "paying the debt" appear from the consciousness of the individual self. In reality, there are no debts to be paid, no debtors, no debtees. The debt and owner of the debt freely come and go within the Dharma Universe *(Hokkai)* of the supra-individual self. Buddhists call this the "dependent origination of all things in the universe" *(Hokkai engi)*, as well as the "Sportive Samadhi" *(yuge zanmai)*[1] of the bodhisattva. But it is within the life of the individual self that one's karma must be exhausted. At this Dōshū was a truly resolute master. In his fierce determination he is reminiscent of Zen master Suzuki Shōsan, who lived many years after him during the first years of Tokugawa rule.

Since Shōsan was a Zen teacher, his attitude toward Buddhist teachings was naturally different from Dōshū's, but as concerns an indomitable will and resolute temperament, there is a close resemblance. I do not remember Shōsan speaking of "repaying the debt," but for teaching purposes he does talk of exhausting karmic hindrances, of exhausting self, of self-abandonment, of "not being deluded by this putrid flesh." He told those who were setting off to make the pilgrimage around the island of Shikoku to mourn the pilgrims who had died along the way and had no one to mourn them. He taught those who chanted dharani that the intent repetition of the dharani's words would remove karmic hindrance. In worshiping Amida by chanting the Nembutsu, you should simply trust in the Buddha's grace and worship for all your worth. By doing that, he said, you would exhaust the karmic hindrance and exhaust the self; and you should not harbor any thought of attaining Buddhahood through such acts. He taught that those who claimed they did not fear karma in the least were proof of the words "Those who do not fear karma are those with the greatest karma." He also said:

> It would be best for a beginner to pray for faith first of all, and then to repeat mantras and dharanis, using up his mind and body. Or, if he invokes an eight-syllable dharani one hundred, two hundred, or even three hundred thousand times, he can use up his karmic hindrances, deepen his faith, and awaken to the truth. He should discard any wish to become a venerable priest and just work earnestly to become one with the earth. (*Roankyō*, 1:16)

The self, in any case, must be eliminated. The self is the karmic hindrance, a debt acquired from a previous existence, an obstacle that prevents you from reaching the supra-individual "Person," that is, from reaching spiritual self-awakening. You have no need to wait for a kick from someone. To pay the debt you should go forward on your own and discover the truth that you are a self that consists of burning passions and desires. You are not able to experience this concretely in your own life simply by hearing of the existence of such passions from someone else. When the passions and desires are experienced as a concrete reality in your own body, the opportunity to attain the believing heart (faith) will appear of itself. The clarity of your faith will be in proportion to the depth and intensity of the reality you experience. First of all, you must grasp that faith experientially, and you must harbor no intention of attaining it. If you did, it would simply be a case of worshiping the Buddha in order to attain Buddhahood oneself.

Dōshū, while he was engaged in the intense training we have described, was advancing along the path of spiritual awakening. Viewed superficially, words such as "absolute passivity," "severe asceticism," "absolute reliance," and "natural, effortless activity" seem to contain many disparities, but upon some reflection it is possible to sense at their depths the spiritual self-awakening *(reisei teki jikaku)* common to them all. I believe that in the manner in which this is sensed is found a form of spiritual self-awakening that can be said to bear a uniquely Japanese character.

Dōshū drew up the "Twenty-One Resolutions" that appear in the following section during the third winter after Rennyo's death. Although ostensibly they are personal admonitions, there is no doubt that Dōshū used them primarily to indicate the right path to the villagers, people who were also his fellow Nembutsu practicers. Since these "Resolutions" reveal practices Dōshū himself had been following, there would have been little need for him to take the trouble of enumerating them in this way. Perhaps, after Rennyo's death, the villagers asked Dōshū to write something for them, and he just dipped into his past experience and came up with these precepts. Since nothing directly pertaining to faith per se appears in them, we may regard them as guides for conduct that he wrote down for his fellow believers (and for himself as well), both to encourage correct practice and to help prevent any tendency to neglect that practice. If faith can be said to figure in any of the resolutions, it would have to be the last part of article twenty-one: "Never breach the laws and rules of society. Preserve within your heart the reliability and blessedness of the 'one thought' *(ichinen)*, while outwardly acting with deep humility toward others."

Compliance with the laws of the world, not making a display of one's faith, simply preserving the constancy and virtue of the "one thought" deep within the heart are words often heard from followers of the Pure Land sects. The admonition against flaunting one's faith, even if it does not necessarily connote keeping it secret, should probably be understood to signify that spiritual self-awakening is a matter that should not be approached in an easy or irresolute manner. In some cases religious insight may lead a person to disregard worldly norms—society's morality, customs, and laws. There were those among the Christian mystics of the European Middle Ages who committed highly dubious acts on the grounds that "I am God. My will is God's will. I may act as I wish." This is something that must be constantly guarded against, and it applies to the followers of all religions. It was probably this point that was Rennyo's and Dōshū's primary concern.

2. *Dōshū's Twenty-One Resolutions*

(1) Do not be forgetful of the One Great Matter [of your rebirth in the Pure Land (NW)] as long as you live.

(2) Should something other than the Buddha-Dharma enter deeply into your heart, consider it shameful and dispatch it forthwith.

(3) You must resolutely break through and sweep away any tendency to indolence, laxity, or self-indulgence.
(4) If you feel something to be shameful in light of the Buddha-Dharma, you must sever immediately and without hesitation all connection with it.
(5) Hold no favoritism in your heart. Do no evil to others.
(6) You are always being watched; therefore, do not think you may do evil just because no one is watching your actions.
(7) You must always respect and honor deeply the Buddha-Dharma, be ever modest yourself, and behave with prudence.
(8) However you look at it, it is shameful to consider using others by means of the Buddha-Dharma. Should such an idea enter your mind, consider that there is no other reason for having faith in the Buddha-Dharma than to assist you in the One Great Matter of this one life, and reject such thoughts.
(9) If you find yourself somewhere that evil is being committed, regardless of its relative merits, you should leave.
(10) The very thought that Amida knows the wretchedness in my heart brings me deep sadness and pain. Though I am well aware he has forgiven me all my prior actions, the fact that he knows my inner state is cause for shame and sorrow. When I think that my heart was anchored in wretchedness in the world before and is now still so, I know a wretchedness beyond description. Even though I chanced to meet Amida my heart would still remain in wretchedness. Oh, wondrous compassion! I beg forgiveness for my prior transgression. I must entrust myself to your compassion.
(11) If you are still alive today or tomorrow and you become lax with regard to the Dharma, you must consider it shameful, sweep the laxity aside, and attend to the Dharma.
(12) If wonder does not rise fully in your heart, you should consider it shameful and wasteful, and resolve that, though you starve to death or freeze to death, you will attain *Ōjō* (birth in the Pure Land). And you should decide the One Great Matter in this present existence, the fulfillment of your desire from beginningless kalpas in the past, and press yourself resolutely in order to recover your sense of wonder. If even then wonder is not obtained, consider that you are probably being punished by the Buddha; break through your laxity and praise the Dharma to fellow devotees, because those acts at least should be matters of wonder.
(13) You must not make the mistake of being self-indulgent, of sleeping away your life in vain, failing to consider the One Great Matter of your life.
(14) Do not make excuses for not having friends. Encountering those of your household, though they may not be conscious of the Dharma, direct their attention to it as best you can; above all ask them about the One Great Matter and be attentive to retaining a sense of wonder in your hearts.

(15) Keep fully in mind that the matters of the temple are important above all else.
(16) You must not hold thoughts of hate or vengeance toward those who hate you.
(17) You must simply keep the One Great Matter deeply and unceasingly in your heart, and follow the suggestions given you by your fellow believers.
(18) Do not become attached to the myriad things of the world; just keep deep in your heart this One Great Matter.
(19) As I write in this way, because my heart is so incorrigible and shameful, even though I consult with it deeply and gain resolve, I wonder if something will be forthcoming. I must follow without fail the advice of others.
(20) I think of nothing but the hope you will give me your incomparable compassion, keep me from going astray, and correct what is in my heart.
(21) Oh, this wretched heart! If I am to resolve the One Great Matter, I cannot think of the fate of this existence. Wherever I am ordered to go, I must go. I must resolve even to journey to China or to India in search of the Dharma. Compared with such resolution, is there anything so easy as following the way of Amida? Consider deeply the transience of the world. One is not long upon this earth. Starving from hunger or freezing to death makes little difference. Do not think twice about such considerations, and constantly work for the One Great Matter. Do not go against these resolutions: strive, be attentive, never breach the laws and rules of society. Preserve within your heart the reliability and blessedness of the "one thought" *(ichinen),* while outwardly acting with deep humility toward others.

II. ASAHARA SAICHI

1. *Myōkōnin Asahara Saichi*

When I first heard of Myōkōnin Saichi from Professor Nishitani Keiji almost two years ago, I wanted very much to read his poems. Then this year I received a book titled *Daijō sōō no chi* (A Land Suited for Mahayana) by Rev. Fuji Shūsui, in which some of Saichi's poems were included. I felt upon reading them that Japanese spiritual self-awakening was manifested here in a pure and unalloyed form. In the following chapter I will quote some of Saichi's poems, together with my own comments. In going about this, I have thought it best to place Saichi's experience within the background of Pure Land thought as a whole, not within the more limited context of the Jōdo or Shin sects in particular.

According to Rev. Fuji, Myōkōnin Saichi—as Asahara Saichi has come to be called—lived in the small country town of Kohama in the province of Iwami, now Shimane Prefecture. He died in December of 1933[2] at the age of eighty-three. Until his fiftieth year he worked as a shipwright, at which time he began making *geta,* a type of wooden clog, an occupation he continued up until his death. His father was a deeply religious man who also lived into his eighties.

While at work making the *geta* Saichi would write poems on the wood shavings that fell from his planer. The poems gradually accumulated and in time reached a considerable number. Carrying on his trade in the midst of a samadhi-like religious joy—a Nembutsu Samadhi—Saichi wrote artlessly of the thoughts that chanced to enter his head, without allowing this to interfere in any way with his work. On the contrary, he accomplished more than any average *geta*-maker. Although those who become immersed in the "ecstasy" of samadhi might be thought of as least fit for the practical side of life, forgetting their work, dropping dishes or stitches, or whatever, Saichi's case was totally different. Saichi's work was itself a blissful Nembutsu Samadhi. Still, the human consciousness being self-reflective, the words of the poems could not help flowing naturally from his heart. Saichi's "poems" are artless; neither shaped nor polished, they are free of technique or artifice of any kind. He uses what small literary skills he possessed and, like a spider spinning out thread, he produces a natural, styleless poetry, without adhering to any set number of syllables. The results are truly wonderful expressions of religious faith.

According to Rev. Fuji, Saichi had a strong desire to seek the Way from the age of eighteen or nineteen, but abandoned his attempts at religious practice after five or six years when they failed to achieve any results. When he was twenty-seven or -eight, realizing that it would no longer be possible for him to abandon his great undertaking for even a single day, he began to pursue his goal once again. He believed that the Way would be revealed to him if he could only travel to the great Honganji Temple in Kyoto and listen to an eminent priest preach. But the long journey from his village in Iwami to the capital was an undertaking of such magnitude, he could not even consider it. Instead he listened to expositions of the Pure Land teaching at local country temples, and visited the houses of lay Buddhists whenever meetings with sermons were conducted. It is said that he did not finally attain *anjin* ("a mind pacified," meaning "faith confirmed") until he had passed the age of fifty. The hard struggle Saichi underwent up to that time can well be imagined, yet we are thankful that his poetry remains free from any trace of formal Shin sect terminology. Those who become too concerned with words and letters to give their attention to actual experience tend to speak in a conceptual manner. This tendency is not found in the *myōkōnin,* who fall directly under the experience itself. The actual taste of this experience must first be known; thought systems can be constructed afterward. To produce the system first and then try to squeeze the experience from it is as profitless as trying to extract blood from turnips.

Saichi's completely artless mode of expression and the lack of connective particles in his poems to indicate relationships between words and phrases are probably the reason why their meaning is at times difficult to grasp. Unavoidably, the reader becomes enmeshed in the words. In such cases, I will just take the initiative and act as interpreter.

2. *The* Namu-amida-butsu *Poems*

What first strikes one about Saichi's poetry is the constant recurrence of *Namu-amida-butsu:* "I'm thankful, *Namu-amida-butsu,*" "I'm miserable, *Namu-amida-butsu,*" "Amida *Oya-sama, Namu-amida-butsu,*" "I'm blessed with Amida's compassion, *Namu-amida-butsu,*" "My breath flows in and out, *Namu-amida-butsu,*" "The day is over, *Namu-amida-butsu,*" "Night is here, *Namu-amida-butsu,*" and on and on. Nembutsu wells forth in an endless stream. The *Namu-amida-butsu* of Saichi's Nembutsu seems to contain many layers of meaning. Here, instead of trying to analyze them one by one, I will begin by plunging directly into *Namu-amida-butsu* itself.

What does his *Namu-amida-butsu* mean? My own answer is that Saichi's entire being has become *Namu-amida-butsu.* Or rather, Saichi is none other than *Namu-amida-butsu* itself. Saying that his consciousness is completely filled with Nembutsu would mean consciousness and Nembutsu have become two, and only perpetuate a dualistic understanding. Saichi's Nembutsu does not emerge from a dualistic standpoint. His central identity is *Namu-amida-butsu* itself. His consciousness is one in which *Namu-amida-butsu* realizes *Namu-amida-butsu.* When Linji's "true man" or Shinran's "I, alone" is realized, there Linji and Shinran are born. It is then that *Namu-amida-butsu* pours forth from his mouth. Saichi did not make the wooden clogs, *Namu-amida-butsu* made them. When this *Namu-amida-butsu* chances to return to the individual self, the uttering of the Name, the repeating of Nembutsu, occurs. *Namu-amida-butsu. Namu-amida-butsu.* Asahara Saichi spent thirty years of his life seeking to attain this experience. He was a lost child who had not strayed a single pace from his own doorstep. Yet had he not once been lost, he would never have understood.

The supra-individual "Person" that has broken through the consciousness of the individual self must tell us what it has done. This exclamation is spiritual self-awakening, the realization of *Namu-amida-butsu.* This is where Saichi's poems all have their genesis.

There would be little sense trying to explain the poems by saying that in Japanese *Namu* is *kimyō,* which means "taking refuge," "adoration," "worshiping," and the like, and that *Amida Butsu* is the Tathagata of Infinite Light. At times such explanations are no doubt needed, but for a *myōkōnin,* as for ordinary devotees, such talk tends only to drive them into paths of illusion. Just *Namu-amida-butsu*—that is all that is needed. The oak tree in the yard does not state, "I am a tree of the cypress family." It simply grows up in the garden as it is. *Namu-amida-butsu* is "meaningless meaning," and if we try to attach some kind of meaning to it, or start to think that some significance should exist within it, then the six-syllable Name is no longer your own; it is farther from you than the highest clouds. Since *Namu-amida-butsu* transcends time and place, if even the slightest bit of discrimination, distinction, or calculation is allowed, the *geta* will not get made, the work will fail, and Saichi as Saichi will disappear. Contradiction alone will be felt, the mind will become turbulent, heart and mind will be obstructed, and joy, the emotion that flows from the supra-individual "Person," will fly.

Whenever I chance to meet with Joy,
Both time and place left unspoken.
I am joyful. You are joyful—
That is the pleasure, *Namu-amida-butsu.*

Saichi's joy is not a conscious product of his individual self. In it, the participation of the supra-individual "Person" can be perceived with utmost clarity. Nor is the joy of a temporal nature, nor can it be limited to any fixed place. It occupies Saichi's consciousness constantly. It is a continual joy free of any distinctions of time or place. For that reason Amida takes part in it as well. Were the joy limited by the consciousness of Saichi's individual self, it would be an accidental and occasional thing, and would inevitably be tinged with the special characteristics of the individual self. It would, in that case, be no different from ordinary joy, and would not belong to the sphere of spiritual self-awakening. In this can be seen the distinctive feature of the religious mind.

3. *Joy and Repentance*

Nembutsu is the Buddha of ceaseless joy and repentance,
The Buddha that is born with *Namu-amida-butsu.*

Repentance is joy, joy is repentance. This constant mixture is, in and of itself, *Namu-amida-butsu.* Thanks to *Namu-amida-butsu,* Saichi is, as he is, fully conscious of his penitence and humility and folly, and is, at the same time, the Buddha of joy. Spiritual self-awakening realizes this contradiction and at the same time knows, intuitively, that there is no contradiction. This can be seen in the following:

When I encounter the chance for repentance,
Both time and person are utterly shameful.
This becomes the source of joy
In *Namu-amida-butsu.*

This is apparently filled with contradiction. Since this *bonbu* ("ordinary man" or "unenlightened person") is mean and shameful, he is repentant. The possibility of realizing his woeful state lies in the "chance" or "opportunity." Without that chance, realization is impossible. Realization is the source of joy. It is joy itself. Shamefulness—repentance—joy—*Namu-amida-butsu:* these are the links in the experiential chain. It is not a straight-line sequence from any one to any other. All occur simultaneously. When this is analyzed by the consciousness of the individual self, the image of a contradictory repentance and joy is seen by the mind as incompatible. But from the vantage point of spiritual self-awakening, repentance and joy, misery and *Namu-amida-butsu,* are interfused; they are three-dimensional, or circular. The body and essence of this is *Namu-amida-butsu, Namu-amida-butsu. Namu-amida-butsu* rejoices in *Namu-amida-butsu.* Or perhaps we might say that Nembutsu says Nembutsu.

> This Dharma is the Dharma of repentance.
> If it is the Dharma of repentance, it is the Dharma of joy.
> If it is the Dharma of joy, *Namu-amida-butsu.*

Repentance and joy and *Namu-amida-butsu* are linked together as in an endless, beginningless circle. If you have any one of them, the others are there naturally. Repentance and joy, joy and repentance, are not two, but one. They are one, yet they are two. The one is the many and the many are the one. Although we cannot deal with this from the standpoint of contradiction, there is another side, thanks to which we are able to carry on with our lives. This is compassion, the compassion of *Namu-amida-butsu.* Saichi's life until the end had this *Namu-amida-butsu* at its center. When he experienced the momentousness and immensity of this center, he experienced the momentousness and immensity of repentance and joy. As he expresses it:

> Much happiness and joy is wretchedness too,
> Much wretchedness.
> The abundance of the mountain streams is also
> Originally from the ocean's boundless seas.
> Thus we know the taste of joy and repentance,
> Repentance and joy is an ocean of compassion,
> The six syllables, *na-mu-a-mi-da-butsu.*

Saichi's poems are always *Namu-amida-butsu* from beginning to end; it is their center as well. There is little doubt that the opening of Saichi's enlightenment was profoundly and thoroughly grounded in the six syllables of the Name.

4. *Receiving Amida*-san *from Amida*-san

By means of *Namu-amida-butsu* Saichi's individual self, wretched and heavily laden with sin, enters straightaway the realm of the *Nyorai,* becoming a Buddha of great merit. This is Amida Nyorai's great compassion. To Saichi, it is Amida's great favor. The great compassion of the Original Prayer (or Vow) and Saichi's thankfulness for Amida's great mercy are two sides of the same coin. When the supra-individual "Person" starts to function, it is called great compassion. When this great compassion touches the individual self of "wretched Saichi," the consciousness of the individual self sees it as the (Buddha's) great favor. Worshiped and worshiper are both *Namu-amida-butsu*. Saichi says:

> I receive Amida-*san* from Amida-*san,*
> He has me say *Namu-amida-butsu.*

"Receiving," "Accepting," "Has me say" are compassion, the Buddha's favor, and the heart of joy. They are *Namu-amida-butsu* itself.

> Compassion is Amida-*san,*
> Compassion that makes me worship him.
> *Namu-amida-butsu*
> Is *Namu-amida-butsu.*

The meeting point of individual self and supra-individual "Person" is *Namu-amida-butsu*. This point is the source of all Saichi's poetry.

> The great favor
> That makes my sin a virtuous Buddha,
> *Namu-amida-butsu.*

Again:

> Great favor, great favor, oh, great favor,
> This Buddha is the Buddha
> Who makes Saichi Buddha,
> The great favor that says *Namu-amida-butsu.*

The Buddha makes this wretched, foolish, sinful Saichi a Buddha; through great favor and compassion *Namu-amida-butsu* is bestowed from the Other and immediately becomes his own *Namu-amida-butsu*. Saichi's awakening to the self-identity that exists amid contradiction becomes all the more clear. Look at this next poem:

> *Namu* Buddha is Saichi, Saichi is the Buddha.
> Saichi's satori comes, *Namu-amida-butsu,*
> And it is received, *Namu-amida-butsu.*

Where Saichi is the Buddha and the Buddha is Saichi, there is *Namu-amida-butsu*. He does not say, "Saichi is identical to the Buddha; the Buddha is identical to Saichi," for there is between them the giving and receiving of *Namu-amida-butsu*. When Saichi realizes this, his satori "opens up." The notion of the self-identity of supra-individual "Person" and individual self may be most appropriate in the context of "holy path" *(jiriki)* Buddhism. Yet in *Namu-amida-butsu,* the intuitive understanding of the Pure Land *(tariki)* tradition has something that should be included here as well. It is the starting point and the goal as well.

5. *Buddha's Saichi—Saichi's Buddha*

What is this *Namu-amida-butsu* that has wretched Saichi on one hand, great compassionate Amida (or *Oya-sama,* author of the great favor) on the other, and *Namu-amida-butsu* as the central point or connecting line? Isn't it the six-syllable Name, a mere stream of sounds coming from the mouth? Doesn't it just mean relying upon Amida Buddha, seeking refuge in him? What incomprehensibility is this, which allows Saichi, the square handle, to be connected to Amida, the round socket?

Saichi, as an ordinary man or *bonbu,* is an actual individual self. The Buddha does not possess ordinary-man Saichi's reality; he has a supra-individual reality that stands in opposition to it. At any rate, the two are at odds, confronting each other from opposite extremes. What is the meaning of the six syllables that connect? Were they merely linked together in a line, they might be considered symbolic. But when in actual practice the six-syllable Name makes the two into one, it is something that cannot be comprehended by the ordinary discriminating consciousness. How then does the supra-individual Buddha through the six syllables enter into Saichi's individual self? Is it not true that the six syllables themselves are not found anywhere within the actuality of Saichi's unworthy existence?

The problem returns once again to the root: What is *Namu-amida-butsu?* Even granting we understand Saichi and the Buddha, what is the six-syllable Name? In reality, however, we do not understand either Saichi or the Buddha. These are matters that cannot be known by the discriminatory intellect no matter how much it searches. The six-syllable Name is more unknowable still. And yet philosophers will try in some way or another to elucidate it by means of logic—a case of the human intellect at work. The only way for the rest of us to settle it is through spiritual self-awakening *(reisei teki chokkaku).* Which is to say that by immediately confronting the six-syllable Name itself and becoming one with it, we are able to understand how Saichi and the Buddha frolic about in this self-identity in which they are one yet two, two yet one.

If the lay mind must produce some kind of statement, it might be something like this: the moment the heart of Saichi—the ordinary man—begins to search for the Way, the six-syllable Name makes its appearance. The appearance of the six-syllable Name occurs when Saichi comes into contact with the great compassion of Amida. When Saichi awakens to this reality, he says *Namu-amida-butsu,* or "I am struck." This is the incomprehensibility spoken of before, which lies outside the bounds of ordinary thought. Here is a Buddhist's view of the Buddha-wisdom's incomprehensibility:

Namu is the name of Amida,
Amida is the name of *Namu*—
This is Saichi's *Namu-amida-butsu.*

Saichi does not speak of theory but expresses his insight as it comes to him, without adornment:

It is not I who heard it,
It is not I who heard it;
Namu-amida-butsu strikes into my heart.
Now I am struck and taken by you.

The third line directly conveys Saichi's sense of being "struck" by the Name. If you yourself are here and the Buddha placed over there, and then you try to connect them, it cannot be done: water and oil do not mix. Without having the realization that you are the Buddha, there is no way you can become the six syllables of the Name.

I do not become Amida,
Amida becomes me—
Namu-amida-butsu.

The Name comes from Amida and "strikes" Saichi. Although Saichi remains Saichi, he is no longer the former Saichi; he is *Namu-amida-butsu.* Viewed from *Namu-amida-butsu,* one side is Amida and the other is Saichi, yet each side is retained. *Namu-amida-butsu* is another name for the insight of spiritual self-awakening. We might call it the substance or content of that insight. Or could we not say that the self-individualization of Amida is *Namu-amida-butsu?* Such seem to be the only conclusions we can reach from examining Saichi's words. Where a philosopher would need to erect a logical sequence of some kind, Saichi says:

My heart is your heart,
Your heart is my heart;
Becoming me is your heart.

To genuinely know this heart is *Namu-amida-butsu.* Or perhaps we could say, if you become *Namu-amida-butsu* you will understand the meaning of "your" in the words, "Becoming me is your heart." In the following,

Compassion and light, all one.
Saichi and Amida, all one.
Namu-amida-butsu.

the place where all are one is *Namu-amida-butsu.* It is *Namu-amida-butsu,* it is light, it is compassion, and it is Saichi. Realization of this is what I call the insight of spiritual self-awakening, and I regard it as being singularly Japanese in its configurations.

How happy I am!
Amida's seal is stamped in my heart.
The seal called *Namu-amida-butsu,*
The seal of *Oya-sama* [the loving parent (JCD)],

His child has received,
And simply says, *Namu-amida-butsu.*

I will consider the parent-child relation between Amida and Saichi later, but first a word concerning the "seal" of *Namu-amida-butsu*. This seal is a bond signifying that Saichi and the Buddha are contradictory yet have a nature of self-identity, which means that this seal is the six-syllable Name. Calling the Nembutsu a "seal" is an unusual choice of words, yet no doubt it clearly reveals what Saichi felt.

If we say that Saichi and Amida-*san* are one, or that *Namu-amida-butsu* is a seal given as proof of this identity, the sense becomes wholly spatial, and a tendency will appear to regard their relation as merely a static one. When this happens, Buddhism takes on a pantheistic character. Even today some Buddhist scholars might assert that it is so, but there could be nothing more mistaken with regard to Buddhism. The self-identity of Saichi and the Buddha has to be seen from the vantage point where space is time and time is space, and probably linked together in an active, dynamic relationship. In any case, Saichi operates within Amida, and Amida moves within Saichi. That is the mode in which *Namu-amida-butsu* must exist. *Namu-amida-butsu* must be *uttered,* in the sense of being spoken through all three spheres of activity—mouth, mind, and body. The Zen sect says, "the feet run, the hands grasp." The Nembutsu schools do not address themselves to this point as distinctly as Zen does. On the other hand, they show more interest in the emotional aspect, speaking of the relation of parent and child, or of the all-pervading light of compassion.

Oya-sama dwells in my fiery hands;
Oya-sama who says *Namu-amida-butsu.*

The phrase "*Oya-sama* dwells in my fiery hands" suggests the endless infinitude of hellish contradictions that seems to make up the boundless passion and endless torment to which human life is subject. Amida dwells within all this. Saichi's "dwell" may suggest passivity or nonaction, something devoid of emotion. But Saichi's actual feeling is not so. It burns intensely together with the flame itself, though Amida remains untouched by the flames. That is how I understand *"Oya-sama* who says *Namu-amida-butsu."* It is not a matter of merely sitting quietly and passively and repeating the Nembutsu. The uttering, the intoning is an act. As the fire burns, *Namu-amida-butsu* burns with it, and *Namu-amida-butsu* is uttered. Each movement of the planer, sweeping wood shavings stroke by stroke to the floor, is the sound of *Namu-amida-butsu. Oya-sama* moves in Saichi's hands and feet, and the wood shavings fall from the plane-strokes until they lie all around his workbench—the hands and feet are not Saichi's. Empty-handed, he grasps the hoe, on foot he rides the bullock, his feet and hands are *Oya-sama*'s. This is the *Namu-amida-butsu* uttered by *Oya-sama.*

Saichi prior to his fiftieth year, striving hard to attain the Way, would probably have said, "Saichi says the Nembutsu." Until "Saichi" was struck and knocked over by the "great wind" of Amida Buddha, he was overly conscious of "Saichi." Afterward "Saichi" was buffeted about and thrown against something—*Namu-amida-butsu*—and from that time on he dwelled in fire; rather, he dwelled together with the fire and came to "taste" fully the life of Nembutsu Samadhi.

> Though we speak of the sameness of illusions,
> Illusion in illusion
> And Dharma in illusion
> Are different—
> Here *tariki* and *jiriki* are known.

In this poem Saichi uncharacteristically assumes an objective, critical attitude. But as he rightly says, insofar as illusion exists in illusion, that is, insofar as it has not emerged from the plane of discrimination, a Nembutsu uttered by *Oya-sama* will be incomprehensible. You need to be knocked down by this wind. The threads tying you to discrimination must be broken and you must be cast into the immense void of nondiscrimination. Yet that in itself is not enough. You must also strike against the Dharma; no, you must be struck by the Dharma. Since this comes from the Other [Amida (NW)], it is not your own act. Karmic opportunity, waiting for time and conditions to mature, has a role to play, but your own part is completely passive. This is where the *tariki* view comes into being. Here the *Oya-sama* of *Namu-amida-butsu* is in reality the *Oya-sama* who says *Namu-amida-butsu*. The two are one and the same. It is Nembutsu that says Nembutsu.

6. Saichi's View of Rebirth in the Pure Land (Ōjō)

One of the most distinguishing features of the poems in Rev. Fuji's book—a collection we might call "Saichi's Nembutsu-samadhi poetry"—is that Saichi never refers to the idea of Pure Land rebirth after death. Not a word about the idea, prevalent among Pure Land followers, that since they will be received into Paradise after they die, they will accept the trials and sorrows of this present life as they come. The Nembutsu sects' view of Pure Land rebirth can be summed up as follows: *shaba,* this world of suffering, stands in direct contrast to *gokuraku* (Paradise, the Land of Bliss), a place of happiness. While living in the *shaba* world, you must above all else practice perseverance, patience, obedience, and the like, and meet the end in quiet composure. All you have to do is trust in Amida's Original Prayer (or Vow) without any doubt that you will attain *Ōjō,* birth in the Pure Land, and spend your days repeating *Namu-amida-butsu.* There is no better way to live your life.

The idea that Amida's heart is your heart, or that you can attain the Pure Land in this *shaba* world, may generally be regarded as belonging only to the "holy [or *jiriki* (JCD)] path," and not appearing in the "Pure Land or *tariki* path." In Saichi's poetry, however, there is no mention at all of a future existence. His heart is filled completely with the Name of six syllables received from *Oya,* and there seems to be no room left over for anything else.

Saichi, where are you going in the next life?
Received into the native place of *Namu-amida-butsu,*
Namu-amida-butsu.

This poem contains the only clue we have for establishing Saichi's view of *Ōjō,* future rebirth in the Pure Land. But the idea of a Pure Land after death does not appear. The native place of *Namu-amida-butsu* is *Namu-amida-butsu,* but whether this is in Saichi's present life or the next is not clear. Saichi notes the usual Pure Land teaching of a future existence, but his *Namu-amida-butsu* is always Saichi himself, the present Saichi at this very moment. Within this, a future life is apparently not included.

You don't go to the Pure Land after death,
You go there before the end has come;
Entrusting *(sumete)* to *Namu-amida-butsu,*
Namu-amida-butsu.

According to this, Paradise, the Pure Land, is clearly attained before you die. You do not go there after you die, but while you are still alive. Saichi is there now. The meaning of the word *sumete* in the third line, which I have rendered as "entrusting," is uncertain, but the implication seems to be that once you have entrusted yourself to, or are "occupied" with, Amida, other, minor considerations need not concern you or cause you worry. For Saichi, all that is needed is *Namu-amida-butsu, Namu-amida-butsu.* Hence his utter lack of concern for whether he goes to Paradise or to hell. Saichi, having become *Namu-amida-butsu,* is no doubt affirming in his poem that such matters should be left to Amida's dispensation and are not the responsibility of this "wretched, undeserving" person. That is because Saichi is a new Buddha and Amida is an old Buddha, and Saichi the ignorant, ordinary person is ready to go anywhere Saichi the new Buddha takes him.

Saichi is the new Buddha,
Amida is the old Buddha;
Old Buddha *Oya-sama,* my *Oya-sama*—
Namu-amida-butsu.

"Amida in one's own body" is a phrase that was coined by the "holy path," and is frequently used in the Zen school. However, Saichi lived constantly within *Namu-amida-butsu.* Even when he uses expressions in an unusual or incomprehensible way, the central *Namu-amida-butsu* is never forgotten.

Although wind and air are two,
They are one wind and one air;

Although Amida and I are two,
The compassion of *Namu-amida-butsu* is one.

Two are one and one is two, and the secret of this wonder is *Namu-amida-butsu. Namu-amida-butsu* is none other than compassion itself. Saichi existed in the six syllables of the Name from beginning to middle to end. He is *Namu-amida-butsu,* and *Namu-amida-butsu* is Saichi. He is wholly and utterly embraced within Amida's great compassion.

Received [by Amida (NW)], my heart makes
Its first visit to the Pure Land,
Then returns to the foulness of the *shaba* world,
Sent back to work for the salvation of all beings.

According to this, Saichi has already finished making his first visit to the Pure Land, and at the present time he has returned. This is the "return and transfer" *(gensō-ekō)* for the sake of all beings. Saichi is truly the adopted son of Amida. He continues sweeping his planer until surrounded by fallen chips and shavings. Can we not see them as the pieces of his sincere heart working for the salvation of all living beings? Is it not obvious why he adds not a single word about going to the Pure Land after death?

Saichi saw himself as someone who had long before finished the business of dying, so naturally for him the question of after death does not exist. He is no longer wandering about in the region of birth-and-death. The next poem clearly reveals this state of mind.

You have seized the end of my life,
My death, my funeral all over.
The joy that follows, *Namu-amida-butsu.*

The expression "you have seized the end of my life" is indeed fresh and stimulating. It expresses marvelously his transcendence of birth-and-death.

Death has not yet come,
But that is no wonder,
It has already passed.
The end of life is past,
Namu-amida-butsu.

In the first of the two preceding poems Saichi says his death is already past; he begins the second by saying it has not come; and in the next, he says his end is now.

Now is the end, my end,
Which is your end;
Joyful, joyful, *Namu-amida-butsu.*

In the *Shūjishō* [On Steadily Holding (to Faith)],[3] it is written:

> When in accordance with the words of a good master you awaken in your ordinary moments one thought of trust in Amida, let this be regarded as your last moment, the end of this world for you.

Not being conceptual, Saichi's expressions are fresh and vivid.

7. The Salvation of Sentient Beings

How did Saichi view the salvation of sentient beings? The line "Sent back to work for the salvation of all beings" quoted above clearly suggests that this salvation is his present work. Yet how should we interpret the following monologue? Since Saichi is deeply immersed in the Nembutsu Samadhi, and occupied with singing of his mental state, he would seem to have little time to worry about scholarly expositions of such things as the salvation of sentient beings. Yet since he does speak of the oneness of *hō* and *ki*,[4] of the thoughts that are irrelevant to a believing heart, of the inability of wise men and saints to enter the Pure Land, he is not incapable of occasionally adopting an objective, critical attitude. This being the case, he probably had given some thought to the salvation of living beings as well.

Saichi-*san,* are you in?
Yes, I'm home.
The head of the house isn't in.
He's gone out, to the salvation of living beings,
He'll be back shortly, please wait.
Namu-amida-butsu, Namu-amida-butsu.
He's back, he's come back!

How should we understand this salvation of sentient beings? Amida has gone somewhere to engage in the salvation of sentient beings, and Saichi is conscious of his absence. Amida's work for the salvation of others is apparently altogether different from Saichi's present activity. Could "not at home" mean that Saichi's work and Saichi's self have separated, that outside, irrelevant ideas have intruded between them? Is this poem a monologue in which Saichi examines himself to determine whether a breach has developed in his practice of right mindfulness? Is he examining himself to test his ability to maintain the Nembutsu Samadhi, that is, his grasp of the believing heart's unconscious consciousness? This is different from the diligence exerted by someone who does not yet possess established faith, as a means of maintaining right mindfulness.

Should the poem perhaps be seen rather as a playful divertissement, a question and answer between Saichi and the master, Amida Buddha? Everyone has this playful spirit. The human consciousness is not always proceeding straight ahead toward a goal of some kind. It also has a need for divertissements. "Following after the fragrant grasses, then pursuing the falling flowers" is a privilege reserved for human beings alone. At times, it leads them to wander about from one illusion to the next.

Be that as it may, the salvation of living beings was for Saichi not something to be planned and carried out through various acts of benevolence. For him, to continuously examine the constancy of his believing heart while fashioning *geta,* and to do so amid a Sportive Samadhi, was surely well suited to the circumstances of his life. This poetic self-dialogue can no doubt be explained in this light. That is, Saichi did not set about working for the salvation of sentient beings by emptying his self, or going outside of his self; he performed this activity in his everyday mind, while living amid a Nembutsu Samadhi. This daily activity was for him the salvation of living beings. The next poem can be read in a similar light.

> The believing heart *(shinjin)* is the "principal"
> For the salvation of living beings;
> I duly receive it, *Namu-amida-butsu.*

The believing heart is the "principal" received from Amida Buddha, thanks to which this life is enabled to function within spiritual self-realization. When you receive the believing heart reverently and thankfully, and become *Namu-amida-butsu,* that is the salvation of living beings. The salvation of sentient beings is our everyday life itself. There is no need to insist on having it signify any other activities. The "capital funds" for a life devoted to the salvation of living beings is granted upon attainment of faith, upon receipt of the believing heart. Life without *Namu-amida-butsu* is a life of empty promises. It is extremely unstable and insecure. Most of us are creatures of just such lives, our actions never attaining the level of effortlessness and purposelessness, our lives never freed from conscious strivings. The salvation of living beings is none other than this kind of purposeless life *(mukuyūtei;* S. *anābhogacaryā).*

The work of salvation must take place within a Sportive Samadhi. Saichi fashions *geta* from blocks of wood in this Sportive Samadhi, a purposeless activity performed for the salvation of sentient beings. Saichi's life was that of a saint, although he himself described it as "playing with *Oya-sama.*" He lived it playing hand in hand with Amida. Amid this play he went to the Pure Land: "By playing, you are taken to the Pure Land." In Zen, a person who has reached this stage of religious attainment is said to be capable of enlightening others at will.

> This wretched unworthy person
> Is now playing with *Oya-sama*
> Within this *shaba* world.
> I'm taken off to Amida's Pure Land
> Playing with *Oya-sama.*

Saichi says that while remaining in this present *shaba* world, in his present unworthy state, he is leading a life of Sportive Samadhi together with Amida, and the Pure Land is no more than an extension of this sport. Only a person who was thoroughly in possession of the believing heart *(shinjin)* could genuinely make such statements. Of course one might be able to fashion something of a similar nature from various notions one has in one's head. But no amount of ordinary practice or training will enable you to produce direct and artless declarations of faith like Saichi's. In Saichi Japanese spiritual insight *(Nihon teki reisei teki chokkaku)* can be said to have crystallized into a gem of great purity and brilliance.

The following poem helps clarify Saichi's previous words about the salvation of living beings:

> This evil person delights in Buddha, *Namu-amida-butsu.*
> Buddha takes delight in Saichi's *ki, Namu-amida-butsu.*
> He has me engage in the salvation of living beings,
> Joyfully, *Namu-amida-butsu.*

Seen in this way, *Namu-amida-butsu* becomes everything's main constituent. Through its mediation, the evil person delights in the Buddha; through its mediation, the Buddha delights in Saichi as a *ki,* delights in the evil person. Saichi's joy is found here and nowhere else. In the acts of the evil person, in Saichi's everyday mind, in the *geta* shavings, in the work in the rice-fields—*Namu-amida-butsu* performs *Namu-amida-butsu.* This is the salvation of sentient beings. To go somewhere else for this, apart from one's self, would mean leaving *Namu-amida-butsu* behind, being absent from one's true home. That could not be the true salvation of living beings. "Living beings" exists in the singular; it is this wicked person, this *ki*—Saichi himself. Unless he can be saved, the salvation of living beings (in the plural), the supra-individual self, and the selves of others are all meaningless. To engage as Saichi does in doing this, however, is a truly joyous, Sportive Samadhi.

8. Saichi's Satori

Saichi was a master of enlightenment. He does not flaunt his attainment as Zen people do. In place of intellectual expressions, he talks of his gratefulness, joyfulness, happiness, and pleasure. This is a characteristic of those associated with the Pure Land tradition, who tend to use emotional or affective language in expressing themselves. Of course things of a more intellectual cast do occasionally appear in their vocabulary. Even Saichi must refer to satori.

> *Namu* Buddha is Saichi's Buddha—he is Saichi.
> Saichi's satori opens up—*Namu-amida-butsu.*
> He's received it but . . . *Namu-amida-butsu.*

The meaning of the first line is rather unclear, but as a whole I think the poem can be explained as follows: Saichi is the Buddha, the Buddha is Saichi. This is realized through the medium of *Namu-amida-butsu.* Buddha and Saichi are linked through *Namu-amida-butsu* in a circular fashion. That is Saichi's satori, which he receives from the six syllables of the Name. Everything is *Namu-amida-butsu,* nothing is apart from it. It is not "Saichi is identical to Buddha," or "Buddha is identical to Saichi." It is *Namu-amida-butsu. Namu-amida-butsu* must not be regarded as an intermediary connecting Saichi and the Buddha. Here they are three and at the same time one. When the discriminatory intellect gets holds of this idea and tries to express it, they become simply three. But within spiritual self-awakening there is *Namu-amida-butsu* and nothing else, no Buddha and no Saichi. He expresses this in the next poem:

> Impermanence is me, this impermanence
> Attains the enlightenment of Nirvana,
> *Namu-amida-butsu.*

Here Saichi dissolves the opposition of Nirvana and impermanence in *Namu-amida-butsu.* Expressed in individual terms, impermanence is Saichi himself, hence Nirvana is Amida Buddha. Their self-identity is *Namu-amida-butsu.* Saichi always uses *Namu-amida-butsu* in an absolutive sense. It is his "Person," Shinran's "one person," the "person" of Linji's "true person of no title," "the only one, alone in all the universe." Lived constantly within *Namu-amida-butsu*'s right mindfulness, Saichi's daily activity was always fresh and vivid. Zen master Juzhi (J. Gutei) had his "one-finger Zen" that he could not use up in a lifetime. Saichi's one finger is *Namu-amida-butsu.* If we are to call Juzhi a man of enlightenment, we must say the same of Saichi. He talks of "uttering *Namu-amida-butsu* walking, standing, sitting, and lying down." Fu Dashi, a great Zen layman of early Chinese Buddhism, said that he lived and worked with Buddha, and then retired and slept with Buddha—that perfectly describes Myōkōnin Saichi's life.

According to the Shin treatise *Anjin ketsujō shō,* "*Namu-amida-butsu* is the form in which *Ōjō,* rebirth in the Pure Land, is attained." Saichi is an actual personification of this form.

> Hearing *Namu-amida-butsu* not as it should be,
> But as though hearing it for the very first time.

Saichi's enlightenment is clearly perceived even in these brief statements. Something "as it should be" has no relation to what is present *now,* actually manifested before one's eyes; it is confined to conceptual reasoning. Saichi's Name is not such a feeble concept. It is an actual, living *Namu-amida-butsu* heard here and now, this very instant. Hence it is always new and fresh. "Each time it appears, it is new, each day it is heard, it is always as though for the first time."

To live is not to have lived; it is not an expectation to live, the potential to live, or "ought to live." It is *living now*, instant by instant, and thus it is continual creation. Saichi says it is "*Namu-amida-butsu* heard as though for the first time." Saichi was definitely a man who had been struck by *Namu-amida-butsu*.

He often uses the word *ataru*, to "hit" or "strike," and when he does, it takes on a truly deep meaning. "Striking into" something or "bumping up against" something are expressions often used in Zen with a similar sense. Saichi vividly and directly describes this same experience.

"*Namu-amida-butsu* strikes against me."

"*Namu-amida-butsu* strikes my heart."

"You strike my heart."

"The Name of Amida strikes my heart, *Namu-amida-butsu*."

"*Namu-amida-butsu* strikes my miserable heart."

Lines like these appear frequently in Saichi's poetry. The word "strike" *(ataru)* signifies Saichi and *Namu-amida-butsu* meeting like two arrows head-on, a meeting that can in no way be avoided. Something that has until now moved continuously forward in a straight line suddenly stops and changes to a new direction or movement. Zen calls this advancing a step beyond the tip of a hundred-foot pole, the moment when something unanticipated and unplanned by the discriminating intellect suddenly opens up. *Ataru* has implications of discontinuity, breaking-out, fortuity, even intuition. Although it is used in various senses with both good and bad connotations, here it indicates a region beyond the reach of the discriminatory intellect. Saichi's questionings—"Is *Namu-amida-butsu* this?" "Is *Namu-amida-butsu* that?"—all miss the mark completely and, unexpectedly, he is "struck." Saichi's *ataru* is after all rather a kind of *magure-atari*, "a chancing to hit," an unexpected or fortuitous encounter.

9. Taste–Experience–Now

The word "taste" also appears quite often in Saichi's poems. Taste is an experience: by tasting something you know whether it is sweet or bitter or salty. You know by yourself whether something is cold or warm. Those who live only on the level of words and letters, for whom all things are conceptual, do not really taste. Someone like Saichi, whose relation to words and letters is a remote one, avoids making verbal distinctions, and speaks of all things from direct experience. For this reason, what he says strikes right to the quick. It is highly refreshing, exhilarating even, to see him put so easily into words matters that lie beyond a scholar's considerations. I am not sure we should even call his jottings poems. They read like the *Anjin ketsujō shō*, or Ippen Shōnin's *Sayings*.

According to Reverend Fuji, Saichi's collection of poems begins with this one:

> *Namu* Amida, proceeding to *Amida Butsu*,
> Savoring *Namu, Namu-amida-butsu*.

Saichi has left in his notebooks, extending over a number of years, a genuine record of his experience. He notes simply and artlessly, without affectation or calculation, as a spider spins out its thread, how he "tasted" *Namu-amida-butsu* according to his daily moods. Like the Zen eccentrics Hanshan (J. Kanzan) and Shide (J. Jittoku) who wrote down their poems on tree trunks and plantain leaves, Saichi took up his brush and as the natural poet of spiritual self-awakening sang unreservedly of *Namu-amida-butsu*.

Clouds are said to rise up mindlessly among the mountain peaks. If the mountains are high, clouds are naturally abundant. If a person's spiritual insight attains a certain depth, he cannot help trying to express that experience in words. Saichi's words, because they are artless and shorn of technique, touch all the more closely the true nature of his experience.

> A joyous heart tasting today,
> A believing heart formed by *Namu-amida-butsu*.
> *Namu-amida-butsu*.

These three brief lines contain boundless meaning. *Namu-amida-butsu* is the incomparable iron hammer wielded by the Buddha's invincible power. Knocked down by this hammer, Saichi attains faith. Now, this very instant, his faith, his believing heart, can be tasted. "Now" is the eternal, or absolute present. It is not a now that proceeds in a straight line from past to present to future. It is the present now that is unattainable in the three periods of past, present, and future. Its center is to be found only within the infinite circle of enlightenment. Here is where Saichi stands; or, rather, Saichi is the center. Here the insight of spiritual self-awakening becomes possible, overflowing the emotional plane as the heart of joy.

Jōdo followers are, in a certain sense, simple people. They refer to this as simpleness of heart, genuineness of mind, and let it go at that. In comparison, Zen people seem almost philosophically minded. Not professional philosophers, to be sure, but somehow we feel something rationalistic about them, and they moreover understand the charge of literary expression. To illustrate this point, let us see what Saichi's "heart of joy tasting today" becomes in the hands of a man of Zen.

Daitō Kokushi (1282–1337), the well-known founder of Daitokuji Temple in Kyoto, is said to have lived as a beggar for more than twenty years, tasting the lowest level of human existence. A beggar's lot in those days might not have been as bad, in some ways, as it is today. But still beggars were despised as being somewhat less than human. I believe Daitō undertook such a life not to experience material poverty, but in order to experience the wretchedness of these outcasts.

When requested by the emperor to found a temple in the north of the capital—Daitokuji—he did so. Daitō's erudition was very helpful to him during his later service as the distinguished abbot of this important temple. I frankly wish, however, that he had left some record of his daily life in addition to writings that reveal his learning, literary ability, and Zen genius.

In the case of Saichi, whose utterances are straight from the heart in the language of everyday speech without undergoing any shaping or polishing whatever, it is possible to see his character in each and every word. Daitō, or any other Zen master for that matter, often uses words and phrases that at first glance are not readily comprehensible. It is true that the written word is addressed to the eye; even so, if one does not possess some special knowledge of Chinese literature, and Zen literature as well, Zen writings are extremely difficult to understand. Not only because one does not have the necessary Zen experience, but because breaking through the shell that covers this experience—which is very thick—and getting the taste within is such an arduous task.

Since Saichi threw off his verses in much the same way that he fashioned his roughhewn *geta,* we can tell pretty much at a glance what they are about. A highly wrought, finely finished art object is fated to be hung in the *tokonoma*—the place of honor. This is not of course to slight Daitō Kokushi's writings. He was confined, as the revered Kokushi, or "National Teacher," by the influences of accumulated convention and the background of the age in which he lived. The following quotation is included in *Kaiankokugo* (Dream Words from the Land of Dreams), Hakuin's commentary on Daitō's poems and sermons. It is a teaching Daitō delivered on New Year's Eve:

> New Year's Eve. The sun rises. The moon rises. The morning comes. The night comes. Twelve months, three hundred and sixty days, reach their culmination here. Tonight the new and the old intermingle and come together. Anyone who allows his body to remain in the old year will not be able to fulfill his true potential in the new. Anyone who allows his mind to remain in the new year will lose his essential and primary function. Because of this, Master Hokuzen roasted the great white bullock [the symbol of highest reality (NW)] that appeared in the courtyard. Master Soō shouldered the lantern at midnight. Although that is the way things are, I am not going to enter dark caverns like these. Why? "December snow packed to the horizon turns all things white; spring winds beating against the doors are extremely cold."

This contains a number of traditional allusions, but I will not attempt to explain them in detail now. The aim of Daitō's words is this: now, with the past year going and the new year about to come, how are we to view the immediate present, the *now* of this moment, this juncture. New Year's Eve is the intersection where the old and the new come together, where past and future change places. "Right now, this very instant, what is it!" Iida Tōin, a modern Japanese Zen master, comments on Daitō's words as follows:

> In the immediate present there is no new and old. The past perishing, the future being born—that takes place as a function of the immediate present. It does not cease

> even for an instant. If you are diligent, the water wheel will find no chance to freeze to a stop. You must rejoice in life in which each and every day is a totally new day. A person's death is like the final day of the year; the following day, the New Year, is immediately the beginning of life. It does not stop for an instant. Even though we attach provisional names such as life and death, the time is always the same time. This activity has continued since beginningless time. Death is a function of a certain time too. Without death, there is no life. In other words, it is the immediate present. Nothing exists apart from the immediate present. The eternal past is also the immediate present, and it is beginningless. In the *Lotus Sutra* the Buddha says of this, "Many kalpas have passed since I attained Buddhahood." The eternity of the entire future is the immediate present as well, and it is endless. So if you would know the beginninglessness and endlessness of the present moment, look right at the immediate present. Eternity is becoming the immediate present. If you would know the eternal future, look at the immediate present. The present extended is the future. Maitreya Buddha who will appear billions of years in the future is only another name for us living here right now. (*Kaiankokugo teishōroku,* 4)

Comparing the remarks of Daitō and the modern Zen master on the theme of "a joyous heart tasting today" with Saichi's own simple words provides an interesting contrast. As Saichi spent his eighteenth through fiftieth years listening to Shin priests preaching the Dharma, we can assume he was conversant with the vocabulary of the Pure Land teachings. In spite of this, we find among his jottings no literary allusions or words from Buddhist scripture. His words come simply, naturally, in a familiar colloquial manner. The Shin terms *ki* (devotee) and *hō* (Dharma) do appear, but most Pure Land believers would be expected to know them.

> Don't listen to principles and theory,
> Be captured by the taste, hear the taste—
> *Namu-amida-butsu.*

"Tasting" in this sense can be said to characterize Saichi's entire life. The words "Be captured by the taste, listen to the taste" have a refreshing resonance. Can we not see within these words the circumstances of Saichi's life immersed within his *Namu-amida-butsu* Samadhi? He was never, from the very first, interested in logical principles or theory. From the age of nineteen or so, when with a sincere heart he first resolved to seek the Way, the voice of Japanese spirituality *(Nihon teki reisei)* was constantly whispering something in his ear. He resolved that one way or another he would hear this voice in its full clarity. There was a spell during this period when, apparently, these efforts slackened. But spirituality does not always appear on the surface of consciousness; it operates constantly in the hidden areas of the unconscious mind as well. So sure enough, Saichi had to throw back his ears once again and plunge ahead with renewed determination in the direction of the whisper. Up until his fiftieth year, he doubtless experienced great difficulties, though there is no record of that period of his life. Yet there is really no reason for him to have written any. He was engaged too busily in savoring the samadhi of his believing heart. Living in the immediate present, by what Zen master Bankei called the "Unborn" *(fushō),* Saichi did not enmesh himself fruitlessly in past experiences and he never ventures to grumble over them. To turn back into one's memories is to remake or reconstruct one's experience. Of course, that is necessary too. The universal salvation of all beings would be impossible without it. But it is accompanied by great evil, inasmuch as it is separated from the world of actual existence and experience. That is why Saichi embraced *taste* and avoided theory and logic. There was no special reason for this. It was simply the natural thing for him to do.

10. The View That the Buddha Is the Ordinary Man, the Ordinary Man Is the Buddha—Guchi *(Ignorance)*

I would now like to examine Saichi's view of the self-identity of the Buddha and the ordinary man, of the world of purity and the world of defilement. Since it was based on his direct experience, we should remain aware that it differs from the views of religious scholars whose deductions are carried out in their heads. That is not to say that such deductions must be rejected. So long as it is rooted in life experience, the human consciousness has need of such logic. There is no reason to disparage religious scholars and teachers out of hand. The key is in determining the degree to which the logic is rooted in the reality of life. We can be sure that Saichi himself had listened for many years to the expositions of Buddhist teachers. At the same time he was jotting down what he experienced on wood shavings in his own unique manner of expression. It is to those utterances we should give our attention. Saichi says:

> The sect founder's death anniversary
> Is the death anniversary of Saichi.
> This is Saichi, isn't it? *Namu-amida-butsu.*

The anniversary of the death of Shinran, the founder of the Shin sect, is at the same time the "death anniversary" of the *geta*-maker Saichi. This is a bold statement indeed. Bold, that is, from the mouth of an ordinary Pure Land follower. For Saichi, it is not in the least out of the ordinary. He utters it as matter-of-factly as he would state that a cat is a cat. Still, it is not something that can easily be said with such artless simplicity.

I have some trouble understanding the word "this" in the line "This is Saichi, isn't it?" Although there are various possible ways of explaining Saichi's intention here, I want to find the answer by leaving the text and putting myself in Saichi's place. Saichi has experienced the realization that today's anniversary of the death of Shinran is his own. So "this" should be the realization that Saichi the *geta*-maker and Shinran the sect-founder are different yet at the same time one. This self-realization is Saichi himself, and is at the same time *Namu-amida-butsu*. The adding of the words "Isn't it?" is merely a playful way of ending the poem. A man of Zen would have nothing of this. He would immediately tweak his opposite's nose, or give him a shove and demand, "What is 'this'?" Saichi belongs to the Jōdo tradition. He cocks his head to one side questioningly, "isn't it?" and goes on sweeping his plane through the woodblock before him, all the while repeating *Namu-amida-butsu*. But isn't it interesting the way this reveals Saichi's personality.

Recall the lines quoted previously: "*Namu* Buddha is Saichi's Buddha, it is Saichi." The *Namu-amida-butsu* functioning within Saichi's heart, the six syllables of the Name that have been granted from Amida, work here with an incalculable force. Were it a realization of Saichi's discriminating intellect, he might have puffed up self-importantly into a lump of unmanageable egotism. But since his realization in *Namu-amida-butsu* is one that grasps the contradiction between Saichi and the Buddha as sameness, it belongs to the realm of nondiscriminatory discrimination, discriminatory nondiscrimination. No matter what else he says, Saichi constantly repeats *Namu-amida-butsu* and uses it to end his poems because the center of his entire consciousness is constantly guided by *Namu-amida-butsu*.

> I don't listen as an ordinary man,
> The ordinary man is a fraud *(bakemono)*.
> You strike my heart.

Being "heart-struck" in this sense is *Namu-amida-butsu*. *Namu-amida-butsu* recites *Namu-amida-butsu* and hears it as well. From someone like Ippen Shōnin, words like these would be quite convincing, but from the lips of Myōkōnin Saichi, they come as something of a surprise. Still, I believe deeper consideration will show that the reality Saichi experienced is essentially Asian in content, and is, above all, a type of intuitive spiritual self-realization that is distinctively Japanese.

> I do not become Amida,
> Amida becomes me,
> *Namu-amida-butsu*.

I—the ordinary man—Saichi, all are the result, product, or idea of the discriminating intellect. This is the "fraud," something that is not grounded in truth. Fraud—that which is produced by discrimination or analysis—is what the consciousness creates conceptually as the objective world. This is Shinran's "hollow apparitions, unreality." Within Saichi's I, or the individual self of the discriminating intellect, there is nothing capable of becoming Amida Buddha. To be able as Saichi does to say that Saichi is the Buddha, the death anniversary of Shinran is his own, is an utterance, or act, conferred by the other-power, by the working of Amida's compassion. Realization of this becomes possible through the direct insight of spiritual self-awakening. This is the content of absolute truth, things as they truly are, concrete reality in the ultimate sense. Saichi, Shinran, and Hōnen all lived within this self-realization.

> Both compassion and [boundless (NW)] light are one.
> Both Saichi and Amida are one,
> *Namu-amida-butsu.*

The reality of Pure Land thought lies here, in the experience of attaining oneness through *Namu-amida-butsu.* Inasmuch as Hōnen, Shinran, and Saichi share this experience, the death anniversary of the founder is Saichi's own death anniversary. Christians say, "For as in Adam all die, even so in Christ shall all be made alive." Pure Land followers say: die in Amida and live in Amida. Saichi is Amida's Saichi and Amida is Saichi's Amida. Realization of this is *Namu-amida-butsu.* The ideas of eternal illusion and eternal enlightenment, Saichi doomed to hell and Amida Buddha abiding in perfect purity, are inevitably and indissolubly opposed, contradictions that are beyond resolution. They are polar opposites, and that is how it must be. The contradiction is a contradiction, yet there must be free and unobstructed interpenetration. To attempt to insert a third element would only endlessly perpetuate the opposition. Since the ordinary person is beyond help, there is no way that Saichi can escape eternal illusion and ignorance. And yet he easily dissolves this away by means of Japanese spiritual self-realization:

> Though I am in eternal illusion,
> My *Oya-sama* is an eternal *Oya;*
> Joyous gratitude, *Namu-amida-butsu.*

If ignorance was eternal, you could never be rid of it. If enlightenment was eternal, you could never fall into ignorance. But enlightenment is the eternal *Oya,* the substance of Amida's eternal Prayer (or Vow). Hence it is within this Prayer alone that enlightenment and illusion are one. A person steeped in ignorance receives this as the great favor, the Buddha's favor. From this a free and unobstructed interpenetration takes place.

While fashioning his *geta,* Saichi scribbled down on the wood shavings the reality of his own experience. Therein lies the great significance of his poems. I believe that it is now the role of scholars to erect something new upon this reality.

Saichi's poems gained in profundity as they flowed forth. The following could come only from someone with Saichi's experience. From a scholar's lips, it would be nothing but a piece of logic with the scent of a secondhand clothing box.

> The world is ignorant, I am ignorant,
> Amida is ignorant too;
> No matter, *Oya-sama* delivers me from ignorance,
> *Namu-amida-butsu.*

"Amida is ignorant too" is a daring assertion. Perhaps only Saichi could have made it. When Vimalakīrti said, "I am ill because all beings are ill," he inserted the word "because" between "I" and "all beings." Saichi inserts nothing, but simply enumerates, "The world is ignorant, I am ignorant, Amida is ignorant too," with no words to connect the three. Then he shifts tack: "No matter, *Oya-sama* delivers me from ignorance." Only then do we know that Amida's ignorance is different from the ignorance of all beings. But Amida does not call upon Saichi and the others to relinquish their ignorance. It remains intact, and they are saved just as they are. This is the distinguishing characteristic of Japanese spiritual awakening. The contradiction remains as it is, unresolved, but the remaining contradiction is not the original one, for it is now invested with a nature of free and unobstructed interpenetration. That is the working of *Namu-amida-butsu.*

The external circumstances of the former Saichi's ignorance are no different from those of the present Saichi, but the present Saichi's ignorance has the support of *Namu-amida-butsu.* It is no longer the ignorance of Saichi's discriminatory consciousness, but ignorance that has been taken in hand by *Oya-sama.* This of course does not mean that Saichi has lost his individual self, but the individual self is now the "Person" of the supra-individual self. It does not mean that his ignorance has been purified, but that it no longer derives from the individual self. Ignorance cannot be purified, since it is eternal, but it is ignorance that is in touch with the eternal *Oya-sama.* In language or ordinary logic, something like this is impossible, but within the self-realization of spiritual insight the contradictions are taken in just as they are and given continuous and vigorous life.

11. Saichi and Zhaozhou (J. Jōshū)

It is interesting to compare Saichi's *guchi* (ignorance) with a Zen master's view of *bonnō* (desires and passions), and Saichi's *Namu-amida-butsu* with the crystal Zhaozhou held up before his assembled monks.

Zhaozhou said:

> This matter is like holding up a transparent crystal in your hand. When a foreigner comes it reflects him as such; when a Chinese comes it reflects him as such. I pick up a blade of grass and make it work like a golden-bodied Buddha sixteen feet high. Then I take hold of a golden-bodied Buddha sixteen feet high and make him work like a blade of grass. The Buddha is in himself human desire *(bonnō).* Human desire is no other than Buddha.
>
> A monk asked, "Who does Buddha arouse desires for?"
>
> "He arouses desires for all sentient beings."
>
> "How does he rid himself of the desires?" asked the monk.
>
> "Why does he want to get rid of them?" answered the master.

Zhaozhou's crystal is Saichi's *Namu-amida-butsu.* All of Saichi is reflected in this Name. If a foreigner comes, a foreigner is reflected as such; if a Chinese comes, he is reflected as such. We may view the Chinese and the foreigner as the *bonnō* of greed, hate, and delusion; we may view them as the world of discrimination. There is nothing that is not illumined by the crystal of spiritual realization *(reisei teki jikaku).* In a perfect oneness with *Namu-amida-butsu,* human consciousness itself becomes a blade of grass, becomes a sixteen-foot Buddha. Where a Zen person's utterances are objective and employ phrases taken from nature, Pure Land followers describe the psychological circumstances of the individual self. Instead of Buddhas, or grass, they talk about something being hateful or endearing, about wretchedness or wrongness, or else love, prayer, and the like. The crystal is the all-seeing Buddha-eye that sees both within and without, sees Saichi and the Buddha, sees mistaken views and enlightenment. Let me repeat that the crystal is *Namu-amida-butsu.*

> I received the eye from you,
> The eye to see you,
> *Namu-amida-butsu.*

"The eye to see you" is none other than the eye that sees Saichi himself, which is *Namu-amida-butsu.* Hence the Buddha's ignorance *(guchi),* Saichi's ignorance, the world's ignorance are all felt, and the identity of Buddha and *bonnō,* and of *bonnō* and Buddha, is made possible. If the eye were merely one-sided, a free and unobstructed intercommunion could not come into play. Thus *bonnō* cannot be excluded. *Bonnō* is the Buddha, the Buddha is the Buddha because he too has *bonnō.* Because of his *bonnō* the Buddha becomes aware of, appreciates, and experiences the *guchi* and *bonnō,* the ignorance and desires, of Saichi and all other living beings, and elicits from within them a purposeless activity. This is the working of the sixteen-foot Buddha. The working of the blade of grass is being blown and rustled about by the wind; it is for this willful self to be accepted and embraced by the parent *Oya-sama.* It is this willful self that is embraced by *Oya* when it is hungry, when it wants milk, when it is bothered by mosquitoes, when it itches.

> The child held by *Oya* is here,
> Embraced by *Oya,*
> *Namu-amida-butsu.*

I'd like to draw attention to the phrase "the child is here." The child, Saichi, is a blade of grass, and is moreover working purposelessly, as he makes his *geta,* for the salvation of sentient beings as well.

In making these remarks I have no interest at all in joining or fusing Pure Land thought and Zen. That is something I will leave to the professional scholars and priests. My sole concern here is to compare the different ways in which [the Chinese Zen master (JCD)] Zhaozhou and Saichi express themselves, one as the crystal itself, the other as *Namu-amida-butsu.* Zen is Zen, Pure Land Buddhism is Pure Land Buddhism. As we examine their differences, we must not overlook their similarities; in examining their similarities, we should always keep in mind their differences. My purpose is simply to call attention to the fact that in both of them is found what I feel deserves to be called the self-awakening of Japanese spirituality *(Nihon teki reisei teki jikaku).*

12. Shaba *and* Jōdo*—the Defiled World and the Pure Land*

Passages such as the previously quoted "I am foolish, Amida is foolish too" and "my thoughts are your thoughts" help us understand the relationship between Saichi and Amida, and give a general idea of the relation of *shaba* and *Jōdo* as well.

Where is Saichi? In the Pure Land?
Here is the Pure Land, *Namu-amida-butsu.*

Saichi's *Namu-amida-butsu* is in fact the Pure Land. There is nothing whatever unusual in that. Inasmuch as Saichi is never divorced from *Namu-amida-butsu,* wherever he is found—the *shaba* world—must also be *Namu-amida-butsu.* There can be no Pure Land apart from this. The *shaba* world must be the Pure Land, the Pure Land the *shaba* world. Yet the *shaba* world is not the same as Pure Land, for in the *shaba* world there is *Namu-amida-butsu. Shaba* is the Pure Land by means of *Namu-amida-butsu,* and by means of *Namu-amida-butsu* the Pure Land transforms into the *shaba* world. It is not simply a self-identity of the two; it must be that the two are one, the one is two. That is *Namu-amida-butsu.*

I am taken to and receive Paradise,
Namu-amida-butsu.
I receive it in this *shaba* world,
Moon of the believing heart.

He says, "I am taken to and receive Paradise," but he does not say he will go there after death. Because this *shaba* world is illuminated by the "moon of the believing heart" *(shinjin no tsuki),* the Pure Land is received. Here *shaba* and *gokuraku* (Paradise) have not become disparate and completely unconnected entities, but neither are they regarded as one. It is *Namu-amida-butsu* of the *shaba* world, *Namu-amida-butsu* of Paradise. Since Saichi exists in the *shaba* world and Buddha exists in Paradise, if Saichi becomes Buddha, there is nothing strange about the *shaba* world becoming Paradise.

I hear the Name of Amida Buddha.
That's the Buddha who becomes Saichi;
That Buddha is *Namu-amida-butsu.*

Again,

Oya-sama makes Saichi Buddha;
The Amida of *Namu-amida-butsu.*

The connection of *shaba* and Paradise, joined by *Namu-amida-butsu,* needs no repeating, yet I feel compelled to reiterate, in the hope it should not be forgotten, that the six syllables of the Name must not be regarded as intervening between two contradictory extremes, or existing in some position above, and connecting, them. The Name operates like the word *soku* (usually translated "is") in the formula "one is two, two is one." The *shaba* world and Paradise are not spatially connected. As it seems to be difficult to grasp the meaning of this "nonconnection," I like to call it the "continuation of noncontinuation." Shinran calls this "leaping sideways" or "passing sideways" *(ōchō),* that is, going directly to the Pure Land. Thus stated, it could be understood spatially as a continuum, leaping from one point to another. But such notions are all those of the discriminating intellect. Here the direct insight of spiritual self-awakening comes into play; without it, the meaning of the Name can never be grasped. But Saichi does not speak of such complexities. He says simply, in an utterance of direct spiritual insight,

> This is the Buddha that becomes Saichi.
> That Buddha is *Namu-amida-butsu.*
>
> This darkness is taken and illumined by the bright moon of the six syllables;
> While in the *shaba* world, I live in the six syllables,
> How joyful!

Saichi lives constantly in the moonlight of the six-syllable Name, though this does not imply that the darkness of the *shaba* world has dissipated. Hence he says, "While in a *shaba* world. . . ." He uncharacteristically fails to say "*Namu-amida-butsu,*" adding instead that he is "living in the six syllables." The next poem quickly clarifies this point:

> *Shaba* is the dawn, the dawn of the Pure Land.
> It opens, it's my joy, *Namu-amida-butsu.*

It might be speculated that the *shaba* dawn is the Pure Land, but, no, it is the dawn of the Pure Land. His joy at the dawning is no other than the awakening of *Namu-amida-butsu.* Without the realization of "living in the six syllables" there is no joy or happiness, and hence no wretchedness. This realization is called *ichinen hokki,* the awakening or arousing of the "one thought" of faith. This is a rare instance when Saichi uses a technical term of the Pure Land tradition.

> Eternity . . . doesn't exist anywhere else,
> This world is the world of eternity,
> Here the arousing of "one thought" occurs,
> *Namu-amida-butsu.*

We may say *shaba* is the Pure Land, the Pure Land is this world, but unless this is based on the experience of *ichinen hokki,* the arising of single-hearted faith in Amida, it is a false, empty Nembutsu. One must strike directly against the truth of

Namu-amida-butsu. That is the awakening of "one thought," that is spiritual self-awakening *(reisei teki chokkaku).* It is not possible to grasp unless you have once experienced the time of death. The golden carp will know for the first time what it will feed upon after it has broken through the net. A person who says that *Namu* is the *ki,* or person who utters the Nembutsu, and Amida Buddha is *hō,* the Dharma, that the oneness of *ki* and *hō* is *Namu-amida-butsu,* is a preacher, not a *myōkōnin.* The latter confines himself to *Namu-amida-butsu* and nothing else, and pays not the slightest attention to whether it is a cause that brings him rebirth in the Pure Land or the cause that sends him falling into hell. And he goes on living within that reality.

When Buddha's six syllables, six essences,
Come to me—*Namu-amida-butsu.*
Oya, who informed me of this,
Is *Namu-amida-butsu.*

The Saichi who is aware that "the six syllables come to me" is the "*Oya* who informed me." In the experience itself, informing and being informed are the same reality. Therefore,

If the eye that sees evil is the eye of *Namu,*
It is possessed by *Amida Butsu;*
That is the six syllables of *Namu-amida-butsu.*

This has come before—the eye that sees Saichi and the eye that sees the Buddha are the same *Namu-amida-butsu.* It does not merely look without or look within; like the "eye" of Eckhart, it looks both within and without at the same time. The time you know is the time it is made known to you. In *kenshō* (seeing into one's own nature), the Zen term for satori, *ken* (seeing) is *shō* (nature), *shō* is *ken.* Although we say this is simultaneous, in fact it does not have a temporal nature. Nor is it to be understood as a spatial sameness of place either. The I—Saichi—who "receives Amida-*san* from Amida-*san*" is this wondrous, incomprehensible eye.

If Saichi's verses were to be collected and classified thematically into groups, it would help us discern the contents of a splendid Japanese spiritual awakening. The next poem has been given before, but it makes a fitting conclusion to this section.

This wretched one is now playing with *Oya-sama*
In this *shaba* world.
I will be taken into the Pure Land of Amida
Playing with *Oya-sama.*

13. Emotional and Intellectual

The most characteristic element in Pure Land thought lies in the way it puts forward Amida Buddha as *Oya-sama,* "the parent." In Saichi's monologues, where he is in a constant parent-child relationship with Amida, this is seen as well. Naturally, the center of Pure Land thought is found within spiritual self-awakening, but it is manifested mainly through the emotions. It contrasts in this respect to Zen, in which the intellect is dominant.

> Amida-*san*—
> You, You
> You're eager to help me, aren't you?
> Thank you.

This is not one of Saichi's poems. It was written by an elderly man in a remote area of Aki, present Hiroshima Prefecture, and is quoted in Rev. Fuji's book. Only in the Pure Land tradition is it possible for the devotee to approach so closely to Amida Buddha in this way. We do not find in Zen this same attitude of familiar congeniality.

> Zhaozhou once said to the assembled monks:
> "I do not like to hear the word 'Buddha.'"
> A monk said, "Yet you work for the sake of other beings, don't you?"
> Zhaozhou immediately answered, "Buddha Buddha."

After Zhaozhou declared that he did not want to hear the word "Buddha," when asked what he would do to save all beings, the word "Buddha" came from his own lips. He might have said, "If it can be of help to others, then say Buddha." Or "Keep Buddha in mind, *Namu-amida-butsu, Namu-amida-butsu.*" At any rate you must not be in thrall to Buddha, or to No-Buddha either. You must leave both existence and nonexistence behind. You must go on living within the contradiction. In other words, you must become Buddha itself. At this point, Pure Land and Zen are the same. Zen wants the negation first—it talks of "prajna that is not prajna." In the Pure Land schools the tendency is to go forward from the affirmation that follows this negation. It then becomes natural for you to walk along with Amida, hand in hand, as parent and child. The intellect always wants to separate itself from things, the emotions to live together with them. Here we see a difference between Zen and Jōdo, but when this difference is understood as being superficial, then affirmation or negation will depend only upon one's own native tendencies and capacities.

> Joy, joy's abundance is wretchedness too.
> This wretchedness, illuminated by the mirror of compassion.
> Now it becomes a mirror within a mirror.

Some points here are obscure, but I think the overall meaning is this: mere bounding excess of joy is not yet sufficiently separated from the consciousness of self. When this joy becomes genuine and pure, it is embraced completely within Amida's compassion. At that very moment it becomes the supra-individual "Person," and the mirror of the individual self is received within the mirror of Amida like two facing mirrors with no image between them. And the joy in the consciousness of the individual self leads immediately to Buddha wisdom—"Great Mirror Wisdom"—where you enter a realm where there is neither joy nor anxiety.

The phrase "mirror within a mirror" is rarely seen in Pure Land texts. It appears as a simile in *The Sutra of Eternal Life,* one of the three main Pure Land sutras, where something is likened to seeing one's face in a bright mirror. Another passage in the same sutra describes the Pure Land and defiled *shaba* world as mirrors facing and reflecting each other. I should perhaps add that the Pure Land faithful themselves have shown little interest in these descriptions.

Saichi's poem here has a Zen flavor. I should emphasize how unusual it is to find the expression "the mirror within a mirror" among the usual vocabulary of compassion, parent and child, gratitude and thankfulness. Its occurrence in a poem of Saichi's, who is usually involved in savoring or tasting *Namu-amida-butsu,* is something worthy of special note.

8

From Saichi's Journals

This essay is a collection of religious poems by the *myōkōnin* Asahara Saichi (1850–1932), which Suzuki assembled and translated into English as an appendix to his book *Mysticism: Christian and Buddhist.* The study of the *myōkōnin* as a religious archetype in Shin Buddhism has undergone two stages of development. The first was in the Tokugawa period (1603–1867) when the religious ideal was originally articulated. Collections of *myōkōnin den,* "accounts of *myōkōnin,*" were compiled and circulated mostly at the popular level, and they continued to be produced into modern times. The figures appearing in them were mostly ordinary and obscure Shin Buddhists who were celebrated in some way for their practice of the nembutsu, or for their gratitude to Amida, or for some memorable occurrence in their life. Stories about them frequently contain accounts of religious conversion or miraculous events or changes of heart or morality tales. It is noteworthy, however, that the collections present few examples of the type of nondual awareness that Suzuki sought to highlight in his concept of spirituality, *reisei.*

Suzuki was drawn to the *myōkōnin* biographies because of their down-to-earth quality and their real-world religiosity, but he struggled to find stories that illustrated a strong nondualistic outlook. In his earlier publications, the most compelling examples of nondualistic thinking in Pure Land Buddhism were drawn from Ippen (1239–1289) and from the *Anjin ketsujō shō* (On the Final Peaceful Settlement of Mind), not from the mainstream Shin Buddhist tradition. All of that changed when Suzuki encountered the religious verses of Asahara Saichi, introduced to him by Nishitani Keiji (1900–1990), the Japanese philosopher and younger intellectual friend of Suzuki. Saichi's verses express in simple but moving words his sense of oneness with Amida Buddha and of identification between this world and the Pure Land, which Suzuki propounded as the hallmark of true Pure Land faith. In the last two or three decades of his life, Suzuki cited Saichi repeatedly as a model of Shin Buddhist piety. In fact, Suzuki singlehandedly raised Saichi to the status of the *myōkōnin* par excellence, even though he was largely unknown prior to that time. Suzuki's work thus represents the second stage in the development of the *myōkōnin* ideal, when the *myōkōnin* figure moved beyond the confines of parochial Shin culture and became a topic in Buddhist studies and religious studies generally. This occurred because of Suzuki's pioneering efforts using Saichi as his paradigm.

This collection of verses, translated from Saichi's voluminous journals, displays a wide variety of themes that captured Saichi's religious imagination: Amida's embrace as *Oya-sama,* the parent; the inseparable identity of Amida and Saichi; Saichi's simultaneous feelings of wretchedness and joy; the presence of the Pure Land in this world and even in hell; the nembutsu, *Namu-amida-butsu,* as the point where all things converge; and so on. These verses convey explicitly or implicitly Suzuki's idea of *sokuhi,* simultaneous identification and differentiation, and express the nondualistic vision that he idealized. In some cases, Saichi betrays a familiarity with doctrinal concepts, perhaps picked up from temple sermons—for instance, *kihō ittai,* the oneness of the unenlightened person and the Buddha (or Dharma); and *hokkai,* the all-encompassing, Dharma-filled universe—even though he was a lowly, semiliterate wooden clog maker. In this text Suzuki presents Saichi's verses with very light annotation in the notes. Though Suzuki had strong feelings about how Saichi should be interpreted, and in other publications he explicated his sayings extensively, here he largely allows Saichi to speak for himself. Though Suzuki was an important modern interpreter of Buddhism for the West, he also sought through his numerous translations to be a straightforward conduit of Buddhist voices from Asia to the West. These verses are an example of that.

The base text for this essay is chapter 10 of *Mysticism: Christian and Buddhist* (London: George Allen & Unwin, 1957), 174–214. A Japanese translation by Bandō Shōjun and Shimizu Shūsetsu was published as Suzuki Daisetsu, *Shinpi shugi: Kirisutokyō to Bukkyō* (Tokyo: Iwanami Shoten, 2004), 235–281, 297–305.

. . .

The following are translations in English of some of Saichi's utterances. As I have said before, there are several thousands of such items in his journals, and there is no doubt that they are good material for students of religious experiences. My attempt here is, however poor the translations, to afford the reader a glimpse into Saichi's inner life. Unless one has a thorough mastery of both languages, Japanese and English, it is impossible to convey to the English reader the deep underlying feelings characterizing Saichi as one of the most conspicuously *myōkōnin* type of Shin followers.

The following selections, numbering 147,[1] are grouped under nine headings. The classification is not at all scientific, since it is often very difficult to classify certain expressions under a certain definite group because they include various ideas interrelated to one another. The nine are as follows:

1. *Nyorai* and Saichi
2. *Oya-sama*
3. The Nembutsu
4. The *Ki* and the *Hō*
5. The Pure Land, This World and Hell
6. The Free Gift
7. The Heart-Searchings
8. Poverty
9. The Inner Life

I. *NYORAI*[2] AND SAICHI[3]

1

I exchange work with Amida:
I worship him who in turn deigns to worship me—
This is the way I exchange work with him.[4]

2

"O Saichi, who is *Nyorai-san?*"
"He is no other than myself."
"Who is the founder [of the Shin teaching]?"
"He is no other than myself."
"What is the canonical text?"
"It is no other than myself."
The ordinary man's heart has no fixed root,
Yet this rootless one takes delight in the *Hō* [i.e., Dharma];
This is because he is given *Oya*'s heart—
The heart of *Namu-amida-butsu.*

3

I am lying,
Amida deigns to worship Saichi,
I too in turn worship Amida—
Namu-amida-butsu!

4

The adorable form of *Nyorai*
Is indeed this wretched self's form—
Namu-amida-butsu, Namu-amida-butsu![5]

5

Buddha is worshiped by [another] Buddha:
The *Namu* is worshiped by Amida,
Amida is worshiped by the *Namu:*
This is the meaning of *kimyō*[6]
As expressed in the *Namu-amida-butsu.*

6

Amida calling on Amida—
This voice—
Namu-amida-butsu, Namu-amida-butsu!

7

Saichi exchanges work with Amida:
When he worships Amida,

Amida in turn deigns to worship him [Saichi]—
This is the way we exchange our work.
How happy I am with the favor!
Namu-amida-butsu, Namu-amida-butsu!

8

When I worship thee, O Buddha,
This is Buddha worshiping [another] Buddha,
And it is thou who makest this fact known to me, O Buddha:
For this favor Saichi is most grateful.

9

What all the Buddhas of the *Hokkai*[7] declare
Is to make this Saichi turn into a Buddha—
Namu-amida-butsu, Namu-amida-butsu!

10

My joy!
How beyond thought!
Self and Amida and the *Namu-amida-butsu.*

11

How fine!
The whole world and vastness of space is Buddha!
And I am in it—*Namu-amida-butsu!*

II. *OYA-SAMA*[8]

12

Oya-sama is Buddha
Who transforms Saichi into a Buddha—
How happy with the favor!
Namu-amida-butsu, Namu-amida-butsu!

13

My heart and *Oya-sama*—
We have just one heart
Of *Namu-amida-butsu.*

14

I am a happy man,
A glad heart is given me;
Amida's gladness is my gladness—
Namu-amida-butsu!

15

The heart that thinks [of Buddha]
Is Buddha's heart,
A Buddha given by Buddha—
Namu-amida-butsu!

16

How grateful I am!
Into my heart has *Oya-sama* entered and fully occupies it.
The cloud of doubt all dispersed,
I am now made to turn westward.
How fortunate I am!
Saying *Namu-amida-butsu* I return west.

17

Are devils[9] come?
Are serpents come?
I know not.
I live my life embraced in the arms of *Oya-sama,*
I am fed with the milk of *Namu-amida-butsu,*
Looking at *Oya-sama*'s face.
Namu-amida-butsu!

18

When he is known as *Oya,*
Worship him as such:
Oya and I are one—
The oneness of *ki* and *hō*
In the *Namu-amida-butsu.*

19

Amida is my *Oya-sama,*
I am child of Amida;
Let me rejoice in *Oya-sama,* in *Namu-amida-butsu.*
The *Namu-amida-butsu* belongs to child as well as to *Oya-sama:*
By this is known the mutual relationship [between Thee and me].

20

My heart and thy heart—
The oneness of hearts—
Namu-amida-butsu!

21

How lucky I am!
Oya is given me!
Oya who turns me into a Buddha is
The *Namu-amida-butsu!*

22

The *Hokkai* is my *Oya*—
Being my *Oya*—
Namu-amida-butsu!

23

Oya and child—
Between them not a shadow of doubt:[10]
This is my joy!

24

The *Namu* and Amida,
Oya and child,
They quarrel: the *Namu* on one side and Amida on the other side.
Repentance and joyfulness—
How intimate!

25

What is Saichi's understanding of the *Namu-amida-butsu?*
Yes, I am an adopted child of *Namu-amida-butsu.*
How do you understand a life of gratitude?
As to being grateful, sometimes I remember it, sometimes I do not.
Really, a wretched man I am!

26

Namu-san[11] and Amida-*san* are talking:
This is the *Namu-amida-butsu* of *Oya* and son.

27

Namu-san and Amida-*san*—both are Amida:
Namu-amida-butsu!
This happiness is my happiness.

28

Namu-amida-butsu!—how grateful I am!
Namu-amida-butsu is the oneness of the worldly and the highest truth.

Namu-amida-butsu!—how happy I am for the favor!
Namu-amida-butsu, Namu-amida-butsu!
Wherefrom is *Namu-amida-butsu?*
It is the mercy issuing from *Oya*'s bosom;
How happy I am with the favor, *Namu-amida-butsu!*
"Wherefore is Saichi bound?"
"Saichi will go to the Land of Bliss."
"With whom?"
"With *Oya-sama* I go—how happy I am!"
Namu-amida-butsu, Namu-amida-butsu!

III. THE NEMBUTSU[12]

29

"O Saichi, do you recite the Nembutsu only when you think of it?
What do you do when you do not think of it?"
"Yes, [well,] when I do not think of it, there is
The *Namu-amida-butsu* [just the same]—
The oneness of *ki* and *hō;*
Even my thinking of [the Nembutsu] rises out of it.
How thankful I am for the favor!"
Namu-amida-butsu, Namu-amida-butsu!

30

Hōnen Shōnin [is said to have recited the Nembutsu] sixty thousand times [a day];
With Saichi it is only now and then.
Sixty-thousand-times and now-and-then—
They are one thing.
How grateful I am for the favor!
Namu-amida-butsu!

31

"O *Nyorai-san,* do you take me—this wretched one such as I am?
Surely because of the presence of such wretched ones as you,
Oya-sama's mercy is needed—
The Name is just meant for you, O Saichi,
And it is yours."
"That is so, I am really grateful,
I am grateful for the favor—
Namu-amida-butsu!"

32
All the miraculous merits accumulated by Amida
Throughout his disciplinary life of innumerable eons
Are filling up this body called Saichi.
Merits are no other than the six syllables *na-mu-a-mi-da-buts(u).*

33
The *Namu-amida-butsu* is inexhaustible,
However much one recites it, it is inexhaustible;
Saichi's heart is inexhaustible;
Oya's heart is inexhaustible.
Oya's heart and Saichi's heart,
Ki and *hō,* are of one body which is the *Namu-amida-butsu.*
However much this is recited, it is inexhaustible.

34
To Saichi such as he is, something wonderful has happened—
That heart of his has turned into Buddhahood!
What an extraordinary event this!
What things beyond imagination are in store within the
Namu-amida-butsu!

35
The *Namu-amida-butsu*
Is like the sun-god,
Is like the world,
Is like the great earth,
Is like the ocean!
Whatever Saichi's heart may be,
He is enveloped in the emptiness of space,
And the emptiness of space is enveloped in *Namu-amida-butsu!*
O my friends, be pleased to hear the *Namu-amida-butsu—*
Namu-amida-butsu that will free you from *jigoku* [hell].

36
The Nembutsu is like vastness of space,
The vastness of space is illumined by *Oya-sama*'s Nembutsu.
My heart is illumined by *Oya-sama.*
Namu-amida-butsu!

37
For what reason it is I do not know,
But the fact is the *Namu-amida-butsu* has come upon me.

38
How wretched! What shall I do?
[But] wretchedness is the *Namu-amida-butsu*—
Namu-amida-butsu, Namu-amida-butsu!

39
There is nothing in the *Hokkai;*
Only one there is,
Which is the *Namu-amida-butsu*—
And this is Saichi's property.

40
The *Namu-amida-butsu* is transformed and I am it,
And it delights in me,
And I am delighted in it.

41
How wretched!
And how joyous!
They are one
[In] the *Namu-amida-butsu.*

42
The Nembutsu of repentance over my wretchedness,
The Nembutsu of joy—
The *Namu-amida-butsu.*

43
I may be in possession of 84,000 evil passions,
And Amida too is 84,000—
This is the meaning of oneness of *Namu-amida-butsu.*

44
The *Namu* is myself,
Amida is the *Namu;*
And both *Namu* and Amida are the *Namu-amida-butsu.*

45
I, bound for death,
Am now made into the immortal *Namu-amida-butsu.*

46
Life's ending means not-dying;
Not-dying is life's ending;
Life's ending is to become *Namu-amida-butsu.*

47
Death has been snatched away from me,
And in its place the *Namu-amida-butsu.*

48
Saichi's heart destined for death when his end comes,
Is now made an immortal heart,
Is made into the *Namu-amida-butsu.*

49
To die—nothing is better than death;
One feels so relieved!
Nothing exceeds this feeling of relief.
Namu-amida-butsu, Namu-amida-butsu!

IV. THE KI AND THE HŌ[13]

50
"O Saichi, let me have what your understanding is."
"Yes, yes, I will:
How miserable, how miserable!
Namu-amida-butsu, Namu-amida-butsu!"
"Is that all, O Saichi?
It will never do."
"Yes, yes, it will do, it will do.
According to Saichi's understanding,
Ki and *hō* are one:
The *Namu-amida-butsu* is no other than he himself.
This is indeed Saichi's understanding:
He has flowers in both hands,
Taken away in one way and given as gift in another way."

51
How happy I am for this favor! *Namu-amida-butsu!*
Now I know where to deposit all my amassed delusions:
It is where the *ki* and the *hō* are one—
The *Namu-amida-butsu.*

52
Such a Buddha! he is really a good Buddha!
He follows me wherever I go,
He takes hold of my heart.
The saving voice of the six syllables

Is heard as the oneness of the *ki* and the *hō*—
As the *Namu-amida-butsu.*
I have altogether no words for this;
How sweet the mercy!

53
No clinging to anything *(katagiru ja nai):*
No clinging to the *ki,*
No clinging to the *hō*—
This is in accord with the Law *(okite ni kanō).*
Namu-amida-butsu!

This on the part of the *ki,*
This on the part of the *hō.*
How grateful I am!
Namu-amida-butsu!

54
How wretched!
What is it that makes up my heart?
It is no other than my own filled with infinitude of guilt,
Into which the two syllables *na-mu* have come,
And by these syllables infinitude of guilt is borne,
It is Amida who bears infinitude of guilt.
The oneness of the *ki* and the *hō*—
Namu-amida-butsu!

55
Saichi's *Nyorai-san,*
Where is he?
Saichi's *Nyorai-san* is no other than the oneness of the *ki* and the *hō.*
How grateful I am! *Namu-amida-butsu!*
Namu-amida-butsu, Namu-amida-butsu!

56
O Saichi, if you wish to see Buddha,
Look within your own heart where the *ki* and the *hō* are one
As the *Namu-amida-butsu*—
This is Saichi's *Oya-sama.*
How happy with the favor!
Namu-amida-butsu, Namu-amida-butsu!

57
If the *Namu* is myself, Amida is myself too:
This is the *Namu-amida-butsu* of six syllables.[14]

58
The *Namu* is worshiped by Amida,
And Amida is worshiped by the *Namu*—
This is the *Namu-amida-butsu* of six syllables.

59
This Saichi is thine,
Thou art mine—
Namu-amida-butsu!

60
As to Saichi's own *Nyorai-san,*
Where is he?
Yes, Saichi's *Nyorai-san* is the oneness of the *ki* and the *hō*.
How grateful I am!
Namu-amida-butsu!
Namu-amida-butsu!

61
"O Saichi, what are you saying to *Oya-sama?*"
"I am saying, '*Amida-bu, Amida-bu.*'"
"What is *Oya-sama* saying?"
"He is saying, 'O *Namu,* O *Namu.*'"
Thus Thou to me, and I to Thee:
This is the oneness of the *ki* and the *hō*.
Namu-amida-butsu!

62
"O Saichi, how do you see 'thee'?"
"To see 'thee' [take] Amida's mirror,
Therein revealed are both *ki* and *hō*.
Beyond that—repentance and joy.
How wonderful, how wonderful!
Grateful indeed I am! *Namu-amida-butsu!*"

63
How wretched!—
This comes out spontaneously.
How grateful for Buddha's favor!—

This too spontaneously.
The *ki* and the *hō,* both are *Oya*'s working.

64
All comes out in perfection.
How grateful for the favor!
And I take no part in it.
How grateful for the favor!
Namu-amida-butsu, Namu-amida-butsu!

V. THE PURE LAND, THIS WORLD AND HELL[15]

65
"O Saichi, what is your pleasure?"
"My pleasure is this world of delusion;
Because it turns into the seed of delight in the Dharma *(hō)*."
Namu-amida-butsu, Namu-amida-butsu!

66
This world *(sahāloka)* and the Pure Land—they are one;
Worlds as numberless as atoms, too, are mine.
Namu-amida-butsu, Namu-amida-butsu!

67
The path to be born into the Land of Bliss
From this world, there is no other, after all,
Than this world itself.
This world is *Namu-amida-butsu*
Just as much as the Land of Bliss is.
How grateful, how grateful I am!
This Saichi's eye[16] is the boundary line
[Between this world and the Land of Bliss].
Namu-amida-butsu, Namu-amida-butsu!

68
Where are you sleeping, O Saichi?
I am sleeping in this world's Pure Land;
When awakened I go to Amida's Pure Land.

69
This is *shaba* (Sanskrit: *sahāloka*),
And my heart is born of *jigoku* (Sanskrit: *naraka*).

70

"O Saichi, when you die, who will be your companion to the Land of Bliss?"
"As to me, Enma-*san*[17] will be my companion."
"O Saichi, you tell us such tales again.
Who has ever gone to the Land of Bliss with Enma-*san* as companion?
O Saichi, you'd better not tell us such nonsense any more."
"In spite of your remark, I say you are mistaken;
Have you not read this in the *Songs?*
'Enma, Great Lord of Justice, respects us; together with lords of the five paths, he stands as guardian day and night.'
You too should rejoice in the company of Enma-*sama*—
Here is *Namu-amida-butsu.*
This world, how enjoyable with Enma-*sama!*
This Saichi too is guarded by Enma-*sama,*
This Saichi and Enma-*sama* both are one *Namu-amida-butsu:*
This is my joy!"
"O Saichi, from whom did you get such a joyous note?"
"Yes, I talked with Enma-*sama* himself who granted this to me—
[He says] 'You are welcome indeed.'
How joyful! how joyful!
Namu-amida-butsu! Namu-amida-butsu!"

71

I'm fortunate indeed!
Not dead I go,
Just as I live,
I go to the Pure Land!
Namu-amida-butsu!

72

Led by *Namu-amida-butsu,*
While living in this world,
I go to *Namu-amida-butsu.*

73[18]

I'm fortunate indeed!
Not dead I go,
Just as I live,

I go to the Pure Land!
Namu-amida-butsu!

74
I am poor and immensely happy at that;
Amida's Pure Land I enjoy while here—
Namu-amida-butsu!

75
If the *shaba* world is different from the Pure Land,
I should never have heard the Dharma:
Myself and this *shaba* world and the Pure Land and Amida—
All is one *Namu-amida-butsu.*

76
This *shaba* world too is yours,
Where Saichi's rebirth is confirmed—
This is your waiting teahouse.

77
This *shaba* turned into the Pure Land,
And myself changing!
Namu-amida-butsu!

78
My joy is that while in this world of *shaba*
I have been given the Pure Land—
Namu-amida-butsu!

79
My birthplace? I am born of *jigoku* (hell);
I am a nobody's dog
Carrying the tail between the legs;
I pass this world of woes,
Saying *Namu-amida-butsu.*

80
How happy I am! *Namu-amida-butsu!*
I am the Land of Bliss;
I am *Oya-sama.*
Namu-amida-butsu!

81

Shining in glory is Amida's Pure Land,
And this is my Pure Land—
Namu-amida-butsu!

82

Heard so much of the Happy Land,
But after all it is not so much [as I expected];
It is good that it is not, indeed,
How at home do I feel with it!
Namu-amida-butsu, Namu-amida-butsu!

83

The Land of Bliss is mine,
Just take *Namu-amida-butsu* as you hear it!

84

How grateful!
While others die,
I do not die:
Not dying, I go
To Amida's Pure Land.

85

Has Saichi ever seen the Land of Bliss?
No, Saichi has never seen it before.
That is good—
The first visit this.

86

How grateful I am!
I live without knowing anything—
Is this living in a natural Pure Land?

87

How grateful I am!
Into my heart has *Oya-sama* entered!
The cloud of doubt is all dispersed,
I am now given to turn westward.
How fortunate I am!
Saying *Namu-amida-butsu,* I turn west.

88

Buddha-wisdom is beyond human thought,
It makes me go to the Pure Land.
Namu-amida-butsu!

89

How dreadful!
This world known as *shaba*
Is where we endlessly commit all kinds of karma.
How thankful!
All this is turned into [the work of] the Pure Land,
Unintermittently!

90

The most wonderful thing is
That Buddha's invisible heart of compassion is visible
While I'm right here;
That the Pure Land, millions of millions of worlds away, is visible
While I'm right here—
Namu-amida-butsu!

91

I am not to go to *jigoku* (hell),
Jigoku is right here,
We are living right in *jigoku,*
Jigoku is no other place than this.

92

The *Hokkai* is never filled
However much we may talk of it—
Which is the Land of Bliss.
Namu-amida-butsu!

93

The *Hokkai* is Saichi's own country—
Namu-amida-butsu!

94

There is a man going back to Amida's Pure Land—
The *Namu* is carried by Amida.
The Pure Land where he returns
Is the *Namu-amida-butsu.*

95
The being reborn means this present moment;
By means of the *Namu-amida-butsu* this is attained;
Namu-amida-butsu!

VI. THE FREE GIFT[19]

96
Let this world go as it does,
Ignorance-debts, all paid up by *Nyorai-san*—
How happy, how happy I am!

97
Whatever we might say, it is all from thy side,
Yes, it is all from thee.
How thankful I am indeed, how happy I am indeed!
Namu-amida-butsu, Namu-amida-butsu!

98
The *Namu-amida-butsu* is as great as the world itself;
All the air is the *Namu-amida-butsu;*
My heart is also a big heart,
My *tsumi* [wrongdoing (JCD)] is filling the world.
However bad Saichi may be, he cannot defeat you, [O Buddha];
My *tsumi* is dragged along by you,
And it is now taken up [by you] to the Pure Land—
This favor of yours, this favor of yours!
Namu-amida-butsu!

99
The treasure of the six syllables was given me by *Oya-sama:*
However much one spends of it, it is never exhausted.
The treasure grows all the more as it is used;
It is the most wondrous treasure,
And I am the recipient of the good thing.
How happy I am with the favor! *Namu-amida-butsu!*

100
"O Saichi, you say, 'I am given, I am given'
And what is it that is given you?"
"Yes, yes, I am given, I am given the Name of Amida!
And this for nothing!

Saichi is thereby set at ease.
To be set at ease means that the *ki* is altogether possessed [by *Oya-sama*].
It is indeed *Oya-sama* who has taken full possession of me,
And this *Oya-sama* of mine is the *Namu-amida-butsu*."

101

Saichi has his heart revealed by Amida's mirror,
How happy for the favor! *Namu-amida-butsu!*
Namu-amida-butsu, Namu-amida-butsu!
Namu-amida-butsu, Namu-amida-butsu!

102

What a miracle! The *Namu-amida-butsu* fills up the whole world,
And this world is given to me by *Oya-sama.*
This is my happiness, *Namu-amida-butsu!*

103

O *Nyorai-san,*
You have given up yourself to me,
And my heart has been made captive by you—
Namu-amida-butsu!

104

How miserable!
Saichi's heart, how miserable!
All kinds of delusion thickly arise all at once!
A hateful fire mixed with evils is burning,
The waves mixed with evils are rising,
How miserable! A fire mixed with follies is burning.

This heretic, how miserable!
Cannot you call a halt?

Saichi's heart, worrying,
A heart in utter confusion,
Saichi's heart rising as high as the sky!

Here comes the wise man giving the warning:
"O Saichi, listen, now is the time!"

How grateful!
"Now that Amida's 'Original Vow' is established as the *Namu-amida-butsu,*
You have no more to worry about yourself,

Listen, listen!
When you hear *Namu-amida-butsu,*
You have your rebirth in the Pure Land.
The *Namu-amida-butsu* is yours."

How happy I am for this favor! *Namu-amida-butsu!*
Now I know where to deposit all my amassed delusions:
It is where the *ki* and *hō* are one—
The *Namu-amida-butsu.*

With this heart [thus identified],
All over the worlds as many as atoms,
I roam playing in company with all Buddhas and Bodhisattvas.

Eating the *Namu-amida-butsu,* this heart passes its time
In happy company with the *Namu-amida-butsu.*

How happy with this favor!
Namu-amida-butsu!

105

O you, my friends, looking at your hearts filled with wretchedness,
Be not led to doubt Amida's mercy,
Though there is indeed this possibility.
But this is the greatest mistake you are apt to commit.
An utter wretchedness we all guilty beings experience
Does surely turn into a priceless treasure—
This you will realize when karma ripens;
For the *Namu-amida-butsu* truly achieves wonders.

That the *Namu-amida-butsu* truly achieves wonders is this:
The oceans, mountains, eatables, waters, wood used for our house-building, and all other things handled by us guilty beings:
They are one and all transformations of the *Namu-amida-butsu.*
O my friends, be pleased to take note of this truth,
For this is all due to *Oya-sama*'s mercy.
How grateful I feel for all this!

Namu-amida-butsu, Namu-amida-butsu!

106

How grateful!
When I think of it, all is by his [Amida's] grace.
O Saichi, what do you mean by it?
Ah, yes, his grace is real fact.

This Saichi was made by his grace;
The dress I wear was made by his grace;
The food I eat was made by his grace;
The footgear I put on was made by his grace;
Every other thing we have in this world was all made by his grace,
Including the bowl and the chopsticks;
Even this workshop where I work was made by his grace:
There is really nothing that is not the *Namu-amida-butsu.*
How happy I am for all this!
Namu-amida-butsu!

107

By your favor I am turned into a Buddha;
Infinitely great is this favor of yours—
Namu-amida-butsu!

108

"Saichi's illness, is it cured by swallowing the *Namu-amida-butsu?*"
"O, no!"
"If so, how is it cured?"
"Yes, Saichi's illness is cured when it is swallowed up by the *Namu-amida-bu-sama.*"
Saichi is now bodily swallowed up by the pill of the six syllables,
And within the six syllables he leads a life of gratitude.
His life of gratitude is indeed a mystery,
The mystery of mysteries this!
How happy I am with the favor!
Namu-amida-butsu!

109

Saichi has something good given him,
The meditation of five Kalpas is given him.
Where can he have a fit place to store such a big thing?
The fact is that he is taken into it.
How grateful I am!
Namu-amida-butsu!
Namu-amida-butsu!

110[20]

Saichi has something good given him,
The meditation of five Kalpas is given him.
Where can he have a fit place to store such a big thing?

The fact is that he is taken into it.
How grateful I am!
Namu-amida-butsu!
Namu-amida-butsu!

111

Namu-amida-butsu is indeed a wonderful Name,
And I have it as gift.
It gushes out of Saichi's heart;
This is as it ought to be:
The *ki* and *hō* are one in the *Namu-amida-butsu.*

112

"O Saichi, tell us what kind of taste[21] is the taste of *Namu-amida-butsu,*
Tell us what kind of taste is the taste of *Namu-amida-butsu.*"
"The taste of the *Namu-amida-butsu* is:
A joy filling up the bosom,
A joy filling up the liver,
Like the rolling swell of the sea—
No words—just the utterance: Oh, Oh!"

113

There is one thing I wish to learn from *Oya-sama:*
How do you wipe out my guilts?
Carrying my guilts as they are
[I am] borne up by the *Namu-amida-butsu!*
How grateful I am!
Namu-amida-butsu, Namu-amida-butsu!

114

The three poisonous passions are in company with the *Namu-amida-butsu,*
And found working with *Namu-amida-butsu!*
How thankful I am for the favor!
Namu-amida-butsu!

115

The love that inspired *Oya-sama* to go through
All the sufferings and all the hardships—
I thought I was simply to listen to the story,
But that was a grievous mistake, I find.

116

[What a wonder] that such a bad man as Saichi whose badness knows no bounds
Has been transformed into a Buddha!
How grateful for the favor, and how happy!
Namu-amida-butsu, Namu-amida-butsu!

117

How wretched I am!
For us ordinary people human calculations are of no avail.
As to the estimation of guilts—this is left to *Oya-sama.*
How grateful for the favor!
Namu-amida-butsu!

118

My heart given up to Thee,
And Thy heart received by me!

VII. THE HEART-SEARCHINGS[22]

119

The *bonbu*[23] cannot live with Buddha,
Because he has no humility and joy;
Lives with Buddha—
Namu-amida-butsu!

120

Saying "I cannot understand,"
They seize upon the *bonnō*[24] and investigate;
But the *bonnō* is the body of merit;
This makes me laugh.

121

If there were no wretchedness,
My life would be wickedness itself;
How fortunate I am that I was given wretchedness
Namu-amida-butsu, Namu-amida-butsu!

122

When the *bonbu* is not understood
It is wickedness;
When understood, it is humility—
Namu-amida-butsu!

123

Saichi feels within himself
An endless flow of folly,
An endless flow of greed;
There is a fire constantly burning—
No wonder, this burning,
For Saichi is an evil spirit.

124

Saichi's heart is all rain,
Saichi's heart, like rain and rain, is all rain;
Saichi's heart is all fog, like fog within a fog.
There is nothing but wretchedness in Saichi's heart.

125

"How wretched I am!"
This is what we all say when we feel humiliated.
But this kind of self-humiliation we say now is all a lie.
[The real one we say is] what we say after we've visited the Pure Land.
This Saichi's self-humiliation is nothing but a lie, monstrous lie, a monstrous, monstrous lie!
And within this lie there is another lie well wrapped!
How shameful!
This "How shameful!" is also a lie bursting out of the mouth.
This Saichi putting on the mask is most irreverently playing upon the saintly masters!
How wretched, how wretched!
There, there, that Saichi is again putting on the mask!
There is nothing in this Saichi but going around in disguise and deceiving everybody;
How wretched!
Anything Saichi says is wretchedness itself.
Even this comes out of the lying lips.
The only real true thing is *Oya-sama,* no other there is!
All my lies have been completely taken away [by him],
[And there remains nothing but]
Namu-amida-butsu!

126

How did you see your own heart?
To see the heart, take Amida's mirror.

How wretched!
The wretchedness of my heart is like space, it has no limits.
How wretched!

127

O Saichi, you are a wretched fellow!
Your stature is hardly five feet,
And yet your heart runs wildly all over the world.
Saichi is a wretched man.
How wretched!

128

They understand who have had sorrows,
But those who had them not can never understand:
There is nothing so excruciating as sighs—
The sighs that refuse to be disposed of.
But they are removed by Amida,
And all I can say now is *Namu-amida-butsu, Namu-amida-butsu!*

129

There is no bottom to Saichi's wickedness;
There is no bottom to Saichi's goodness:
How happy I am with the favor!
Namu-amida-butsu!

130

The wretched heart of contrition—
The thankful heart of joy—
The *Namu-amida-butsu* of contrition and joy![25]

VIII. POVERTY[26]

131

Nothing is left to Saichi,
Except a joyful heart nothing is left to him.
Neither good nor bad has he, all is taken away from him;
Nothing is left to him!
To have nothing—how completely satisfying!
Everything has been carried away by the *Namu-amida-butsu.*
He is thoroughly at home with himself:
This is indeed the *Namu-amida-butsu!*

132
My avarice has all been taken away,
And the world has turned into my *Namu-amida-butsu.*

133
Everything of mine has been carried away by Thee,
And Thou hast given me the Nembutsu—*Namu-amida-butsu.*

IX. THE INNER LIFE[27]

134
To be grateful is all a lie,
The truth is—there is nothing the matter;
And beyond this there is no peace of mind—
Namu-amida-butsu, Namu-amida-butsu, Namu-amida-butsu!
(With this peacefully I retire.)

135
There's nothing with me, nothing's the matter with me—
To have nothing the matter is the *Namu-amida-butsu.*

136
That this Saichi is turned into a Buddha,
Even while I knew nothing of it:
So I am told.

137
How wretched!
Wretchedness too is of suchness.[28]
How thankful!
Buddha's favor too is of suchness.
Both *ki* and *hō* are *Oya-sama's* work.[29]
All out, nothing kept back![30]
How grateful for the favor!
Nothing's left for me to do.
How grateful for the favor!
Namu-amida-butsu!

138
As regards myself, nothing is the matter:
Called by the voice the mind has been made captive,
And *Namu-amida-butsu!*

139
To say, "How grateful!" is a lie;
The truth is: there is nothing the matter with one;
And there is nothing more that makes one feel at home—
Namu-amida-butsu! Namu-amida-butsu!

140
O Saichi, such as you are, are you grateful?
Nothing's the matter [with me],
However much I listen [to the sermons], nothing's the matter with me.
And no inquiries are to be made.

141
Nothing's the matter, nothing's the matter with me;
That there's nothing the matter—this is the *Namu-amida-butsu.*

142
To be grateful is not *anjin;*[31]
Nothing happening is nothing happening.
To be grateful is a fraud—[32]
'Tis true, 'tis true!

143
Whether I'm falling [to hell]
Or bound for the Pure Land—
I have no knowledge:
All is left to Amida's Vow.
Namu-amida-butsu!

144
Doubts have been taken away—
I know not how and when!
How to be thankful for the favor—I know not!
Namu-amida-butsu!

145
I am happy!
The root of sinfulness[33] is cut off;
Though still functioning, it is the same as non-existent.
How happy I am!
Born of happiness is the *Namu-amida-butsu.*

146

"O Saichi, won't you tell us about *tariki?*"
"Yes, but there is neither *tariki* nor *jiriki,*
What is, is the graceful acceptance only."

147

Where are Saichi's evil desires gone?
They are still here:
I hate, I love, I crave—
How wretched, how wretched I am!

9

Infinite Light

This essay, which developed from presentations that Suzuki gave in California in 1950 and 1952, was edited and published after his death. In it Suzuki explicates the imagery of light in the Pure Land sutras, specifically the infinite light of Amida Buddha. Though ubiquitous in the sutras, the theme of light was not as prominent in the Shin Buddhist exegetical tradition as Amida's vows and name were. Suzuki singles out light as a symbol for various Buddhist ideals—for example, the Buddha's wisdom, love, and power—and employs it to convey his own nondualistic understanding of Pure Land Buddhism.

Suzuki makes a distinction between Light (with a capital L) and ordinary light, the antithesis of darkness. He treats the Buddha's Light as an ontological reality undergirding both light and darkness and pervading not only the Pure Land but also this flawed world, *sahāloka,* and even hell, *naraka.* Light transcends the world but also suffuses it, making possible the path to deliverance as well as the realms of suffering and torment themselves. Amida's Light thereby embraces and subsumes all the conflicts and contradictions of the world, rather than rivaling or standing apart from them. Suzuki thus propounds a philosophy of interpenetration and nonduality—with Light as the fundamental stuff underlying and permeating all reality.

Using his explication of Light as a model, Suzuki applies this type of analysis to the multitude of distinct and opposing entities in the world. Amid their differences, Suzuki extols them as one; and while confirming them as one, he simultaneously recognizes them as different. This analysis is applied particularly to the idea of the Pure Land itself. Suzuki emphasizes that the Pure Land is not a separate realm from this world, *sahāloka,* nor even from hell, *naraka.* Anyone with an awakened religious consciousness will realize that they are identical. Suzuki acknowledges that this interpretation of Light and the Pure Land may be at odds with the views of most Shin Buddhists. But he maintains that their truth will be self-evident to people based on their inmost experience.

In explicating Amida's Light and Pure Land, Suzuki uses some of the same themes and strategies that Western proponents of religion did in the twentieth century. First of all, he emphasizes religious experience. He differentiates it from intellectual comprehension and moral discipline without necessarily dismissing their value in real life. Suzuki believes that religious experience arises at the point where humans confront the limits of their own intellection and moral perfection. It is noteworthy that in explaining religious experience—or "enlightenment-experience" as Suzuki styles it—he does not describe it in terms of mysticism or spirituality as he does in his earlier writings. Instead, he characterizes it as a state of awareness in which the "self" is superseded by the "Self," a rhetorical strategy found also in Western religious thought and psychology of religion in the twentieth century. For Suzuki, this experience is tantamount to realizing the nondualistic nature of all things.

A second parallel between Suzuki and Western thought is their treatment of religious myth. Both of them find the literal interpretation of scripture, such as the premodern account of the Pure Land paradise, to be problematic. One approach in addressing this issue was the twentieth-century theological attempt to demythologize religious texts. This essay by Suzuki, without explicitly deploying demythologization as a method, treats scripture as a rich repository of themes and symbols that lend themselves to modern appropriation. The infinite Light of Amida Buddha, which Suzuki explicates independent of Pure Land's prescientific cosmology, is a prime example of this.

The base text for this essay is "Infinite Light," *The Eastern Buddhist* (New Series) 4, no. 2 (1971): 1–29. It was republished in Daisetz Teitarō Suzuki, *Collected Writings on Shin Buddhism* (CWSB), ed. The Eastern Buddhist Society (Kyoto: Shinshū Ōtaniha, 1973), 129–152; and again in *Matsugaoka Bunko kenkyū nenpō* 26 (2012): 57–85. A Japanese translation by Sakai Tsutomu was published as "Muryōkō," *Matsugaoka Bunko kenkyū nenpō* 26 (2012): 4–41. Earlier versions of this essay—under the titles "Amida, the Buddha of Infinite Light" (1950), "The Pure Land Reflected in This *Sahāloka*" (1950), and "Amitābha, the Buddha of Infinite Light" (1952)—are preserved in manuscript form at the Matsugaoka Bunko in Kamakura.

• • •

AMITĀBHA, THE BUDDHA OF INFINITE LIGHT

Those who are at all acquainted with Buddhist sutras, especially those belonging to the Mahayana school, must have noticed that all the Buddhas are described as enveloped in light, as emanating rays of light from various parts of their bodies, riding on light-emitting clouds, etc. Not only the Buddhas themselves but anything connected with them also becomes luminous. For example: in the *Avataṃsaka Sūtra (Kegonkyō)* we observe that upon Buddha's entering a state of enlightenment the ground which surrounds him, the tree under which he sits, and the lion-seat which he occupies—all shine out in glorious light. In other words, wherever a Buddha appears, the environment including everything existing around him is miraculously transformed and finds itself enveloped in light.

The *Sukhāvatī-vyūha Sūtra* and others belonging to the Pure Land school thus also describe Buddhas and their lands in terms of dazzling light. Indeed, the name of the Buddha himself is "infinite light," *amitābha* in Sanskrit.[1] It is no wonder then that the sutras bearing his name portray him and his land in terms of light throughout. Śākyamuni who is the narrator of the story of Amida (or rather, the one who transmits the story as having been told by Śākyamuni) exhausts his arts trying to impress this point in the minds and hearts of the readers or hearers. This is seen in his description of Amida's shining dignity which goes beyond human measurements. Infinite Light together with eternal Life are the two characteristics of Amida Nyorai.

Let me quote from Shinran's *Wasan,* "Songs in Praise of Amitābha," translated by B. L. Suzuki:

Since the attainment of Buddhahood by Amitābha,
Ten kalpas[2] have now passed away;
The Light radiating from the Dharmakaya[3] has no limits:
It illuminates the world's blindness and darkness.

The Light of His wisdom is measureless,
All conditional forms without exception
Are enveloped in the dawning Light;
Therefore, take refuge in the True Light.

Amida's Light is like a wheel radiating without bounds.
Buddha[4] declared that all things touched by His[5] Light
Are freed from all forms of being and not-being.
Take refuge in the One who is universally enlightened.

The clouds of Light have, like space, no hindrances;
All that have obstructions are not impeded by them;
There is no one who is not embraced in His Soft Light:
Take refuge in Him who is beyond thought.

Nothing can be compared to His Pure Light;
The result of encountering this Light
Destroys all karma-bondage:
So take refuge in Him who is the Ultimate Haven.

Amida Buddha's illuminating Light is above all,
So He is called the Sovereign Buddha of Flaming Light,
The darkness of the three evil paths[6] is opened:
Take refuge in the Great Arhat.[7]

The radiance of His Light of Truth surpasses all,
So He is called the Buddha of Pure Light:
Those who are embraced in the Light
Are cleansed from the dirt of karma and attain emancipation.

However far His Light illumines, love penetrates,
The joy of faith is attained,

So we are told.
Take refuge in the Great One who gives comfort.

He is known as the Buddha of the Light of Prajna,[8]
Because He dispels the darkness of ignorance;
The Buddhas and the beings of the Three Vehicles[9]
All join in praising Him.

As there is a constant flow of Light,
He is known as the Buddha of Constancy;
Because of perceiving the power of Light with uninterrupted faith,
We are born into the Pure Land.

As the Buddha of Light knows naught of measurement,
He is known as the Buddha of Unthinkable Light:
All other Buddhas praise the *Ōjō*[10]
And the virtues of Buddha Amida are extolled.

As His Wondrous Light transcends form and description,
He is known as the Buddha of Inexpressible Light;
His Light has the power to enlighten all beings:
So he is praised by all the Buddhas.

As His Light surpasses that of the Sun and the Moon,
He is known as the Sun-and-Moon-Surpassing Light;
Śākyamuni could not praise Him enough:
Take refuge in the One who is peerless.

Amida therefore is the Buddha whose Light fills all the worlds with his illuminating rays, and any of the sentient beings who happens to be struck by it is assuredly cleansed of all his defilements and his body becomes soft and his heart overflowing with goodness is filled with joy and happiness. Indeed, the features of Śākyamuni himself who gives the account of Amida radiate with a light attracting the attention of the whole congregation that is gathered around him.

The following may just as well be applied to Śākyamuni though it is ascribed to Buddha Lokeśvararāja[11] under whom Amida made his solemn announcement of the forty-eight vows.[12] In fact, unless Śākyamuni did not shine in the same Light as Amida and Lokeśvararāja he could never give the story of Amida as he did to his congregation on Mount Vulture. They were all enveloped, each one of the three, in one and the same Light of surpassing beauty and splendor which defies all our human efforts of description.

His radiant features are majestic and inspire awe,
His divine dignity knows no limits;
To such brilliancy of light
There is nothing comparable;
The suns and moons and *maṇi*-jewels,

> However much they may shine in their way,
> Every one of them appears darkly covered,
> And is no more than a black mass of coal.[13]

The Light that illumines the Pure Land is also of this nature. If we, therefore, try to paint it in the color we ordinarily see about us, we can never see it, even at our death as is told by the followers of the Jōdo school. Amida and his Land are of the same nature, they belong to an order higher than and altogether transcending ours. The Light pervading the Buddha-land and everything in it has no shadow; it is not to be measured by the hypothesis of wavelengths; it is neither short nor long, neither broad nor narrow. As it is of this nature Amida can take us into it with all our defilements, moral or otherwise. If it could be measured by its wavelengths, our entering into it would at once cast a shadow all around and the whole land would be turned into a world of darkness. The reason why we of this *sahāloka*[14] can be inhabitants of the Pure Land is because the Light there is of such nature that it penetrates everything and transforms it into its own color-light as it pervades the Pure Land. So we read in the *Larger Sukhāvatī-vyūha Sūtra:*

> If those who are born in my country, upon my obtaining Buddhahood, should not all shine in golden color, may I not attain the highest enlightenment. (Vow 3)

Again:

> If those who are born in my country, upon my obtaining Buddhahood, should not all be of one form and one color, showing no difference in look, may I not attain the highest enlightenment. (Vow 4)

THE LIGHT, *SAHĀLOKA* AND *NARAKA*

What strikes us ordinary beings living in this *sahāloka* most strange and beyond comprehension is the fact that the Light also shines here and that we are in it. Most of us would surely argue in this way: If we are in the Light and this world shares in its splendor, why does not this world with everything in it partake of the same golden color as in the Pure Land? Why do we have here the three evil paths? Why are we tainted with defilements[15] as we actually are? Why are we so ugly and deformed as to make us feel utterly disgusted? Some such questions would arise endlessly. And how shall we dispose of them if the Light is really shining upon us and within us?

The answer is this: If we were not ugly, deformed, and tainted with all kinds of defilement, there would be no Pure Land, and hence no Light, and the very existence of this *sahāloka* would be impossible. The reason we raise questions such as above is due to the fact that the Light of Amida is right here with us, in us, and around us. If this were not the case, we would never give rise to any question as to the presence of the Light anywhere. It is the Light of Amida indeed that prompts us and makes us ask about Amida. For as soon as the Light of Amida enters here, the shadowless Light acquires a shadow and begins to torment us, as it were, with a shadow of doubt and a feeling of uncertainty. We of this world are bound to feel the darkness though the Light shines absolutely unobstructed in the Land of Amida.

We would therefore commit a most grievous mistake and suffer the consequence of it if we should persuade ourselves to think that Amida with his Land exists somewhere outside and impassably separated from this world of ours. We would commit yet another most grievous mistake and suffer if we should imagine that this world itself is the Pure Land and that we are all its inhabitants by indisputable right. These two notions are to be carefully avoided.

Another strange, perhaps the most strange, thing is that the Light of Amida also shines in *naraka*[16] (or *jigoku* in Japanese). Without this Light *naraka* too could not come into existence and keep on existing. Without this Light *naraka* would be in a state of utter darkness, which means nonexistence. Since we can talk about it and see so many of us actually going through all forms of torment and torture, there must be some light even in *naraka,* and this light however darkish must come from Amida's Light, for no light of whatever nature could come from anywhere else but from Amida. The reason why Yama, lord of the underworld, could have his "mirror of judgment" beside him is because it reflects the Light of Amida. [Amida (CWSB)] is not a judge in the sense taught in some other religions, but in his own way he judges. While he never punishes he is fully aware of all the defilements with which we sentient beings are inevitably tainted as beings of finitude and relativity.

Without Amida's Light reaching *naraka,* Yama's mirror of judgment can never be bright enough, impartial enough, free from egoistic taints. Without the Light Yama cannot see anything from his own light, which being conditioned and limited produces shadows all around. His light which is his judgment is of no worth unless it reflects something of Amida's. Indeed, if Amida's Light could not penetrate *naraka,* it would be nothing but that of wavelengths.

When we talk about Amida's Light extending to this world of ours, we may feel here a sort of contradiction. But we can say that here is a far more serious, or rather an ominous form of contradiction as regards the relation of *naraka* to Amida's Light. Whether or not it is serious or ominous or threatening, there is no doubt that we have here a contradiction. In fact, *naraka* is no more than the extension of *sahāloka,* and if Amida's Light is penetrating to *sahāloka,* there is no reason why the Light should not also illuminate *naraka.* It is true that light and darkness contradict each other, for where the one is the other cannot be. This kind of light which stands against darkness is not the shadowless Light of Amida. If it is shadowless, it transcends all forms of contradiction. Amida's Light covers everything and makes it look like one uniform color of solid gold. Contradictions are human and logical. Amida knows of no logicalness nor of illogicalness. He transcends contradictions. *Naraka* as well as *sahāloka* is Amida's Light.

The trouble with us human beings when we at all begin to think is that we divide the thinking into two terms, object and subject, and endeavor to carry on this process endlessly. Dividing thus is the essence of thought, and on account of this division the one is made to stand always directly contrasted to the other, as if there could be no common ground between the two, while in reality there is always oneness, however deeply hidden from sight, at the basis of the opposition, whereby the two opposing terms can be brought out for a synthesis. Contradictions, therefore, of whatever nature can always be unified by making them transcend themselves. The reason for contradiction is thus the reason for mutual relationship and for a higher unification.

We establish a sharp division and an uncrossable gap between the Pure Land and *naraka,* thinking that the one can never be brought out to make a close approach to the other. But unless the Pure Land is not penetrating even to the depths of *naraka,* the Light cannot be said to be all-illuminating. In Amida's Land, it is true, there is no *naraka,* no *sahāloka,* but the shadowless Light of Amida is above discriminations—it is the Pure Land and also is *sahāloka* and *naraka,* and for this reason the Light can be touched or seen by inhabitants of all other countries other than the Pure Land, including *sahāloka* and *naraka.* If not for this fact, not only *naraka,* but *sahāloka* too, could never be recovered into the Pure Land. The latter reflects itself anywhere there are fully matured conditions. And such conditions are available anywhere throughout the worlds whose numbers, according to Buddhism, are inexhaustible.

Amida's Light reflects itself negatively as well as positively in *naraka* and *sahāloka.* Otherwise, there would be no chances whatever for dwellers of *naraka.* This is the reason for making Shinran[17] say that "the evil-minded are really Amida's objectives of salvation." Amida is really more concerned with *naraka.* This means that the Light has greater chances to enter *naraka.* Paradoxically, we can state thus: Because of the very contradiction, from the human point [of (CWSB)] view, between the Pure Land and *naraka,* Amida comes down to *naraka* and picks up Yama's victims, and on this account the Pure Land increases its Light ever more radiantly where we humans consider there are more obstacles.

> The unimpeded Light illuminating all the ten quarters
> Shines through the darkness of ignorance;
> It leads most assuredly to Nirvana
> All those who are gladdened by [the experience of] one-mindedness *(ichinen).*
>
> Benefited by the unimpeded Light,
> Faith is attained, great in power

Whereby the ice of evil passions melts
Into the water of enlightenment.

Karma-hindrance is the substance of merit:
It is like water and ice—
Much ice produces much water,
The more impediment, the more merit.[18]

Naraka is not a region of pure darkness; there is no such thing as pure darkness. The darkness here is of such nature as to conceal the Light, or we can say that by the very reason of darkness *naraka* obtains its light from Amida and is saved from itself. As long as one stays in *naraka* one can never understand this mystery of mysteries.

I repeat, *naraka* can never see itself, for it has no light of its own. Yama's mirror is bright and free from dust because of its reflecting the Light of the Pure Land. Yama has no power by himself over the inhabitants of his realm except for the Light coming from the Beyond. The eternal fire burning in *naraka* effects its transformation into the cooling lotus pond at the very moment the inhabitants realize that even *naraka* reflects the Light of Amida.

A woman *myōkōnin*[19] of Hawaii expresses her experience:

Being told to fall,
I fall;
And lo! I find myself
Held within the lotus petals!

"To fall" is to fall into *naraka,* as this is the sure destination of all sentient beings conditioned by finitude and relativity. Most of us, however, are afraid of this inevitableness and struggle to escape it. But the more we struggle the deeper we are involved in the dilemma and stand looking despairingly into the bottomless abyss. The crisis is transcended by jumping right into the gaping maw of the devil. The decision is not the outcome of despair, it is the deed of giving up relativity, it is the supreme moment of the Light breaking through the darkness of the self-power of *naraka.* For this reason the bottomless abyss, the relative, empirical consciousness calculated to jump into, is now transformed into the lotus flower radiating in the Light of Amida.

The Light is a creative activity and where it touches there takes place not only a transformation of old things but the creation of new things. If it were an event to be measured by lights and shades, by the length of wave-movements, it could never work miracles. If it created the Pure Land it could also create *sahāloka* and *naraka* as well. If it could create space and time and causation, it could also wipe out all these things of relativity by just striking them with one of its shafts. This is the reason why our "sins"[20] of hundreds of thousands of *koṭis*[21] of kalpas could be effaced by "one thought"[22] *(ekakṣaṇa)* of *Namu-amida-butsu.*[23]

As long as the Light is conceived spatially and intellectually, there are contradictions galore: the Pure Land versus *naraka,* self-power versus other-power,[24] *pṛthagjana*[25] (*bonpu* in Japanese) versus Buddha, *kleśa*[26] *(bonnō)* versus *bodhi*[27] *(satori)* or *nirvāṇa*[28] *(nehan),* etc. But as soon as this way of interpreting the Light is given up and expressed in terms of time, everything becomes possible, wonders cease to be wonders. The *bonpu* of yesterday is the Buddha of today; the jackal has turned into the lion; *naraka* flooded with blood and fire is transformed into a lotus pond filled with clear limpid waters, lightly kissed by a refreshing breeze; there are no traces of a lurid fire here, all is of one golden color shining in beauty and splendor.

Not only are there spatial transformations here by the Light striking on *naraka,* but time itself loses its relative order of sequence, the past becomes the present and the future is no more an anticipation. This is demonstrated by Amida's vows 5 to 15. Let me quote one of them by way of illustrating my point:

> If those who are born in my country, upon my obtaining Buddhahood, should not be endowed with the heavenly ear so as at least to be able to hear and retain in memory all the Buddhas' preaching in hundreds of thousands of *koṭi*s of Buddha-countries, may I not attain the highest enlightenment. (Vow 8)

From the ordinary, relative point of view prevailing in this world of *sahāloka,* this acquiring of the heavenly ears or eyes or similar other powers of sense when we are in the Pure Land, as mentioned in these vows, is of no significance whatever. For what would the inhabitants of the Pure Land have to do with such extraordinary sensitiveness of the senses? They are already in the Pure Land where all earthly relationships have lost their values. The heavenly eyes or ears may be something highly desirable while here, but in the Pure Land even remembering all the Buddhas' preachings or seeing all the Buddha-lands in the ten quarters will be a kind of superfluity or even nuisance which adds nothing of worth to what the residents in Amida's country already have. They enjoy everything there which is given in Buddhas' teachings, in fact they are living them; the Pure Land is the very symbol of the fullness of all things, and its occupants can really have nothing wanting. If they still had something wanting in the Pure Land it would no more be the Pure Land.

All the wonderful powers and experiences promised in Amida's vows are no more than demonstrating the transcendental nature of the Pure Land where such conceptions as space, time, and causation are of no avail. The Pure Land is the enlightenment-experience itself and all the details given in the vows of Amida are its contents as were conceivable in India in those days when the sutras were compiled.

The Pure Land is not to be interpreted in terms of *sahāloka* though it is full of imageries belonging to the latter. Where Amida's Light is given description in its own way altogether ignoring the significance attachable to those imageries, we must use a different measurement not belonging to this world. When I said that Amida's Light is not to be explained by the theory of wavelengths, implications were that we are here dealing with a subject quite unique and beyond our intellectual postulates.

The fact that there is no other way of describing the Pure Land except for resorting to *sahāloka* imageries shows to that extent that the Pure Land is not a region beyond *sahāloka* and *naraka* as well.

If Amida's Light did not reach *naraka* as well as *sahāloka,* the Pure Land would cease to be a Pure Land and Amida's vows would come to naught. If we, on the other hand, conceived this world (and for that matter *naraka*) from our intellectual standpoint to be a realm independent of the Pure Land, existing unrelated to the Pure Land, we would be taking this world away from Amida's Light and at the same time denying the all-illuminating nature of the Light. Here too Amida's vows would be of no significance.

THE LIGHT IN *SAHĀLOKA*

The statement that unless the Pure Land reflected itself in this world of particulars and relativities, Amida's vows would be in vain, may be contested by most of the Shin Buddhists, though the statement to my thinking is almost one of self-evidence and does not require a specific process of rationalization. In order to show that the statement is based on the scriptural authority and supported by our inmost experience, the following is quoted from the *Larger Sukhāvatī-vyūha Sūtra* (Chinese translation by Saṃghavarman). Ānanda expresses his desire to see the Pure Land and, Buddha granting it, the following scene ensues:

> Instantly, the Buddha of Eternal Life radiating his infinite light universally illumined all the Buddha-countries including the Diamond-enclosed mountains, Mount Sumeru, and all the other mountains large and small, and also everything that could be found there. They were then all of one color.
>
> It was like a great flood at the end of the kalpa, which would deluge all the worlds, submerging everything in them and burying them far below the surface, so that as far as one's eye could survey there would be nothing but the surging, swelling, rolling waters.
>
> The rays of light emitted by the Buddha were also like these waters: those of the Sravakas and Bodhisattvas were covered by the Buddha's and could not at all be seen. There was nothing but the light of the Buddha radiating in its utmost brilliancy.
>
> Ānanda then immediately saw the Buddha of Eternal Life in his august dignity like Mount Sumeru towering high above all other worlds. There was nothing that escaped the all-illuminating rays of light which emanated from the Buddha's [Amitābha's] body. All four groups of the congregation were then able to see everything instantly. Those [of the Pure Land] saw also this land as the latter saw the other.

The quotation is clear enough to show that this world is fully reflected in the Pure Land, showing that Amida's Light reaches here whereby the latter shines enough to make itself visible to the host of the other side. This is intelligible, but how do we of this side come to the knowledge that those of the other side saw us as we saw them? This knowledge on our part is only possible when there is a mutual reflection between *sahāloka* and the Pure Land, and this not once, as is recorded in the sutra, but must be taking place constantly between here and yonder, because this is in the nature of the Light itself.

Listen to the experience of the *myōkōnin* which is perfectly in accord with this view of the Light. I will quote some lines from the "notebooks" of the *myōkōnin,* Saichi:

> Amida is here,
> Here is Amida,
> Here in this very spot.
> *Namu* and Amida,
> As *Namu-amida-butsu,*
> Here we are both together!
>
> O *Nyorai-san,* you have given me all of yourself,
> And I've been taken captive by you, body and soul—
> *Namu-amida-butsu!*
>
> He makes me call upon him,
> And he gives himself up to me:
> This is Amida's voice of summons—
> *Namu-amida-butsu!*
>
> It is Amida's will
> To make my thought turn to him:
> I utter *Namu!*
> In perfect obedience to Amida's will.
>
> *Namu-amida-bu* and 'Mida-*sama*
> Are one and not two.
> *Namu-amida-bu* is myself,
> And 'Mida-*sama* is my *Oya-sama:*
> Here is the oneness of *Namu-amida-butsu.*
> How happy for this favor!
> *Namu-amida-butsu!*
>
> "O Saichi, where is your Land of Bliss?"
> "My Land of Bliss is right here."
> "Where is the line dividing the Land of Bliss from this world?"
> "Between this world and the Land of Bliss
> The eye is the dividing line."

From these utterances of one who went through the Shin Buddhist experience, we realize that there is a most intimate mutual relationship between the Pure Land and this *sahāloka.* The *myōkōnin* calls Amida or 'Mida-*sama* his *Oya-sama,* which means both father and mother, and this *Oya-sama* is with him and in him, declares Saichi the *myōkōnin.* The *Oya-sama* in him called upon him and made him turn to *Oya-sama,* who in turn faced him and willingly became the object of the devotee's wholehearted homage. In other words, Amida divided himself, made the one turn toward the other, in order to pay homage, as it were, to each other. In terms of light, Amida makes the Pure Land reflect itself in this world and this world in the Pure Land, and this mutual fusion of light takes place instantly between them, between this world and the Pure Land, when we have an enlightenment-experience. And I must add that this mutual fusion of light is taking place constantly between this world and the Pure Land, between Amida and ourselves.

How is this mutual reflection possible?

This can take place only under the hypothesis that Amida's Light illuminates both worlds, making it possible for each of them to reflect itself in the other, so that each can see its image as it is in the other. This means in turn that the Pure Land and this world are interpenetrating and that between them there are no separating obstructions. If there were not such interpenetration or interfusion, we could never picture to ourselves what is happening in the Pure Land whereby we are made to deplore the present state of our finite existence and to aspire to be born into the Pure Land. But this deploring and aspiring could never take place without Amida's infusing his Light deeply into our hearts. To use official Shin terminology, we could not come to the consciousness of the Pure Land without the mediation of the other-power. The self-power is discriminative, relative, and limited, and unless it draws its life from Amida's Light it could never see the Pure Land and be born there. Only by means of the Light of the other-power can we of *sahāloka* transcend ourselves.

Dialectically speaking, the absolute contradiction between the Pure Land and the defiled land of ours is synthesized only by going through the mediumship of Amida's infinite Light. Without this we could never say that the Pure Land is here or that outside this world of finitude and defilement there is no Pure Land.

Again, from the point of the Shin Buddhist experience, we who are heavily laden with all kinds of evil passions and most decidedly destined for *naraka* could not expect to be born in the Pure Land unless with our defilements there is in us the other-power working all the time for enlightenment. In fact, the defilements so-called are the other-power itself, and it is only through these defilements that we could realize the presence of the other-power within ourselves. We can never get rid of our defilements inasmuch as we are finite beings and limited in every sense of the word. But by being awakened to the fact that there is in us Amida's saving Light, all those defilements lose their power of binding us to this world or making us go to *naraka.* We are finite and yet infinite; we are destined to pass out of this individual existence as far as we are in time, yet by becoming conscious of the other-power we die and yet live; we are endowed with eternal life.

So we read in one of Shinran's hymns:

> Since we heard the vow of compassion surpassing anything of this world,
> We are no more ordinary mortals going through births and deaths.
> While this finite body of defilements may remain the same,
> The mind is already visiting the Land of Purity.

We must not think that this mutual reflection between the Pure Land and this world took place only once in historical time, while Śākyamuni and Ānanda and his congregation appeared in India two thousand and five hundred years ago, as Christ appeared in the history of the Jewish people. From the point of view of the religious consciousness Ānanda and the whole congregation including the Buddha himself are no other than ourselves who are gathered here tonight. We cannot say exactly or individually who is Ānanda, or who is Buddha among us. Such questions are nonsensical. We are in fact all Ānandas, Buddhas, Maitreyas, Mahākāśyapas, Śāriputras, and all the rest of the congregation who were present when this sutra was delivered on Mount Vulture. The main point is that the question Ānanda asked is the question we are asking of ourselves all the time. That is to say, the Ānanda in each of us is asking this question all the time to the Buddha in each of us. For in each of us there is an Ānanda who asks questions and a Buddha who is ready to answer them.

However this may be, Amida's Light envelops not only the Pure Land and this world, but also *naraka,* for even *naraka* cannot escape being enclosed within the Light, for *naraka* is a kind of intensified shadow of *sahāloka.* It is for this reason that Yama, lord of *naraka,* including all the *oni* (devils) and all the instruments and conditions of torture, could not be made visible not only to the inhabitants in *naraka* but to this human world; the mirror of purity standing before Yama could not have the power of illuminating all the "sins" committed by the inhabitants while they were in *sahāloka.* The mirror is no other than the Light.

There is no doubt that Amida's Light penetrates all the three worlds, Pure Land, *sahāloka,* and *naraka.* However divergent and mutually contradicting they may appear, all these are ultimately one reality; they are three aspects of one identical reality, which reflects itself variously because of conditions prevailing there. It is we, addicted to or endowed with the intellect which discriminates, who see the one differentiated as three. It is we who separate one reality, one Light, into three facets and take each as contrasted to the others.

It is due to this discrimination exercised by the intellect, or to a light accompanied by a shadow, that we often think this world as a kind of connecting link between *naraka* and the Pure Land, and ourselves standing on the middle section of a straight line whose one end points to *naraka* and the other to the Pure Land. But when we stand right on the line itself, as in the Light of Amida, the straight line itself is this Light and all the three are also in it. Even when we are all inevitably destined for *naraka* as is taught by Jōdo people, we are nevertheless able to climb up the ladder of the Pure Land, or rather we can at once leap over to Amida's realm, because we are right in the middle of his Light which is like a straight line stretched out infinitely at either end. It is the privilege of the human mind that it can grasp the infinite while right in it.

In this sense, the following statement is true: *Sahāloka* is the Pure Land itself shining in its absolutely serene Light; each one of us is nobody else than Amida himself. At the same time we must remember that this kind of insight never comes to one whose eyesight is dimmed by discrimination.

The eye that sees the shadowless Light of Amida is not the eye that we all have as one of the senses. There must be a third eye like the one possessed by the heavenly god, Maheśvara. But let me remind you of this: Though this eye does not belong to this world of relativity, it is not something different from the eye which we use in surveying the world. This is very confusing, you might say. Yes, so it is. But what is needed for the transformation is to change the direction in which it is used to looking. Let the same eye turn within instead of without, and it works wonders. It is just this turning, this changing of direction, that is needed for transformation. So long as we are relying on our own light which is mere reflection, this will never be effected. There must be an inner experience, which is known as "crosswise leaping."

By virtue of this transformation or "crosswise leaping" the three poisonous passions and the five self-centered desires are also transformed into so many merit-producing virtues. This has already been noticed in connection with Saichi's idea of the eye as the dividing line between this world and the Pure Land. It will be interesting to note that Eckhart makes a similar reference to the eye, saying that it is the same eye that sees God as well as the external world.

It is indeed the eye-curtain that separates this world from the Pure Land; when the curtain is drawn up one sees *sahāloka* in the Pure Land and the Pure Land in *sahāloka*. Let me quote Saichi again:

> "Where is Saichi sleeping?"
> "I am sleeping in the Pure Land which is this world;
> When I am awakened, I shall be in 'Mida's Pure Land."

In another place, he has:

> *Sahāloka* is no other than here where I am,
> The Land of Happiness is also no other than here where I am.
> This means the removing of the eye-curtain.

It is the eye-curtain, not very heavy nor unwieldy, but as long as it is there the Pure Land is furthest away from our view and utterly inaccessible.

According to Saichi, while he is alive, that is, while he is leading this life of relativity and discrimination, he is in the Pure Land belonging to this world, *sahāloka,* and as such he cannot escape all the karma-conditions which characterize this world. But upon his death, that is, when he parts with this life of relativity and discrimination, he enters into the Pure Land where these conditions are no more in operation. But judging from the whole trend of his writings, he does not seem to care where he is actually living, in this land of suffering or in the land of bliss; wherever he may be he is happy and thankful for the favor which he finds everywhere he goes. Amida's Light is always with him, he is with Amida all the time, in fact he is Amida, he cannot get away from him, he is taken captive by him. This being the case, it does not matter where he is.

With all these inner feelings which he cherishes, his expressions follow the old traditional, conventional modes; he does not try to invent a new terminology, for he is not a thinker, he is just an ordinary devotee of Shin faith which he has experienced to the very core of his being, and for that reason he cannot help giving expression to it to the best of his learning and thinking. He is happy with that and with handmaking the footgear according to the fashion of his day.

Saichi, however, makes distinction between "sleeping" and "awake" which corresponds to the Pure Land conditioned and the Pure Land in its absolute purity. While "sleeping," which is our actual state in this world, we are indeed in the Pure Land yet as conditioned by relativity. When "awake," however, whatever this may mean, we are in the Pure Land itself shorn of all its conditions. As long as Saichi finds himself to be living in this world of birth-and-death, of sleep and wakefulness, he cannot help thinking dualistically as none of us can.

It is significant that he speaks here of being in sleep and being awakened, instead of living and dying. While he is sleeping he sees the finite aspect of the Pure Land, and when he is awakened he faces the infinity-aspect of the Pure Land, where Amida's Light shines in its shadowlessness. He thus transcends his *sahāloka* existence.

When the eye-curtain is down, we sleep, and while thus sleeping we cannot perceive the eternal shadowless beams of the Light; what we see is conditioned, differentiated, where we have an interplay of lights and shades. But it is the same light even when it is seen thus conditioned; it is no other light than the one illuminating the Pure Land.

When the curtain is fully up and we are no more asleep and ushered into the Pure Land, we may see something like the following prevailing there:

The *Larger Sukhāvatī-vyūha Sūtra* describes in another place the lotus flower in the Pure Land which is significant in view of the interfusion of Light taking place everywhere throughout the worlds whose numbers are beyond our limited survey:

> The lotus flowers of precious jewels fill the entire land, and attached to every one of the jewel flowers there are hundreds of thousands of myriads of petals. The rays of light issuing from the flowers are infinitely multicolored: from blue flowers, blue rays issue; from white flowers, white rays; from the deep-colored, from the yellow, from

> the vermilion, from the violet, issue each its corresponding light. Their brilliantly radiating lights far exceed those of the suns and moons.
>
> From each one of the petals there emanate thirty-six hundreds of thousands of myriads of rays and from each one of these rays issue thirty-six hundreds of thousands of myriads of Buddhas, whose bodies most excellently formed are golden-colored. From each one of these Buddhas also emanate hundreds of thousands of rays of light illuminating all the ten quarters, and the most wonderful Dharma is preached.
>
> Each one of these Buddhas thus leads innumerable numbers of sentient beings to be securely established in the right path of Buddhahood.

The lotus flower described in such high lights symbolizes each one of us sentient beings. For each one of us is a Bodhisattva, a possible Buddha—each one of us in his individual coloring, that is to say, not necessarily in one uniform color but each in his own unique tinge, which may be violet or yellow or red or any one of the infinitely variable hues. And all these color-lights are infinitely interfused as described above. And this interfusion explains the nature of the enlightenment-experience which always demands expression of some kind, in words, in sounds, in colors, in actions.

AMIDA AND HIS ORIGINAL VOW

When this Light is translated in terms of religious experience, that which makes us turn toward the Pure Land is Amida's Power of Vow *(pūrva-praṇidhāna-bala)*, which is known as the other-power in the system of Shinran. He bases this on the eighteenth vow:

> If, upon my obtaining Buddhahood, all beings in the ten quarters should not desire in sincerity and trustfulness to be born in my country, and if they should not be born by only thinking of me, say, ten times, . . . may I not attain the highest enlightenment.

Shin Buddhism makes this eighteenth vow the very foundation of all its teachings, asserting that if not for this vow on the part of Amida no sentient beings can ever expect to be born into the Pure Land and there to attain enlightenment. Vows 19 and 20 emphasize the awakening of the enlightenment-mind and the accumulation of meritorious deeds based on moral discipline. However strong and sincere a man's desire to be born in the Pure Land may be, his morality and intellection alone will never take him to Amida's Land; that is, he can never hope to achieve his end of bringing about the enlightenment-experience. For this, something more is needed, which does not belong in the order of moral merit or intellectual acumen. This something must come from a higher realm of values. Things belonging to the moral or intellectual order are necessarily conditioned, and what we aspire for is to transcend this and to realize enlightenment, which is the ground of all Buddhas' teachings, and also of our relative existence. Amida's Original Vow alone, according to Shin teaching, makes us reach this ground. Vows 19 and 20 are, respectively:

> If, upon my obtaining Buddhahood, all beings in the ten quarters awakening their thoughts to enlightenment and practicing all deeds of merit should cherish the desire in sincerity to be born in my country and if I should not, surrounded by a large company, appear before them at the time of their death, may I not attain the highest enlightenment.
>
> If, upon my obtaining Buddhahood, all beings in the ten quarters hearing my Name should cherish the thought of my country and planting all the roots of merit turn them in sincerity over to being born in my country, and if they should fail in obtaining the result of it, may I not attain the highest enlightenment.

In these vows there is no reference to "thinking of the *myōgō*" *(nāmadheya),* that is identified with *Namu-amida-butsu.* This thinking of *myōgō* is what distinguishes vow 18 from vows 19 and 20.

In our ordinary way of reasoning, mere thinking of Amida's Name cannot be regarded as having the power of working such wonders as to make our birth in the Pure Land possible where conditions are all ready [for (CWSB)] our attainment of enlightenment. Moral discipline especially, far more than merely thinking of Amida's Name and making it take possession of one's entire consciousness, is naturally to be considered of greater weight and consequence in the attainment of enlightenment either in this life or after, and we must feel certainly justified to attach more significance to the nineteenth and the twentieth vows than to the eighteenth.

How then is it that Shin upholds the eighteenth vow as the only means to transcend finitude and relativity, even to the extent that its followers tend to ignore the value of the nineteenth and the twentieth?

I will not try here to explain the basic ideas underlying the Shin doctrine of salvation through thinking or reciting Amida's Name. This I will do somewhere else. Let me just state this: moral discipline, the accumulation of merits, or the exercising of intellectual powers, or these activities together, cannot, even when the enlightenment-mind is awakened, reach the bedrock of our consciousness;[29] and unless this bedrock is shaken up and broken through, there cannot be any transcending this relative existence; and so long as this existence is not transcended there cannot be any enlightenment-experience, which alone gives us a final sense of rest and peace.

What then is this bedrock of consciousness?

This is the will or the Self as I call it, but the self not in its psychological sense, but in its most fundamental sense beyond which we cannot go. Enlightenment consists in knowing what this Self is, what the will is. This knowing, however, is not a knowledge as we understand it ordinarily. In another word, the will is faith, and faith is enlightenment-experience.

To realize this, moral discipline must exhaust itself, intellection must reach its limits, for in these activities there is always the sense of a relative self which obstructs the way to self-realization, to the awakening of the Self.

The Self we thus ultimately reach is Amida's Name or Amida's Light, whichever we may choose to call it. The Light, which is shadowless, illumines not only the Pure Land but all the worlds, including *sahāloka* and *naraka* as well. The Name, as is also repeatedly told in the sutra, reverberates throughout all the Buddha-lands in the ten quarters. To give instances of the miraculous power of the Name, let me cite two more vows:

> If, upon my obtaining Buddhahood, all the Buddhas, immeasurable in number in the ten quarters, do not approvingly proclaim my name, may I not attain the highest enlightenment. (Vow 17)
>
> If, upon my obtaining Buddhahood, all the Bodhisattvas in other lands by hearing my Name should not instantly reach the stage of no-turning-back, may I not attain the highest enlightenment. (Vow 47)

Amida puts his own life into his Name and declares that he may not attain enlightenment unless his Name is approvingly accepted by all the Buddhas and effective enough to bring all beings into his Pure Land by hearing it, reciting it, thinking of it, holding it, believing it—and all this "in sincerity and trustfulness." As Amida is no Amida without his Light, he cannot really be himself without his Name. He is Light, he is Name; Name and Light are one. Seeing the Light is hearing the Name. As the Light is shadowless and beyond the measurement of wavelengths, so is the Name not anything attached to something. It stands all by itself; it is the Self.

Instead of going into a detailed explanation of all the ideas presented in this paper, which will be done later under special headings, I wish to make this remark here. By Amida's Name Shinran points to the awakening of the Self—not the self in the self-power, but the one within the innermost depths of our religious consciousness; in other words, he points to the assertion of Amida's Vow-power which is our willpower transcending every form of finitude and relativity. In Shin terminology, this supreme moment is known as Amida addressing himself to the soul of his devotee, or the devotee's giving up his self-power, or his being taken captive in the hands of Amida.

On the moral plane of religious consciousness, the Self cannot be revealed in its own light; what morality conceives is still under the guise of relativity; the selflessness of the Self is still far from being realized. The inner urge which is identifiable with the awakening of the enlightenment-mind is still on the plane of relative empirical self standing opposed to Amida. There is yet no state of consciousness to be designated as one-minded-ness, which is Amida's assertion of himself in our soul, Amida's self-identification with the Self which constitutes the reason of our being. When this takes place there is what is known as the awakening of faith, the realizing of absolute sincerity as given us by Amida who is sincerity itself. As long as we are on the plane of relativity and finitude, there is no sincerity or truth in us, no Amida, no one-minded-ness, no awakening of karuna-heart which is the Buddha-heart itself; or viewed from different angles of human consciousness, we may call it the Buddha-mind, the Buddha-nature, or Buddhahood, or faith, or enlightenment.

THE ORIGINAL VOW AND THE SELF

The power of the Original Vow is conceived by Shin followers objectively as coming from Amida; but, speaking from our primal religious consciousness, it is what is innately abiding in every one of us. The inmost Self as distinguished from the relative psychological self is the abode of the power; and it is no other than this power that makes us realize the relativity and limitation of our finite existence and condemn ourselves as burning with fiery evil passions and destined for *naraka*. It is in this way that the Self, as opposed to the relative self, expresses its dissatisfaction with the conditions under which it is placed; or we can say that in this way the Self makes itself known to our relative consciousness.

This relative consciousness or rather this relative empirical self is always ready to work mischief. It is always ready to assert itself like an autocrat with whatever powers it possesses. The autocrat deceives himself by imagining that he is the actual owner of the power and forgetting altogether the fact that he himself is a hireling and cannot shine by his own light. Quite well-meaningly he calculates, when he feels that something is not altogether right with him, to amend the situation by his own efforts. This is all very well if he does not deceive himself by thinking that he can by his own power and by that alone achieve the end he seeks. In such cases what is wrong with him is that he is not conscious of the limits of his power, that whatever power he may think he has is all derived from a deeper source. It is this deeper source which is really concerned with the unsatisfactory conditions prevailing on the relative plane of consciousness.

Moral discipline which belongs in the order of relativity is not enough, inasmuch as we are finite beings, to attain the infinite. It is only when we have attained the infinite that we realize that the infinite is really in the finite and conversely. But so long as we have not attained this insight we fail to know that the finite has no power to take hold of the infinite, because there is an absolute gap between the finite and the infinite. The bridging takes place only from the side of the infinite and not from the finite side. This is an important consideration we have to make when we are dealing with religious subjects.

Moral discipline as such will never lead us to the realization of the Self which is the absolute subjectum of our being, for morality relies on the self-power and the self-power can never transcend itself to do this; the self-power must negate itself, which means to abandon itself, deny itself, abrogate its claims to be the means of reaching the infinite. This abrogation on the part of morality of its claims for self-transcendence does by no means involve effacing itself. For the discipline as discipline has quite an independent role in perfecting human character as such. Morality has its own function to perform in human society. Only, we must remember that we cannot reach religion by means of morality, for religion belongs in a higher order of meaning or values. To awaken the religious consciousness, to open up the realm of infinite Light and eternal Life, to receive Amida's Original Vow-power, to penetrate into the Self, we must resort to another method of discipline than mere morality and intellection, both of which belong in the plane of relativity.

Amida's Light shines on everything, inclusive of all forms of self-power: moral discipline, intellectual speculation, and rationalistic calculation. The Light, therefore, must be approachable from every avenue conceivable to our consciousness. It is not right to open just one approach and condemn the rest as incapable of reaching the end. Amida is all-comprehensive and will favor any means. The choice is determined by the various circumstances, internal and external, surrounding any particular personality. The only thing most important and essential, without which Amida's Light or his Original Vow-power can never be apperceived within oneself, is that the self-power in whatever pattern it may assume in the personality of the Amida aspirant is to be carried on until it finds itself utterly exhausted, being at the end of its powers and devices.

Intellectual speculation is a form of self-power, so is moral discipline, and as such they are not conducive to the realization of the other-power. But as the other-power is at the infinite end of those human calculations born of self-power, the self-power is to be severely tried until it finds itself entirely wanting. It is not in the nature of self-power to be despaired of its own limitations without first putting itself to trial. Mere reasoning or persuasion is not sufficient. The self-power, a most aggressive, most conceited power, will never be convinced of its impotency until it has exercised itself to its utmost and acknowledged its defeat. Frequently it so happens that the self-power refuses to push its efforts to the limits where it is forced to admit its powerlessness, for the self-power from its own baseness hesitates, falters, swerves, intoxicated with its human conceit and deep-seated delusion. The awakening of the enlightenment-mind is just the beginning of the self-power coming to the knowledge of itself. It is just an incipient stage of self-realization. One has to go through with bitter frustrations one after another, otherwise the self-power can never see itself totally bared before the other-power. But, in reality, that the self-power can bare itself shorn of all its self-conceit and self-delusions is due to the presence of the other-power within itself. In other words, it is the working of the power of Original Vow in our relative consciousness that the self-power finally comes to acknowledge its complete defeat.

In terms of the Self, the relative, empirical, psychological self which we conceive to be an ego at the center of personality is not final reality, but a pseudo-representative of the Self. The psychological ego, however, conceals something of the real Self underneath it, and it is due to the working of this Self that the superficial self comes to acknowledge its deceptive, spurious nature.

To recapitulate:

When the exhaustion of the self-power takes place, it discerns that it is nothing so long as it remains in itself, that it is really the other-power that makes the self-power use itself up. Therefore, what is needed for the experience of the other-power is to exhaust the self-power, whatever form it may take, moral or intellectual.

I repeat, that moral discipline itself is not to be condemned, nor is intellection. Why? When it is deeply tainted with the pride and self-conceit of the self-power, it proves to be the stumbling block to the waking of the Vow-power *(praṇidhāna-bala)* in oneself. But it is this very conceit and delusion that causes the final downfall of the self-power. So with the intellect: doubt is indeed the opposite of faith. No one is expected to attain enlightenment without removing doubt. It is this doubt, however, that leads one ultimately to faith. The denser the clouds of doubt the brighter the Light when it reveals itself. One is first to struggle desperately with doubt and self-power; this is what makes Shinran declare that the evil-minded are the objects of Amida's Original Vow.

We are always apt to forget this fact and think that moral discipline is useless and that the intellectual attempt at reaching reality is fruitless; and the worst thing is that we for this reason relegate morality and intellect to the furthest recesses of the religious consciousness as if they were positive hindrances rather than negative unessentials. It is not that they in themselves are fruitless or useless, but that they are so when they are separated from the other-power which in fact they are.

A tendency to moral laxity is a phenomenon we frequently notice among Shin Buddhist followers. I am inclined to think this is due to their inadequate appreciation of the other-power, and probably principally to their leaders' imperfect, half-way interpretation of the vows 19 and 20 in relation to vow 18.

When these descriptions are translated into more humanly intelligible language, we may have something like this: After a good night sleep, I get up. The sun is shining into the room, a refreshing breeze comes through the windows, I breathe deeply. Probably I had a dream, but I do not remember now what it was. I am ready for the day's work. I meet people, greet them, and they greet me back. They look pleased, so am I. As I am a writer, I sit by the desk, take up my pen, or have the typewriter ready. I collect my thoughts, or look up books needed for reference. After some hours' work I feel tired. I go down into the garden, take a walk among flowers, for I like them, and the garden is filled with them. About this time of the year in Japan, the morning glories begin to shoot out their young tender leaves. It is interesting to watch them grow. They have to be carefully taken care of if we wish to see them bloom fine in summer. When the summer comes the first thing I do in the morning is to go around in the garden and admire the flowers refreshingly full of life. They can well be compared with those lotus flowers blooming in the water of merits in the Pure Land. Nature is generally thought to be dumb, but the trouble is not on her side, but on ours: she speaks eloquently in her own way and it is we who fail to understand her. In the Pure Land every tree, every leaf, every flower is described as singing in praise of the triple treasure. So do things on this side of the world. Swedenborg's doctrine of correspondence holds good in Buddhism too. Amida's Light illuminates this *sahāloka* as much as the Pure Land. Amida attained his enlightenment and his Pure Land came into existence. We attain ours and this *sahāloka* too must transform itself into a Pure Land. When we have our absolute faith established firmly in Amida, we do not go to Amida's Pure Land, but the Pure Land comes to us along with Amida. Amida is born in our minds with his Land. This *sahāloka* becomes a Pure Land, and we Amida. For are we not devoted followers of *tariki,* the other-power? After this musing I come back to my study and resume my work. The inner world is another "nature." Beautiful flowers are here along with rampant weeds; the sweet-singing birds are here along with poisonous snakes; the star-sprinkled skies reflect themselves on mud-filled ponds perhaps harboring noxious plants. All kinds of *bonnō* are in company with high-flying ideals and a tenderly yielding heart.

10

The Spirit of Shinran Shōnin

This brief essay is an address that Suzuki gave during the installation ceremony of a large bronze statue of Shinran (1173–1262) at the American Buddhist Academy in New York on September 11, 1955. Shinran was the celebrated proponent of Pure Land teachings of the Kamakura period (1185–1333) and the founder of Shin Buddhism in Japan. Suzuki was residing in New York at the time, lecturing at Columbia University. He was invited by Rev. Hōzen Seki (1903–1991), the founder of the Academy, to offer the address at the ceremony. The statue that was installed depicts Shinran in the classical garb of an itinerant Japanese preacher of the Dharma: wide-rim straw hat, robe, rain cape, walking staff, and straw sandals. This particular statue has an extraordinary background. It was originally erected in Hiroshima in 1937 and survived the atomic bomb blast in 1945. Subsequently, the wealthy industrialist and devout Buddhist donor Hirose Seiichi (1895–1979), who had the statue cast, collaborated with Rev. Seki to move it to New York as an inspiration for world peace.

The gist of Suzuki's talk is that, in order to see the true Shinran, one must look beyond the physical appearance of his statue, and also beyond his historical identity, to a living Shinran inside every person. Implicit in his statements is a radical subjectivism. It points to the inside of a person as the starting point from which the world is reordered. The discovery of one's own humanity leads to the advancement of everyone's humanity. In Suzuki's writings throughout his career he tended to avoid conflating religious experience with morality. In this talk, though, he seems to imply that a humanized, moral world begins with a religious awakening internally—one's own inner Shinran.

The base text for this essay is a transcription made by Hoshina Seki and edited by James C. Dobbins from an audio-recording of this previously unpublished talk. Published by permission of the American Buddhist Study Center, Inc., 331 Riverside Drive, New York, NY 10025.

Statue of Shinran (1173–1262) as an itinerant Buddhist preacher in Japan's Kamakura period (1185–1333), located in front of the New York Buddhist Church, 332 Riverside Drive, New York. Photograph by Hoshina Seki.

. . .

Ladies and Gentlemen,

Many years ago there was a great Buddhist government officer. He once visited a Buddhist monastery and the monks took him to a room where many portraits were hung on the wall. The governor, then a high government officer, pointed at one of the portraits and asked the monks, "Who is he?"

The monks answered, "This is the abbot's portrait, who recently passed away."

The governor asked, "The portrait is here, but where is the man?"

The monks did not know how to answer that question, so they confessed, "We do not know where the man is." But the governor insisted he wanted to know where the man was, or rather where the man is, instead of the portrait.

The monks did not know how to answer that question, so they consulted among themselves and came to this conclusion. There was a strange monk who came around and was staying with them for a while. He was very likely to answer this question as proposed by the governor. So they hunted him up and brought him into the presence of the governor. Then the governor said to this monk, a quite insignificant looking monk, "Reverend Sir, I wish to ask you a question. Would you be kind enough to answer it?" Then he said, "Yes, whatever question you may ask I will answer."

Now the governor said, "As you see, here is a portrait of the abbot, but I want to know where the man is." Then the monk, a gardener, loudly called out, "O governor!" And the governor said, "Yes, Reverend Sir, I am here." Then the monk said, "Here is the man."

This concluded the question and the answer.

Now this is most significant on this occasion where the Shinran Shōnin statue has been unveiled. Here we see a great big statue of Shinran Shōnin unveiled, which is cast in bronze, so many feet high, and so many pounds in weight, coming over the great ocean of the Pacific and across a long distance to this side of the Atlantic. His serene expression is full of tender feelings, evidently desirous to transmit the message of "brotherhood and equality," though according to my view Americans are in no special need for such a message, because equality is the principle of democracy and brotherhood is one of the favorite themes taught by Christianity. Americans are really overfed with this kind of diet. The presentation of this statue is in fact bringing coals to New Castle, or recently one of your high American government officers would interpret it as bringing saké to Nada.

I am not, however, concerned with the American feeling, nor with the political meaning of this Shinran statue as revealed here. What concerns me most is the person of Shinran Shōnin and not his statue. However I may call out his name now, he remains dumb, he shows no signs of life.

Ladies and gentlemen, what we want most seriously, most urgently at this very moment is not Shinran Shōnin's statue, but his person most vivaciously alive, and not the person coming out of the pages of history, but the person who properly understands the spirit of the modern world and knows perfectly well how to adjust his teachings to the needs of modern man.

I want not a Shinran statue who has gone to the Pure Land so many years ago, but the Shinran Shōnin who is back from his long trip to the Land of Bliss to this *shaba* world, *sahālokadhātu,* this world filled with all forms of inequity or inequality in spite of our loud and boisterous proclamations, a world also filled with things tending toward a direction altogether opposite of universal brotherhood so-called.

Such a Shinran—not one Shinran, but Shinrans, who thoroughly understand the spirit of the modern world—must be discovered among our fellow Buddhists gathered here today. Let them announce not necessarily loudly, but quietly and persistently and in most practical ways what not the dead Shinran but the living Shinran would say and do, not as he said and did in those Kamakura days, but in this modern world where the atomic bombs may at any moment explode again.

The present state of things that we are facing everywhere—politically, economically, morally, intellectually, and spiritually—is no doubt the result of our past thoughts and deeds we have committed as human beings through the whole length of history (how many years we cannot count) through eons of existence, not only individually but collectively. As such, we are, every one of us, responsible for the present world situation filled with awesome forebodings. The bombing of Hiroshima was not after all the doing of the American armies, but the doing of mankind as a whole, and as such, we, not only the Japanese and Americans but the whole world, are to be held responsible for the wholesale slaughter witnessed ten years ago in Japan.

What then is the meaning of this celebration we see going on now about us?

As far as I can see, it must be in finding the living Shinran Shōnin who is surely among us answering to the call of his name; only we have not been able to hear his response. Our ears have not yet been fully opened innerly as well as externally to the still small voice. Perhaps we can hear it, at least a little portion of Shinran's voice, when the Buddhist Academy begins to operate properly equipped not only in externalities but in spirit and personnel. No doubt, Shinran Shōnin will find many more things to do besides establishing a school. As it happens, let him start with it and steadily go on doing things not only educational in its narrower sense, but more comprehensively social and spiritual.

We must realize that modern civilization is thoroughly oriented toward dehumanizing humanity in every possible way, that is to say, we are fast turning into robots and statues with no human souls. Our task is to get humanized once more. In conclusion I wish to call out again: "O Shinran Shōnin, here we have the statue, but where is the person? Where are you?"

Thank you.

NOTES

INTRODUCTION

1. For instance, see Suzuki and Soga, "Dialogue: Zen and Shin," 88, in which Suzuki acknowledged that Shin adherents tend to treat his explanations of Shin Buddhism as influenced by Zen. Suzuki himself admitted that most Shin Buddhists would contest his ideas. See "Infinite Light," 11 (also chapter 9 in this volume).

2. The following brief summary of Suzuki's life is drawn from a variety of sources, but principally from Kirita, *Suzuki Daisetsu kenkyū kiso shiryō,* "Nenpu," 9–227; Suzuki, *Watakushi no rirekisho,* SDZ 26:499–539; Suzuki, *Yafūryūan jiden,* SDZ 29:147–163; and Suzuki, "Early Memories," 3–12, and "An Autobiographical Account," 13–26. SDZ is used in reference to Suzuki Daisetsu, *Suzuki Daisetsu zenshū.*

3. Ōtani Daigaku Shinshū Sōgō Kenkyūjo, *Ōtani Daigaku kindai hyakunen no ayumi,* 55.

4. Suzuki's lectures to the Emperor were published in 1947 as *Bukkyō no daii,* SDZ 7:1–79.

5. Officially, Suzuki's father's family was affiliated with a Rinzai Zen temple, though his father was actually more interested in Chinese classics and Confucian texts. *Yafūryūan jiden,* SDZ 29:148.

6. Akizuki, *Suzuki Daisetsu,* 21–22. For a study of secret teachings in Shin Buddhism, see Chilson, *Secrecy's Power.* Ordinarily, in Shin secret initiation ceremonies such as this, the initiate would chant *tasuketamae* (Please save me) repeatedly instead of the nembutsu. Whether Suzuki misremembered this detail from his own initiation or whether the nembutsu was actually chanted in his case is unclear. There do exist a few accounts of the nembutsu being chanted instead of *tasuketamae* in such initiations, though they are rare. For an example, see Kadoya, *Kakushi nenbutsu,* 166–169. I am indebted to Clark Chilson for indicating this example as well as for his assistance with this topic.

7. The title of Sōen's address to the World's Parliament of Religions, which Suzuki translated, was "The Law of Cause and Effect, as Taught by the Buddha." For the complete text,

see Yokoyama, "Two Addresses by Shaku Sōen," 134–137. It was originally published in Barrows, *The World's Parliament of Religions,* 2:829–831.

8. For confirmation of Suzuki's use of Carus's ideas in writing *Shin shūkyō ron,* see Letter 35 (1895.6.3), SDZ 36:57; Letter 36 (1895.8.26), SDZ 36:57–58; and Letter 49 (1896.5.14), SDZ 36:75–76.

9. For references to these figures, see Letter 74 (1897.11.26), SDZ 36:110–112; Letter 75 (1897.12.10), SDZ 36:112–116; Letter 77 (1897.12.29), SDZ 36:119–122; Letter 78 (1898.1.20), SDZ 36:123–126; Letter 80 (1898.2.13), SDZ 36:128; Letter 82 (1898.3.7), SDZ 36:133–134; Letter 108 (1899.12.24), SDZ 36:176–179; Letter 111 (1900.5.3), SDZ 36:184–185; Letter 120 (1900.11.12), SDZ 36:196–198; Letter 141 (1902.9.23), SDZ 36:221–223; and Letter 211 (1907.5.21), SDZ 36:303–306.

10. In Letter 100 (1899.1.27), SDZ 36:166–167, Suzuki thanks Carus for allowing him to borrow books frequently from Carus's personal library.

11. On this concept, see Carus, *Religion of Science.* See also Meyer, "Paul Carus and the Religion of Science," and Henderson, *Catalyst for Controversy,* 45–63.

12. In Letter 141 (1902.9.23), SDZ 36:222, Suzuki explicitly cites William James's book, *The Varieties of Religious Experience,* and urges his friend Nishida Kitarō to read it. He focuses on James's idea of religious experience *(shūkyō teki keiken)* and applies it specifically to an episode in his life when he felt a loss of self and an identification with the trees while practicing Zen at Engakuji monastery. He also indicates that James's approach to religion is distinctly different from that of Paul Carus.

13. Suzuki's chronology indicates that he was still using James's *The Varieties of Religious Experience* as a textbook in his classes in the 1930s and 1940s; see Kirita, *Suzuki Daisetsu kenkyū kiso shiryō,* 75 (1931), 79 (1932), 84 (1933), and 125 (1943).

14. Kirita, *Suzuki Daisetsu kenkyū kiso shiryō,* 24–25 (Sōen's lecture in New York on 1906.4.8 and subsequent meeting with Beatrice Lane on 1906.4.18).

15. Concerning Beatrice's and D. T. Suzuki's deep involvement in Theosophy, see Algeo, "Beatrice Lane Suzuki and Theosophy in Japan." See also the frequent notations of "T. S." (Theosophical Society) in Suzuki's diaries from 1920 to 1928 in Suzuki, "D. T. Suzuki's English Diaries," *Matsugaoka bunko nenpō* 19 (2005): 39, 42, 43, 73, 78, 82, 92, 96, 123, and 145.

16. In *Watakushi no rirekisho,* SDZ 26:520, Suzuki indicates that, while teaching English at an elementary school on the Noto Peninsula in 1889, he became acquainted with a local Shin priest who was well versed in Buddhist *Yuishiki* thought.

17. Suzuki's knowledge of Rev. Shūe Sonoda of the Honganji mission in San Francisco is indicated in Letter 107 (1899.11.21), SDZ 36:175. Suzuki's stay in San Francisco is recorded in Letter 152 (1903.8.4), SDZ 36:230–231; Letter 153 (1903.8.30), SDZ 36:231–232; Letter 154 (1903.9.17), SDZ 36:232–233; and Letter 155 (1903.10.2), SDZ 36:234.

18. Suzuki was the English translator of Okusa, *Principal Teachings of the True Sect of Pure Land;* and the cotranslator with Sasaki Gesshō of *The Life of the Shonin Shinran.*

19. The text that Suzuki read was Akegarasu, *Shinkō gobusho,* mentioned in the memorial lecture to Kiyozawa Manshi that Suzuki presented at Otani University in 1963. For an English translation of the lecture, see Suzuki, "Kiyozawa's Living Presence: A 1963 Commemorative Lecture," 3.

20. "Jiriki to tariki," SDZ 30:434–437.

21. Concerning the ouster of Soga and Kaneko, see Ōtani Daigaku Hyakunenshi Henshū Iinkai, *Ōtani Daigaku hyakunenshi,* 1:335–354; and Ōtani Daigaku Shinshū Sōgō Kenkyūjo, *Ōtani Daigaku kindai hyakunen no ayumi,* 67–72.

22. For example, see Yokogawa, "Shin Buddhism as the Religion of Hearing."

23. Two important studies presenting a critical, historical analysis of the development of the concept of religious experience are Sharf, "Experience," and Proudfoot, *Religious Experience.*

24. For a simple overview of Suzuki's understanding of religion, see Suzuki, "What Is Religion?" There he describes religion as mysticism and in terms of an inward and fundamental experience, and he relates it specifically to concepts in Buddhism. These ideas were foreshadowed in 1896 in Suzuki's earliest treatise on religion, *Shin shūkyō ron,* SDZ 23: 16–28, where Suzuki speaks of the "religious heart or mind" *(shūkyōshin)* and "religious feelings or emotions" *(shūkyō teki kanjō),* pp. 16, 17, 18, 20, and 22, though he does not yet present a strong demarcation between internal feelings and empirical experience of the external world. Suzuki's ideas became more focused and crisply articulated in this way only after his encounter with William James's writings on religious experience *(shūkyō teki keiken)* in 1902.

25. See James, *The Varieties of Religious Experience,* 31, for his classic definition of religion, which stresses feelings and experiences over doctrines and institutional practices: "Religion, therefore, as I now ask you arbitrarily to take it, shall mean for us *the feelings, acts, and experiences of individual men in their solitude, so far as they apprehend themselves to stand in relation to whatever they may consider the divine.* Since the relation may be either moral, physical, or ritual, it is evident that out of religion in the sense in which we take it, theologies, philosophies, and ecclesiastical organizations may secondarily grow" (italics are James's).

26. For an example of this type of analysis, see Suzuki, *Introduction to Zen Buddhism,* chap. 7, "Satori, or Acquiring a New Viewpoint," 88, 94–98.

27. Suzuki, Letter 141 (1902.9.22), SDZ 36:222.

28. For further discussion of these contrasting depictions of Buddhism—as religious experience versus religious lifestyle—see Dobbins, "D. T. Suzuki and the Construction of Modern Buddhism."

29. For Suzuki's views on mysticism, see, inter alia, Suzuki, "The Koan Exercise," in *Essays in Zen Buddhism (Second Series),* 157–159 (also chapter 3 in this volume); "Sayings of a Modern Tariki Mystic," 98–100 (also chapter 6 in this volume); and *Introduction to Zen Buddhism,* 35–37, 44–45.

30. Suzuki lists these three among the various characteristics of satori in Suzuki, *Zen Buddhism,* chap. 4: "Satori, or Enlightenment," 103–108. These roughly parallel the first three characteristics of mysticism identified by James, *The Varieties of Religious Experience,* chap. 16 and 17, 379–382: ineffability, noetic quality, and transiency. The fourth characteristic listed by James is passivity, which Suzuki emphasizes in his very long essay, "Passivity in the Buddhist Life," in *Essays in Zen Buddhism (Second Series),* 233–302.

31. For a brief description of the breakdown of a sense of dualism in the mystic's experience, see Suzuki, "The Koan Exercise," in *Essays in Zen Buddhism (Second Series),* 149 (also chapter 3 in this volume).

32. For Pure Land examples presented in this study, see Suzuki, *Mysticism: Christian and Buddhist,* 143–214 (also chapter 8 in this volume).

33. Suzuki, "Book Review: *A History of Zen Buddhism,* by Heinrich Dumoulin," 123–126.

34. *Nihon teki reisei,* SDZ 8:21–22 (updated translation by Norman Waddell); for Waddell's original translation, see Suzuki, *Japanese Spirituality,* 15.

35. This term first appeared in *Jōdokei shisōron,* SDZ 6:77. See Yokoyama, "Nishida Kitaro and D.T. Suzuki's Logic of *Soku-hi*—with a Translation of Suzuki's 'Gokuraku to Shaba' (1942)."

36. *Nihon teki reisei,* SDZ 8:45–51; for the English translation, see Suzuki, *Japanese Spirituality,* 40–46.

37. See specifically chapter 4, "Myōkōnin," of *Nihon teki reisei,* SDZ, 8:171–223; for the English translation, see chapter 7 in this volume and also Suzuki, *Japanese Spirituality,* 167–213.

38. Concerning the three Pure Land sutras, see Inagaki, *The Three Pure Land Sutras,* and Gómez, *The Land of Bliss.*

39. For an overview of the teachings and development of Pure Land Buddhism in Japan, specifically those related to the Shin Buddhist tradition, see Dobbins, *Jōdo Shinshū.*

40. *Shin shūkyō ron,* SDZ 23:7–8.

41. For Suzuki's critique of the *mappō* or *masse* theme, see *Nihon teki reisei,* SDZ 8:53–56; for the English translation, see chapter 5 in this volume and also Suzuki, *Japanese Spirituality,* 48–50.

42. For Suzuki's idealization of the *Tannishō* and criticism of the *Kyōgyōshinshō,* see *Nihon teki reisei,* SDZ 8:84–87; for the English translation, see chapter 5 in this volume and also Suzuki, *Japanese Spirituality,* 80–82. These sentiments are expressed even more strongly in Suzuki's 1928 essay "Shinshū zakkan," SDZ 31:385–388.

43. For Suzuki's translation of the first four fascicles of the *Kyōgyōshinshō,* see Shinran, *The Kyōgyōshinshō.*

44. For an example in Shinran's teaching of the primacy of *tariki* over *jiriki,* see *Mattōshō,* in Shinshū Shōgyō Zensho Hensanjo, *Shinshū shōgyō zensho,* 2:658–661 (Letter 2). For an English translation, see Shinran, *The Collected Works of Shinran,* 1:525–527. Hereafter, *Shinshū shōgyō zensho* is cited as SSZ, and *The Collected Works of Shinran* as CWS.

45. Concerning James's two categories of conversion, volitional and self-surrender, see James, *The Varieties of Religious Experience,* 204–212.

46. "Jiriki to tariki" (1911), SDZ 30:434–437.

47. Suzuki's comparison of the nembutsu to repeating the name of Allah in Islam and to the koan is in Suzuki, "The Koan Exercise," in *Essays in Zen Buddhism (Second Series),* 145 and 151 (also chapter 3 in this volume).

48. See, for example, ibid., 151–153; and *Nihon teki reisei,* SDZ 8:57–59 (for the English translation, see chapter 5 in this volume and also Suzuki, *Japanese Spirituality,* 53–54).

49. For examples of Suzuki citing Ippen, see Suzuki, "Zen and Jōdo, Two Types of Buddhist Experience," 116 (also chapter 2 in this volume); and Suzuki, "The Koan Exercise," in *Essays in Zen Buddhism (Second Series),* 153–154 (also chapter 3 in this volume).

50. *Nihon teki reisei,* SDZ 8:182–223 (for the English translation, see chapter 7 in this volume and also Suzuki, *Japanese Spirituality,* 177–213).

51. This theme is found, for instance, in *Nihon teki reisei,* SDZ 8:217–221 (for the English translation, see chapter 7 in this volume and also Suzuki, *Japanese Spirituality,* 207–211); Suzuki, *Mysticism: Christian and Buddhist,* 191–197 (also chapter 8 in this volume); and Suzuki, "Infinite Light," 5–19 (also chapter 9 in this volume).

52. *The Platform Sutra* (Dunhuang version), citing a theme from the *Vimalakīrti Sūtra*, declares, "In accordance with the purity of the mind, the Buddha-land is pure." See Yampolsky, *The Platform Sutra of the Sixth Patriarch*, 157. For the quotation from the *Vimalakīrti Sūtra*, see *Yuimagyō*, in *Taishō shinshū daizōkyō*, 14:538c. A similar theme from the *Vimalakīrti Sūtra* can be found in the *Taishō shinshū Daizōkyō* edition of *The Platform Sutra* (which differs from the Dunhuang version) at 48:352c: "... the straightforward mind is the Pure Land." For a translation, see McRae, *The Platform Sutra of the Sixth Patriarch*, 42.

53. Concerning the tendency toward dualistic pairs in Pure Land Buddhism, see Suzuki, "Zen and Jōdo, Two Types of Buddhist Experience," 99–100 (also chapter 2 in this volume).

54. On *kihō ittai*, see, for example, ibid., 116–120; and Suzuki, *Mysticism: Christian and Buddhist*, 187–190 (also chapter 8 in this volume).

55. *Jōdokei shisōron*, SDZ 6:212–58 (chapter 5: "Tariki no shinjin ni tsukite—*Kyōgyōshinshō* o yomite").

56. In *Jōdokei shisōron*, SDZ 6:216, Suzuki makes the statement: "Shin religious experience (*Shinshū no shinkō taiken*) at its base [means] in one respect that great Nirvana is great Faith itself." In *Jōdokei shisōron*, SDZ 6:75–78 inter alia, Suzuki also uses extensively the ideas of *reisei*, spirituality, and *sokuhi no ronri*, the logic of simultaneous identification and differentiation, applying them to various Pure Land themes a year before he published his major work on Japanese spirituality, *Nihon teki reisei*.

57. Shinran makes this point obliquely in his *Kyōgyōshinshō*, SSZ, 2:73, where he indicates that the three dimensions of the mind of faith are in fact a single mind, and that mind is none other than the "diamond-like true mind" *(kongō no shinshin)*, that is, the enlightened mind or the mind of the Buddha. For an English translation of this passage, see CWS 1:114. See also Dobbins, *Jōdo Shinshū*, 35. Suzuki highlights this point from Shinran in *Jōdokei shisōron*, SDZ 6:213, 225, 228.

58. For example, in Suzuki, "Infinite Light," 17 (also chapter 9 in this volume) Suzuki makes the statement, "faith is enlightenment-experience."

59. For an example of Shinran's declaration that people of faith are in a state "equivalent to enlightenment" *(tōshōgaku)* and "equal to the buddhas" *(shobutsu tōdō)*, see *Mattōshō*, SSZ 2:661–662, 666–668 (Letters 3 and 7). For English translations, see CWS 1:528, 532–533. See also Dobbins, *Jōdo Shinshū*, 42–43.

60. Shinran's classic statement on *jinen hōni* is found in *Mattōshō*, SSZ 2:663–624 (Letter 5); and *Shōzōmatsu wasan*, SSZ 2:530. For English translations, see CWS 1:530, 427–428. See also Dobbins, *Jōdo Shinshū*, 43–45.

61. Suzuki, *Mysticism: Christian and Buddhist*, 154–158 (also chapter 8 in this volume). For an earlier exposition by Suzuki of *jinen hōni*, see his lecture "Jinen hōni," SDZ 27:452–476, which was presented in 1938.

62. For an orthodox Shin Buddhist interpretation of the *hō no jinshin* and *ki no jinshin* doctrine, see Okamura, *Shinshū daijiten*, 3:1704–1710, s.v. "Nishu jinshin" (Two Types of Deep Faith). The idea of equal emphasis on these two types of deep faith has become a standard "article of faith" *(anjin rondai)* in the orthodox dogma of the Shinshū Honganjiha. See Kiritani, *Kōza Shinshū no anjin rondai*, 73–88. Suzuki does not overlook the *ki no jinshin* side of the two completely, for it does come out in some of Saichi's verses where he calls himself "wretched," for example, Suzuki, *Mysticism: Christian and Buddhist*, 181–190, 205–214 (also chapter 8 in this volume).

1. THE DEVELOPMENT OF THE PURE LAND DOCTRINE IN BUDDHISM

1. Historically, as far as the doctrine of the Pure Land goes, it originated in India and made notable progress in China soon after the introduction of Buddhism there. But it never came to be recognized as an independent school of Buddhism as for instance Zen or Tendai did. Its position was somewhat secondary or subsidiary to the main sects. It was in Japan that the Pure Land school attained its full growth even to the extent of overshadowing all the other forms of Buddhism.

2. Sanskrit, *sukhāvatī*. The term "Pure Land" is much more frequently in use in Japanese and Chinese Buddhist literature though the sutras have "Blissful Land," or "Pure Land of Happiness," instead of simple "Pure Land."

3. In this isolation we can trace the mystic tendency of the Pure Land school. The idea that in the name itself there is a miraculous power to save us from misery and bondage evidently suggests the symbolic mysticism of the Shingon. When Amida attained the Supreme Enlightenment, he compressed all the merit he had acquired through the spiritual discipline of innumerable kalpas into this one phrase, *na-mu-a-mi-da-bu-tsu*. For this reason when this one phrase, or dharani in a sense, is recited with singleness of purpose and with all the intensity of feeling, all the merit contained in it is miraculously transferred into the soul of the devotee, and he is at once embraced into the light of Amida. The miraculous power thus lying latent in the name of Amida belongs to the unfathomability of the Buddha-wisdom, and the only thing we ignorant mortals can do or have to do for our own salvation is to believe the wisdom and invoke the name just for once; for the "other-power" achieves the rest for us. In one sense, "Amida" is a kind of mystic "Om," a spiritual "sesame," or a mantram which unlocks the secrets of life. Does this not remind us of Tennyson's experience in connection with the repeating of his own name? "I have," writes the poet, "never had any revelations through anesthetics, but a kind of waking trance—this for a lack of a better word—I have frequently had, quite up from boyhood, when I have been all alone. This has come upon me through repeating my own name silently, till all at once, as it were out of the intensity of the consciousness of individuality, individuality itself seemed to dissolve and fade away into boundless being, and this not a confused state but the clearest, the surest of the surest, utterly beyond words—where death was an almost laughable possibility—the loss of personality (if so it were) seeming no extinction, but the only true life. I am ashamed of my feeble description. Have I not said the state is utterly beyond words?" We may say, "What's in a name?" but after all we have to own "the magic of a name." That, instead of mentally dwelling on the superhuman qualities of the Buddha, the nembutsu came to be merely reciting the name is highly significant as showing how much mysticism is cherished in the hearts of *tariki* followers. I shall have occasion later to refer to the psychology of the nembutsu.

4. Japanese "Amida" stands both for Amitābha (infinite light) and for Amitāyus (eternal life). According to the Pure Land school, the author of the Original Vows is Infinite Light and Eternal Life, though he assumed temporarily the form of the Bhikshu Dharmākara in order to go through with the human discipline or experience known as the six virtues of perfection *(pāramitā)*.

5. The number of the Vows vary according to the different versions of the text, or rather to the different texts. I have followed here the teaching of the Japanese Pure Land school.

6. [Johannes Tauler, c. 1300–1361. JCD]

7. These are the titles of the Sanskrit MSS. edited by Max Müller and Nanjō Bun'yū in 1883, forming a volume in the "Anecdota Oxoniensia." Max Müller's English translations appeared in 1894 as S.B.E., Vol. XLIX. The Chinese translations of the *Larger Sukhāvatī* by Saṃghavarman and of the Smaller one by Kumārajīva bear different titles: the former is known as the *Muryōjukyō (Amitāyuḥ-sūtra)* and the latter simply as the *Amidakyō (Amita-sūtra).*

8. The five subjects are generally: Impurity, Compassion, Breathing, Causality, and Buddha. The ten are: Buddha, Dharma, Sangha, Morality, Charity, the Heavenly worlds, Solitude, Breathing, the Physical Body, and Death.

9. These quotations here are from William Law's "The Spirit is Life," edited and arranged by M. M. Schofield.

10. Cf. Gessho Sasaki's *Study of Shin Buddhism,* p. 57 et seq.

11. *Li* corresponds to mile and *sun* to inch.

12. *Dīgha-nikāya,* XVI, 2, 26. [The prevailing view among scholars when Suzuki wrote this essay was that the expression *attadīpā* means "Be ye a lamp unto yourself." But later scholarship has shown that it actually means "Be ye an island unto yourself." JCD]

13. To be directly perceived, beyond limits of time, to be personally experienced, altogether persuasive, and to be cognized by the wise, each by himself.

14. *Evam etaṃ yathābhūtaṃ sammappaññāya daṭṭhabbaṃ.*

15. *Anjin ketsujō shō* ("On the Attainment of Spiritual Peace"). The author is not known, but the book is one of the most important of all the Shin writings.

16. Here is a Western version of Vimalakīrti:

> The whole earth's filled with Heaven,
> And every common bush afire with God;
> But only he who sees takes off his shoes,
> The rest sit round it, and pluck blackberries.

[Paraphrased quotation from Elizabeth Barrett Browning (1806–1861). JCD]

2. ZEN AND JŌDO, TWO TYPES OF BUDDHIST EXPERIENCE

As this article presupposes some knowledge of the teachings of the Pure Land (Jōdo) and the Zen school, the reader is referred to the author's previous essays on the subjects which have already appeared in this magazine [*The Eastern Buddhist* (JCD)].

1. Hōnen was the founder of the Japanese Pure Land sect. While there were some devout Buddhists prior to him who advocated the nembutsu it was due to Hōnen's influence that the Pure Land or Nembutsu sect came to be recognized as an independent denomination in the body of Buddhism. Shinran following him advanced a step further and developed the deeper meaning implied in the teaching of Hōnen. The one constant refrain that runs through all those devotees of the nembutsu is their unmistakable detestation of this mundane life which is filled with the three poisonous passions and the five nauseating desires, and at the same time their utter inability to escape these fetters by their own efforts. Hence their faith in the saving power of Amida's Original Vow.

2. [The original text mistakenly identifies the Sanskrit equivalent of Hossō as Dharmalakṣa. JCD]

3. Zendō (C. Shandao, 613–681) was a great advocate of the Pure Land doctrine in China, and always so strongly conscious of his sinful life in this world of defilements, he was ready at any moment to depart for Amida's country where everything was pure and perfect.

4. *Hōnen, The Buddhist Saint,* pp. 186–188.

5. As to what is meant by "Nembutsu," literally "thinking of the Buddha," see below, and also my article on "The Development of the Pure Land Doctrine," which appeared in *The Eastern Buddhist* 3, no. 3.

6. *Tannishō,* a short collection of Shinran's sayings compiled by Yuienbō, one of his immediate disciples.

7. Literally, "If you wish to use, use!" "It" is supplied by the translator, meaning the truth of Zen. The idea is that we are distracted too much by things external, including selfish desires and passions, and for that reason we fail to realize the sense of inner freedom which we all have and which constitutes the ultimate truth of all religion.

8. From the *Sayings of Rinzai* (C. *Linji lu,* J. *Rinzai roku*) somewhat freely rendered.

9. *The Gutokushō.*

10. In *Hōnen, The Buddhist Saint,* p. 187f., we have this record: Following the examples of Zendō and Genshin, Hōnen repeated the nembutsu over sixty thousand times a day; and when he came nearer to the end of his life, he added ten thousand more making it altogether seventy thousand times a day. It is said that he then did nothing else but repeating the nembutsu day and night; even when he had visitors and inquirers about his religion, he seemed to be listening to their talk as he lowered his voice, but in fact he never ceased repeating the nembutsu. The followers of Hōnen have often a special week devoted to the nembutsu when they expect to say it one million times. As to the all-importance of the nembutsu, read the following extract from Hōnen's *Life* (p. 734): "Whether a man is rich and noble, or poor and mean, whether he is kind or unkind, avaricious or morose, indeed no matter what he is, if he only repeats the nembutsu, in dependence upon the mysterious power of the Original Vow, his rebirth is certain."

11. 己身彌陀、唯心浄土.

12. The whole text, more or less liberally translated, is given here in order to show where lies the principle of life that regulates the ideals of the Buddhist monk generally.

13. From Shinran's *Notes on the Yuishinshō (Yuishinshō mon'i),* a little treatise on the doctrine of faith alone.

14. From the *Shūjishō* ["Tract on Steadily Holding to the Faith." JCD], in which are recorded some of the most important sayings of Shinran. Compiled 1326.

15. *Letters of Shinran (Goshōsokushū).*

16. *Sayings of Ippen (Ippen Shōnin goroku).*

17. The *Anjin ketsujō shō* is one of the finest and deepest expositions of the *tariki* doctrine of salvation. The central idea is a mystic unification of the mortal sinful being called *ki* and Amida designated as *hō,* and is technically known as the doctrine of *kihō ittai,* that is, the identity of *ki* and *hō. Ki* is a very difficult term to translate into any other language, it is generally understood to mean potentiality, affectability, and the possibility of getting related to others. Sentient beings have within themselves a certain capacity to get related to the merciful heart or Original Vow of Amida and be recipients of the merit of his deeds performed for the realization of enlightenment. There is something spiritual though potential

even in every one of us who are mortal, sinful, and ignorant, and through this something Amida works in us in order to carry out his Original Vow. What is this something? If it does not partake somewhat of the nature of Amida himself, how can the latter come to stand in any manner of relationship to it? The wisdom of Amida may be beyond the calculation of human understanding, and his way of achieving salvation may be a miracle as far as it transcends the law of moral causation. But unless the subject, that is, *ki* itself, has some possibility of being affected by the Original Vow, it will be like throwing pearls before swine, there is no unity of interest, no sympathetic response, no mutual relationship; hence absolutely no understanding between them. The *ki* therefore must be regarded as reflecting something of Amida, as holding in it a potentiality of Amidaship, and by virtue of this the *ki* is affected by the latter's loving heart and gets related to it. When the heart of the *ki* is finally occupied by Amida whose Original Vow is ever ready to function whenever the *ki* opens itself to its influence, the *ki* is said to have entered upon the order of steadfastness and attained to a peaceful state of mind called *anjin. Ki* and *hō* are thus said to be of one substance. Without this fact, the Shin scholar argues, Amida and his devotees would be two entirely independent terms with no connection whatever between them. The whole edifice of *tariki* salvation will then indeed topple down even with Amida under its ruins.

Hō which is ordinarily the Chinese equivalent for Dharma stands here for Amida as the embodiment of truth, or as ultimate reality itself, or, in the terminology of the Jōdo school, the author of the Original Vow. But sometimes, especially by scholars of the Shin, *hō* is understood to signify the virtue or power of Amida whereby the salvation of all beings is effected, and not Amida himself in whose personality lies this saving power. In this case *ki* means not mortal sinners as they are, but their believing heart directed toward Amida. When this heart gets united to the power or loving heart of Amida in the expression of *Namu-amida-butsu,* they say there is the identification of *ki* and *hō.*

18. Originally, *Buddhānusmṛti-samādhi* in Sanskrit. This is a mental state in which the nembutsu follower finds himself completely unified with the nembutsu itself, or a state of perfect identity in which self and not-self, or subject and object, are merged as one.

19. Physical movements, speech, and mentation in its wider sense.

20. Walking, standing, sitting, and lying.

21. Buddhist theology has a fine comprehensive theory to explain the manifold types of experience in Buddhism, which look so contradicting to each other. In fact, the history of Chinese Buddhism is a series of attempts to reconcile its diverse schools, all claiming to base their authority on the sacred writings of Buddhism. Various ways of classification and reconciliation were offered, and when they thought they succeeded in the attempt, their conclusion was this: Buddhism supplies us with so many gates to enter into the truth because of such a variety of human characters and temperaments and environments due to diversities of karma. This is plainly depicted and taught by the Buddha himself when he says that the same water drunk by the cow and the cobra turns in one case into nourishing milk and in the other into deadly poison, and that medicine is to be given according to disease. This is called the doctrine of means or device *(upāya),* and the broad-mindedness of Buddhists is explained on this ground. The doctrine of *upāya* has its background in the Buddhist conception of the highest being as the embodiment of wisdom *(prajñā)* and love *(karuṇā).*

3. *SELECTION FROM* THE KOAN EXERCISE

1. [Popular name for Zhiyi (538–597). JCD]
2. *Shi chan boluomi cidi famen* (J. *Shaku zen haramitsu shidai hōmon*), Book IV.
3. [Octavius 18:8. JCD]
4. See the *Sukhāvatī-vyūha Sūtra*.
5. This is one of the three principal sutras belonging to the Pure Land School. The three are: 1. *Sukhāvatī-vyūha*, which treats of the Land of Bliss inhabited by Amitābha Buddha, and of the forty-eight (forty-three in the Sanskrit text) vows of the same Amitābha; 2. *Sūtra of the Meditations on Buddha Amitāyus*, in which Queen Vaidehī is instructed by Śākyamumi to practice sixteen forms of meditation regarding the Land of Bliss and its Lord; and 3. *The Sūtra of Amitābha*, which is generally known as the *Smaller Sukhāvatī-vyūha*, as it also describes the Land of Bliss. Amitāyus (Eternal Life) and Amitābha (Infinite Light) refer to one and the same Buddha.
6. Max Müller, p. 15, l. 4.
7. Max Müller, p. 14, l. 15.
8. Max Müller, p. 47, ll. 2, 3.
9. *Hanju zanmaikyō*.
10. [Or Lokakṣema. JCD]
11. J. Dōshaku (562–645), one of the foremost devotees of the Pure Land teaching.
12. *Daijū gatsuzōkyō*.
13. J. *Anrakushū* (Book of Peace and Happiness).
14. J. Tennyo Isoku. *Jingtu huowen* (J. *Jōdo wakumon*).
15. J. *A-mi-da Butsu*.
16. It is not quite proper to use a scholastic term in this connection, but my idea is to distinguish here the aspect of the Nembutsu exercise in which the significance of the name is held up more emphatically against all other considerations. By "nominalism," therefore, I wish to indicate roughly the principle operating in the emphatical upholding of the name as efficacious to mature the Samadhi of Oneness, or in being born in the Pure Land of Amitābha. "Idealism" or "conceptualism" will then mean the attitude of Prajñāpāramitā philosophers who endeavor to describe the ultimate nature of Reality by means of highly abstract, conceptualistic terms which are generally negativistic.
17. There are three Chinese translations of this sutra, the first of which appeared in A.D. 503 and the last in A.D. 693. It is generally known as a sutra on Prajñāpāramitā, expounded by Mañjuśrī. The Buddhist Tripitaka, Taishō Edition, nos. 232, 233, and 220 (7).
18. J. *ichigyō sanmai*, "Samadhi of One Deed (?)," in Mantuoluo's version, is the "Samadhi of One Form Array" (*ekanimitta* [?] *vyūhasamādhi*) in Xuanzang's translation. In the Sanskrit text now extant this Samadhi is called *ekavyūhasamādhi*. *Vyūha* is generally rendered as *zhuangyan* in Chinese, meaning "embellishment," "array," or "arrangement in order." The sense is, however, not to arrange things merely for the sake of decoration; it is to fill the abstract barrenness of Reality with multiplicities, and it may be regarded sometimes as synonymous with "individualization," or "particular objects." *Ekavyūha*, therefore, may mean "one particular object" and *ekavyūhasamādhi* "a samadhi with one object in view." It is difficult to take *xing* to be equivalent to *vyūha*, for *xing* is usually *caryā*.

The passage containing the account of the *yixing* samadhi is missing in Saṃghapāla's (Sengqiepoluo?) translation, which fact suggests its later addition. Probably the earlier text of the *Saptaśatikā-prajñāpāramitā Sūtra* thoroughly retained the characteristic features of Prajñāpāramitā philosophy with no admixture of the visualizing meditation and also of the nominalistic trend of thought.

19. In the Xuanzang version no reference is made to the recitation *(cheng),* thus: "If sons and daughters of good family wish to enter upon this Samadhi, let them retire to a solitary place away from confusions, and sit cross-legged without thinking of forms of any kind; let them, in order to benefit all sentient beings, single-mindedly and collectively take hold of the [Buddha's] name and reflect well on his personality, while turning in the direction where the Buddha is and facing him in the proper attitude. To have their thoughts continually fixed on this one Buddha is thereby to see all the Buddhas of the past, present, and future."

In the Sanskrit *Saptaśatikā*, we have simply *tasya nāmadheyaṃ grahitavyam.*

20. This is also known as the *Bhadrapāla Bodhisattva Sūtra* because this is the name of the interlocutor in the sutra. There are four extant Chinese translations of it. The first one was done by Loujiachen as early as A.D. 179. It is one of the authoritative sources of the Pure Land teaching. See [below for more detail. JCD]

21. J. Zendō, died A.D. 681.

22. J. Zendō.

23. From Hōnen's *Passages Relative to the Nembutsu and Original Vows* (*Senchaku hongan nenbutsushū.* JCD), Fas. I. In this Hōnen attempts to explain his position as founder of the Nembutsu school in Japan.

24. *Ōjōyōshū.* Genshin, comp.

25. Zhizhe Dashi. *Mohezhiguan.* The Taishō Tripitaka, no. 1911.

26. Soon after this, Genshin quotes another authority in the Jōdo teaching, Huaigan: "According to the *Sutra of the Meditations,* this one harassed to the extreme has no time to think of the Buddha; but being advised by good friends he recites the name of the Buddha Amitābha, and thereby he is enabled to keep up his recitation uninterruptedly and with sincerity of heart. In a similar manner, let those who wish to attain a Samadhi in the Nembutsu keep up their recitation audibly without stopping, and they will surely realize the Samadhi and see the holy congregation of the Buddhas right before them as in the daylight. The louder you recite the name of the Buddha at the top of your voice the easier the attainment of the Samadhi of the Nembutsu. When your recitation is not loud enough, the mind is liable to distraction. This will be found out by the Yogin himself without being told by others."

27. From his *Senchakushū.*

28. *Anecdota Oxoniensia,* Aryan series, Vol. I, Part II, p. 96.

29. 歸依無量光佛 (J. *kie muryōkō butsu*).

30. [Genshin is the name that should appear here. Genkū is an alternate name for Hōnen, and is mistakenly used in the original text. The Japanese translation of this essay corrects the name to Genshin. JCD]

31. Quoted by Hōnen in his *Senchakushū,* Fas. I.

32. J. *Daijū gatsuzōkyō* (S. *Candragarbha),* translated into the Chinese by Narendrayaśas, A.D. 550–577.

33. 大念見大佛. 小念見小佛. 大念者大聲稱佛也. 小念者聲稱佛也.

34. 今日也無無. 明日也無無. In one of Konggu Long's letters.

35. In the practical recitation, this is pronounced something like *nam-man-da-bu, nam-man-da-bu, . . .*

36. Pp. 7–9.

37. C. *Pusa nianfo sanmei jing*. Sui dynasty. Dharmagupta (C. Damojiduo), trans.

38. Cf. Hakuin's story of the two Jōdo devotees [not included in this selection. JCD]

39. *Jōdo ōjōden* (C. *Jingtu wangsheng zhuan*).

40. Translated into Chinese for the first time by Zhi Loujiachen who came to China in the latter half of the second century, during the latter Han dynasty. The English translation is drawn from Jñānagupta's Chinese translation (A.D. 586) instead of from Zhi Loujiachen (A.D. 179), for Jñānagupta's is more intelligible, though Zhi Loujiachen is better known to students of the Pure Land school. The Taishō Tripitaka, nos. 416–419.

41. *Shūjishō.*

42. From *Yuishinshō mon'i.*

43. Op. cit.

44. The founder of the Ji sect of the Pure Land School, 1239–1289. His *Sayings* is full of mystic thoughts.

45. *Mattōshō.* This is a collection of Shinran's letters, twenty-three in all.

46. *The Mattōsho.*

47. J. *myōgō.*

48. J. *shōmyō.*

4. THE SHIN SECT OF BUDDHISM

1. Transcendental wisdom, or intuitive knowledge—one of the specifically Buddhist terms requiring a somewhat lengthy explanation.

2. The Chinese version adopted by the Jōdo followers counts forty-eight, for which see [below. JCD]

3. *Ta* = other, *riki* = power, and *ji* = self.

4. In Sanskrit *a* is a privative prefix and *akarma* means the negation or absence of karma.

5. Cf. my *Studies in the Laṅkāvatāra,* Pt. III, Chapter III, pp. 308ff.

6. *Daimuryōjukyō* (S. *Sukhāvatī-vyūha Sūtra*).

7. [The word "not" has been deleted from the original sentence, which mistakenly stated, "unless the following forty-eight conditions were *not* fulfilled. . . . " JCD and CWSB]

8. According to Shin, "entering into Nirvana" means "attaining enlightenment," and the attaining of enlightenment which takes place in the Pure Land is to be preceded by joining while here with the group of the faithful.

9. "The Unborn Dharma" means Reality in the absolute aspect, that is, the Dharma not affected by birth-and-death.

10. This is the stage where faith is firmly established and no retrogression ever takes place. *Avaivartika* in Sanskrit.

11. For further discussion see [below in this essay. JCD]

12. In Sanskrit, *buddhasmṛti,* literally, "thinking of the Buddha." But it has come to be synonymous with *shōmyō,* "reciting or pronouncing the Name." For the Jōdo followers *nem-*

butsu means *shōmyō,* to think of the Buddha is to pronounce his Name, Amida. For further remarks see below and also my *Zen Essays* [*(Second Series),* "The Koan Exercise," Pt. II. JCD]

13. *Anjin ketsujō shō.* The author is unknown, but this short treatise contains a remarkably clear exposition of the *tariki* teaching. *Anjin* means "peaceful mind," *ketsujō* "final settlement," and *shō* "treatise"; and the whole title may be rendered "On the Final Peaceful Settlement of Mind." The work has contributed greatly to the philosophy of the Shin.

14. The following is more or less a free translation.

15. Dharmākara, the name of Amida still in the stage of Bodhisattvahood.

16. That is, the Pure Land proper.

17. [This final section does not appear in this format in the original 1939 version of the essay. There the five enumerated parts are presented only as "Notes." In the 1949 version used here these notes are given a new seven-paragraph introduction and changed into the final section (VII) of the essay. JCD]

18. See [above in this essay. JCD]

19. My *Zen Essays* [*(Third Series),* "The Bodhisattva's Abode." JCD], p. 123 et seq.

5. *SELECTIONS FROM* JAPANESE SPIRITUALITY

1. [I have generally rendered the rare and difficult Japanese term *reisei* as both "religious consciousness" and "spirituality." The former has the approval of the author, who remarked that *reisei* is virtually synonymous with *shūkyō ishiki* (religious consciousness). He also wrote in a postcard dated May 3, 1947, (SDZ 37:172–173) that he didn't feel "spiritual" was an adequate translation of *reisei.* Despite its drawbacks, I have nonetheless decided to use "spirituality" on occasions when it seemed preferable for syntactic reasons. NW]

2. [Shinran described the Shin Buddhist path as *ōchō,* a "sidewise leap" or "leaping crosswise." Suzuki elucidates this to mean, instead of following a continuous logical passage of ratiocination, to abandon all intellectual calculations and to jump right down into what seems to be a dark bottomless abyss of the absolute, where the white road to the Pure Land opens up before one. Thus, the way to absolute assurance of rebirth in the Pure Land *(Ōjō)* is wholehearted acceptance of the Original Prayer (or Vow) proclaimed by Amida. NW]

3. [*Sokuhi,* literally, "is and is not." Suzuki formulated the logic of prajna-intuition, which he called the logic of *sokuhi,* as "A is not A and therefore A is A." See Suzuki, *Studies in Zen,* 119ff. NW]

4. [Original Prayer is a translation of the term *hongan,* referring to Amida's forty-eight Vows or Prayers (particularly the eighteenth one) at the beginning of his career as a bodhisattva, which are detailed in the *Sukhāvatī-vyūha Sūtra,* the principal text of Pure Land Buddhism. Suzuki used two different translations of *hongan* over the course of his career, "Original Vow" and "Original Prayer," but late in life he tended to prefer the latter, which the translator has opted to use in this translation. The term "prayer" sounds somewhat un-Buddhistic. But Suzuki maintains that, if prayer is understood as having no specified petitionary objective, as is often the case in Christian and Buddhist prayers, then it may be preferable to the term "vow," which has its own problems. JCD and NW]

6. SAYINGS OF A MODERN TARIKI MYSTIC

1. *Pūrva-praṇidhāna* in Sanskrit. They were made by Amitābha Buddha innumerable ages ago when he was still a Bodhisattva practicing the six paramitas. Finally he realized supreme enlightenment and became the Buddha, which fact, according to the Shinshū followers, most conclusively proves that all his vows are fulfilled. They are forty-eight in number and the most important one, the eighteenth, is that salvation or rebirth in his Land is promised to all beings who would even once sincerely think of him.

2. Amida is the Japanese reading of the Sanskrit Amitābha, which literally means "Infinite Light."

3. Gidō, sometimes called Irikiin, 1805–1881. The translation is a free rendering of the injunctions which he left for his disciples.

4. *Naraka* or [*niraya* (CWSB)] is Buddhist hell. It is divided into many compartments. The principal difference between hell and *naraka* is that in the latter sinners suffer only as long as their karma is effective, for their souls are never condemned to eternal suffering as is traditionally taught in Christianity. [Suzuki's original text mistakenly substitutes *Nirṛti* for *niraya* in this note, which has been corrected here. JCD]

5. [Suzuki's original essay mistakenly gives Shichiri's personal name as Kōjun, but is corrected to Gōjun in later versions. JCD]

6. Invoking the name of Amida.

7. [1697–1769. JCD]

7. THE MYŌKŌNIN

1. [*Yuge zanmai*—a conception describing the life of a bodhisattva which is free from every kind of constraint and restraint. It is like the fowls of the air and the lilies of the field, and yet there is in him a great compassionate heart functioning all the time freely and self-sufficiently. NW]

2. [Actually Saichi died in the previous year, 1932. JCD]

3. [By the Shin master Kakunyo Shōnin (1270–1351). NW]

4. [*Hō* is the Dharma and *ki* the recipient of the Dharma. *Ki,* originally meaning "hinge," signifies in Shin Buddhism especially the devotee who approaches Amida in the attitude of dependence. He stands as far as his "self-power" is concerned against Amida. *Hō* is "Dharma," "Reality," "Amida," and the "other-power." This opposition appears to our intellect as contradiction and to our will as a situation implying anxiety, fear, and insecurity. When *ki* and *hō* are united in the *myōgō,* or sacred Name of Amida, as *Namu-amida-butsu,* the Shin devotee attains *anjin,* "peace of mind." NW]

8. FROM SAICHI'S JOURNALS

1. [The number given in the original text is 148, but only 147 actually appear below. JCD]

2. *Nyorai* is the Japanese reading for Chinese *rulai,* which is the translation of the Sanskrit *Tathāgata.* It means "one who thus comes (or goes)" [and is used to refer to the Buddha. JCD]

3. Cf. Angelus Silesius [1624–1677 (JCD)], German mystic-poet:

I know that without me
God can no moment live;
Were I to die, then He
No longer could survive.

I am as great as God,
And He is small like me;
He cannot be above,
Nor I below Him be.

4. The Japanese for "worship" is *ogamu,* which literally means "to bow to an object reverentially and devotionally." "Worship" may sound too strong, but if it is understood in the sense of "religious reverence and homage" as it is ordinarily done, there is no harm in the use of the term.

5. Dreamed on the night of May 22.

6. *Kimyō* is the Japanese for *namu,* meaning "taking refuge," "adoration," "worshiping," etc. The author here probably intends to mean that mutual worshiping of *Namu* and Amida is the meaning of *Namu-amida-butsu,* or that *Namu-amida-butsu* symbolizes the oneness of Amida and every one of us.

7. *Hokkai* is *dharmadhātu* in Sanskrit, meaning the universe as the totality of all things.

8. *Oya* has no English equivalent. It is both motherhood and fatherhood, not in their biological sense but as the symbol of loving-kindness. *Sama,* an honorific particle, is sometimes shortened to *san* which is less formal and more friendly and intimate.

9. *Oni* in Japanese, evil spirits under the King of Death (Yamarāja).

10. Meaning absolute trust between Amida as *Oya-sama* and Saichi as child.

11. This is Saichi himself. *Namu* is personified here.

12. The Nembutsu (literally, "thinking of Buddha") and the *Myōgō* ("name") are often interchangeable. Both refer to the six syllables: *na-mu-a-mi-da-buts(u).* The syllables serve three purposes: (1) as the *Myōgō* itself, (2) as an actual invocation, and (3) as the symbol of identity.

13. The following equations hold: the *ki* = *jiriki* ("self-power") = the *Namu* = the supplicating individual = the sinner = Saichi. The *hō* = Amida = Buddha = Enlightenment = *tariki* ("other-power") = Reality = the Dharma = *Oya-sama* = Tathagata.

14. Saichi generally declares *Namu* to be himself and Amida to be *Oya-sama.* To identify himself with both *Namu* and Amida is unusual. We may however remark that Saichi often equates himself with *Namu-amida-butsu,* which means that he is Amida as well as *Namu.*

15. *Jigoku* is hell generally, *Gokuraku* is the Land of Bliss, *Jōdo* is the Pure Land, and *shaba* is "this world" or *sahālokadhātu* in Sanskrit.

16. This does not necessarily mean that when the eyes are closed, which symbolize death, we are in the Pure Land and that while they are kept open we are in this world. Saichi's idea probably is metaphysical or dialectical, though of course this is not to say that Saichi has reasoned out all these things consciously after the fashion of a philosopher. Saichi's allusion to the eye reminds us of Eckhart's remark on it.

17. [Enma is the chief magistrate of hell. JCD]

18. [This verse is identical to 71 in all English editions of the text. The Japanese translation of the work, however, presents a different verse here. See Suzuki Daisetsu, *Shinpi shugi:*

Kirisutokyō to Bukkyō, trans. Bandō Shōjun and Shimizu Shūsetsu (Tokyo: Iwanami Shoten, 2004), 258. JCD]

19. The gift or favor coming from Amida is a free one, for he never asks anything in exchange or in compensation. When the sinner *(ki)* utters *Namu-amida-butsu* in all sincerity he is at once made conscious of his being from the first with Amida and in Amida. There has never been any sort of alienation or estrangement between Amida and sinner. It was all due to the latter's illusive ideas cherished about himself. When they are wiped away, he realizes that the sun has always been there and finds himself basking in its light of infinity.

20. [This verse is identical to the previous one, apparently repeated inadvertently in the text. The Japanese translation of this work omits this verse, reducing the total number to 146. See Suzuki Daisetsu, *Shinpi shugi: Kirisutokyō to Bukkyō,* 270. JCD]

21. "Taste"—Bible reference: *Imitation of Christ,* Chapter XXXIV. "To him who tasteth Thee, what can be distasteful? And to him who tasteth Thee not, what is there which can make him joyous?"

22. While at the moment of exaltation Saichi feels he is Amida himself in company with Buddhas and Bodhisattvas who fill the whole universe, there are occasions when he feels the contrary. He then is the most despicable creature, like a homeless dog with his tail between the legs. He would cry: "How wretched, how worthless, how full of 84,000 evil thoughts am I!" But he never remains long in this state of self-commiseration, for he soon rises from it triumphantly, praising Buddha's infinite love for him. The psychologist may take him as a good example of manic-depressive psychosis. But the trouble is that Saichi is very much saner than most ordinary minds including scholars. He belongs to the group of "steadfastness," he has "something" occupying the very core of his being as Eckhart would say. Students of the religious consciousness know well that there is something of ambivalence in every devout soul. In this respect Saichi's utterances are of unusual importance.

23. *Bonbu* is the unenlightened and stands in contrast to Buddha.

24. *Kleśa* in Sanskrit, generally rendered "evil passions." They are the product of ignorance *(avidyā)* and thirst *(tṛṣṇā).*

25. Logically speaking, this is a case of identity in absolute contradiction. Saichi demonstrates this experientially. When he is conscious of his finiteness, being bound to the law of karmic causation, his heart is filled with contrition. But as soon as he feels that it is because of this consciousness that he has been taken up in the arms of *Oya-sama,* his joy knows no limits. The *Namu-amida-butsu* symbolizes the unification or rather identification of utter wretchedness and elated joyfulness.

26. Poverty means that all that one thinks to be one's own is taken or carried away by Amida or *Oya-sama,* that the self-power *(jiriki)* finds itself of no avail whatever. More positively, it is a state of self-realization that Amida is all in all.

27. The inner life is the life of suchness, of *kono-mama,* of the "nothing's the matter," of the "I know not what," of the horse galloping on the heath (Eckhart), of the flea in God's is-ness.

28. The original Japanese reads *onozukara,* which means "as-it-is-ness," "being natural," "being perfect in itself," or "being sufficient in itself." This is *kono-mama* or *sono-mama.*

29. *Hataraki* in the original means "function," "action," or "operation."

30. *Marude deru,* meaning "to come out in all nakedness," "nothing wanting," "in perfection," or "in full operation."

31. *Anjin*, literally, "mind pacified," meaning "faith confirmed."

32. Literally, *bakemono* is "something unreal," "something temporarily assuming a certain shape but not at all genuine."

33. *Bonbu* in Japanese. Saichi uses the term also in an abstract sense, in the sense of *bonbu*-hood, making it contrast with Buddhahood. Sinfulness here is not to be understood in its Christian sense.

9. INFINITE LIGHT

Editor's note (*The Eastern Buddhist*, 1971): The editors thank the Matsugaoka Library for permission to publish this paper, which seems to have been written around 1950. Most likely it began as a series of talks the author gave in California and was later combined and rewritten to form this single essay. The typescript contains indications where the author had intended to supply footnotes. These have been added by Dr. Suzuki's secretary, Miss Okamura Mihoko, who has gleaned them wherever possible from the author's English writings.

1. *Amida* in Japanese.

2. Kalpa: a long period of time.

3. Dharmakaya: generally translated "Law-Body." The highest reality or personality.

4. Buddha, that is, Śākyamuni.

5. His, that is, Amida's.

6. Three evil paths: the hungry ghosts, the animal world, and hell.

7. Arhat: one of the titles of the Buddha; he who is worthy of respect.

8. Prajna: transcendental knowledge or source of all knowledge.

9. Three Vehicles: (1) The Bodhisattva, being of enlightenment, (2) Pratyekabuddha, solitary Buddha, and (3) Sravaka, hearer.

10. "*Ōjō* means literally 'to go and be born,' that is, assurance of rebirth in the Pure Land."

11. It was a long time ago, indeed in an innumerable, immeasurable, incomprehensible kalpa before now, that Dharmākara (the name assumed by Amida while still in the stage of Bodhisattvahood) studied and practiced the Dharma under the guidance of a Tathagata called Lokeśvararāja . . . and vowed in the presence not only of this Buddha but of all the celestial beings, evil spirits, Brahmā, gods, and all other beings that unless the . . . forty-eight conditions were fulfilled he might not attain the highest enlightenment. . . . he completed all the virtues belonging to the life of a Bodhisattva, which consists of the realization of Love *(karuṇā)* and Wisdom *(prajñā)*. [The word "not" has been deleted from the sentence above, which originally stated mistakenly, "unless the . . . forty-eight conditions were *not* fulfilled." JCD]

12. "The Original Vow, the expression of Amida's Will or Karuna ('love' or 'compassion') which he cherishes over all beings, is specified, itemized, or particularized in forty-eight ways, each a practical situation in which we may find ourselves in the course of an individual life . . . the Original Vow is Amida himself expressed in human terms."

13. Taken from the *Kanmuryōjukyō (The Sutra of Meditation)*. This sutra "records how Śākyamuni accompanied by Ānanda came to the royal palace in Rājagṛha where Queen Vaidehī was imprisoned and what he preached to her concerning the possibility of all sentient beings to be reborn in the Pure Land of Amida after the deliverance from this world of

suffering. It was translated into Chinese in 424 A.D. by Kālayaśas." [This quotation actually comes from the *Muryōjukyō (Larger Sukhāvatī-vyūha Sūtra)* rather than the *Kanmuryōjukyō*. See this essay in *Collected Writings on Shin Buddhism* (CWSB, 1973), note 4. JCD]

14. More fully, *sahālokadhātu* in Sanskrit; *shaba* in Japanese. Dr. Suzuki has translated this term variously "this world of suffering," "the world of particulars," "this relative world of finitude and limitation," "this world of patience and endurance."

15. "Being finite means being defiled . . . ," "a taint of finitude or relativity . . . means defilement or karma or sin . . . As long as we are what we are, we have to continue to commit deeds of defilement and thus accumulate chances of falling into evil paths. There is no escape from this, there is no alternative other path. The self-power of relativity . . . constitutes our being . . . "

16. "Buddhists are more concerned—which is natural—with *naraka* (hells) than heavens. After death we generally go to Yama, who rules the spirits of the dead . . . He has a bright mirror before him. When we appear before him, we see ourselves reflected in it. It illuminates our entire being, and we cannot hide anything from it . . . Yama looks at it and knows at once what kind of person each of us was while living in this world. Besides this, he has a book before him in which everything we did is minutely recorded . . . His penetrating eye reads not only consciousness but also our unconscious. He is naturally legalistic, but he is not devoid of kindheartedness, for he is always ready to discover in the unconscious something which may help the criminal to save himself."

17. Shinran (1173–1262), the founder of the Shin school of Pure Land teaching. "The Shin school is the culmination of Pure Land thought, and that took place in Japan . . . Shinran had a profound understanding of the needs of the common people."

18. Taken from the *Kōsō wasan*, "Hymns dedicated to the Seven Great Fathers of Shin Buddhism, in India, China, and Japan."

19. "There is a class of people among the devotees of Shin Buddhism who are popularly known as *Myōkōnin* which means 'wondrously happy (or good) men.' They are distinguished generally by their good-heartedness, unworldliness, piousness, and lastly by their illiteracy, that is, their not being learned in the lore of their religion and not being at all argumentative about what they believe. This last quality is probably what differentiates them most sharply from the rest of the Shin devotees. They are in fact true Shin followers. They do not argue, they are not intellectually demonstrative, they just go on practicing what they have innerly experienced. When they express themselves at all, they are unaffected, their words come directly from their inmost hearts and refer directly to the truth of their faith. This is really what Shin Buddhism claims to do for its followers."

20. "In Buddhism sin means ignorance, that is, ignorance as to the meaning of the individual or the ultimate destiny of the self. Positively, sin is the affirmation of the self as a final *svabhāva* (self-substance) in deed, thought, and speech. When a man is above these two hindrances, ignorance and self-assertion, he is said to be sinless . . . That we are sinful does not mean in Buddhism that we have so many evil impulses, desires, or proclivities, which, when released, are apt to cause the ruination of oneself as well as others; the idea goes deeper and is rooted in our being itself, for it is sin to imagine and act as if individuality were a final fact. As long as we are what we are, we have no way to escape from sin, and this is at the root of all our spiritual tribulations. This is what the followers of Shin Buddhism mean when they say that all works, even when they are generally considered morally good,

are contaminated, as long as they are the efforts of 'self-power,' and do not lift us from the bondage of Karma."

21. A very large number, variously rendered as ten million, one hundred million, etc.

22. "'One Thought' is a momentous term in the philosophy of Shin and Jōdo. Its Sanskrit original . . . means 'one instant' or 'one moment.' As we say in English 'quick as thought' or 'quick as a flash,' 'one thought' represents in terms of time the shortest possible duration, which is to say, one instant. The one instant of faith-establishment is the moment when Amida's Eternal Life cuts crosswise the flow of birth-and-death, or when his Infinite Light flashes into the darkening succession of love and hate which is experienced by our relative consciousness. This event takes place in 'one thought' and is never repeated, and therefore is known . . . as 'the last moment' . . . This moment of 'one thought' is the one in our life most deeply impregnated with meaning, and for that reason must come to us in our 'ordinary moments of life' and not wait for 'the last moment' in its relative sense."

23. "*Namu-amida-butsu* is the Japanese reading of the original Sanskrit phrase 'namo amitābhabuddhāya,' meaning 'Adoration of the Buddha of Infinite Light.' But with followers of the Pure Land teaching, the phrase is far more than mere adoration for [Amitābha-buddha (CWSB)], or Amida, for by this they express their absolute faith in Amida as one who makes it possible for them to be born in his Land of Purity and Bliss . . . the phrase often serves as a metaphysical formula symbolizing the identity of subject and object of the devotee and Amida, of the 'sin-laden' individual and the all-saving and all-merciful *Oya-sama,* of all beings *(sarvasattva)* and Buddha, of *ki* and *hō,* of human yearnings and the supreme enlightenment."

24. See further on in this essay.

25. *Bonpu* or "*Bonbu* is the unenlightened and stands in contrast to Buddha."

26. See note 15 [above on defilement. JCD]

27. "It is . . . another name for Enlightenment *(anuttarā samyaksaṃbodhi),* which is the word used by the Buddha and his Indian followers ever since his realization under the Bodhi-tree by the River Nairañjanā." "Enlightenment means perfected personality—one who is perfect in Prajna ('transcendental or intuitive knowledge') and Karuna ('love')."

28. "Nirvana [is] nothing else in its essence than Enlightenment, the content [is] identical . . . Enlightenment [is] Nirvana reached while yet in the flesh, and no Nirvana [is] ever possible without obtaining Enlightenment. The latter may have a more intellectual note in it than the former, which is a psychological state realized through Enlightenment . . . Generally Nirvana is understood in its negative aspect as the total extinction of everything, body and soul, but in the actuality of life no such negativist conception could ever prevail, and the Buddha never meant Nirvana to be so interpreted."

29. Editor's note (*The Eastern Buddhist,* 1971): This seems to mean that the enlightenment-mind though awakened often retains the characteristic of the self-power. In Zen the saying is: "Enlightenment which smells of enlightenment is not true enlightenment." "The bedrock of our consciousness," which is the Self, stands at a distance from us as a bottom which must be broken through.

GLOSSARY OF JAPANESE AND CHINESE TERMS

Note: When multiple pronunciations are given, the alternative pronunciations are marked "C." (Chinese), "J." (Japanese), or "S." (Sanskrit).

Akanuma Chizen (1884–1937)	赤沼智善
Akao	赤尾
Aki	安芸
Amakasu no Tarō Tadatsuna (d. 1192)	甘糟太郎忠綱
Amida	阿弥陀
Amida Butsu	阿弥陀仏
Amida-butsu	阿弥陀仏
Amidakyō	阿弥陀経
anjin	安心
Anjin ketsujō shō	安心決定抄
anjin rondai	安心論題
Anleji (J. *Anrakushū*)	安楽集
Anrakushū (C. *Anleji*)	安楽集
Asahara Saichi (1850–1932)	浅原才市
Asōzu	麻生津
Ataka Yakichi (1873–1949)	安宅弥吉
ataru	当る
bakemono	ばけもの (化物)

Bankei (1622–1693)	盤珪
Biwa	琵琶
bonbu	凡夫
bonnō	煩悩
bonpu	凡夫
Bosatsu nenbutsu zanmaikyō (C. *Pusa nianfo sanmei jing*)	菩薩念仏三味経
Bukkyō no daii	仏教の大意
butsu	仏
cheng (J. *shō*)	称
chengming (J. *shōmyō*)	称名
Chigi (C. Zhiyi, 538–597)	智顗
Chisha Daishi (C. Zhizhe Dashi, 538–597)	智者大師
chō koonore	超個己
Chokushū goden	勅修御伝
Chokushū Hōnen Shōnin den	勅修法然上人伝
Cimin (J. Jimin, 679–748)	慈愍
Dahui (J. Daie, 1089–1163)	大慧
Daie (C. Dahui, 1089–1163)	大慧
Daijō sōō no chi	大乗相応の地
Daijū gatsuzōkyō (C. *Daji yuezang jing*)	大集月蔵経
Daikyō	大経
Daitō Kokushi (1282–1337)	大燈国師
Daitokuji	大徳寺
Daji yuezang jing (J. *Daijū gatsuzōkyō*)	大集月藏經
Damojiduo (S. Dharmagupta, d. 619)	達磨笈多
Daochuo (J. Dōshaku, 562–645)	道綽
Dashi	大師
Dengyō Daishi (aka Saichō, 767–822)	伝教大師/最澄
Donran (C. Tanluan, 476–542)	曇鸞
Dōshaku (C. Daochuo, 562–645)	道綽
Dōshū (d. 1516)	道宗
Echigo	越後
Echizen	越前
Emituo Fo	阿彌陀佛
Enma	閻魔
Eshin Sōzu (aka Genshin, 942–1017)	恵心僧都/源信

Etchū	越中
Fazang (643–712)	法藏
fotu (J. *butsudo*)	佛土
Fu Dashi (497–569)	傅大士
Fuji Shūsui (1885–1983)	藤秀璻
Funanguo	扶南国
fushō	不生
Gakushūin	学習院
Genkū (aka Hōnen, 1133–1212)	源空 / 法然
Genshin (aka Eshin Sōzu, 942–1017)	源信 / 恵心僧都
gensō-ekō	還相回向
geta	下駄
Gidō (aka Irikiin, 1805–1881)	義導 / 威力院
Go-Daigo (1288–1339)	後醍醐
Goichidaiki kikigaki	御一代記聞書
gokuraku	極楽
gong'an (J. *kōan*)	公案
Goshōsokushū	御消息集
Guanjingshu (J. *Kangyōsho*)	観經疏
guchi	愚痴
guiyi wuliang guang fo (J. *kie muryōkō butsu*)	歸依無量光佛
Gutei (C. Juzhi, 9th cent.)	倶胝
gutoku	愚禿
Gutokushō	愚禿抄
Haibutsu kishaku	廃仏毀釈
hakarai	はからい
Hakata	博多
Hakuin (1685–1768)	白隠
Hamaguchi Eshō	濱口恵璋
Hanju zanmai	般舟三昧
Hanju zanmaikyō	般舟三昧経
Hanshan (J. Kanzan, 9th cent.)	寒山
hataraki	はたらき (働き)
Heian	平安
Hiei	比叡
hiji bōmon	秘事法門

Hirose Seiichi (1895–1979)	広瀬精一
Hiroshima	広島
hō	法
hokkai	法界
hokkai engi	法界縁起
Hokuzen	北禅
Hōnen (aka Genkū, 1133–1212)	法然 / 源空
Hōnen Shōnin gyōjō	法然上人行状
hongan	本願
Honganji	本願寺
hōni	法爾
hō no jinshin	法深信
Hossō	法相
Hōzō	法蔵
Huaigan (J. Ekan, ca. 7th–8th cent.)	懐感
Huayan (J. Kegon)	華嚴
Huike (J. Eka, 486–593)	慧可
Huiyuan (J. Eon, 334–416)	慧遠
Huizhong (J. Echū, 675–775)	慧忠
ichidaiji	一大事
ichigyō sanmai (C. *yixing sanmei*)	一行三昧
ichinen	一念
ichinen hokki	一念発起
Iida Tōin (1862-1937)	飯田欓隠
Inami	井波
Ippen (1239–1289)	一遍
Ippen Shōnin goroku	一遍上人語録
Irikiin (aka Gidō, 1805–1881)	威力院 / 義導
Irin (C. Weilin, 1615–1702)	為霖
isshin	一心
ittai	一体
Iwakura Seiji (1903–2000)	岩倉政治
Iwami	石見
Ji	時
jigoku	地獄
Jimin (C. Cimin, 679–748)	慈愍

jinen	自然
jinen hōni	自然法爾
jingtu (J. *jōdo*)	浄土
Jingtu huowen (J. *Jōdo wakumon*)	浄土或問
Jingtu wangsheng zhuan (J. *Jōdo ōjōden*)	浄土往生伝
jiriki	自力
Jishū	時宗
Jittoku (C. Shide, 9th cent.)	拾得
Jōdo	浄土
jōdo (C. *jingtu*)	浄土
Jōdokei shisōron	浄土系思想論
Jōdo ōjōden (C. *Jingtu wangsheng zhuan*)	浄土往生伝
Jōdo Shinshū	浄土真宗
Jōdo wakumon (C. *Jingtu huowen*)	浄土或問
Jōgahana	城端
Jōshū (C. Zhaozhou)	趙州
Jōtoku	浄徳
Juzhi (J. Gutei, 9th cent.)	倶胝
Kaiankokugo	槐安國語
Kaiankokugo teishōroku	槐安國語提唱錄
kakkontō	葛根湯
Kakunyo (1270–1351)	覚如
Kamakura	鎌倉
Kanazawa	金沢
Kaneko Daiei (1881–1976)	金子大栄
Kang Sengkai (J. Kōsōgai, S. Saṃghavarman)	康僧鎧
Kangyō	観経
Kangyōsho (C. *Guanjingshu*)	観経疏
Kanmuryōjukyō	観無量寿経
Kantō	関東
Kanzan (C. Hanshan, 9th cent.)	寒山
katagiru ja nai	かたぎるじゃない
Kegon (C. Huayan)	華厳
Kegonkyō	華厳経
keiken	経験
Keiō	慶應

ken	見
kenshō	見性
ki	機
kihō ittai	機法一体
kimyō	帰命
Kinmei (539–571)	欽明
ki no jinshin	機深信
Kiyozawa Manshi (1863–1903)	清沢満之
kōan (C. *gong'an*)	公案
Kōbō Daishi (aka Kūkai, 774–835)	弘法大師 / 空海
Kohama	小浜
Koizumi Ryōtai (1851–1938)	小泉了諦
kokoro	心
Kokushi	国師
Kōkyō Shoin	興教書院
Konggu Long	空谷隆
kongō no shinshin	金剛真心
kono-mama	このまま
koonore	個己
koshin no Mida, yuishin no Jōdo	己身弥陀、唯心浄土
Kōsōgai (C. Kang Sengkai, S. Saṃghavarman)	康僧鎧
Kōsō wasan	高僧和讃
Kūkai (aka Kōbō Daishi, 774–835)	空海 / 弘法大師
kunshi	君子
Kurodani	黒谷
Kyōgyōshinshō	教行信証
Kyōshin (d. 866)	教信
li	里
Linji (J. Rinzai, d. 867)	臨済
Linji lu (J. *Rinzai roku*)	臨済録
Loujiachen (S. Lokakṣema)	婁迦讖
magureatari	まぐれ当り
Makashikan (C. *Mohezhiguan*)	摩訶止観
Mantuoluo Xian	曼陀羅仙
mappō	末法
marude deru	まるででる

masse	末世
Mattōshō	末燈抄
Meiji	明治
Mikawa	三河
minghao (J. *myōgō*)	名號
Mohezhiguan (J. *Makashikan*)	摩訶止観
monogatari	物語
Mu (C. *Wu*)	無
mukuyūtei	無功用底
Muryōjukyō	無量寿経
Myōe (1173–1232)	明恵
myōgō (C. *minghao*)	名号
myōkōnin	妙好人
Myōkōnin den	妙好人伝
Nada	灘
Namo-emituo-fo (J. *Namu-amida-butsu*)	南無阿彌陀佛
Namu	南無
na-mu-a-mi-da-bu/buts/butsu	南無阿弥陀仏
Namu-amida-butsu (C. *Namo-emituo-fo*)	南無阿弥陀仏
Nanjō Bun'yū (1849–1927)	南条文雄
Nanyang Huizhong Guoshi (J. Nan'yō Echū Kokushi, 675–775)	南陽慧忠国師
Nara	奈良
nehan	涅槃
nen (C. *nian*)	念
nenbutsu (same as nembutsu, C. *nianfo*)	念仏
nian (J. *nen*)	念
nianfo (J. *nenbutsu*)	念佛
Nihon teki reisei	日本的霊性
Nimai kishōmon	二枚起請文
Nishida Kitarō (1870–1945)	西田幾多郎
Nishi Honganji	西本願寺
Nishitani Keiji (1900–1990)	西谷啓二
nishu jinshin	二種深信
Noto	能登
nyorai (C. *rulai*)	如来

ōchō	横超
ogamu	拝む
ōjō (C. *wangsheng*)	往生
Ōjōyōshū	往生要集
okite ni kanō	掟にかなう
on	恩
oni	鬼
onozukara	自ずから
ōsō-ekō	往相回向
Ōtani	大谷
Oya	をや (親)
Oya-sama	をやさま (親様)
Pusa nianfo sanmei jing (J. *Bosatsu nenbutsu zanmaikyō*)	菩薩念佛三味經
raigō	来迎
reisei	霊性
reisei teki chokkaku	霊性的直覚
reisei teki jikaku	霊性的自覚
Rennyo (1415–1499)	蓮如
Rinzai (C. Linji, d. 867)	臨済
Rinzai roku (C. *Linji lu*)	臨済録
Roankyō	驢鞍橋
Rokuso dangyō	六祖壇経
rōnin	浪人
rulai (J. *nyorai*)	如來
Saichi (1850–1932)	才市
Saichō (aka Dengyō Daishi, 767–822)	最澄/伝教大師
saké	酒
-sama	さま
-san	さん
sanmai (C. *sanmei*, S. *samādhi*)	三昧
sanmei (J. *sanmai*, S. *samādhi*)	三昧
Sanuki	讃岐
sanze inga	三世因果
Sasaki Gesshō (1875–1926)	佐々木月樵
satori	悟り
seishin	精神

Seizan 西山

Seki Hōzen (1903–1991) 関法善

Senchaku hongan nenbutsushū 選択本願念仏集

Senchakushū 選択集

Sengoku 戦国

Sengqiepoluo (S. Saṃghapāla) 僧伽婆羅

senju 専修

senju nenbutsu 専修念仏

senrei 洗礼

shaba 娑婆

Shaku Sōen (1859–1919) 釈宗演

Shaku zen haramitsu shidai hōmon (C. *Shi chan boluomi cidi famen*) 釈禅波羅蜜次第法門

Shandao (J. Zendō, 613–681) 善導

sheng (J. *shō*) 声

shengming (J. *shōmyō*) 声名

Shenzan 神讃

Shi chan boluomi cidi famen (J. *Shaku zen haramitsu shidai hōmon*) 釋禪波羅蜜次第法門

Shichiri Gōjun (1835–1900) 七里恒順

Shichiri Rōshi goroku 七里老師語録

Shichiri Wajō genkōroku 七里和上言行録

Shide (J. Jittoku, 9th cent.) 拾得

Shikoku 四国

Shimane 島根

shin 信

Shin 真

Shingon 真言

shinjin 信心

shinjin no tsuki しんじん(信心)の月

Shinran (1173–1262) 親鸞

shinri teki na henka 心理的な変化

Shinshū 真宗

Shin shūkyō ron 新宗教論

Shinshū no shinkō taiken 真宗の信仰体験

shishin ekō 至心廻向

shō	性
shō (C. *cheng*)	称
shō (C. *sheng*)	声
Shō (River)	庄
shōbō	正法
shobutsu tōdō	諸仏等同
Shōkū (1177–1247)	証空
Shōkyō	小経
Shōma (or Shōmatsu, 1799–1871)	庄松
shōmyō (C. *chengming*)	称名
shōmyō (C. *shengming*)	声名
Shōnin	上人 or 聖人
Shōsokushū	消息集
Shōtoku (573–622)	聖徳
Shūjishō	執持抄
Shukō (C. Zhuhong, 1535–1615)	袾宏
shūkyō ishiki	宗教意識
Shūkyō keiken no jijitsu	宗教経験の事実
shūkyōshin	宗教心
shūkyō teki kanjō	宗教的感情
shūkyō teki keiken	宗教的経験
Soga Ryōjin (1875–1971)	曽我量深
soku	即
sokuhi	即非
sokuhi no ronri	即非の論理
Sonoda Shūe (1862–1922)	薗田宗恵
sono-mama	そのまま
Soō	祖翁
Sugihira Shizutoshi (1899–1984)	杉平顗智
sumete	すめて
sun	寸
Suzuki Daisetsu Teitarō (1870–1966)	鈴木大拙貞太郎
Suzuki Shōsan (1579–1655)	鈴木正三
taiken	体験
Taishō	大正
Tanluan (J. Donran, 476–542)	曇鸞

Tannishō	歎異抄
tariki	他力
tasuketamae	たすけたまへ (助け給へ)
Tendai (C. Tiantai)	天台
Tennyo Isoku (C. Tianru Weize, 1286–1354)	天如惟則
Tianru Weize (J. Tennyo Isoku, 1286–1354)	天如惟則
Tiantai (J. Tendai)	天台
tokonoma	床の間
Tokugawa	徳川
tokusa	砥草 or 木賊
Tōkyō	東京
tōshōgaku	等正覚
Toyama	富山
Tsukushi	筑紫
tsumi	罪
uguisu	鶯
Wajō	和上
wangsheng (J. *ōjō*)	往生
wasan	和讃
Waseda	早稲田
Weilin (J. Irin, 1615–1702)	爲霖
Wu (J. *Mu*)	無
wutingxin	五停心
Xi	西
xing	行
Xuanzang (602–664)	玄奘
Yamabe Shūgaku (1882–1944)	山辺習学
Yashichi	弥七
yixing sanmei (J. *ichigyō sanmai*)	一行三昧
Yokogawa	横川
Yokogawa Kenshō (1904–1940)	横川顕正
Yuan	元
yuge zanmai	游戯三昧
Yuimagyō	維摩経
Yuishiki	唯識
Yuishinshō mon'i	唯信抄文意

Yūzū	融通
Zen	禅
Zendō (C. Shandao, 613–681)	善導
Zhaozhou (J. Jōshū)	趙州
zhichi	執持
Zhi Loujiachen (S. Lokakṣema)	支婁迦讖
Zhiyi (J. Chigi, 538–597)	智顗
Zhizhe Dashi (J. Chisha Daishi, 538–597)	智者大師
zhuangyan (J. *shōgon*)	莊嚴
Zhuhong (J. Shukō, 1535–1615)	袾宏
Zoku Shinshū taikei	続真宗体系

BIBLIOGRAPHY

ABBREVIATIONS

CWS Shinran. *The Collected Works of Shinran.* 2 vols. Translated by Dennis Hirota et al. Kyoto: Jōdo Shinshū Hongwanji-ha, 1997.

CWSB Suzuki, Daisetz Teitarō. *Collected Writings on Shin Buddhism.* Edited by The Eastern Buddhist Society. Kyoto: Shinshū Ōtaniha, 1973.

SDZ Suzuki Daisetsu 鈴木大拙. *Suzuki Daisetsu zenshū* 鈴木大拙全集. 40 vols. Edited by Hisamatsu Shin'ichi 久松真一, Yamaguchi Susumu 山口益, and Furuta Shōkin 古田紹欽. Tokyo: Iwanami Shoten, 1999–2003.

SSZ Shinshū Shōgyō Zensho Hensanjo 真宗聖教全書編纂所, ed. *Shinshū shōgyō zensho* 真宗聖教全書. 5 vols. Kyoto: Kōkyō Shoin, 1940–1941.

PRIMARY AND SECONDARY SOURCES

Abe, Masao, ed. *A Zen Life: D. T. Suzuki Remembered.* New York and Tokyo: Weatherhill, 1986.

Akegarasu Haya 暁烏敏, ed. *Shinkō gobusho* 信仰五部書. Tokyo: Muga Sanbō, 1909.

Akizuki Ryōmin 秋月龍珉. *Suzuki Daisetsu* 鈴木大拙. 1967; Tokyo: Kōdansha, 2004.

Algeo, Adele S. "Beatrice Lane Suzuki and Theosophy in Japan." *Theosophical History* 11, no. 3 (July 2005): 3–16.

Bandō Shōjun 坂東性純. "D. T. Suzuki and Pure Land Buddhism." *The Eastern Buddhist* (New Series) 14, no. 2 (1981): 132–136.

———. "D. T. Suzuki's Life in La Salle." *The Eastern Buddhist* (New Series) 2, no. 1 (1967): 137–146.

———. "Suzuki Daisetsu: Reisei to Jōdokyō" 鈴木大拙–霊性と浄土教. In *Jōdo Bukkyō shisō,* 15:1–126. Tokyo: Kōdansha, 1993.

Barrows, John Henry, ed. *The World's Parliament of Religions*. Chicago: Parliament, 1893.

Blum, Mark L. "Standing Alone in the Faith of Non-Obedience: Suzuki Daisetsu and Pure Land Buddhism." *The Eastern Buddhist* (New Series) 39, no. 2 (2008): 27–68.

Carus, Paul. *Religion of Science*. Chicago: Open Court, 1893.

Chilson, Clark. *Secrecy's Power: Covert Shin Buddhists in Japan and Contradictions of Concealment*. Honolulu: University of Hawaii Press, 2014.

Coates, Harper Havelock, and Ryugaku Ishizuka, trans. *Honen, The Buddhist Saint: His Life and Teachings*. Kyoto: Chion'in, 1925.

DeMartino, Richard J. "Karen Horney, Daisetz T. Suzuki, and Zen Buddhism." *American Journal of Psychoanalysis* 51, no. 3 (1991): 267–283.

Dobbins, James C. "D. T. Suzuki and the Construction of Modern Buddhism." In *Buddhist Tradition and Human Life: Perspectives toward Research on Shinran's Thought*, edited by the Committee for the Publication of a Festschrift in Honor of Yasutomi Shin'ya, 73–97. Kyoto: Hōzōkan, 2014.

———. "D. T. Suzuki in Transition: 1949–1953." Unpublished manuscript.

———. *Jōdo Shinshū: Shin Buddhism in Medieval Japan*. 1989; Honolulu: University of Hawaii Press, 2002.

———. *Letters of the Nun Eshinni: Images of Pure Land Buddhism in Medieval Japan*. Honolulu: University of Hawaii Press, 2004.

———. "The Many Faces of Shinran: Images from D. T. Suzuki and *The Eastern Buddhist*." *The Eastern Buddhist* (New Series) 42, no. 2 (2011): 1–24.

Faure, Bernard. *Chan Insights and Oversights: An Epistemological Critique of the Chan Tradition*. Princeton: Princeton University Press, 1993.

Gómez, Luis O. *The Land of Bliss: The Paradise of the Buddha of Measureless Light*. Honolulu: University of Hawaii Press, 1996.

Hashimoto Mineo. "Two Models of the Modernization of Japanese Buddhism: Kiyozawa Manshi and D. T. Suzuki." *The Eastern Buddhist* (New Series) 35, no. 1/2 (2003): 6–41.

Hayashida Kumino 林田久美野. *Ōji Suzuki Daisetsu kara no tegami* 大叔父鈴木大拙からの手紙. Kyoto: Hōzōkan, 1995.

Henderson, Harold. *Catalyst for Controversy: Paul Carus of Open Court*. Carbondale: Southern Illinois University Press, 1993.

Hisamatsu Shin'ichi 久松真一, Yamaguchi Susumu 山口益, and Furuta Shōkin 古田紹欽, eds. *Suzuki Daisetsu: Hito to shisō* 鈴木大拙–人と思想. Tokyo: Iwanami Shoten, 1971.

Hokkoku Shinbunsha Henshūkyoku 北國新聞社編集局, ed. *Zen: Suzuki Daisetsu botsugo 40 nen* 禅–鈴木大拙没後４０年. Kanazawa: Jirinsha, 2006.

Inagaki, Hisao. *The Three Pure Land Sutras*. Kyoto: Nagata Bunshōdō, 1994.

Iwakura Masaji 岩倉政治. *Shinnin Suzuki Daisetsu* 真人鈴木大拙. Kyoto: Hōzōkan, 1986.

Jackson, Carl T. "D. T. Suzuki, 'Suzuki Zen,' and the American Reception of Zen Buddhism." In *American Buddhism as a Way of Life*, edited by Gary Storhoff and John Whalen-Bridge, 39–56. Albany: SUNY Press, 2010.

Jaffe, Richard M. "Introduction." In *Zen and Japanese Culture*, by Daizetz T. Suzuki, vii–xxviii. Princeton: Princeton University Press, 2010.

James, William. *The Varieties of Religious Experience*. 1902; London: Longmans, Green, 1911.

Kadoya Mitsuaki 門屋光昭. *Kakushi nenbutsu* 隠し念仏. Tokyo: Tōkyōdō Shuppan, 1989.

Kaneko Tsutomu 金子務, ed. *Tsuisō Suzuki Daisetsu: Botsugo yonjūnen kinen kikōshū* 追想鈴木大拙–没後四十年記念寄稿集. Kamakura: Matsugaoka Bunko, 2006.

Kasulis, Thomas P. "Reading D. T. Suzuki Today." *The Eastern Buddhist* (New Series) 38, no. 1/2 (2007): 41–57.

Ketelaar, James Edward. *Of Heretics and Martyrs in Meiji Japan: Buddhism and Its Persecution.* Princeton: Princeton University Press, 1990.

Kirita Kiyohide 桐田清秀. "D. T. Suzuki on Society and State." In *Rude Awakenings: Zen, the Kyoto School, and the Question of Nationalism,* edited by James W. Heisig and John C. Maraldo, 52–74. Honolulu: University of Hawaii Press, 1995.

———. "Matsugaoka Bunko to Suzuki Daisetsu kenkyū" 松ヶ岡文庫と鈴木大拙研究. *Matsugaoka Bunko kenkyū nenpō* 18 (2004): 83–93.

———, comp. *Suzuki Daisetsu kenkyū kiso shiryō* 鈴木大拙研究基礎資料. Kamakura: Matsugaoka Bunko, 2005.

———. "Young D. T. Suzuki's Views on Society." *The Eastern Buddhist* (New Series) 29, no. 1 (1996): 109–133.

Kiritani Junnin 桐渓順忍. *Kōza Shinshū no anjin rondai* 講座真宗の安心論題. Tokyo: Kyōiku Shinchōsha, 1983.

Matsugaoka Bunko 松ヶ岡文庫, ed. *Suzuki Daisetsu: Botsugo yonjūnen* 鈴木大拙–没後４０年. Tokyo: Kawade Shobō, 2006.

McRae, John R., trans. *The Platform Sutra of the Sixth Patriarch.* BDK English Tripiṭaka Series. Berkeley: Numata Center for Buddhist Translation and Research, 2000.

Meyer, Donald H. "Paul Carus and the Religion of Science." *American Quarterly* 14, no. 4 (Winter 1962): 597–607.

Moore, Charles A. "Suzuki: The Man and the Scholar." *The Eastern Buddhist* (New Series) 2, no. 1 (1967): 10–18.

Moriya Tomoe. "'A Note from a Rural Town in America': The Young Suzuki Daisetsu and the Significance of Religious Experience." *The Eastern Buddhist* (New Series) 38, no. 1/2 (2007): 58–68.

———. "Social Ethics of 'New Buddhists' at the Turn of the Twentieth Century." *Japanese Journal of Religious Studies* 32, no. 2 (2005): 283–304.

Nishimura Eshin 西村恵信. *Suzuki Daisetsu no genfūkei* 鈴木大拙の原風景. Tokyo: Daitō Shuppan, 1993.

Okamura Mihoko 岡村美穂子 and Ueda Shizuteru 上田閑照. *Daisetsu no fūkei—Suzuki Daisetsu to wa dare ka* 大拙の風景–鈴木大拙とは誰か. Kyoto: Tōeisha, 1999.

———. *Omoide no kobako kara—Suzuki Daisetsu no koto* 思い出の小箱から–鈴木大拙のこと. Kyoto: Tōeisha, 1997.

Okamura Shūsatsu 岡村周薩, ed. *Shinshū daijiten* 真宗大辞典. 3 vols. 1936; Kyoto: Nagata Bunshōdō, 1972.

Okusa Yejitsu, ed. *Principal Teachings of the True Sect of Pure Land.* Tokyo: Asakusa Hongwanji, 1910.

Ōtani Daigaku Hakubutsukan 大谷大学博物館, ed. *Suzuki Daisetsu: Botsugo yonjūnen kinenten* 鈴木大拙没後四十年記念展. Kyoto: Ōtani Daigaku Hakubutsukan, 2006.

Ōtani Daigaku Hyakunenshi Henshū Iinkai 大谷大学百年史編集委員会, ed. *Ōtani Daigaku hyakunenshi* 大谷大学百年史. 2 vols. Kyoto: Ōtani Daigaku, 2001.

Ōtani Daigaku Shinshū Sōgō Kenkyūjo 大谷大学真宗総合研究所, ed. *Ōtani Daigaku kindai hyakunen no ayumi* 大谷大学近代百年のあゆみ. Kyoto: Ōtani Daigaku, 1997.

Proudfoot, Wayne. *Religious Experience*. Berkeley: University of California Press, 1985.

Pye, Michael. "Hans-Martin Barth and Suzuki Daisetsu on Amida and the Pure Land." In *Buddhist Tradition and Human Life: Perspectives toward Research on Shinran's Thought*, edited by the Committee for the Publication of a Festschrift in Honor of Yasutomi Shin'ya, 101–129. Kyoto: Hōzōkan, 2014.

———. "Suzuki Daisetsu's View of Buddhism and the Encounter between Eastern and Western Thought." *The Eastern Buddhist* (New Series) 39, no. 2 (2008): 1–25.

Sasaki, Gessho. *A Study of Shin Buddhism*. Kyoto: The Eastern Buddhist Society, 1925.

Sasaki, Gessho, and Daisetz Teitaro Suzuki, trans. *The Life of the Shonin Shinran*. Tokyo: Buddhist Text Translation Society, 1911.

Sharf, Robert H. "Experience." In *Critical Terms for Religious Studies*, edited by Mark C. Taylor, 94–116. Chicago: University of Chicago Press, 1998.

———. "The Zen of Japanese Nationalism." In *Curators of the Buddha*, edited by Donald S. Lopez, Jr., 107–160. Chicago: Chicago University Press, 1995.

Shinran. *The Collected Works of Shinran*. 2 vols. Translated by Dennis Hirota et al. Kyoto: Jōdo Shinshū Hongwanji-ha, 1997.

———. *Kyōgyōshinshō* 教行信証. SSZ 2:1–203.

———. *The Kyōgyōshinshō: The Collection of Passages Expounding the True Teaching, Living, Faith, and Realizing of the Pure Land*. Translated by Daisetz Teitarō Suzuki. Kyoto: Shinshū Ōtaniha, 1973. Reprinted in Oxford by Oxford University Press in 2012.

———. *Mattōshō* 末燈鈔. SSZ 2:656–694.

———. *Shōzōmatsu wasan* 正像末和讃. SSZ 2:516–531.

Shinshū Shōgyō Zensho Hensanjo 真宗聖教全書編纂所, ed. *Shinshū shōgyō zensho* 真宗聖教全書. 5 vols. Kyoto: Kōkyō Shoin, 1940–1941.

Snodgrass, Judith. "*Budda no fukuin*: The Deployment of Paul Carus's *Gospel of Buddha* in Meiji Japan." *Japanese Journal of Religious Studies* 25, no. 3/4 (1998): 319–344.

———. *Presenting Japanese Buddhism to the West: Orientalism, Occidentalism, and the Columbian Exposition*. Chapel Hill: University of North Carolina Press, 2003.

Sueki Fumihiko 末木文美士. "Daisetsu hihan saikō" 大拙批判再考. *Matsugaoka Bunko kenkyū nenpō* 24 (2010): 19–35.

———. "Suzuki Daisetsu no reiseiron to sensō hihan" 鈴木大拙の霊性論と戦争批判. In *Kindai Nihon no shisō, saikō 3: Tasha shisha tachi no kindai* 近代日本の思想、再考３−他者死者たちの近代, 98–119. Tokyo: Transview, 2010.

Suzuki, Beatrice Erskine Lane. *Impressions of Mahayana Buddhism*. Edited by Daisetz Teitaro Suzuki. Kyoto: The Eastern Buddhist Society; and London: Luzac, 1940.

———. *In Memoriam: Emma Erskine Lane Hahn (1846–1927)*. Kyoto: Suzuki Teitarō, 1929.

Suzuki, Daisetsu (Daisetz) Teitarō 鈴木大拙貞太郎. "An Autobiographical Account." In *A Zen Life: D. T. Suzuki Remembered*, edited by Masao Abe, 13–26. New York and Tokyo: Weatherhill, 1986.

———. "Àpropos of Shin." In *The Buddha Eye: An Anthology of the Kyoto School*, edited by Frederick Franck, 211–220. New York: Crossroad, 1982.

———. "Book Review: *A History of Zen Buddhism*, by Heinrich Dumoulin." *The Eastern Buddhist* (New Series) 1, no. 1 (1965): 123–126.

———. *Buddha of Infinite Light*. With an introduction and notes by Taitetsu Unno. Boston: Shambhala, 1997.

———. "Bukkyō ni okeru Jōdo kyōri no hattatsu" 仏教における浄土教理の発達. SDZ 11:352–400.

———. *Bukkyō no daii* 仏教の大意. SDZ 7:1–79.

———. *Collected Writings on Shin Buddhism*. Edited by The Eastern Buddhist Society. Kyoto: Shinshū Ōtaniha, 1973.

———. *Daisetsu Zen o kataru: Sekai o kandō saseta mitsu no eigo kōen* 大拙禅を語る–世界を感動させた三つの英語講演. Tokyo: Aato Deizu (Art Days), 2006.

———. "The Development of the Pure Land Doctrine in Buddhism." *The Eastern Buddhist* (Old Series) 3, no. 4 (1925): 285–326.

———. "D. T. Suzuki's English Diaries." Edited by Kirita Kiyohide. *Matsugaoka Bunko kenkyū nenpō* 19–28 (2005–2014).

———. "Early Memories." In *A Zen Life: D. T. Suzuki Remembered,* edited by Masao Abe, 3–12. New York and Tokyo: Weatherhill, 1986.

———. *Eight Lectures on Chan*. Kamakura: Matsugaoka Bunko, 2011.

———. *Essays in Zen Buddhism (First Series)*. London: Luzac, 1927. Reprinted in London by Rider in 1949.

———. *Essays in Zen Buddhism (Second Series)*. London: Luzac, 1933. Reprinted in London by Rider in 1950.

———. *Essays in Zen Buddhism (Third Series)*. London: Luzac, 1934. Reprinted in London by Rider in 1953.

———. *The Field of Zen*. Edited by Christmas Humphreys. New York: Harper and Row, 1970.

———. "Hashigaki to omoide" はしがきと思い出. In *Seiren Bukkyō shōkan* 青蓮仏教小観. SDZ 35:16–28.

———. "Infinite Light." *The Eastern Buddhist* (New Series) 4, no. 2 (1971): 1–29.

———. *Introduction to Zen Buddhism*. 1934; New York: Grove, 1964.

———. *Japanese Spirituality*. Translated by Norman Waddell. Tokyo: Japan Society for the Promotion of Science, 1972.

———. "Jiriki to tariki" 自力と他力. SDZ 30:434–437.

———. *Jōdokei shisōron* 浄土系思想論. Kyoto: Hōzōkan, 1942. Reprinted in SDZ 6:1–320.

———. "Kiyozawa's Living Presence: A 1963 Commemorative Lecture." Translated by Satō Taira and W. S. Yokoyama. *The Eastern Buddhist* (New Series) 26, no. 2 (1993): 1–10.

———. *A Miscellany on the Shin Teaching of Buddhism*. Kyoto: Shinshu Otaniha Shumusho, 1949.

———. "Muryōkō" 無量光. Translated by Sakai Tsutomu 酒井懋. *Matsugaoka Bunko kenkyū nenpō* 26 (2012): 4–41.

———. *Mysticism: Christian and Buddhist*. London: George Allen & Unwin, 1957.

———. *Nihon Bukkyō no soko o nagareru mono* 日本仏教の底を流れるもの. Translated by Kusunoki Kyō 楠恭. Kyoto: Ōtani Shuppansha, 1950.

———. *Nihon teki reisei* 日本的霊性. Tokyo: Daitō Shuppansha, 1944. Reprinted in SDZ 8:1–223.

———. *Outlines of Mahayana Buddhism*. London: Luzac, 1907.

———. "Sayings of a Modern Tariki Mystic." *The Eastern Buddhist* (Old Series) 3, no. 2 (1924): 93–116.

———. *Shin Buddhism*. New York: Harper and Row, 1970.

———. *Shinpi shugi: Kirisutokyō to Bukkyō* 神秘主義–キリスト教と仏教. Translated by Bandō Shōjun 坂東性純 and Shimizu Shūsetsu 清水守拙. Tokyo: Iwanami Shoten, 2004.

———. "The Shin Sect of Buddhism." *The Eastern Buddhist* (Old Series) 7, no. 3/4 (1939): 227–284.

———. "Shinshū kanken" 真宗管見. SDZ 6:7–69.

———. *Shin shūkyō ron* 新宗教論. Kyoto: Baiyō Shoin, 1896. Reprinted in SDZ 23:1–147.

———. "Shinshū zakkan" 真宗雑観. SDZ 31:385–388.

———. "The Spirit of Shinran Shōnin." Unpublished talk presented at the American Buddhist Academy in New York on September 11, 1955.

———. *Studies in Zen*. Edited by Christmas Humphreys. New York: Dell, 1955.

———. *Suzuki Daisetsu no hito to gakumon* 鈴木大拙の人と学問. Suzuki Daisetsu Zenshū. Bekkan. Tokyo: Shunjūsha, 1975.

———. *Suzuki Daisetsu zenshū* 鈴木大拙全集. 40 vols. Edited by Hisamatsu Shin'ichi 久松真一, Yamaguchi Susumu 山口益, and Furuta Shōkin 古田紹欽. Tokyo: Iwanami Shoten, 1999–2003.

———. *Swedenborg: Buddha of the North*. Translated by Andrew Bernstein. West Chester, PA: Swedenborg Foundation, 1996.

———. *Watakushi no rirekisho* 私の履歴書. SDZ 26:499–539.

———. "What Is Religion?" *Buddhism in England* 14, no. 5 (1940): 138–139.

———. "The Wondrous Good Man." *Japan Quarterly* 11, no. 2 (1964): 157–161.

———. *Yafūryūan jiden* 也風流案自伝. SDZ 29:147–163.

———. "Zen and Jōdo, Two Types of Buddhist Experience." *The Eastern Buddhist* (Old Series) 4, no. 2 (1927): 89–121.

———. *Zen Buddhism: Selected Writings of D. T. Suzuki*. Edited by William Barrett. Garden City, NY: Doubleday, 1956.

———. *Zen ni ikeru: Suzuki Daisetsu korekushon* 禅に生きる–鈴木大拙コレクション. Edited by Moriya Tomoe 守屋友江. Tokyo: Chikuma Shobo, 2012.

———. *Zen to nenbutsu no shinrigaku teki kiso* 禅と念仏の心理学的基礎. Translated by Yokogawa Kenshō 横川顕正. Tokyo: Daitō Shuppansha, 1937. Reprinted in SDZ 4:187–369.

Suzuki, D. T., and Soga Ryōjin. "Dialogue: Zen and Shin." *The Eastern Buddhist* (New Series) 27, no. 1 (1994): 78–95.

Switzer, A. Irwin, III. *D. T. Suzuki: A Biography by A. Irwin Switzer III*. Edited and enlarged by John Snelling. London: Buddhist Society, 1985.

Taishō shinshū Daizōkyō 大正新脩大蔵経. 85 vols. Edited by Takakusu Junjirō 高楠順次郎 and Watanabe Kaikyoku 渡辺海旭. Tokyo: Taishō Issaikyō Kankōkai, 1924–1932.

Tweed, Thomas A. "American Occultism and Japanese Buddhism: Albert J. Edmunds, D. T. Suzuki, and Translocative History." *Japanese Journal of Religious Studies* 32, no. 2 (2005): 249–281.

Ueda Yoshifumi. "Reflections on the Study of Buddhism: Ui Hakuju and D. T. Suzuki." *The Eastern Buddhist* (New Series) 18, no. 2 (1985): 114–130.

Yampolsky, Philip B. *The Platform Sutra of the Sixth Patriarch*. New York: Columbia University Press, 1967.

Yasutomi Shin'ya 安富信也. *Kindai Nihon to Shinran: Shin no saisei* 近代日本と親鸞：信の再生. Tokyo: Chikuma Shobō, 2010.

Yokogawa, Kenshō. "Shin Buddhism as the Religion of Hearing." *The Eastern Buddhist* (Old Series) 7, no. 3/4 (1939): 296–341.

Yokoyama, W. S. "Bannen no Suzuki Daisetsu no shisōka to shite no shōzō: Matsugaoka Bunko no sengo genkō aakaibu no igi" 晩年の鈴木大拙の思想家としての肖像：松ヶ岡文庫の戦後原稿アーカイブの意義. *Matsugaoka Bunko kenkyū nenpō* 21 (2007): 139–185.

———. "Nishida Kitaro and D. T. Suzuki's Logic of *Soku-hi*—with a Translation of Suzuki's 'Gokuraku to Shaba' (1942)." *Hanazono Daigaku Bungakubu kenkyū kiyō* 33 (March 2001): 18–49.

———. "Two Addresses by Shaku Sōen." *The Eastern Buddhist* (New Series) 26, no. 2 (1993): 131–148.

Yoshinaga Shin'ichi. "After Olcott Left: Theosophy and 'New Buddhists' at the Turn of the Century." *The Eastern Buddhist* (New Series) 43, no. 1/2 (2012): 103–132.

———. "Suzuki Daisetsu and Swedenborg: A Historical Background." In *Modern Buddhism in Japan,* edited by Hayashi Makoto, Ōtani Eiichi, and Paul L. Swanson, 112–143. Nagoya: Nanzan, 2014.

———. "Theosophy and Buddhist Reformers in the Middle of the Meiji Period: An Introduction." *Japanese Religions* 34, no. 2 (2009): 119–131.

———. "Three Boys on a Great Vehicle: 'Mahayana Buddhism' and a Trans-National Network." *Contemporary Buddhism: An Interdisciplinary Journal* 14, no. 1 (2013): 52–65.

INDEX